1001

GREATEST FOOTBALL MOMENTS

First published in 2007 as
1001 Football Moments by
Carlton Books Limited,
20 Mortimer Street,
London W1T 3JW

This revised paperback edition
published in 2009 by Carlton Books

10 9 8 7 6 5 4 3 2 1

A CIP catalogue record for this book is available
from the British Library.

Paperback ISBN: 978-1-84732-367-5

Project Art Editor: Luke Griffin
Editorial: Lisa Hughes and John Behan
Picture Research: Paul Langan
Production: Kate Pimm
Index: Chris Bell

Introduction by Rob Wightman

Printed in Dubai

1001

GREATEST FOOTBALL MOMENTS

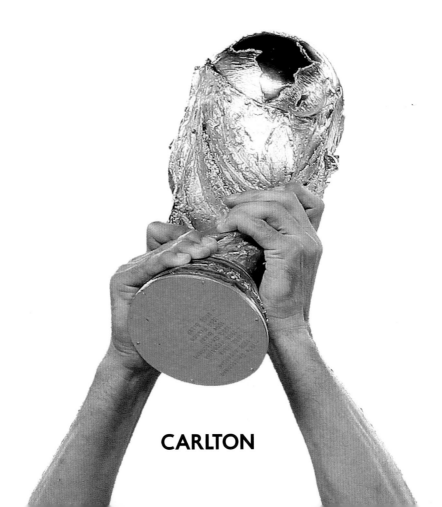

CARLTON

INTRODUCTION

From the creation of the Football Association in 1863 to a look ahead to the 2010 World Cup, *1001 Greatest Football Moments* is a literary and pictorial journey through the beautiful game's most significant, wonderful, tragic, obscene, hilarious and downright bizarre occurrences. It charts changes in the laws, attitudes, customs and profile of a sport that is now a global obsession and highly lucrative industry.

There is Pelé's artistry throughout the 1970 World Cup, the 'Cruyff Turn' four years later and Maradona's brilliant second goal against England in 1986. When these superstars were producing their magic week in, week out, it was rarely in front of a worldwide television audience. Instead, fans relied on iconic examples of such brilliance, mainly during World Cups, and, for many, such moments encapsulate the careers of these great players.

Football would be nowhere without its icons, so this book includes the likes of Billy Meredith, Manchester United's toothpick-chewing winger of the early 20th century, Denis Compton – the original Brylcreem boy, Paul Gascoigne and his tears at Italia 90, Roger Milla's funky goal celebrations and David Beckham's development from halfway-line hero to LA Galaxy and AC Milan star.

This book has not glossed over the darker side of football, for there have been times when even the most passionate supporter has had to concede that it really is only a game. The tragedies that are infamous to a British audience, such as the 1902 Ibrox disaster, the Munich air crash and Hillsborough, are relived in these pages. However, also covered are disasters less well-known in the UK, including the Superga air crash, in which Torino's great side of the late 1940s perished, and the Bastia stadium tragedy of 1992, when 18 fans died at a French Cup match.

Whenever that heady combination of kudos and money are at stake, scandal is close by. Way back in 1906, Parliament passed a law to stymie corruption in the English game amid suggestions that players had attempted to pay off rivals. But football often gives scope for rehabilitation and redemption. No better example of this can be Paolo Rossi who, after serving a lengthy ban for match-fixing, returned to be the goal-scoring hero of Italy's 1982 World Cup success.

Giant-killings are the lifeblood of the football romantic, who can relive the days when Wimbledon stole the FA Cup from Liverpool and late entrants Denmark fought their way to a shock triumph at Euro 92. There are also plenty of moments that chart the development of the game including entries about the first shin pads, floodlit match, referee's whistle and two-handed throw-ins.

Then there are the great comebacks. Nobody has forgotten Manchester United's last-gasp defeat of Bayern Munich in 1999 or Liverpool's Champions League comeback in 2005, but how many know that 70 years earlier Spain overturned a two-goal deficit to become the first team from outside the British Isles to defeat England?

It is easy to regard the formative decades of professional football as an age of innocence when players turned out just for fun and the game was not sullied by the greed and arrogance of modern times. But football has always had its fair share of political intrigue and infighting. Most European nations refused to travel to Uruguay for the first World Cup, in 1930, despite the host nation's agreement to cover all their costs. In retaliation, Uruguay spurned the opportunity to defend their crown in Italy four years later. Which just shows that football is a simple game but that nothing surrounding it is ever simple.

This book has required painstaking research to assemble such a huge collection of football moments, and we hope football fans everywhere will enjoy this particular result.

CONTENTS

'FOOTBALL EH, BLOODY HELL!'

Sir Alex Ferguson following Manchester United's 1999 Champions League final win over Bayern Munich. Substitute Ole Gunnar Solskjær scored the winning goal with just seconds remaining.

1863

FOOTBALL ASSOCIATION FORMED

The Football Association (FA) was formed on 26 October 1863 at the Freemasons Tavern in London, following a meeting of 12 interested club and school representatives. It was the world's first official football body.

The game was to be referred to as 'association football' in order to distinguish it from 'rugby football' and the rules adopted on that October morning were largely based on the earlier work of a group of Cambridge University undergraduates, who had attempted to formulate a set of rules in the mid to late 1840s.

Before the formation of the Football Association, there was no formalised set of rules for the game. Ebenezer Cobb Morley, founder and captain of Barnes Football Club, had written to a newspaper in 1863 to advocate the establishment of a governing body to run the game and indeed Morley's words were the catalyst for the first meeting and creation of the FA. As well as being a founding member, Morley also became the first secretary of the FA.

The first ever official exhibition game played under the newly formed rules occurred on 9 January 1864 at Battersea Park in south-west London. Although the FA rules had been set up, they were only adhered to in and around London, as elsewhere localised rules continued to be followed for some time.

Notts County was formed in 1862 and therefore predates the creation of the FA. County are the oldest league club in England and also the oldest surviving professional football club in the world. Naturally the Nottingham side were one of the founding members of the Football League.

SEE ALSO 'FORMATION OF THE FOOTBALL LEAGUE' (page 32); 'THE FORMATION OF FIFA' (page 55).

Morley's article was the catalyst for the creation of the Football Association. The 'Three Lions' was to be become the official emblem of the English FA.

Ebenezer Cobb Morley set about to draft the first set of football rules. The aim was to offer a distinction between this modern game and rugby.

MORLEY DRAFTS THE FIRST LAWS

The first set of laws governing the game of football was drafted by Ebenezer Cobb Morley at his home in Barnes, London. Morley devised 14 laws, which provided the basis for the first set of rules and these were put before the Football Association (FA) for approval at a third meeting in late 1863. These initial FA meetings were integral to the formation of the modern game of football and its distinction from rugby. In particular, there were two practices that Morley wanted to outlaw: running with the ball in hand and hacking – or kicking – opposition players in the shins.

SEE ALSO **'LAWS EXPANDED TO 17'** (page 42); **'LAWS AMENDED TO INCLUDE GOALKEEPERS'** (page 18).

Blackheath strongly objected to the new Football Association rules. They withdrew but later became a prominent rugby football club.

LAWS ADOPTED – BUT BLACKHEATH WALK OUT

On 8 December 1863, at the sixth meeting of the newly formed Football Association, the first comprehensive set of rules for football were finally agreed upon and published. The previous meeting had decided that carrying the ball and hacking were to be banned and this was largely supported. However, FW Campbell, the first FA treasurer and the Blackheath representative, strongly objected and withdrew his club (Blackheath later joined the Rugby Football Union). Surprisingly, in addition to stipulating a maximum length for pitches and the definition of various terms, including offside, the new rules actually allowed the ball to be caught.

SEE ALSO **'MANCHESTER UNITED LEAD TALK OF A BREAKAWAY'** (page 63); **'HOME NATIONS UNITE TO BOYCOTT FIFA'** (page 86).

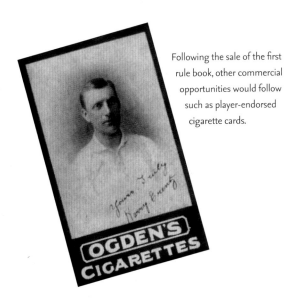

Following the sale of the first rule book, other commercial opportunities would follow such as player-endorsed cigarette cards.

FA'S FIRST COMMERCIAL VENTURE

Once the Football Association (FA) had agreed upon its first set of rules following that 8 December 1863 meeting, it also agreed that those rules needed publishing. So it was that the FA embarked upon its first commercial venture and John Lillywhite of Euston Square, London, was given the sole rights to publish and sell the first rule book. This important volume retailed at a shilling (12p) for a pocket-sized book and one shilling and six pence (18p) for a larger sized set of rules, designed for club rooms.

SEE ALSO 'MORLEY DRAFTS THE FIRST LAWS' (page 14); 'SPOT THE BALL' LAUNCHED' (page 106).

The first game under FA rules ended disappointingly goalless. Further games would take place, here, 45,000 spectators enjoy a match in 1893.

FIRST GAME UNDER FA RULES

After the Football Association (FA) had finally agreed upon a universal set of rules, the first fixture was scheduled for 2 January 1864 at Battersea Park, London, although it was subsequently postponed by a week. However, the members of the FA were understandably impatient to get out on the park and play the first-ever game under the new code, so it was therefore decided to have a match between Barnes and Richmond. This took place on 19 December 1863 at Mortlake, the home of Barnes. Historically speaking, it was an auspicious occasion, but not an auspicious result and the game ended goalless. Richmond were obviously disappointed by the lack of goals, for they went on to help in the 1871 formation of the Rugby Football Union.

SEE ALSO 'MORLEY DRAFTS FIRST LAWS' (page 14). 'LAWS AMENDED TO INCLUDE GOALKEEPERS' (page 18).

The founding of Buenos Aires FC began a great football tradition. Here, Argentinian goalkeeper Juan Botasso dives bravely in the 1930 World Cup.

BUENOS AIRES FC FORMED

Football arrived in Argentina in the late 19th century, at the port of Buenos Aires, but it was the large British expatriate community, rather than the locals, who introduced it and it was the Brits who, at a meeting on 9 May 1867, formed the Buenos Aires Football Club. The Buenos Aires Cricket Club allowed the football team to play on their field and it was there that the first recorded game took place, between two British merchant teams. The Argentinian Football Association wasn't founded until 1893 and then mainly British teams competed in the first league, although Italian immigrants later helped to popularise the game in Argentina.

SEE ALSO 'ARGENTINA INAUGURATES NATIONAL CHAMPIONSHIP' (page 38); 'ENGLISH CLUBS TOUR BRAZIL AND ARGENTINA' (page 67).

In 1865, it was decided that a tape should be stretched from one goalpost to another at a height of eight feet. As depicted here in a game in 1872.

TAPE USED FOR FIRST CROSSBAR

The early Football Association rules didn't specify a fixture between the goalposts, so in effect there wasn't a height restriction. The only stipulation was that the upright posts had to be a distance of eight yards apart. In 1865, though, it was decided that tape should be stretched from one goalpost to the other at a height of eight feet. Then ten years later the crossbar was introduced, with tape being outlawed in 1882. It was not until 1902 when the two lines spanning the width of the pitch, 12 and 18 yards from each goal line, were replaced and the penalty area markings we're familiar with today were brought in.

SEE ALSO 'GOAL NETS MAKE AN APPEARANCE' (page 35); 'MEXICO AND BULGARIA ALL FALL DOWN' (page 477).

DIFFERENT RULES... SAME GAME

Sheffield Football Club, formed in 1857, is acknowledged by both the Football Association (FA) and the world's governing body FIFA as the oldest club still playing association football today – and indeed it's the oldest documented club in any code of football.

   Although the team became members of the FA in 1863, they continued to play under their own set of laws, known as the Sheffield Rules. These rules differed from the FA's version in several ways. For example, there was no offside and you were allowed to push opposition players. When, on 31 March 1866, a Sheffield representative side played a London team in the capital's Battersea Park, the match was played under a slight variation of the FA rules, but despite this fixture the Sheffield club didn't sign up to the FA rule book until 1878. However, following the 1866 match between the two cities the FA elected to restrict the handling of the ball to just one player on each side – the goalkeeper.

SEE ALSO 'NORTHERNERS INVADE LONDON' (page 28);
'FIRST 100,000 ATTENDANCE AT FA CUP FINAL' (page 46-47).

Sheffield United did not sign up to the FA rule book until 1878. Their 1895 team are shown above.

In an incident in 1933, referee G C Denton rules out a Chelsea goal for offside. Hughie Gallacher appeals vehemently against the decision.

OFFSIDE RULE INTRODUCED

The FA introduced offside in 1863, although the concept did already exist in other sports. The original ruling, that any player in front of the kicker was offside, encouraged an excess of dribbling and was amended in 1866 so that the attacking player had to have three players between him and the goal line when the ball was played by a team-mate. FA secretary Charles W Alcock was the first player to be officially caught offside, during London's match against Sheffield in March 1866. The law was updated in 1925 so that the two players were required to be between the attacker and goal line.

SEE ALSO **'McCRACKEN SETS OFFSIDE TRAP'** (page 53); **'INTERNATIONAL BOARD AMENDS OFFSIDE LAW'** (page 98).

LAWS AMENDED TO INCLUDE GOALKEEPERS

Originally, any one player was permitted to punch the ball away from goal provided they were the deepest player on the team, but in 1870 the Football Association (FA) introduced the concept of designated goalkeepers. The rule was further adapted in 1871, when the FA deemed that only the goalkeeper was allowed to handle the ball. During this embryonic stage of the game, the goalkeeper was allowed to handle the ball anywhere within his own half of the pitch, with handling not restricted to within the penalty area until 1912.

SEE ALSO **'11 PLAYERS VERSUS 1 GOALKEEPER'** (page 36); **'GOALKEEPERS BARRED FROM HANDLING OUTSIDE AREA'** (page 71).

The new rules led to goalkeepers being formally recognised. One future star was Sheffield United's William Foulke, seen here, in the 1901 FA Cup.

FA CUP INAUGURATED

Following a Football Association (FA) committee meeting on 20 July 1871, secretary Charles W Alcock presented his grand plan for a Football Association Challenge Cup competition. The committee consented to Alcock's idea for a knockout Cup competition for its member clubs and so the FA Cup was born. Within three months the rules had been drafted and 15 clubs had signed up to take part, although three later pulled out without playing a match.

The FA Cup competition kicked off for the first time on 11 November 1871, when four first-round ties were played, with the first goal being scored by Jarvis Kenrick of Clapham Rovers. The inaugural final took place between Wanderers and Royal Engineers on 16 March 1872, with 2000 spectators in attendance – each had paid a shilling (12p) for the privilege – at the Kennington Oval in London, now better known as the home of Surrey County Cricket Club.

Despite Royal Engineers being the favourites, it was Wanderers who won 1-0 and entered the history books as the first winners of the famous trophy. Morton Betts scored the winning goal to become the first scorer of an FA Cup final goal.

The Kennington Oval went on to host all the Cup finals bar one until 1892, with Wanderers going on to triumph on four more occasions, and the FA Cup proved to be a great success. The number of clubs wanting to participate grew quickly and, indeed, the competition's popularity gave considerable impetus to the universal acceptance of a standard set of rules, as stipulated by the FA.

SEE ALSO **'FIRST 100,000 ATTENDANCE AT FA CUP FINAL'** (page 46-47); **'MONARCH ATTENDS THE FA CUP FINAL'** (page 75).

The original FA Cup. The knock-out tournament would quickly become the most famous club competition in the world.

FOOTBALL CROSSES THE CHANNEL

Following the growth of its popularity in England, football quickly began to spread further afield and it was the British who brought the game to France. British sailors began playing football in the port of Le Havre in the 19th century, encouraging the French to take up the game, and in 1872 the first French football club – Le Havre Athletic Club – was established. Football began to be played regularly in France from 1894 onwards and it wasn't long before France became a major European footballing nation, joining FIFA as a founding member in 1904.

SEE ALSO 'FOOTBALL REACHES BRAZIL' (page 34); 'WOOLWICH ARSENAL 26 PARIS 1' (page 56).

England's Roy Goodall and France's Edmond Delfour are joined by three girls in French national dress before an international in 1933.

THE FIRST INTERNATIONAL MATCH

The world's first international football fixture took place between Scotland and England on 30 November 1872 at Hamilton Crescent, Glasgow, in Scotland. Despite the differences in the teams' styles of play – England dribbled, Scotland passed – the game finished 0-0 and started a long-standing tradition of fiercely fought contests between the two countries, which lasted until the regular home nation fixtures were scrapped in 1984. Although the game, played in front of a crowd of 4000, was the first official meeting, there had previously been a number of unofficial games played between the two countries, organised by the English Football Association.

SEE ALSO 'THE FIRST INTERNATIONAL GOAL' (page 21); 'FIRST INTERNATIONAL TOURNAMENT ESTABLISHED' (page 27).

An artist's impression of an early match between England and Scotland. The first official game finished 0-0 and was played in front of a crowd of 4,000.

THE FIRST INTERNATIONAL GOAL

The first-ever international goal was scored during England's return encounter with Scotland on 8 March 1873. This, only the second international match staged, took place at the Kennington Oval in London and after the goalless draw of the first meeting between the two countries in Glasgow, it took England just a minute to take the lead. William S Kenyon-Stanley claimed the prestigious honour of scoring the inaugural goal in international football, before going on to notch England's third in a 4-2 victory. England were no doubt aided in their quest for goals by adopting a 2-2-6 formation, although this wasn't unusual at the time.

SEE ALSO **'FOOTBALL'S FIRST LEAGUE GOAL'** (page 33); **'LAURENT MAKES HISTORY'** (page 114).

In a later international meeting in 1903, Scotland goalkeeper Ned Doig makes an unorthodox save during the match against England.

SHIN PADS INTRODUCED

The first known use of the shin pad can be traced back to 1874, when Nottingham Forest captain and England player Sam Weller Widdowson cut down some cricket pads and then wore them on the outside of his stockings. The early shin pads were used as protection against hacking, or deliberate kicking of the shins, which was still prevalent in some areas of England, despite being outlawed by the Football Association. As the game progressed and got quicker, shin pads became smaller and many players then elected not to wear them. It wasn't until 100 years after Widdowson's first shin pad that the FA deemed them compulsory equipment.

SEE ALSO **'ADIDAS INNOVATE WITH SCREW-IN STUDS'** (page 190); **'EX-FOOTBALLER INVENTS THE 'PREDATOR' BOOT'** (page 472).

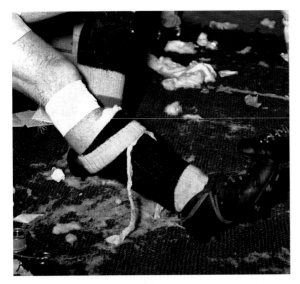

Inspired by cricket, the protection afforded by shin pads meant they were essential, despite the practice of hacking having been outlawed.

FOOTBALL REACHES SWEDEN

In 1875 British expatriates introduced football into Sweden on two fronts. Embassy officials started playing the game in the Swedish capital Stockholm and around the same time Scottish textile workers brought the game to Gothenburg. The first known football club in Sweden was Goteborgs Bollklubb, founded in 1875. Although it was actually a sports club, football was one of the activities played. Goteborgs, along with Stockholm's leading clubs Stockholms Bollklubb and Visby Bollklubb helped to standardise the rules for Swedish football in 1885, although it was a further ten years before the code was updated in line with the English FA.

SEE ALSO **'SWEDEN WIN OLYMPIC GOLD'** (page 164). **'GOTHENBURG WIN UEFA CUP'** (page 381).

Young Swedish fans waiting for their football heroes before the 1958 World Cup semi-final between Sweden and West Germany.

THE REFEREE'S WHISTLE SOUNDS ITS ARRIVAL

According to legend, the first time a referee (or umpire as the official used to be called) used a whistle was in a match between Nottingham Forest and Sheffield Norfolk in 1878. However, the Forest secretary-treasurer Walter Roe Lymbery recorded that he purchased an 'umpire's whistle' in December 1872, so it is quite possible that one was used in matches prior to the generally accepted 1878 date. Before the use of the whistle became commonplace, the referee would wave a handkerchief to gain players' attention, but as crowd attendances increased this method inevitably became unworkable.

SEE ALSO **'ENTER: A REFEREE AND TWO LINESMEN'** (page 36). **'REFEREE BLOWS FULL-TIME EARLY'** (page 357).

The use of the referee's whistle was generally accepted in 1878. It is hard to imagine how a referee could ever have controlled a match without one.

FLOODLIT FOOTBALL
SHOWS THE WAY

1878

On 14 October 1878 Bramall Lane hosted the first ever football match played under floodlights. Approximately 20,000 spectators poured into the ground for the historic match, played between a team chosen by the Sheffield Association and a combination of players from local clubs, with the Association side winning 2-0. The ground-breaking feat was made possible by two portable engines, one behind each goal, which generated the electric power to illuminate four lamps. Each lamp stood on 10-metre high wooden towers, with one lamp placed in each corner of the ground.

SEE ALSO **'FLOODLIGHTS FINALLY ADOPTED'** (page 179); **'FIRST WORLD CUP GAME PLAYED INDOORS'** (page 475).

To test the possibilities of floodlit football, a tryout match was convened at the Arsenal practice ground.

Fergie Suter is regarded as being one of football's first professionals. He gave up his job as a stonemason shortly before playing for Darwen FC.

THE FIRST PROFESSIONALS

When Lancashire club Darwen played Scottish players Fergie Suter and Jimmy Love in the quarter-final of the still strictly amateur 1879 FA Cup against Old Etonians, there was a request that the pair be withdrawn from the competition on account of rumours that they were paid professionals. However, the request was overruled and the tie eventually went to two replays, before Old Etonians emerged victorious, winning 6-2.

Speculation that Suter was indeed a professional footballer was fuelled after he gave up his job as a stonemason shortly after leaving his Scottish club Partick Thistle and moving to England to play for Darwen.

SEE ALSO **'PROFESSIONALISM LEGALIZED'** (page 30); **'£4 A WEEK MAXIMUM WAGE INTRODUCED BY FA'** (page 49).

55 years after Uruguay's first club was formed the national team go on a victory lap following their win over Switzerland in the 1924 Olympic final.

FOOTBALL IN URUGUAY KICKS OFF

Uruguay's first football team was founded by an English professor at Montevideo University in 1882, but it wasn't until 1891 and the formation of a club called the Central Uruguay Railway Cricket Club (CURCC) that football really began to increase in popularity. CURCC was a sporting club formed by British railway engineers and it started out by playing football matches against British colleges and teams made up of sailors from ships docked in Montevideo harbour. CURCC was to become one of the most famous clubs in Uruguay when, in 1913, it was renamed as Club Atletico Penarol. It is now generally acknowledged to be the oldest club in Uruguay.

SEE ALSO **'URUGUAY DEFEND OLYMPIC TITLE'** (page 108); **'PENAROL WIN COPA LIBERTADORES'** (page 232).

TWO-HANDED
THROW-INS INTRODUCED

In 1882, 19 years after the formation of the Football Association, the rules were changed to allow two-handed thrown-ins. Prior to this innovation, a throw-in could be taken with one hand only, a law which had originally been set out in the Cambridge football rules of 1848. Two years before the two-handed method was introduced, there had been another amendment to the rules which permitted throw-ins to be taken in any direction. It had previously been stipulated that the ball had to be thrown back into play at right angles to the touchline, but this change further differentiated football from rugby.

SEE ALSO **'TEN YARD RULE INTRODUCED'** (page 73);
'GOALS DIRECT FROM CORNER KICKS ALLOWED' (page 97).

The two-handed throw-in in any direction was designed to further differentiate between football and rugby.

BLACKBURN OLYMPIC BREAK SOUTHERN DOMINANCE AND WIN CUP FINAL

By winning the 1883 FA Cup final Blackburn Olympic made history. On 31 March the Lancashire club defeated Old Etonians 2-1 after extra-time and became the first club from north of London to win the competition, thus breaking the domination of southern amateur clubs.

Blackburn Olympic were only founded in 1877, following the merger of two smaller clubs, Black Star and James Street, but were well coached in the still uncommon passing style of play by Jack Hunter. He also had the unusual idea of taking his team into Blackpool for a few days of relaxation prior to the final, something which no doubt precipitated the move towards professionalism. At the time of the 1883 FA Cup final, the team's full-time jobs included dental assistant (Thomas James Hacking), a cotton machine operator (James Thomas Ward) and a picture framer (Arthur Matthews).

SEE ALSO **'NORTHERNERS INVADE LONDON'** (page 28).
'CARDIFF CITY TAKE THE FA CUP OUT OF ENGLAND' (page 104).

Blackburn's achievement of winning the FA Cup was commemorated on a set a cigarette cards.

FIRST INTERNATIONAL TOURNAMENT ESTABLISHED

In a Home Championship international in 1905, Scotland goalkeeper John Lyall prepares to kick the ball downfield during against England.

After a series of friendlies during the late 1870s and early 1880s, England, Scotland, Wales and Ireland agreed to contest the British Home Championships – the world's first international competition. The first fixture, on 24 January 1884, saw Scotland visit Ireland and win 5-0. Due to the advanced development of British football, as well as the logistics of international travel, the four home nations continued to play each other for almost four decades before they met opponents from any further afield. The competition continued until 1984 when England and Scotland withdrew citing falling attendances and hooliganism among their reasons.

SEE ALSO **'FIRST EUROPEAN INTERNATIONAL'** (page 52); **'MEISL CREATES THE MITROPA CUP...'** (page 104).

FOOTBALL TAKES OFF DOWN UNDER

The popularity of the Australian rules football did not prevent the formation of a Football Association and the first clubs.

In 1880 the first football match under FA rules took place in Australia, when Parramatta Common in Sydney hosted a match between students from The King's School and a team called The Wanderers. The latter were Australia's first official football club, founded by school teacher John Walter Fletcher. In 1882 he had gone on to help form the South British Football Soccer Association (now the New South Wales Association) and the following year the first interstate match took place between New South Wales and Victoria. In 1884 Victoria's own footballing body, named the Anglo-Australian Football Association, was founded and its Queensland counterpart was formed a short time later.

SEE ALSO **'AUSTRALIA LAUNCHES NEW LEAGUE TO ATTRACT STAR PLAYERS'** (page 593). **'AUSTRALIA'S FIRST WORLD CUP GOAL'** (page 599).

Rovers ensured that the FA Cup would stay in Blackburn for another season, following their 2-1 win over Scottish side Queen's Park.

NORTHERNERS INVADE LONDON

Following in the footsteps of local rivals Blackburn Olympic a year earlier, on 19 March 1884 Blackburn Rovers became the second team from the north of England to win the FA Cup, beating Queen's Park 2-1. Scottish amateur side Queen's Park themselves made history by being the first non-English side to get to the Cup final. They reached it again in 1885, but again lost out to Rovers. With two teams from outside London contesting the Cup, there was inevitably an invasion of supporters from the north, with an estimated 4,000 fans in attendance at the Kennington Oval in South London.

SEE ALSO **'THE GREAT MERSEY SPLIT'** (page 37); **'FIRST 100,000 ATTENDANCE AT FA CUP FINAL'** (page 46-47).

England's 2-3-5 formation was considered cautious and defensive in a time when teams would play with six or seven strikers.

ENGLAND GO ON THE DEFENSIVE

During the 19th century it was common for both domestic and international teams to adopt line-ups featuring as many as six or seven attacking players. When England began their inaugural British Home Championships campaign against Ireland in February 1884 they used the then standard 2-2-6 (two defenders, two midfielders, six strikers) formation, winning handsomely 8-1. However, when they played Scotland away in March, England elected to go into the game using a radical formation of 2-3-5. At the time this was considered cautious and defensive, and indeed the match did turn out to be the lowest scoring of the Championships, with Scotland, ultimate winners of the competition, 1-0 victors.

SEE ALSO **'ARSENAL'S WM FORMATION'** (page 101); **'ROCCO INVENTS THE 'CATENACCIO'** (page 162).

ILLEGAL PAYMENTS TO PLAYERS EXPOSED

Following Accrington's 1883 expulsion from the Football Association for paying players, the issue of professionalism came to a head a year later when Preston North End were disqualified from the FA Cup, after a protest by their beaten opponents Upton Park. The strictly amateur club from London had complained to the Football Association that Preston had fielded players who were being paid. In fact, the practice of remunerating players for representing their clubs was spreading throughout the north of England and it was thought that both Blackburn Olympic and Blackburn Rovers were paying players, with Rovers winning the Cup for the three years following Blackburn Olympic's 1883 victory.

SEE ALSO **'FA THREATENED FROM WITHIN'** (page 29); **'PROFESSIONALISM LEGALIZED'** (page 30).

Illegal payments to players were on the increase. The three-time FA Cup-winning side Blackburn Rovers, above, were strongly suspected.

FA THREATENED FROM WITHIN

The British Football Association (BFA) was formed in 1884 in response to the ban by the Football Association (FA) on professional players playing for clubs under its jurisdiction. Rumours of players being paid spread from 1879 onwards when Darwen were thought to have fielded two Scottish semi-professionals in an FA Cup tie. In 1883 Accrington were disqualified from the FA Cup for paying players and the FA expelled Preston North End during the 1884 competition after the Lancashire club admitted it had been doing the same. The BFA signed up 31 members, but existed for less than a year, as on 20 July 1885 the FA legalized professionalism.

SEE ALSO **'PROFESSIONALISM LEGALIZED'** (page 30); **'THE FIRST 'WORLD CHAMPIONS'** (page 32).

A late nineteenth-century photograph of a crowd of football spectators, one of whom has climbed a telegraph pole for a better view.

1885

PROFESSIONALISM LEGALIZED

In 1884 the Football Association (FA) had sought to protect the amateur status of the game by imposing several rules, such as not allowing Scottish players, many of whom were professionals who'd moved to clubs based in northern England, to play in the FA Cup, and these restrictions led to the formation of the breakaway British Football Association.

However, in April 1885 the FA sent a questionnaire to each of its clubs, primarily asking whether paid players should be permitted to play in the FA Cup. At a special general meeting held on 20 July 1885 professionalism was subsequently legalized, the rival association was disbanded and the structure of football was changed forever. The FA imposed strict conditions on professional players and both Bolton Wanderers and Preston North End were thrown out of the 1885-86 competition for breaking the rules, but the legalization of professionalism ultimately led to the formation of the Football League, as clubs sought additional revenue to meet their growing wage bills.

SEE ALSO **'FORMATION OF THE FOOTBALL LEAGUE** (page 32).
'£4 A WEEK MAXIMUM WAGE INTRODUCED BY FA' (page 49).

Professionalism led to the formation of the Football League with Blackburn Rovers one of the founding members.

INTERNATIONAL BOARD FORMED TO SPREAD THE GAME

The inaugural meeting of the International Football Association Board (IFAB) took place on 2 June 1886 in Manchester at the behest of the English Football Association. The aim of the organisation was to standardise the rules of the game internationally and the meeting was attended by the English FA and its Scottish, Welsh and Irish counterparts. After world governing body FIFA was founded in 1904, it quickly sought to team up with the IFAB and incorporate the rules it had established. FIFA went on to join IFAB in 1913 and today has four representatives on the board, along with one from each United Kingdom association.

SEE ALSO **'THE FIRST EUROPEAN INTERNATIONAL'** (page 52); **'FORMATION OF FIFA'** (page 55).

The ball is hacked clear from a corner during a Manchester United and Portsmouth match in 1907. The smoke is from a local chemical works.

ARTHUR WHARTON TURNS OUT FOR PRESTON

Arthur Wharton became the first black professional footballer when he signed for Preston North End in 1886. Wharton, born in Ghana, West Africa, had gone to Cleveland College in Darlington in 1882 to train to be a Methodist preacher. However, he began to excel at several sports, including cycling and sprinting, and actually won the 100 yards at the 1886 national championships. He was spotted by Darlington and represented the north-east club as a goalkeeper, before joining Preston as a semi-professional. He helped Preston reach the FA Cup semi-finals in 1887, before returning to athletics for a year and then signing as a full professional for Rotherham United in 1889.

SEE ALSO **'BLACK POWER EMERGES AT WEMBLEY'** (page 258); **'ANDERSON BECOMES ENGLAND'S FIRST BLACK INTERNATIONAL'** (page 365).

Football's first black professional, Arthur Wharton, played for Preston North End and Rotherham United as well as being a champion sprinter.

THE FIRST 'WORLD CHAMPIONS'

Renton Football Club, a village team from West Dunbartonshire in Scotland, became the first club to lay claim to the grand title of 'Champions of the world'. Renton were one of the foremost clubs during the early years of Scottish football, winning the Scottish Cup in 1885 and again in 1888. Their second triumph led to an unofficial encounter with the English FA Cup holders, West Bromwich Albion, on 19 May 1888 at Second Hampden in Glasgow. Despite terrible weather conditions the game went ahead, with Renton winning convincingly 4-1 to become the unlikely 'Champions of the United Kingdom and the world'.

SEE ALSO **'ONE ARMED FORWARD SEALS FINAL'** (page 116); **'SCOTS CLAIM 'WORLD CHAMPION' STATUS'** (page 281).

Following their Scottish Cup triumph Renton played English Cup winners West Bromwich for the title of 'Champions of the World'.

Aston Villa director William McGregor is regarded as the father of the Football League following his letter to five clubs proposing its formation.

FORMATION OF THE FOOTBALL LEAGUE

Following the advent of professionalism in 1885, the number of professional clubs increased, but those clubs were without regular or guaranteed fixtures. The FA Cup remained the main competition, but although friendly matches organized by the clubs themselves also took place, the income generated was seen as being too unreliable.

The move to a regular set of games was instigated by a Birmingham shopkeeper, Scotsman William McGregor, who was also a director of Aston Villa. On 2 March 1888 he wrote to five clubs proposing the formation of a league.

SEE ALSO **'FOOTBALL'S FIRST LEAGUE GOAL'** (page 33); **'A SECOND TIER IS REALIZED'** (page 37).

FOOTBALL'S FIRST LEAGUE GOAL

The first ever goal in the Football League is thought to have been scored by Aston Villa's Gershom Cox on 8 September 1888. Unfortunately for the Villa player, though, the ball went in at the wrong end and so also goes down as the first ever own-goal. Luckily for Cox, Villa later equalized and the game against Wolverhampton Wanderers finished 1-1. The uncertainty over the first ever goal scorer exists because matches had staggered kick-off times. Preston's Fred Dewhurst opened the scoring in their 5-2 victory over Burnley after only three minutes, but that match started some 50 minutes later than the Villa between Wanderers game.

SEE ALSO **'DIXIE DEAN SCORES 60 LEAGUE GOALS'** (page 107); **'LAURENT MAKES HISTORY'** (page 114).

Having scored after three minutes, Fred Dewhurst had valid claim to the first league goal. Unfortunately his match kicked off 50 minutes late.

PRESTON PROVE 'INVINCIBLE'

Preston North End became the first club to win the double, winning both the Football League Championship and FA Cup in the 1888-89 season. Preston's achievement came at the end of the inaugural Football League season, meaning that it was the first time the feat had been even possible. The Preston side were dubbed the 'Invincibles' after going through the entire season undefeated, winning 18 out of their 22 league games. They also managed to secure the FA Cup without conceding a goal, beating Wolverhampton Wanderers 3-0 in the final. Aston Villa claimed the double in 1897, but then no one won it again until Tottenham Hotspur's 1961 triumphs.

SEE ALSO **'SPURS WIN THE DOUBLE'** (page 238); **'ARSENAL'S UNBEATEN SEASON'** (page 575).

Preston's double winning 'Invincibles'. They went through the league unbeaten and did not concede a goal in their FA Cup winning run.

1888 BRAZIL'S FIRST CLUB FOUNDED

The first sports club in Brazil was the São Paulo Athletic Club, founded on 15 May 1888. The club was formed by different groups of English immigrants, from a combination of English employees at the São Paulo Companhia de Gas (gas company), the São Paulo Railway and London Bank. It's likely that sports other than football, in particular cricket, were more popular during the early years, for it was not until the return to the city of Brazilian-born Englishman Charles Miller in 1894 that football was introduced and started to take off in Brazil.

SEE ALSO **'CHARLES MILLER 'GIVES' FOOTBALL TO BRAZIL'** (page 40).

The founding of São Paulo Athletic Club was the start of Brazil's love affair with football. It would lead them to be viewed as its greatest exponents.

1889 THE DANES JOIN THE GAME

The oldest existing organised body for football outside of England is the Danish Football Association, known as the Dansk Boldspil-Union (DBU). The DBU was founded on 18 May 1889 and its first official football competition began later the same year. Denmark's first club, Kjobenhavns Boldklub, was founded on 26 April 1876 and several others were formed during the 1880s, but it was a man named F I A Markmann who helped to model the Danish rules on the English game, as well as importing balls, shoes and shirts from England for Danish clubs. Markmann was later elected the first chairman of the DBU.

SEE ALSO **'FOOTBALL REACHES SWEDEN'** (page 22); **'ITALY'S FIRST CLUB'** (page 38).

Markmann kicked-off Denmark's long association with football. Danish international Jensen scores a dynamic header in 1973.

GOAL NETS MAKE AN APPEARANCE

1890

Football had managed to survive without the use of goal nets until Professor John Alexander Brodie invented them in 1890. Brodie, who was appointed city engineer for Liverpool in 1898 and famously designed the Mersey Tunnel, witnessed a dispute over whether the ball had passed through the goal posts while watching an Everton game. As a result, he formed the idea of a net 'pocket', to be attached to the goal posts. Goal nets were first used in a match on New Year's Day 1891, in a match between Nottingham Forest and Bolton Wanderers, and they proved to be a great success.

SEE ALSO **'BROOKING'S GETS STUCK IN WITH FREAK SHOT'** (page 376).

After witnessing a dispute over whether a ball had passed through the goal, Professor Brodie formed the idea of a net 'pocket'.

CORINTHIANS REFUSE PENALTIES

1891

Amateur football club Corinthians was founded in 1882 and attracted many of the most talented players of the time. Although they were undoubtedly a top team, true to their amateur status they refused to join the Football League or take part in the FA Cup, abiding by their rule forbidding them to 'compete for any cup or prizes'. Perhaps a further symptom of the trend towards professionalism was the FA's introduction of penalty kicks in 1891. This was a rule change that was strictly against the Corinthians' ideals, for they believed a gentleman would never deliberately commit a foul. They upheld this principle to the extent that they would refuse to take a penalty if one were awarded to them, or attempt to save a penalty given against them.

SEE ALSO **'ENGLAND FIELDS A CORINTHIAN'S XI'** (page 39); **'BAGGIO'S PENALTY PRINCIPLES'** (page 454).

The principled Corinthians amateur outfit thrashed Manchester United 11-3 in 1904. This remains the 'Red Devils' largest defeat.

ENTER: A REFEREE AND TWO LINESMEN

In early football matches there was no referee and any disputes were discussed between team captains. Then umpires nominated by each team were introduced to arbitrate on disputed decisions, but only when called upon, and they were not allowed onto the pitch. In 1880 a referee joined the two umpires as a neutral presence and gradually the power of referees increased until, in 1891, they were allowed onto the pitch and umpires became linesmen. Finally, in 1894, the referee was given sole control of the game, so players no longer needed to appeal for a decision to be given.

SEE ALSO 'REFEREE FELLED' (page 584); 'ITALIAN REFEREES GO ON STRIKE' (page 100).

The neutral presence of the referee and his linesmen. In 1891, the referee was given sole control of the game removing the need for player appeals.

LONE KEEPER FACES 11 OPPONENTS

Local derby encounters are often competitive and occasionally controversial, but the December 1891 meeting between rivals Burnley and Blackburn Rovers was more eventful than most. At the interval Rovers found themselves 3-0 behind and after the regulation ten-minute break they initially failed to reappear. When they eventually emerged, the referee was forced to send off two of their players for fighting and with that the other outfield players decided to depart, too, leaving just the Rovers goalkeeper Herby Arthur remaining. The game continued for a while with 11 against one, before the referee abandoned the game. The Rovers players later said they'd left early because of the cold weather.

SEE ALSO 'SCOTLAND'S OPPONENTS DON'T SHOW' (page 503).

Herbie Arthur the Blackburn Rovers goalkeeper who was left to fend for himself against the eleven men of Burnley after his team left the field.

THE GREAT MERSEY SPLIT

Liverpool Football Club was formed on 15 March 1892 following a dispute involving Everton's home ground… Anfield. Everton chairman John Houlding had become embroiled in a dispute with some of the Everton board after he purchased the ground in 1891, so Everton subsequently moved to Goodison Park, leaving Houlding and some of his supporters behind. Houlding convened a meeting at his Anfield Road home and Liverpool was born (the Football League rejected his original name – Everton Athletic). Liverpool won the Lancashire League at the first attempt and were elected to the Football League Second Division in 1893, ending the 1893-94 season as unbeaten champions.

SEE ALSO 'MILAN SPLIT CREATES INTER' (page 61).

A portrait of the Liverpool team who were promoted to the Football League Second Division in 1893 following their split from Everton.

A SECOND TIER IS REALIZED

The Football League added a second tier in 1892 after merging with the Football Alliance League. The latter had been formed in 1889 and consisted of 12 clubs from the Midlands, north-west and east of England. The new division was largely made up of Football Alliance clubs, with its three strongest sides joining Division One. Automatic promotion and relegation didn't exist until 1898. Instead, the top Division Two sides played a series of 'test matches' against the bottom Division One clubs. The inaugural Division Two champions Small Heath (now Birmingham City) lost out in the test matches, but runners-up Sheffield United overcame Accrington to become the first side to be promoted.

SEE ALSO 'LEAGUE EXTENDED TO 44 CLUBS' (page 84).

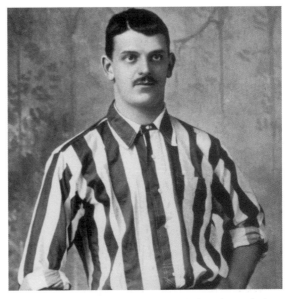

Mick Whitham of Sheffield United, who were the first side to make the leap from the newly created Second Division into the elite English League.

ARGENTINA INAUGURATES NATIONAL CHAMPIONSHIP

Argentina became the first country outside the United Kingdom to organise a national football league championship when the Argentinian Association Football League (renamed the Argentinian Football Association in 1903) was founded on 21 February 1893. Lomas Athletic Club, founded on 15 March 1891 by English immigrants, became the most successful side during the 1890s, winning the championship on five occasions. Former pupils of the English High School then formed Alumni Football Club and from 1900 won a total of ten league titles in 14 years, proving themselves to be the most successful club of the amateur era.

SEE ALSO **'ENGLISH CLUBS TOUR BRAZIL AND ARGENTINA'** (page 67).

Spectators look on as photographers race across the pitch to get pictures of the USA team before their World Cup match with Argentina in 1930.

ITALY'S FIRST CLUB FORMED

Genoa Cricket and Football Club became the first football team in Italy when it was formed on 7 September 1893. Based in northern Italy, it was set up by British expatriates, including the British diplomat Sir Charles Alfred Payton, and went on to win the Italian Championship a total of nine times, including the inaugural title in 1898. The club was created with the aim of representing England abroad and consequently the team was kitted out in white shirts as a tribute to the English national side. Being a private club, Italians were not allowed to play in those formative years.

SEE ALSO **'GENOA WIN FIRST ITALIAN CHAMPIONSHIP'** (page 42); **'GENOA EMPLOY 'MISTER' GARBUTT'** (page 72).

The Italian and Genoa player Fosco Beccatini was a member of the club team who won the Serie A title in 1946-47.

A portrait of Charles Wexford-Brown, a famous Corinthians player here seen wearing the England strip with it's familiar three lions crest.

ENGLAND FIELDS A CORINTHIANS XI

The famous amateur side Corinthians contained many of the best players of the era. Indeed, on 12 March 1894, in a British Home Championship match against Wales in Wrexham, the England national side was made up entirely of Corinthians. The players' familiarity with each other certainly seemed to help and England won 5-1. The following year the selection was repeated. Interestingly though, these statistics are not officially ratified, as the Football Association states that most of the Corinthians players had a primary association with another team, in most cases an English University side.

SEE ALSO **'CORINTHIANS REFUSE TO TAKE PENALTIES'** (page 35). **'THE AMATEURS FIGHT BACK'** (page 60).

Aston Villa pose with their inspirational captain John Devey, centre, and the FA Cup which was stolen from a shop window in 1895.

THE FA CUP IS STOLEN

After Aston Villa had won the 1895 FA Cup final with a 1-0 victory over Midlands rivals West Bromwich Albion, the club decided to put the trophy on public display as a reward for their loyal supporters. The Cup was presented to Birmingham sports shop owner William Shillcock, who placed it in his window on 11 September 1895, but that very night the shop was broken into and the Cup stolen. Despite the offer of a £10 reward, the original FA Cup was never found. The Football Association subsequently fined Villa £25 to meet the cost of the replacement trophy, which was an exact copy of the original.

SEE ALSO **'BRAND NEW FA CUP RETURNS TO BRADFORD'** (page 69); **'WORLD CUP STOLEN'** (page 266).

Charles Miller, the man who is credited with helping football attain its significant role in Brazilian culture.

CHARLES MILLER 'GIVES' FOOTBALL TO BRAZIL

The birth and lift-off of football in Brazil coincided with the return to the country after a ten-year absence of a British man named Charles Alexander Miller.

In 1884, when he was nine, his Scottish expatriate father, an engineer working on a railway in the Brazilian city of Sao Paulo, sent him to England to receive the best possible education. However, the young Miller's education may not have been quite what his father had in mind, as at 19 he came back to Brazil to pass on all he had learnt about a fast-growing sport in England called football, and when he disembarked at Santos he began to teach the game to anyone who was interested.

Before long a match was organised between the mainly British employees of the local railway and gas companies and within a few short years many Brazilians were playing the game. As a lasting legacy to the role Miller played in helping the game attain its hugely significant role in Brazilian culture, a São Paulo street is named in his honour.

SEE ALSO **'BRAZIL FACE MIGHTY EXETER CITY'** (page 76); **'BRAZILIAN SOCIOLOGIST FOCUSES ON FOOTBALL'** (page 142).

JUVENTUS FORMED

Formed in 1897 by a group of Turin students and local British residents, Juventus were only the fourth team to be founded in the city, but by 1905 they were champions of Italy and would go on to become the country's biggest and most famous club, with 27 Scudettos to date and an estimated following of ten million across Italy. A year after the 'Old Lady' was formed, Milan Cricket and Football Club was founded by locals and British residents. They soon changed their name to AC Milan and would go on to become Italy's second most domestically successful club and its most successful in European competition.

SEE ALSO **'JUVENTUS KIT FADES IN THE WASH'** (page 53); **'EDOARDO AGNELLI TAKES CONTROL OF JUVENTUS'** (page 94).

Juventus were formed in 1897 by Turin students and British residents. Within ten years they were champions and widely supported in Italy.

PLAYERS FORM A UNION

Given the strength of the 19th-century trade union movement and the tendency of clubs to simply cold-shoulder injured players it was hardly surprising that, within 13 years of the Football Association reluctantly conceding that professionalism existed, and a decade after the Football League gave the season a structure and tied players to teams, the booted workers clubbed together to protect their own interests. Manchester hosted the meeting, with United and City players joined by others from the north and the Midlands to create the Players' Union of Associated Players, which would later become the Professional Footballers' Association (PFA).

SEE ALSO **'PLAYERS' UNION FINALLY GETS OFF THE GROUND'** (page 60).

Manchester City players were among those present at the first Players' Union meeting. Here, the team can be seen posing with the FA Cup in 1904.

One of Athletic Bilbao's most famous sons, Telmo Zarraonandia. He was a prolific goalscorer, winning the *Pichichi* award for top scorer six times.

ATHLETIC BILBAO FORMED

'Atletico' play in Madrid. The similarly striped team in the northern port of Bilbao is 'Athletic', a testament to their British roots. Itinerant miners from Sunderland met dockers from Southampton and quickly formed a team – Bilbao FC – and it must have taken seconds to decide on a kit of red and white stripes. Meanwhile, the richer locals were returning from their studies in England enthused with the new game and in 1898 they formed the Athletic Club, spelt the English way. Four years later, the two teams combined forces to play in the Copa del Rey and returned from Barcelona with the trophy. A club was born.

SEE ALSO **'WANTED – A FOOTBALL TEAM!'** (page 44). **'REAL MADRID FORM – AND MAKE AN ENEMY'** (page 49).

Four of the new laws concerned 'dead ball' situations including throw-ins. To this day, the basic rules of the game still stand at 17.

LAWS EXPANDED TO 17

The first Laws of Association Football were set at 13 in 1863 and that number was increased to 17 in 1898 by the International Football Association Board (IFAB), which was made up of the football associations of the four home nations and which had formed in 1892. Until then, rules for international games had to be agreed beforehand between the two participating countries. The four new laws all concerned the introduction of new 'dead ball' situations or set pieces – the penalty-kick, the throw-in, the goal-kick and the corner-kick. To this day, the basic rules of the game still stand at 17.

SEE ALSO **'MORLEY DRAFTS THE FIRST LAWS'** (page 14).

Newcastle United were one of the first teams to benefit from the new systems when they were promoted to an expanded 18-team top flight.

PROMOTION AND RELEGATION ADD TO THE COMPETITION

The Football League's 12 clubs soon grew in number as in 1892 it merged with the Football Alliance, creating a dozen-strong Second Division. For several years the bottom two First Division clubs faced the Second Division's top two in 'test matches' – a mini-league of play-offs. However, in 1898 when Stoke and Burnley played for a draw in their final test match, knowing that this would see them both promoted the following season, time was up for the system. From then on, automatic promotion and relegation saw two teams swap positions, while Newcastle United – the victims of Stoke and Burnley's collusion – were promoted to an expanded 18-team top flight.

SEE ALSO **'THE UPS AND DOWNS OF THE FOOTBALL LEAGUE'** (page 328); **'PLAY-OFFS INTRODUCED BY FOOTBALL LEAGUE'** (page 418).

The first Italian league was contested by just four teams over one day. It was the start of the avid Italian following the game would attract.

GENOA WIN FIRST ITALIAN CHAMPIONSHIP

Widely recognised as Italy's first football club – formed by a bunch of Englishmen, no less, in 1893 – Genoa Cricket and Football Club claimed the country's first league title in 1898, after the Italian football federation (FIGC) had been founded earlier that year. The format was slightly different to the modern day Serie A, however. It was contested between just four teams, with the other three – International Torino, FC Torinese, Ginnastica Torino – all coming from Turin, and was played over the course of just one day. Genoa emerged victorious, but, alas, were relegated five years later as other clubs emerged to challenge their dominance.

SEE ALSO **'ITALY'S FIRST CLUB FORMED'** (page 38). **'GENOA EMPLOY 'MISTER' GARBUTT'** (page 72).

WANTED – A FOOTBALL CLUB!

In 1898, on his way to set up some sugar trading companies in Africa, Swiss-born 21-year-old Hans Kamper popped into Barcelona to visit an uncle. He liked the place so much that he stayed, learned Catalan and changed his name to Joan Kamper. A year later he placed an ad in the newspaper Los Deportes to see if anyone fancied setting up a football club. A selection of Catalan, British and Swiss enthusiasts responded, and on 29 November they founded Football Club Barcelona. Nominated captain, Gamper scored more than 100 goals in 48 appearances and went on to become club president.

SEE ALSO **'REAL MADRID FORM – AND MAKE AN ENEMY'** (page 49).
'EULOGIO MARTINEZ RAMIRO SCORES THE NOU CAMP'S FIRST GOAL' (page 210).

The original advert as posted by Joan Kamper. He requests 'that everyone who likes this sport contact him'. It led to the formation of FC Barcelona.

NOTAS DE SPORT

Nuestro amigo y compañero Mr. Kans Kamper, de la Sección de Foot-Vall de la «Sociedad Los Deportes» y antiguo campeón suizo, deseoso de poder organizar algunos partidos en Barcelona, ruega á cuantos sientan aficiones por el referido deporte se sirvan ponerse en relación con el, dignándose al efecto pasar por esta redacción los martes y viernes por la noche de 9 á 11.

ENGLAND TAKE ON THE GERMANS

With football clubs springing up on the continent, English emissaries soon took to touring and in late 1899 a Football Association representative team were dispatched to the continent for a whirlwind four-game tour, opening in Berlin. The locals were easily beaten 13-2 in a friendly encounter, but proved themselves impeccable hosts, treating the visitors to dinner and displaying a huge desire to learn the game. The next morning the English again triumphed 10-2 and then later the same day nipped over to Prague to beat a German-Austrian team. After handing out a final 8-0 beating in Karlsruhe, the English headed home – and the Germans started practicing.

SEE ALSO **'PRINCE WILHELM PRESENTS CUP'** (page 59); **'GERMANY FIELDS TWO NATIONAL SIDES'** (page 66).

The Football Association dispatched a representative team to Berlin in response to increasing popularity of the sport throughout Europe.

The Dade brothers, Hans and Johan were two of the four founding members of arguably Holland's greatest club side, Ajax Amsterdam.

AJAX AMSTERDAM FORMED

Holland's most famous club endured troubled beginnings. Their first incarnation, as the Foothball Club Ajax in 1894, was shortlived and Ajax Amsterdam, as they are now known, were founded on 18 March 1900 by Floris Stempel, Carel Reeser and the Dade brothers, Hans and Johan. In 1911, they were promoted to the Dutch First Division under their first official coach, John Kirwan, and in the same year they changed the original colours of their kit to adopt those of Holland's then most successful club, Sparta Rotterdam. The famous red and white combination still adorns Ajax's home strip to this day.

SEE ALSO **'AJAX INTRODUCE THEIR YOUTH SYSTEM'** (page 82); **'RINUS BRINGS 'TOTAL FOOTBALL' TO AJAX'** (page 255).

FIRST 100,000 ATTENDANCE AT FA CUP FINAL

Having defeated four good First Division teams on their way to the 1901 FA Cup final, Tottenham Hotspur of the Southern League met the mighty Sheffield United in front of 110,000 at Crystal Palace's vast bowl. A 2-2 draw seemed a commendable enough result for the non-league side, but at 2-1 behind, Sheffield United were inexplicably awarded a goal by the referee when it should have been a goal-kick or a corner and Spurs, having had the better of the game, were forced to travel north to Burden Park in Bolton for a replay.

On 27 April only 20,000 turned up, very few of them from London, because the Lancashire and Yorkshire Rail Company refused to issue cheap tickets to supporters travelling to the game. In poor weather conditions, Spurs went behind as they had in the first game, but equalized soon after and scored twice more in the last 15 minutes to secure a surprising, but deserved, 3-1 victory.

At their post-match dinner, Spurs began a tradition that still stands today, when they tied ribbons in the club's colours to the handles of the trophy. Although it was the first time a team from London had reached the FA Cup final for 21 years, Tottenham's victory was further proof of the south's growing influence on a domestic game that had previously been dominated by teams from the north and the Midlands.

Spurs had to wait another seven years before, in 1909, they were elected to Football League Division Two. They earned promotion to the First Division in their first season.

SEE ALSO **'THE WHITE HORSE FINAL'** (page 93).

Second Division Tottenham Hotspur's Tom Morris runs back onto the pitch after taking a throw-in. His team took Sheffield United to a replay where they triumphed 3-1.

Proving the popularity of the game, 100,000 spectators flocked to Crystal Palace for the 1901 final.

Uruguay and Argentina are credited with playing the first international outside Britain. They would notably meet in the 1930 World Cup final.

ETERNAL ENEMIES LAND THEIR FIRST PUNCHES

With 161 fixtures and counting, no international teams have lined up against each other more often than Argentina and Uruguay. The first clash came in 1901 and was officially the first international to be held outside Britain (Canada had played the USA twice, but neither country's football association formally recognizes the games). With the South American neighbours both mad for the new ball game, it was natural that they should face each other and Uruguay invited Argentina over for a game, which the visitors duly won 3-2. Over the next 15 years Uruguay would play 30 more games, all but one of them against Argentina.

SEE ALSO **'ARGENTINA PUTS UP A FENCE'** (page 97).

King Edward VII played a pivotal role in helping football spread throughout Europe in his position as patron of the Football Association.

KING EDWARD VII HEADS THE FA

When Queen Victoria died in January 1901, Edward VII became the second oldest man to ascend to the British throne. Not, you would think, the ideal person to become patron of a football association that was renowned for its fuddy-duddyism. However, despite being 59, Edward was well known for his interest in foreign affairs – he was fluent in French and German – at a time when the Football Association (FA) viewed foreign meddling in an essentially English game with great suspicion, so Edward's links with Europe were particularly handy in 1904 when FIFA was formed. England joined a year later and Edward became known as the 'Uncle of Europe'.

SEE ALSO **'PRINCE WILHELM PRESENTS CUP'** (page 59).

£4 A WEEK MAXIMUM WAGE INTRODUCED BY THE FA

Naturally amateur in outlook, the gentlemen of the Football Association (FA) were clearly rattled by the financial power of the game's most crucial protagonists – the players. Having only reluctantly agreed to clubs being allowed to pay fees, the FA were reasonably quick to react to the nascent players' union – and publicly proclaim an interest in 'levelling the field' – by setting a maximum wage of £4 a week and attempting to abolish all bonuses. Within three years, exasperated by clubs persistently finding their way around the rules to benefit key players, the FA handed over responsibility for all financial matters between club and player to the Football League.

SEE ALSO **'PLAYERS THREATEN TO STRIKE'** (page 65).

Representative of the battle over players wages, Scottish professional outfit Queens Park play the vehemently amateur Corinthians.

The kit of Sociedad Madrid, or Real Madrid as they would become, of white shirts, shorts and blue socks was inspired by London Corinthians.

REAL MADRID FORM – AND MAKE AN ENEMY

At the turn of the 20th century English graduates took part in scratch football games at Madrid's Institution Libre de Ensenanza, soon forming the Football Sky Club. After a couple of name changes and splits, they sat down on 6 March 1902 and settled on a new name – Sociedad Madrid FC. Although the King of Spain didn't grant them the title 'Real' (royal) until 1920, this was the birth of Real Madrid.

Already symbolizing Catalan pride, FC Barcelona were to become a natural foil for the capital club and sure enough the two were quickly drawn together in the Copa del Rey. Barcelona took the honours in the first 'el clasico' game, winning 3-1 in Madrid, and it would be 14 painful years and 10 attempts before Madrid beat Barcelona.

SEE ALSO **'BARCELONA WALK OFF IN PROTEST'** (page 83).

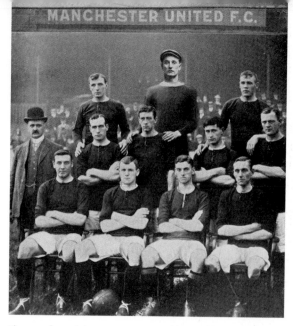

The team formerly known as Newton Heath pose for a photograph three years after they were bought and renamed Manchester United.

NEWTON HEATH BECOME MANCHESTER UNITED

Languishing in the Second Division with dwindling crowds and spiraling debts, Newton Heath were on the verge of bankruptcy when fate intervened in the form of a St Bernard. An attraction at a fund-raising bazaar for the club, the dog's escape brought together Heath captain Harry Stafford and two local businessmen, James Taylor and JH Davies. Along with J Brown and W Deakin, they agreed to pay the £2000 required to keep the club afloat in return for a direct interest in the running of the club. When it was suggested that the club should be renamed 'Manchester United', the new owners unanimously agreed.

SEE ALSO 'MANCHESTER UNITED SNAP UP CITY TALENT' (page 58).

Mexico lay claim to Central America's first organized league. Here, future international Jose Luis Gonzalez takes a break from training in 1966.

MEXICAN FOOTBALL GETS ORGANIZED

Scratch games, friendly fixtures and impromptu cups had been taking place in Central and South America for a few years, but Mexico can lay claim to the region's first organized league. Curiously kicking off at the height of summer, the Mexican Football League was initially contested by four teams and won by the Reforma Athletic Club of Pachuca, which had been founded two years previously by Cornish miners. They beat off competition from El Orizaba FC, El Mexico Cricket Club (also formed by Englishmen) and no, this isn't a fictitious name – El British Club FC.

SEE ALSO 'THE MEXICAN WAVE SAYS HELLO' (page 410).

Injured spectators are carried away on makeshift stretchers after a section of wooden terracing collapsed at Ibrox Park.

THE IBROX DISASTER KILLS 25

Chosen to host international games because of its modern facilities, Rangers' Ibrox Park in Glasgow was the scene of a major disaster in April 1902, when 25 people plunged to their death and 500 were injured after a section of terracing collapsed under the weight of the crowd as Scotland played England. Although the match was only a few minutes old, play continued and many spectators didn't learn of the tragic events until they read about it in the evening newspaper. The 1-1 draw was later declared unofficial and the match was replayed at Villa Park a month later, with receipts going to the disaster fund.

SEE ALSO **'TRAGEDY RETURNS TO IBROX'** (page 312); **'THE BASTIA DISASTER'** (page 457).

1902

FIRST EUROPEAN INTERNATIONAL

By the turn of the century football had spread throughout Europe and South America, thanks largely to British settlers and touring sides. And so, 30 years after England played Scotland in the first recognized game between two international football teams, two countries from outside the United Kingdom met in an international match for the first time – or so the history books tell us.

In fact, Austria's 5-0 victory over near-neighbours Hungary in Vienna in October 1902 was actually a game between two cities – the Austrian capital versus Budapest– and in reality Austria and Hungary enjoyed dual sovereignty as the Empire of Austria and the Kingdom of Hungary. The Austrian Football Association wasn't even founded until 18 March 1904, but in 1908 the game was reclassified as an international.

In 1901 the first game between two South American sides took place when Argentina played Uruguay.

SEE ALSO 'THE FORMATION OF FIFA' (page 55).

International fixtures soon became a common occurrence. Here, Czech goalkeeper Frantisek Planicka scrambles for the ball during a match in 1932.

JUVENTUS STRIP FADES IN WASH

Despite being known as the 'Bianconeri' (Black and whites) Juventus spent the first six years of their existence playing in a feminine shade of pink. However, in 1903, after their already-pale kit faded in the wash, they sent English team member John Savage back home in search of some new team colours. Savage returned with replicas of Notts County's no-nonsense black and white stripes, Juve won the title two years later and have worn the colours ever since. Several European clubs adopted the colours of English clubs and Leeds United returned the favour in 1961, copying Real Madrid's all-white apparel.

SEE ALSO **'CAMEROON'S SHIRTS CUT TO SIZE'** (page 553).

Notts County's 1894 FA Cup-winning team. Having adopted a similar black and white kit in 1903, Juventus then won the Italian league.

McCRACKEN SETS OFFSIDE TRAP

Cunning Bill McCracken is widely considered to have invented the offside trap during a successful spell at Newcastle United between 1904 and 1924. The Ulster-born full-back became so adept at employing the tactic of stepping up to catch attackers offside that he infuriated fans, opponents and officials, even provoking a pitch invasion on one occasion. Some thought the tactic bordered on cheating, but McCracken was an integral part of the Newcastle side that won the League title three times between 1905 and 1909. In 1925, the Football Association felt obliged to change the offside laws to give attackers a better chance of scoring.

SEE ALSO **'CHEDGZOY'S CHUTZPAH'** (page 99).

McCracken's tactic of stepping up to catch strikers offside infuriated fans, opponents and officials, and even provoked a pitch invasion.

1904

BILLY MEREDITH WINS FA CUP

Billy Meredith was the game's first superstar. A charismatic right-winger who played while chewing a toothpick, he instantly endeared himself to fans of Manchester City within a week of his October 1894 arrival by scoring two in the first Manchester derby against Newton Heath (later Manchester United). Five years later he led City to the top flight and in 1904 to their first trophy, with a 1-0 win over local rivals Bolton Wanderers in the FA Cup final at Crystal Palace. He was voted Player of the Year, but circumstances would soon change for the mercurial Meredith.

SEE ALSO 'MANCHESTER UNITED SNAP UP CITY TALENT' (page 58); 'BILLY MEREDITH RETIRES AGED 49' (page 95).

Billy Meredith charges down the wing in the 1904 FA Cup final leaving two Bolton Wanderers opponents trailing in his wake.

THE FORMATION OF FIFA

"Tired of the struggle and recognizing that the Englishmen, true to tradition, wanted to wait and watch, I undertook to invite delegates myself." These are the words of Robert Guerin of the Union of French Sports Clubs, who, after several frustrating meetings with the top brass of the English Football Association (FA), had grown tired of waiting for the modern game's founders to take the lead in the formation of an international governing body. Consequently, on 31 May 1904, a meeting was called in the French capital to coincide with the Congress of Paris and FIFA was born.

With representatives from Holland, Belgium (both of whom had also tried and failed to persuade the English to join the new body), Switzerland, Spain, Sweden and Denmark joining the French, FIFA had seven founder members. Two months later football was introduced as an exhibition sport in the Paris Olympics.

Typically, the FA, having reluctantly given the other countries their blessing, then set up a committee to review the establishment of FIFA and its potential implications for the game. Remaining defiant and suspicious, the following Easter they turned down an invitation from FIFA to play in an international tournament, before finally bowing to the inevitable and joining in July 1905.

SEE ALSO **'ENGLAND JOIN FIFA'** (page 58); **'FIFA CELEBRATE CENTENARY'** (page 576).

GRUPPE I		GRUPPE II		GRUPPE III		GRUPPE IV	
1	Chile	5	Spanien-Jugosl.	9	Niederlande	13	Haiti
2	BR Deutschland	6	Brasilien	10	Uruguay	14	Italien
3	DDR	7	Zaire	11	Schweden	15	Polen
4	Australien	8	Schottland	12	Bulgarien	16	Argentinien

The formation of FIFA opened up the game, something which the FA seemed reluctant to do.

Woolwich Arsenal were selected as a typical English side against which the Parisian side could test themselves. Arsenal won by 25 goals.

WOOLWICH ARSENAL 26 PARIS 1

The French influence on Arsenal didn't start with Monsieur Wenger. Still nine years away from moving to north London, recently promoted Woolwich Arsenal were happy to boost their profile by playing host to a visiting Parisian side, which was widely believed to be the best side the French had to offer. In fact, it was effectively the France national team, coming over the channel in order to assess their strength against a typical English team. The result was sobering, as a rampant Arsenal racked up 26 goals against the visitors, who managed a single goal in reply.

SEE ALSO **'NORRIS ANNOUNCES ARSENAL'S MOVE TO HIGHBURY'** (page 73).

Nottingham Forest keeper, Harry Linacre, looks outfield. In 1905 a law was passed preventing goalkeepers from rushing off their line at penalties.

GOALKEEPERS TIED TO THE LINE FOR PENALTIES

When the penalty was finally introduced in 1891 (with the injured party allowed to kick from anywhere along a line 12 yards from goal), goalkeepers were allowed to charge up to six yards out of their goal – half way to the ball, no mean distance if the goalkeeper in question was giant custodian William 'Fatty' Foulke. With too many penalties being saved to the lawmakers' liking, in 1905 they ruled that a goalkeeper must stay 'on his own goal line until the ball is kicked'. In 1929, the goalkeeper was also prevented from moving along his goal line, a rule which has since been relaxed.

SEE ALSO **'GOALKEEPERS ORDERED TO STAND STILL'** (page 91).

FOOTBALL'S FIRST £1000 TRANSFER

Desperate times call for desperate measures. Facing relegation and without an away win for more than two years, Middlesbrough signed England inside-forward Alf Common from rivals Sunderland for £1000. This caused widespread outrage and Charles Clegg of Sheffield United was particularly angry, having sold Common to Sunderland for just a few hundred pounds, and his mood was unlikely to have improved when Common scored against the Blades on his Middlesbrough debut to give them a long-awaited away victory. Boro were then fined by the FA for making unauthorised payments to players, but their fans were not bothered, as Common's goals eventually helped them avoid relegation by two points.

SEE ALSO **'FOOTBALL ASSOCIATION IMPOSE MAXIMUM TRANSFER FEE'** (page 61).

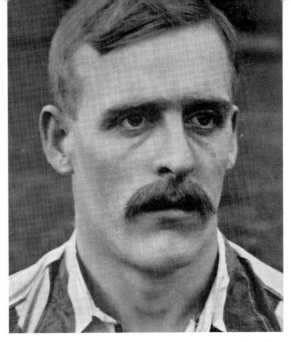

"When will it end?" An MP's question in Parliament following Alf Common's £1000 transfer from Sunderland to Middlesbrough.

NEWLY MINTED CHELSEA WALK INTO THE LEAGUE

Chelsea FC didn't have to search for a home ground – they were formed to fill one. Gus Mears had bought the Stamford Bridge Athletics Ground in west London to stage first-class matches, although when a rent dispute dissuaded nearby Fulham from moving in Mears briefly considered selling the land to the railways. However, instead he decided to found a club of his own, which he duly did on 14 March 1905 at the Rising Sun pub opposite the ground. Denied entry to the Southern League because Fulham and Tottenham objected, they were welcomed into the predominantly northern Football League at that organization's very next AGM.

SEE ALSO **'ABRAMOVICH BUYS CHELSEA – AND SUCCESS'** (page 571).

The Chelsea team who were formed in 1905 to fill Stamford Bridge. Their goalkeeper Willie Foulke was affectionately nicknamed 'Fatty'.

ENGLAND FINALLY JOINS FIFA

Having shunned the opportunity to take a lead role in the formation of football's world governing body only a year earlier, in July 1905 a Football Association (FA) delegation attended a FIFA conference in Berne and one of them, Daniel Woolfall, was duly elected as its first president. It was an uneasy alliance, however. With England's previous apathy and suspicion of the rest of the world, the seven other member countries – all of them European – now questioned England's motives for joining, and the Scottish and Irish FAs were initially refused membership, because it was thought they would be puppets of the FA.

SEE ALSO **'HOME NATIONS TO BOYCOTT FIFA'** (page 86).

England's Herbert Smith in action during the match at the Crystal Palace in a home championship match against Scotland.

The Manchester City team before the corruption scandal erupted. The club was found guilty of making illegal payments to 17 players.

MANCHESTER UNITED SNAP UP CITY TALENT

Having won the FA Cup and finished runners-up in the League in 1904, 1905 was to prove Manchester City's annus horribilis. A Football Association inquiry found the club guilty of making illegal payments to 17 of their players, who were banned from playing for City for life and from all forms of football until January 1907.

City called a meeting, inviting clubs to bid for the players, but Manchester United manager Ernest Mangnall had already approached many of them beforehand and, despite other clubs' protestations, the transfers of three of City's suspended players had already been sanctioned.

SEE ALSO **'LEEDS CITY PLAYERS UP FOR AUCTION'** (page 84).

The enthusiastic endorsement from the future army general helped legitimize football among Germany's upper social classes.

PRINCE WILHELM PRESENTS CUP

On the morning of 29 April 1905 Germania Berlin were excitedly readying themselves for the visit of an English amateur side. Preparations cranked up a notch or two when they received a telegram saying 'His Imperial Highness Crown Prince Wilhelm will arrive at 5.30 today for the football competition.' Sure enough, the 20-year-old son of the Emperor turned up and was so thrilled to see Germania beat the visitors 3-2 that he personally presented them with a trophy. This enthusiastic endorsement from a future army general helped legitimize the game among Germany's upper social classes, which had long distrusted 'English' sports.

SEE ALSO **'WAR SUSPENDS FOOTBALL'** (page 81).

Goalkeeper Jack Hillman's attempts to bribe his opposite number led to his suspension and the passing of the Prevention of Corruption Act.

GOVERNMENT ACT TO STAMP OUT CORRUPTION

Attempted match-fixing had begun to creep into the English game in the early 20th century. First, Burnley captain Jack Hillman had tried to pay off his Nottingham Forest opposite number as the Clarets fought relegation from the First Division in 1900. Then in 1905 Manchester City star Billy Meredith was found guilty of trying to bribe an Aston Villa player as City chased the league title. Passed by Parliament in 1906, the Prevention of Corruption Act made any such misdemeanour punishable by up to seven years in prison, but in football at least this proved to be less of a deterrent than the authorities had hoped.

SEE ALSO **'MATCH FIXING SCANDAL ROCKS ENGLISH FOOTBALL'** (page 80).

THE AMATEURS FIGHT BACK

The Football Association (FA) may have legalized professionalism in 1885, but many in football – particularly the old-school-tie 'gentlemen footballers' whose teams dominated the early decades of the FA Cup – remained adamantly against it. When the FA instructed all its county associations to admit professional clubs, some rebelled and formed their own organization to protect the amateur ideals of fair play and respect toward opponents. Initially known robustly as the Amateur Football Defence Foundation, the quickly renamed Amateur Football Association exists to this day as the Amateur Football Alliance. It and its members are fully affiliated to the FA, but they just don't believe that players should be paid to play.

SEE ALSO **'PROFESSIONALISM LEGALIZED'** (page 30).

A capacity crowd watches South Bank and Oxford City contest the FA Amateur Cup final at Stamford Bridge in 1913.

PLAYERS' UNION FINALLY GETS OFF THE GROUND

Although a players' union had been formed in 1898, it lacked teeth and footballers were still struggling to get their employers to recognize their rights as trade unionists. Their main grievances were over the maximum wage and their inability to move freely to other clubs. However, in December 1907 Manchester United's Billy Meredith chaired the first official meeting of the Players' Union, which comprised of 500 players, mainly from the north and the Midlands. Meredith and five others were tasked with drawing up a constitution, and the room agreed to join with footballers in London. Thus the Professional Footballers' Association was born.

SEE ALSO **'PLAYERS THREATEN TO STRIKE'** (page 65).

Manchester United's Billy Meredith chaired the first official meeting of the Players Union, which 500 players attended.

MAXIMUM TRANSFER FEE CEILING COLLAPSES

After Alf Common's controversial four-figure transfer fee, the Football Association (FA) attempted to emulate the imposition of the maximum wage by introducing a maximum transfer fee of £350. Unlike the wage ceiling, though, it was doomed to fail, because while clubs were happy to limit their overheads, they wanted the best possible players. This meant that when players like Southend United's Harold Halse were sold to a big club, in his case Manchester United, for the top price, a 'makeweight' player would also move – also for the full fee. Unusually quick to acknowledge their failings, by April the FA had scrapped the rule.

SEE ALSO 'FOOTBALL'S FIRST £1000 TRANSFER' (page 57).

Attempts to impose a maximum transfer fee failed. Some 50 years on United signing, Denis Law smiles at Matt Busby as he puts pen to paper.

The Milan split created a great rivalry between Inter's middle-class 'bauscia' (braggarts) and Milan's working-class 'casciavit' (screwdrivers).

MILAN SPLIT CREATES INTER

Formed by a British ex-pat in 1899 as the Milan Football and Cricket Club, the Rossoneri had scooped three national league titles in 1901, 1906 and 1907.

However, the quest for a hat-trick of league titles was scuppered by infighting over selection policy. By now the Milan line-ups were almost exclusively Italian, to the displeasure of a faction within the club who thought the club should have a more inclusive feel. Inevitably, these dissatisfied souls formed their own club, logically named Internazionale, with a stated aim of being open to foreign players.

It worked fairly quickly, with the new club lifting the title in 1910, while their old pals had to wait until 1951 for their next Scudetto.

SEE ALSO 'MILAN WIN EUROPEAN CUP' (page 248).
'INTER MILAN WIN EUROPEAN CUP' (page 252).

The highest scoring Charity Shield was Manchester United's 8-4 win over Swindon in 1913. It's now the traditional curtain-raiser to the season.

THE FIRST CHARITY SHIELD

Until 1974 the Charity Shield was played away from Wembley and before 1959 it was played at the end of the season, often between two teams who hadn't won any trophies, rather than the League champions and FA Cup holders. The first game took place in 1908 when League champions Manchester United required a replay to beat Southern League champions Queens Park Rangers 4-0 after a 1-1 draw in the first game. Both games were played at Stamford Bridge and this was the only Charity Shield to go to a replay.

SEE ALSO 'THE LATIN CUP KICKS OFF' (page 168); 'CHARITY BEGINS AT HOME' (page 566).

In the same year that they would win Olympic gold, the England squad played their first ever match in continental Europe.

ENGLAND PLAY FIRST INTERNATIONAL ON FOREIGN SOIL

In 1902 Austria had beaten Hungary 5-0 in the continent's first international match, so it was no surprise that the England team's debut venture abroad should be to Central Europe, starting in Vienna. The visitors were three up by half-time and romped to a 6-1 win, almost doubling that two days later with an 11-1 victory over the Austrians, before popping off to beat Hungary 7-0 and Bohemia (now part of the Czech Republic) 4-0. The tour was such a success that England returned the following summer for three more games against Austria and Hungary, their last games abroad for 12 long years.

SEE ALSO 'ENGLISH CLUBS TOUR BRAZIL AND ARGENTINA' (page 67).

GREAT BRITAIN WIN OLYMPIC GOLD

Having only been an exhibition sport at the first three Olympics, football was finally given official status at the London Games in 1908 – and indeed it was fitting the hosts and founding fathers of the modern game ran out the winners. However, the credibility of the tournament was somewhat questionable. To begin with, the football competition was played in October, three months after the rest of the Games, and only five countries were involved, with France entering two teams. Great Britain's team of amateurs were too strong for everybody, though, beating Denmark 2-0 in the final to become unofficial world champions. It was a superiority complex that would remain for some time.

SEE ALSO 'OLYMPIC GAMES BRUTALITY' (page 87); 'URUGUAY DEFEND OLYMPIC TITLE' (page 108).

The Great Britain squad were gold medal winners as hosts in the London Games of 1908. Could the feat be repeated in 2012?

MANCHESTER UNITED LEAD TALK OF 'BREAK AWAY'

Against the wishes of both the Football League and the Football Association (FA) Manchester United organized a game against Newcastle United to raise funds for the newly-formed Professional Footballers' Association. But despite threats by United and other big clubs to break away and pay better wages to players, the smaller clubs wanted the maximum wage to be retained – for obvious financial reasons – and the FA dismissed United's threats, insisting that players' contracts should feature a loyalty clause and failing to recognize any official link between the players' union and their clubs. Manchester United refused to sign the loyalty clause and a strike loomed...

SEE ALSO 'FA THREATENED FROM WITHIN' (page 29). 'G-14 FORMED' (page 538).

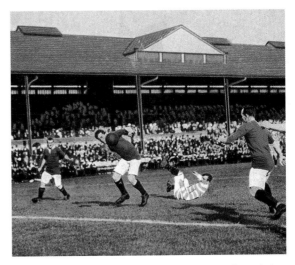

Manchester United on the attack. Away from events on the pitch they were the ringleaders of a plan to organize their own Super League.

AMATEUR TEAM WIN 'WORLD CUP'

Having been made a Knight of the Grand Order of Italy, millionaire tea baron Sir Thomas Lipton wanted to return the favour and the Italians suggested he organize a 'world football tournament' in Turin. Typically, the English Football Association refused to sanction the release of England's professional players, but one of Lipton's employees had contacts at a County Durham amateur team, West Auckland Town, and persuaded them to be England's representatives. The team of poverty-stricken miners beat German outfit Stuttgarter Sportfreunde in the semi-finals, before overcoming FC Winterthur of Switzerland to lift the trophy known as the 'Crown of Italy World Cup'.

SEE ALSO **'THE FIRST 'WORLD CHAMPIONS'** (page 32).
'SCOTS CLAIM 'WORLD CHAMPION' STATUS' (page 281).

Sir Thomas Lipton made his home and fortune in Italy. He used his considerable contacts in England to organize an early 'World Cup'.

CUP FINAL ENDS IN RIOT

Who won the Scottish Cup in 1909? Nobody. Why? Because Celtic and Rangers fans rioted – but not with each other. After the final ended 2-2, rumours spread that draws were being pre-arranged by the Scottish Football Association (SFA) to boost gate revenue. When the replay ended 1-1 and a Tannoy announcement revealed the game would be staged again, rather than go to extra-time, 60,000 fans united to invade the pitch. The goalposts were torn up, wood was set alight, fire brigade hoses were cut, police horses were stoned and more than 50 policemen were injured. The SFA acquiesced to the clubs' request to abandon the game.

SEE ALSO **'SCOTS INVADE WEMBLEY PITCH'** (page 350).

Celtic's Tommy McInally hooks the ball over his head towards goal during an early Old Firm derby with their fierce rivals Rangers.

The Manchester United squad of 1908-09 were used as adverts for Wincarnis in another example of the club being ahead of its time.

MANCHESTER UNITED ADVERTISE TONIC WINE

A hundred years ago health cures were just as big a business as they are nowadays, but whereas today's shelves are stuffed with offerings endorsed by TV experts, those of the early 20th century featured tonics such as Wincarnis, a vitamin- and herb-infused 'wine of life' described as 'suitable alike for the robust, the invalid and the convalescent'. The increasing popularity of football and muscularity of its players made a tie-up inevitable, and so it was that Manchester United broke new ground by endorsing Wincarnis, a full 70 years before the first top-flight shirt sponsorship.

SEE ALSO **'CROMPTON BECOMES 'BRYLCREEM BOY'** (page 170). **'LIVERPOOL GET A SHIRT SPONSOR'** (page 367).

'The Outcasts FC' of Manchester United who were prominent supporters of the players strike over rights to union membership.

PLAYERS THREATEN TO STRIKE

With the Professional Footballers' Association (PFA) having spent the 1908-09 season trying to secure affiliation with the Federation of Trade Unions, on the eve of the 1909-10 season the Football Association and Football League declared that any player who admitted being a member of the PFA should be suspended from playing without pay. But PFA members, chiefly Manchester United's players, who posed for a famous photograph as 'The Outcasts FC', stuck to their guns and with several other clubs in danger of being unable to fulfill their opening day fixtures, the authorities were forced to back down. The players' union was officially recognized on 31 August 1909.

SEE ALSO **'WAGE CUT TO £8 A WEEK'** (page 90).

GERMANY FIELDS
TWO NATIONAL SIDES

It's fair, if surprising, to say that the German national team started off somewhat chaotically. Symptomatic of a parochial country which didn't have a professional national league until 1963, Germany's first official national line-up featured players from 11 different clubs, while the first nine fixtures featured seven different goalkeepers. No surprise, then, that while a team including half a dozen Berliners faced Hungary in Budapest, Karlsruhe hosted an international against Switzerland. Ominously for the rest of Europe, Germany had the depth of talent – the 'home' team won, while the boys in Budapest battled to a draw. All the country needed now was a unifying force.

SEE ALSO **'WEST GERMANY LOSE TO EAST GERMANY'** (page 337);
'FIRST INTERNATIONAL AFTER REUNIFICATION' (page 451).

ENGLISH CLUBS TOUR BRAZIL AND ARGENTINA

South American football owes Britain. Public schoolboy Charles Miller set up Brazil's first league in 1902, while later in the decade one of Miller's old teams helped to popularize the sport. Marginalised amateurs in England, the gentlemen of Corinthians toured and taught the world: Real Madrid adopted their white strip, while awestruck Brazilians started a club of the same name. Meanwhile, Tottenham and Everton toured Argentina in 1910, playing each other and local sides, who were amazed that these fellows passed rather than dribbled. In the prescient words of a contemporary newspaper, 'The example of our visitors can be followed to advantage.'

SEE ALSO **'BRAZIL FACE MIGHTY EXETER CITY'** (page 76).

Everton were one of the English teams that undertook the long journey to Latin America and spread the influence of English football.

Despite being the oldest club in England the Magpies have always had to play second fiddle to their neighbours across the Trent.

CASH-STRAPPED COUNTY SELL HOME RIGHTS OF FA CUP TIE

Notts County may have been English football's first professional football club, but they weren't the most popular, even in their home city. Having been drawn at home against newly promoted Bradford City in the first round of the FA Cup, cash-strapped County feared the game would be overshadowed by near-neighbours Nottingham Forest's own FA Cup tie against Sheffield United at the City Ground. So County agreed to switch their game to Bradford in exchange for £1000, but the decision backfired badly on both clubs – Notts County were thumped 4-2 and Bradford's crowd was too small to take enough gate receipts to cover the payment.

SEE ALSO **'MANCHESTER UNITED WITHDRAW FROM FA CUP'** (page 531).

MANCHESTER UNITED
MOVE TO OLD TRAFFORD

After nearly going bankrupt at the turn of the century, Newton Heath had renamed themselves Manchester United, restructured their finances and set about moving from their Bank Street ground in Clayton. Identifying a site in Trafford near Lancashire County Cricket Club's home ground, they employed renowned stadium architect Archibald Leitch, fresh from redeveloping Rangers' Ibrox home. Initial plans were for a capacity of 100,000, although these were scaled back to 80,000, but even with only the South Stand covered Old Trafford still cost an eye-watering £60,000 to build. The first match was an inauspicious 4-3 defeat to Liverpool, but one of football's most famous theatres was open for business.

SEE ALSO **'OLD TRAFFORD BOMBED'** (page 146);
'REAL MADRID'S BERNABEU OPENS' (page 160).

General view of Old Trafford, home of Manchester United. Building work continues to extend the stadium's capacity still further to this day.

ITALY MAKE INTERNATIONAL DEBUT

Although the Italian national team's 6-2 win over France on 15 May 1910 was their first, they could not yet call themselves the Azzurri. Intriguingly, the Italians wore white shirts at the Arena Stadium in Milan that day, because they were the cheapest available and could be substituted for 'an ordinary white shirt or a rowing singlet'. Indeed, it wasn't until eight months later in their third international – a 1-0 defeat to Hungary at the same venue – that the blue shirts were worn, in homage to the house of Savoy, Italy's then royal family.

SEE ALSO **'ITALY FIGHT BACK TO TAKE WORLD CUP'** (page 129).

The Italians quickly established themselves as one of Europe's best sides and adopted their famous blue shirts to become the Azzurri.

The national football teams of Argentina, left, and Ecuador line up to sing their national anthems during the 1947 South American Championship.

ARGENTINA CROWNED FIRST SOUTH AMERICAN CHAMPIONS

Emboldened by British visitors and keen to extend their boundaries, Argentina invited their western neighbours Chile over the Andes for a three-way face-off with eternal rivals Uruguay – and in doing so, introduced South America to the idea of international tournaments. Chile went down 3-0 to Uruguay on 29 May 1910, then 5-1 to the hosts a week later, setting up a showdown between old chums Argentina and Uruguay. The visitors were duly beaten 4-1, making Argentina the kings of South America – even if no trophy was presented and the tournament remains unofficial because it took place six years before the inauguration of the continent's ruling football body Conmebol.

SEE ALSO **'ARGENTINA SCRAPE PAST FRANCE'** (page 114).

Bradford City's FA Cup winning team proudly pose with the newly designed FA Cup trophy after their defeat of Newcastle United.

BRAND NEW FA CUP RETURNS TO BRADFORD

The FA Cup that is now held aloft in May is the fourth trophy. The first vanished in 1895; the second was presented to the Football Association (FA) president Lord Kinnaird in 1910. The FA then commissioned a grander trophy, designed and manufactured by Bradford firm Fattorini's. It was fitting, then, that the Cup should first be hoisted by Bradford City, whose replay win condemned Newcastle United to their fourth FA Cup final loss in seven years. This remains the only time a Bradford team has reached the final. The increasingly fragile trophy was replicated in 1992.

SEE ALSO **'MONARCH ATTENDS THE FA CUP FINAL'** (page 75).

1912

15 YEAR OLD HITS DEBUT HAT-TRICK FOR BARCELONA

Paulino Alcantara Riestra was aged just 15 years, four months and 18 days when he made his debut for Barcelona against Catala SC in the Championat de Catalunya and his hat-trick – the first three goals in a 9-0 win – was a sign of things to come. He would go on to become Barça's all-time record scorer, with 356 goals in 357 games.

Born in the Philippines to a Spanish father, Alcantara was the first Asian to play for a European club and went on to win a Copa del Rey and two Championat de Catalunyas, but his parents took him back to the Philippines in 1916 and Barcelona failed to win a trophy in his absence. Their pleas for Alcantara's return were rejected, but when he contracted malaria in 1917 he refused to take his medication unless his parents allowed him to return.

Also a gifted table tennis player, Alcantara became a doctor when he retired from playing in 1927 at the age of 31 and also had a brief spell coaching Spain.

SEE ALSO '356 GOALS IN 357 GAMES' (page 102).

Precocious talent and prolific scorer Paulino Alcantara in action for the Catalan giants.

LANCASTRIAN PIONEER HELPS COACH EUROPE

Jimmy Hogan's coaching popularized football in Austria and Switzerland, and improved it elsewhere. A fairly average player who adored the 'Scottish' passing game, he helped coach Austria as early as 1912, spent the 1920s teaching the Dutch, Swiss and Hungarians how to play and was tempted back by Austrian Football Association chief Hugo Meisl to shape the formidable 'Wunderteam' of the early 1930s, the first continental side to beat Scotland. With remarkable foresight, Hogan controlled players' diets by cutting down on meat and increasing fruit and veg.

England captain Billy Wright leads his team out alongside the formidable Hungary XI of 1953 – a team Jimmy Hogan greatly influenced.

SEE ALSO 'AUSTRIA'S 'WUNDERTEAM'' (page 122).

GOALKEEPERS BARRED FROM HANDLING OUTSIDE PENALTY AREA

Fittingly, 1912 was a titanic year for goalkeepers – they got their colour, but had their special powers restricted. Three years previously, a League meeting had decreed that the goalkeeper should be visually distinctive from other players by dressing in a scarlet, royal blue or white top. Then, in 1912 the list was expanded to include green, which was less common among outfielders and therefore quickly became the default colour for a goalkeeper's jersey. However, keepers also had their wings clipped as, 51 years after breaking away from the rugby code, football finally restricted goalkeepers' handling powers to within their own penalty area.

Newcastle United goalkeeper Jimmy Lawrence concedes a corner. The rule change undoubtedly meant that 'keepers had to up their game.

SEE ALSO 'BACK-PASSES TO GOALKEEPERS OUTLAWED' (page 464).

GERMANY HIT RUSSIA FOR 16

The 1912 Olympic football tournament unfolded in much the same way as the 1908 competition. Well, almost. Again inspired by captain Vivian Woodward, Great Britain emerged victorious with a second consecutive win over Denmark in the final. They also demonstrated the Corinthian spirit in the semi-final by deliberately missing what they thought was an unfairly awarded penalty against Finland. Such generosity was absent from the consolation tournament, though, which was organized for the seven teams who had been knocked out in the first round. Germany's Gottfried Fuchs set an international goalscoring record against Russia, finding the net ten times in a 16-0 win.

SEE ALSO 'HUNGARY PUT TEN PAST EL SALVADOR' (page 382); 'SAMOA OUT FOR THE COUNT' (page 544).

Great Britain's 1912 Olympic gold medallists. They emerged victorious with a second consecutive win over Denmark in the final.

Garbutt revolutionized coaching in Italy and was also the first English coach called 'Mister' – a term of respect, loosely meaning 'trainer'.

GENOA EMPLOY 'MISTER' GARBUTT

After a short and undistinguished playing career, Lancastrian William Garbutt moved to Genoa to find work on the docks. With no previous experience, he was appointed head coach of Genoa CFC at just 29.

In 15 years at the club Garbutt revolutionized coaching in Italy, introducing structured training regimes with an emphasis on physical fitness and tactics. He oversaw Italy's first paid-for transfers and Genoa became the first Italian club to play abroad when Garbutt used his connections at old club Reading to organize a friendly.

In 1927 Garbutt became Roma's first full-time coach. He also coached in Naples, Milan and Bilbao, before two more spells with Genoa either side of World War Two.

SEE ALSO 'GENOA WIN SUCCESSIVE TITLES' (page 96). 'WENGER ARRIVES AT HIGHBURY' (page 503).

ARSENAL MOVE TO HIGHBURY

Property development magnate Henry Norris was an ambitious man. Already a director of Fulham, he took over Woolwich Arsenal in 1910 when the ailing south London club was in liquidation. After the Football League blocked his attempt to merge his two clubs, Norris decided to move Arsenal into more populous north London. On 5 March 1913 Norris told the Arsenal board he had found a site in Highbury. Six months and £125,000 later, the Arsenal Stadium opened with a 2-1 win over Leicester Fosse (later City). By the end of the season the Football League agreed to the dropping of the club's now-redundant 'Woolwich' prefix.

SEE ALSO **'HIGHBURY – THE FILM STAR'** (page 143); **'LAST MATCH AT HIGHBURY'** (page 597).

Arsenal's Ray Bowden beats Leeds United's Jack Milburn in an aerial contest. It's difficult to believe Arsenal began life south of the Thames.

10-YARD RULE INTRODUCED

Before 1913 very few goals were scored direct from a free-kick, which was hardly surprising given the weight of the balls and the fact that opposing defenders only had to retreat six yards from the ball when the free-kick was being taken. So in order to encourage attacking play, the Football Association (FA) amended law 13 and increased the distance defenders had to retreat to ten yards (9.15 metres) for the 1913–14 season. But the FA didn't stop there. Wanting to give yet further advantage to the attacking team, for the following season they extended the rule to include corner-kicks.

SEE ALSO **'ROBERTO CARLOS' SPECTACULAR FREE KICK'** (page 507); **'ZAIRE KICK UP A STORM AT THEIR FIRST WORLD CUP'** (page 336).

With the 10-yard rule giving the strikers a clearer sight of goal, Wales' international William 'Willie' Evans gets in some shooting practice.

FIRST INTERNATIONAL IN ASIA

Pressed to name Asia's first national team, you might take a few stabs before hitting on the Philippines. However, introduced to football by British sailors from Hong Kong, the Filipinos were only too happy to play the game at the inaugural multi-sport Far Eastern Championship Games, which opened in Manila in 1913. Of the other five participants – China, Japan, Hong Kong, Thailand and the British East Indies (now Malaysia) – only the Chinese could muster a football team. So it was then, that with a 2-1 win over China on the games' opening day, the Philippines won Asia's first ever international match.

SEE ALSO **'ASIAN CONFEDERATION FORMED'** (page 189): **'BECKHAM MANIA HITS JAPAN'** (page 557).

Football in China has developed slowly but steadily. In 2002 they made their first ever appearance at the World Cup in Japan and South Korea.

PRO VERCELLI BECOME ITALY'S FIRST GREAT TEAM

Though teams from Milan and Turin would eventually become more well known, it was another club from northern Italy who formed the country's first footballing dynasty. Founded in 1892, Societa Ginnastica Pro Vercelli were admitted to the Italian National League in 1907 and won five of the next six league titles (it would have been all six had it not been for a dispute with the Italian Football Federation). Nine of that team, nicknamed the 'Leoni' or Lions formed the backbone of the first Italian national sides, including the 'Midfield Line of Wonders', comprising Ara, Milano I and Leone.

SEE ALSO **'ENGLAND FIELD A CORINTHIANS XI'** (page 39).

Once Italy's greatest team, Pro Vercelli's glory days are well behind them. Still in existence they now play in Italy's fourth division – Serie C2.

GERMAN CUP FINAL
DECIDED IN 153RD MINUTE

Taught 'the Scottish passing game' by former Arsenal and Blackburn Rovers player William Townley, SpVgg Fürth went into the last German championship final before World War One as firm favourites to beat VfB Leipzig. However, long before the days of golden goals and penalty shootouts, the underdogs from the east fought doggedly to force the game into extra-time at 2-2. Under the rules of the day the teams then had to play on until a winning goal was scored and, after an hour of extra-time, SpVgg finally obliged. "Leipzig fought bitterly despite being wounded and weakened," read one report.

SEE ALSO **'PENALTY SHOOT-OUTS MAKE THEIR DEBUT'** (page 290).

Billy Townley is credited with introducing 'the Scottish passing game' to SpVgg Fürth. Despite this his team lost the match in the 153rd minute.

MONARCH ATTENDS
THE FA CUP FINAL

Football had been growing in popularity, particularly among the working class, for decades, but aside from Southern League Tottenham's 1901 win, no club based further south than Wolverhampton had won the FA Cup since 1882. With war looming it was a simple act of class and geographical unity for King George V to apply the royal seal of approval by becoming the first reigning monarch to attend the FA Cup final. As it transpired, he was delayed by heavy traffic and heaving crowds around the Crystal Palace ground, but he was in place to witness the game's only goal, in the 58th minute from Burnley's forward Bert Freeman.

SEE ALSO **'PRINCE WILHELM PRESENTS THE CUP'** (page 59); **'CHURCHILL SUPPORTS FOOTBALL'** (page 147).

Reigning monarch George V gives the FA Cup the royal seal of approval at Crystal Palace. Present heir, Prince William is now president of the FA.

Exeter City face QPR – more plausible opponents than Brazil. In 2004 a Brazilian 'Masters' team took on an Exeter XI to mark their first encounter.

BRAZIL FACE MIGHTY EXETER CITY

If you had to pick an English team mythologised by Brazilians, you might not plump for Exeter, but as war clouds gathered in Europe the Grecians sailed for South America to ease their overdraft. They were the first professional team to tour Brazil and the national team's first opponents, drawing 3-3 at Rio's Laranjeiras Stadium. "Your players are clever in dribbling and fast," said the Exeter trainer at the post-match banquet, "but their weak point is that they are individualists and each try to shine above their fellows. They will never achieve real success until they recognize that it takes 11 men to score a goal."

SEE ALSO **'BRAZIL MAKE THEIR MARK'** (page 83).

Steve Bloomer of Derby County and England. His presence in Germany during the First World War led to his four-year internment.

STEVE BLOOMER INTERNED

Steve 'Paleface' Bloomer was arguably the first superstar of English football. Small, quick and two-footed, the inside-right's 'shoot on sight' approach earned him 28 goals in just 23 games for his country and, with 352 goals during a 21-year club career with Derby County, he is the third highest goalscorer in English league history, behind Dixie Dean and Jimmy Greaves. Having retired from playing in early 1914, just short of his 40th birthday, to take a coaching job in Berlin, when war broke out Bloomer was interned at Ruhleben Civilian Detention Camp and didn't return home until hostilities were over in 1918.

SEE ALSO **'FRITZ WALTER AVOIDS FORCED MARCH'** (page 151).

THE BEGINNING OF A GREAT RIVALRY

Although an Argentinian touring team had played some matches in Rio in 1908, Brazil's first game as a country came against a visiting Exeter City side in 1914. Brazil then played their first international later that year when they lost 3-0 to Argentina in Buenos Aires, Brazil wearing an all-white kit with blue stripes on the shirt sleeves (the famous yellow shirts were not introduced until 1954). Argentina had made their international debut 13 years earlier, winning 3-2 against Uruguay in Montevideo, and although a fierce rivalry between Argentina and Brazil would eventually develop, both Argentina and Uruguay retained footballing superiority over Brazil for many years.

SEE ALSO **'BRAZIL, ARGENTINA AND BROKEN BONES'** (page 153);
'THE HAND OF THE DEVIL' (page 488).

Argentina's goalkeeper Americo Tesorieri lies on the field in a 1925 American Cup match between Argentina and Brazil. The game finished 2-2.

PEACE – AND FOOTBALL – BREAKS OUT IN NO-MAN'S LAND

George Orwell famously described sport as "war minus the shooting", while a large amount of football terminology is military in origin – from fundamental ideas like attack and defence to specifics like long-range strikes, shootout, aerial assault, howitzers, war of attrition and supplying ammunition to the sharpshooters. But on one occasion, it seems that a war was temporarily stopped and opposing forces indulged in a goodwill game of football.

Although accounts of events on the first Christmas Day of the Great War vary, several eyewitness accounts testify to a temporary truce in several areas. With the guns silenced, soldiers who had spent weeks trying to kill each other cautiously emerged from the trenches and swapped drinks, stories and bonhomie. Soon enough, in the words of Lieutenant Johannes Niemann of the 133rd Royal Saxon Regiment, "A Scottish soldier appeared with a football... the Scots marked their goalmouth with their strange caps and we did the same with ours. It was far from easy to play on the frozen ground, but we continued, keeping rigorously to the rules, despite the fact that it only lasted an hour and that we had no referee. A great many of the passes went wide, but all the amateur footballers, although they must have been very tired, played with huge enthusiasm."

It couldn't last, of course; the higher-ranking officers were against the idea, and artillery bombardments took place on all subsequent wartime Christmas Eves to discourage further truces, while troops were rotated to avoid overfamiliarity with the enemy.

SEE ALSO **'WAR SUSPENDS FOOTBALL'** (page 81);
'MATCH STARTS A SHOOTING WAR' (page 291).

On Christmas day hostilities
ceased in favour of football.

1915

MATCH FIXING SCANDAL ROCKS ENGLISH FOOTBALL

On Good Friday 1915 Liverpool turned in such a poor performance against Manchester United in a 2-0 loss that one bookmaker refused to pay out on the flood of bets that had been made on that scoreline at odds of 7-1. His suspicions of foul play proved correct as a subsequent Football League investigation revealed that several players from both teams had hatched a plot to fix the match in a Manchester pub, while many other players were aware of what was happening.

Four players from each team were banned from for life, including alleged ringleader Jackie Sheldon, who had played for both clubs. However, the ban was lifted on seven of the players in 1918 in recognition of their efforts in fighting for their country during World War One. One of those, Sandy Turnball, was killed in action, while the only player of the eight to actually play in the game in question, Enock 'Knocker' West, didn't have his ban lifted until after World War Two, despite continuing to protest his innocence.

SEE ALSO **'MATCH FIXING ENDS CAREERS'** (page 256); **'ROSSI IN MATCH-FIXING SCANDAL** (page 374).

Match fixing was a problem as far back as 1915 as the game developed at pace.

Sheffield United's win was overshadowed by the First World War. The massed ranks of khaki-clad spectators offering a constant reminder.

THE 'KHAKI CUP FINAL'

World War One had been under way for almost nine months when the football season limped to a halt with the FA Cup final, relocated from London to Old Trafford to avoid congestion in the capital. Sheffield United beat Chelsea 3-0, but the match is better remembered for off-field activities. Indeed, the large numbers of uniformed Army personnel on the terraces led to it being known as the 'Khaki Cup final'. Football soon realized its relative unimportance, with players signing up to represent their country, from the humble to the mighty, such as Sunderland's Charles Buchan, who signed up for the Grenadier Guards mere days after the final.

SEE ALSO **'TRAUTMANN VOTED FOOTBALLER OF THE YEAR'** (page 203).

Behind their lines young German troops play a game under the ever-watchful eyes of their commanding officers and their fellow soldiers.

WAR SUSPENDS FOOTBALL

When Britain went to war with Germany in August 1914 it was thought the fighting would be over by Christmas, so football carried on regardless. After receiving criticism in the press for using men who would be more appropriately deployed on the battlefield, the FA staged recruitment drives at matches and after the FA Cup final it was finally decided that the League, the Cup and international matches would be suspended and replaced with regional competitions as war continued to range on the Western Front. Any player who didn't enlist was also required to take a job that helped the war effort.

SEE ALSO **'WAR SUSPENDS COMPETITIONS'** (page 144).

Since its inception, Ajax's youth scheme has provided a steady stream of world-class players. It has been a great advert for the Dutch game.

AJAX INTRODUCE YOUTH SYSTEM

Under the stewardship of Englishman Jack Reynolds, Ajax established a youth system that is still envied throughout the world. Reynolds was one of football's great pioneers and during his 25 seasons at the Amsterdam club he drummed into the players the attacking style for which Ajax are famous. At youth level, Reynolds recognized the importance of developing players' skill, passing ability and teamwork, so that they could take these attributes with them into the senior side. The Ajax youth set-up has produced some of the world's finest players, including Johan Cruyff, Johan Neeskens, Marco van Basten, Frank Rijkaard and Dennis Bergkamp.

SEE ALSO **'FRENCH YOUTH SYSTEM ESTABLISHED'** (page 472); **RINUS BRINGS 'TOTAL FOOTBALL' TO AJAX'** (page 255).

Sandwiched between two of football's superpowers Uruguay has long punched above its weight in South American and world football.

THE FIRST CONTINENTAL CONFEDERATION IS FORMED

Journalists aren't all hot air and bad attitude. Uruguayan football writer Hector Rivadavia Gomez united disparate South American national sides into football's first continental confederation. Gomez had long seen the advantages of co-operation and struck on 9 July 1916. Argentina had invited Brazil, Chile and Uruguay to a South American Championship held to celebrate the 100th anniversary of Argentinian independence. On the very day of the anniversary, the four fledgling football associations met and approved Gomez's dream, forming what came to be known as the Confederacion Sudamericana de Futbol – or, much more easily, Conmebol.

SEE ALSO **'L'EQUIPE SUGGESTS A EUROPEAN CUP'** (page 199).

BARCELONA WALK OFF IN PROTEST

The game in which the seeds of one of football's great rivalries were sown was in the second replay of the King's Cup semi-finals in 1916. Real Madrid players were allegedly showered with missiles by Barca fans in the first replay and, after Madrid went 4-2 up early in the second half of the second replay, Barcelona's players resorted to brutal, underhand tactics. It made little difference, however, and their captain Massana ordered them from the field, citing biased refereeing against his team. The rivalry would intensify under the pro-Madrid dictatorships of Primo de Rivera and, most notably, Francisco Franco.

SEE ALSO **'BARCELONA CROWD WHISTLES DURING ANTHEM'** (page 99).

In a continuation of the great rivalry, Madrid's players show their disbelief at the disallowing of a goal against Barcelona in the 1960 European Cup.

BRAZIL MAKE THEIR MARK

The first signs that Brazil could dominate international football for decades to come came in the 1919 South American Championships. Inspired by Artur Friedenreich, the son of a German immigrant and a black Brazilian, the first-time hosts prevailed 1-0 in the final and wowed crowds with their unique brand of football, with a high emphasis on skill and little emphasis on tactics. One newspaper article, headlined 'Brazilian Innovation', highlighted the difference between the traditionally British style of football and the Brazilian way, noting that 'shots were taken from any distance' It also marveled at the 'precision' and 'devastating speed' of Brazil's attacking play.

SEE ALSO **'BRAZIL'S PLACE IN HISTORY IS ASSURED'** (page 307).

Brazilian flair and the players' dazzling individual skill were on display in 1909 and sounded a warning to other international teams.

1919 LEAGUE EXTENDED TO 44 CLUBS

World War One didn't do much to dampen English enthusiasm for football and the first post-war season saw both Football League divisions swell from 20 to 22, a figure they settled at until the late 1980s (subsequent further expansion being achieved by adding divisions). The four newcomers were West Ham, Coventry City, Stoke and Rotherham, but further up it all got a bit murky: north London newcomers Arsenal, fifth in the previous Second Division, were somehow promoted to the top flight above third-placed Barnsley and fourth-placed Wolves, much to the chagrin of relegated Tottenham, whose righteous indignation drove them to a new record points total for the Second Division.

SEE ALSO 'THE ENGLISH FOOTBALL LEAGUE EXPANDS TO 92 CLUBS' (page 176).

After their promotion to the top flight Arsenal splashed out on Liverpool's Fred Pagnam, seen here at Highbury watching his new team.

1919 AUCTION OF LEEDS CITY PLAYERS

Founded in 1904 and elected to the Football League a year later, Leeds City didn't have the happiest of histories. Attendances were low, the First Division was never reached and, just as Herbert Chapman started to point them upwards, war broke out. City were found guilty of financial irregularities during wartime, including paying players, which was expressly forbidden, and dissolved in 1919. At the Metropole Hotel in Leeds on 17 October, in what the *Yorkshire Post* described as a 'melancholy spectacle,' the playing staff were auctioned off, along with the club's other assets. Nine clubs bought the 16 players for a total of £9,250. Leeds United was formed the next year.

SEE ALSO 'MANCHESTER UNITED SNAP UP CITY TALENT' (page 58); 'HERBERT CHAPMAN TRANSFORMS ARSENAL' (page 100).

Fred Parnell was a right-winger with Leeds City from 1905. He was released in 1908 – eleven years prior to the ignominious player sell-off.

CHILEAN INVENTS BICYCLE KICK

The bicycle kick's origins are somewhat indistinct. Some call it the Pelé kick, despite the fact that it predates Pelé, while the Norwegians call it the Brassespark – literally the 'Brazilian kick'. Early Brazilian exponent Leonidas da Silva credited it to compatriot Petrolinho de Brito and Italians credit Carlo Parola and Silvio Piola, while controversial former Aston Villa chairman Doug Ellis has often claimed to have invented it himself. However, the strongest claim seems to be that of Ramon Unzaga Asla, a Basque-born half-back who played for his adoptive country Chile in the 1920 Copa America. So impressive was Unzaga's technique that visiting Argentinian journalists christened the move 'la Chilena'.

SEE ALSO **'DONKEY KICK BOOTED OUT'** (page 311); **'RIVALDO'S LAST GASP ACROBATICS WORTH MILLIONS'** (page 550).

The bicycle kick is one of the most difficult skills to execute. Pelé, arguably the greatest player the world has ever seen, shows how it's done.

RIMET TAKES FIRST STEPS TOWARDS FIFA PRESIDENCY

Jules Rimet first considered running for the FIFA Presidency in 1920 and with his formal election the following year, he would go on to become organisation's longest-serving president, holding office from 1921 to 1954. For much of this time he was also president of the French FA and one of a group of French administrators who wanted an international competition that would build on the success of the football tournaments at the Olympic Games.

SEE ALSO **'HAVELANGE ELECTED FIFA PRESIDENT'** (page 334); **'BLATTER ELECTED TO FIFA TOP JOB'** (page 510).

In his 33-year reign as FIFA president, Jules Rimet was dedicated to promoting the game across the world, not simply in Europe.

Playing with a white chrome ball under powerful electric lights, a drawing of Dick Kerr's Ladies on the Burnley Cricket Club ground.

DICK KERR'S LADIES DRAW SELL-OUT CROWDS

Formed by the female employees of a railway equipment factory in 1917, when the men were away fighting for the greater good, Dick Kerr's Ladies team became something of a phenomenon. After office administrator Alfred Frankland organised a charity match for the ladies at Preston's Deepdale, a crowd of 10,000 turned up. They attracted another 35,000 at St James' Park in 1919 and in 1920 they also played in front of bumper crowds at Anfield, Old Trafford and Goodison Park, where 53,000 saw them beat St Helens and another 10,000 were turned away.

SEE ALSO **'WOMEN BANNED FROM PLAYING ON LEAGUE GROUNDS'** (page 89).

International football relations were damaged in 1914-18. The Home Nations boycotted any organisation that included their recent enemies.

HOME NATIONS UNITE TO BOYCOTT FIFA

Two years after the end of the First World War, the home nations made it clear that they had no desire to resume sporting relations with Germany, their principal enemy in the conflict, and England, Scotland, Ireland and Wales decided to withdraw from FIFA in protest at Germany being allowed membership. The home nations were largely unenthusiastic members of FIFA during its early years, even though Englishman Daniel Burley Woolfall was the organisation's president from 1906 to 1918, and indeed relations between the home nations and FIFA would break down time and again in the years before the Second World War.

SEE ALSO **'HOME NATIONS REJOIN FIFA'** (page 94).

OLYMPIC GAMES BRUTALITY

On 1 September, when Spain met Sweden at the Antwerp Olympics, both sides were just two wins away from a medal. Spain came back from 1-0 down to win 2-1, although Sweden missed a late penalty, but the game is remembered because of the violent approach employed by the teams. Spain ended the game with eight men and Sweden with seven, because of the number of injuries sustained, and one Spanish newspaper described it as 'the most barbaric and brutal game ever seen on a football field'. Spain went on to defeat Italy and then dispose of Holland in the second place final, thus claiming the silver medal.

SEE ALSO **'HARD FOUGHT COPA URUGUAYA FINAL'** (page 127). **'THE BATTLE OF SANTIAGO'** (page 242-3).

The Anvers Stadium in Antwerp witnessed one of the most violent and ill-disciplined international matches football had ever seen.

FOOTBALL POOLS BEGIN

Cash betting on football was banned when Littlewoods, the UK's biggest football pools company, was formed. However, the pools didn't classify as cash betting because it was done on credit, with participants paying up the week after the matches in question. From the weekend programme, competitors had to pick a line of eight matches whose results would be worth the most points according to the pools scoring system. Those with the highest scores then received a proportion of the combined entry fees from all players. By the 1930s, more people did the pools than attended matches, and the industry employed around 30,000 people.

SEE ALSO **"SPOT THE BALL' LAUNCHED'** (page 106); **'LEAGUE'S DISPUTE WITH POOLS PROMOTERS'** (page 131).

Chairman of the Pools Panel, Lord Brabazon, shares a joke with fellow panel members Tom Finney, Tommy Lawton and George Young.

THE IRISH FA SPLITS

Between 1880 and 1921 the Belfast-based Irish Football
Association (IFA) was the game's governing body
throughout Ireland. But those in the South often
accused the IFA of pro-Belfast bias and the situation
wasn't helped by the fact that the Belfast members were
predominantly Unionist and the Dublin members
mainly Nationalist. Tensions between the factions
reached a climax in April 1921, when, for security reasons,
the IFA ordered that an Irish Cup semi-final be played
in Belfast, not Dublin, so in September the south of the
country, which would become the Republic of Ireland,
broke away to form its own organisation, the Football
Association of Ireland (FAI).

SEE ALSO **'ENGLAND DEFEATED AT HOME BY THE
REPUBLIC OF IRELAND'** (page 168).

Northern Ireland fans display their support for their team as they
attend an international match against Scotland in Glasgow in 1954.

RANGERS BUY DANISH EXPORT

While Brian Laudrup is the most famous Dane to have
played for Rangers, he was not the first. That honour
belonged to Carl 'Skoma'r' (Shoemaker) Hansen, who
became the first Danish footballer to play professionally
outside his homeland three quarters of a century before
Laudrup joined the Glasgow club. The attacker arrived
in Glasgow at the age of 23 and played under legendary
manager Bill Struth, who guided Rangers to seven
titles in the 1920s. When the Germans later occupied
his country, Hansen became involved in the Danish
Resistance, and was arrested and imprisoned in his native
Copenhagen in 1943, but released four months later.

SEE ALSO **'SIMONSEN IS DENMARK'S FIRST EUROPEAN
FOOTBALLER OF THE YEAR'** (page 351).

Bill Struth, Rangers manager. He was in charge for an astonishing 34
years and brought 18 Scottish League titles to Ibrox in that time.

WOMEN BANNED FROM FOOTBALL LEAGUE GROUNDS

The first recorded match between two women's teams took place in 1895, but in December 1921 the Football Association (FA) banned women from playing on Football League grounds after deciding that 'the game of football is quite unsuitable for females and ought not to be encouraged'. The FA arrived at its decision despite the huge popularity of women's football – a game in December 1920 had attracted 53,000 spectators – but complaints had apparently been made to the FA, and it felt compelled to act. Because of the ban, which would last for 40 years, public interest in the women's game fell away dramatically.

SEE ALSO 'ITALIAN WOMEN TAKE THE LEAD' (page 295).
'THE WOMEN'S WORLD CUP ARRIVES' (page 455).

The Scottish FA was more enlightened. Edinburgh Ladies (hoops) play Alloa's Paton and Baldwins Ltd FC in 1937.

The San Mames Stadium, home of Athletic Bilbao and the location of a commemorative bust of legendary centre-forward 'Pichichi'.

PICHICHI DIES YOUNG

The great Athletic Bilbao goal-scorer Rafael Moreno Aranzadi, known throughout Spain as 'Pichichi', died of typhus on 2 March, aged 29, just a year after his retirement. His premature death brought an outpouring of public grief, and four years later a commemorative bust of the legendary centre-forward was unveiled at Athletic's stadium, the San Mames. Pichichi helped Athletic to four Copa del Rey triumphs and won the silver medal with Spain at the 1920 Olympics. Since 1928, the leading scorer in Spain's top flight has been awarded the Pichichi Trophy. Winners have included Alfredo Di Stefano, Ferenc Puskas, Romario, Ronaldo and Raul.

SEE ALSO 'ATHLETIC BILBAO FORMED' (page 42).

Harry Leddy left Goodison Park, the home of Everton, for Chesterfield and fought hard and was victorious seeing his contract honoured.

WAGES CUT TO £8 A WEEK

Since many clubs were facing mounting losses, the Football League reduced its costs by slashing the players' maximum wage from £9 per week to £8, and the incensed players threatened to strike. Although this didn't materialise, centre-half Harry Leddy sued Chesterfield for £99 in lost wages, helped by the Professional Footballers' Association. Leddy successfully argued in the High Court that Chesterfield should be bound by the agreement they made with him when he had signed from Everton in March 1922, stating that he would be paid £9 per week. The Leddy test case was a major victory for the players and the PFA.

SEE ALSO 'THE BOSMAN RULING' (page 491).

GOALKEEPERS ORDERED TO STAND STILL

On 29 April, Stamford Bridge played host to a dull FA Cup final in which Huddersfield Town defeated Preston North End 1-0, with a dubious penalty. In the 67th minute, Billy Smith was brought down just outside the penalty area, but referee JWD Fowler pointed to the spot. Smith slotted his kick past James Frederick Mitchell, Preston's bespectacled amateur goalkeeper, who tried to distract Smith by dancing along his line and waving his arms. It was the first time an FA Cup final had been decided by a penalty-kick. Because of Mitchell's antics, a new rule was brought in forbidding goalkeepers to move before a spot-kick was taken.

SEE ALSO **'GOALKEEPERS PERMITTED TO CHARGE AT PENALTIES'** (page 56).

Slowly but surely, the advantage was moving to the penalty takers, though goalkeepers continued to look for ways to bend the rules.

60,000 TURN UP IN LEIPZIG

An estimated 60,000 fans turned up on 6 August to watch the German Championship play-off replay between HSV Hamburg and Nuremberg, although the capacity of the Probstheidaer Stadion, Leipzig, was only 40,000. The sides had drawn 2-2 in Berlin almost two months earlier in a match that lasted 189 minutes and only finished because it got dark. The replay was equally bizarre. Referee Dr Peco Bauwens ended proceedings after 112 minutes, when the score was 1-1, because Nuremberg had been reduced to seven men. The German Football Association (DFB) awarded the championship to Hamburg, but urged them to decline it to show good sportsmanship, which they did.

SEE ALSO **'THE FLA-FLU DERBY SETS ATTENDANCE RECORD'** (page 251).

Huge attendances were becoming a feature of big matches across Europe. Important games often drew crowds well above capacity.

FIRST SIGHT OF WEMBLEY'S TWIN TOWERS

The Empire Stadium, to give it its original name, was built in just 300 days at a cost of £750,000 on the site of the old Wembley Park Leisure Ground. Wembley, as it soon became known, was designed by architects Sir John Simpson and Maxwell Ayerton to be the centrepiece of the British Empire Exhibition of 1924. The engineer Sir Owen Williams oversaw the construction of the stadium, from 25,000 tons of ferro concrete, 1000 tons of steel and over half a million rivets. Wembley's first public event was the 1923 Cup final, which took place just five days after construction was completed.

SEE ALSO 'WEMBLEY RE-OPENS – AT LAST' (page 616).

After its construction, Wembley soon came to be regarded as the home of English football.

THE 'WHITE HORSE FINAL'

The first ever Wembley Cup final, on 28 April 1923, between Bolton Wanderers and West Ham United, became known as the 'white horse final' and provided one of the most enduring images of the stadium's history. It earned this epithet as a result of the role played by PC George Scorey, on his white horse Billy, in keeping spectators calm after they spilled onto the pitch before kick-off. The overspill was caused by 200,000 people attempting to squeeze into a stadium built to accommodate 125,000.

Though the crowd was good-natured, it was miraculous that Scorey and his colleagues were able to clear the pitch and avoid a disaster, while the FA secretary informed King George V, "I fear, sir, that the match may not be played." Scorey, who didn't like football, said, "Billy knew what to do. He pushed forward quietly but firmly, and the crowd made way for him. They seemed to respect him."

After a 45-minute delay, it was not long before David Jack gave Bolton the lead. Spectators covered every inch of grass between the stands and the touchline, which meant players and the ball regularly disappeared. And because of the overcrowding, the players stayed on the pitch at half-time. Eight minutes after the break, John Smith struck Bolton's controversial second. West Ham players complained that a Bolton fan had kicked the ball back into play in the run-up to the goal, but their protests were ignored. Bolton saw out a 2-0 victory.

SEE ALSO **'THE MATTHEWS FINAL'** (page 183).

PC Scorey and his mount Billy make their way through the sea of fans who had burst through barriers onto the pitch.

1923

EDOARDO AGNELLI TAKES CONTROL OF JUVENTUS

After assuming control of Juventus, Edoardo Agnelli invested heavily to consolidate the club's status as one of the leading lights in Italian football. Agnelli, whose family owned the car manufacturer Fiat, built state-of-the art training facilities and a private stadium at Villar Perosa, near Turin. The investment soon produced positive results as Juventus secured their second Italian Championship in 1925-26. This competition became Serie A in 1929, and Juve soon established themselves as the dominant force, winning the League in five of its first six seasons. Agnelli died in 1935, but his family still owns the majority shareholding in the Turin club.

SEE ALSO **'SILVIO BERLUSCONI BUYS AC MILAN'** (page 406).

Known as the 'Old Lady' of Italian football and still backed by the Agnelli family's Fiat empire, Juve are the most successful Italian club in history.

1924

HOME NATIONS REJOIN FIFA

The home nations made their peace with FIFA, now under the presidency of Jules Rimet, and rejoined the organisation after a four-year absence. The boycott was a protest at the presence of their World War One enemies Germany, Austria and Hungary in the organisation. By this time, all the continental European countries had joined FIFA, whose membership had mushroomed from the six original countries to 40 national associations. However, the Football Association (FA) still had a somewhat strained relationship with FIFA, especially since the FA refused to pay FIFA a share of the revenue generated by international fixtures and rejected any FIFA attempt to intervene in domestic matters.

SEE ALSO **'HOME NATIONS WITHDRAW FROM FIFA – AGAIN'** (page 105).

The home nations' decision to end their boycott allowed the resumption of international football – six years after the war ended.

Communal train travel was less of a problem for Chelsea's 1934 team, members of which can be seen here looking out at St Pancras station.

PLAYERS ON DIFFERENT TRACKS

Nuremberg and Furth had been linked by Germany's first railway line since 1835, but in April 1924 the animosity between the these local rivals was so intense that their players went in separate trains to Amsterdam when they played for Germany against Holland. The sides had recently contested a bitter local derby, which included a large number of fouls and several brawls. Germany beat Holland 1-0 on 21 April, but when Auer scored he celebrated only with his Furth colleagues; the Nuremberg players, including Hans Kalb who had created the goal, ignored him.

SEE ALSO **'DUTCH SQUAD REVOLT'** (page 473).

BILLY MEREDITH RETIRES AGED 49

Billy Meredith bowed out of football at the grand old age of 49 years and 245 days by appearing in Manchester City's 2-0 FA Cup semi-final defeat to Newcastle United at St Andrews, Birmingham, on 29 March 1924. He is the oldest footballer to have taken to the field in the Cup. The Welshman was a speedy, skilful player who always played with a toothpick sticking out of his mouth. He won the FA Cup with both Manchester clubs, as well as two League titles with United. Meredith also set a record as the oldest international of all time when he played for Wales aged 45 years and eight months.

SEE ALSO **'BILLY MEREDITH WINS FA CUP'** (page 54); **'SIR STANLEY BOWS OUT'** (page 257).

William Meredith. Manchester United

Meredith was Manchester United's first 'Welsh Wizard', much-loved despite his long association with the blue half of the city.

FIRST WEMBLEY INTERNATIONAL

On 12 April a home championship clash between the game's fiercest rivals was a perfect first international fixture for the new Wembley Stadium. England, skippered by Aston Villa's Frank Moss, made a bad start as the visitors took the lead on 40 minutes after William Cowan's shot rebounded off the post, hit goalkeeper Ted Taylor and flew into the net. But 20 minutes into the second half, Villa inside-left Billy Walker struck England's equaliser, their first goal at Wembley. Surprisingly, the game drew a crowd of just 37,250, and another strange aspect of the match was that it was refereed by a Scot, Thomas Dougray.

SEE ALSO 'SCOTS INVADE WEMBLEY PITCH' (page 350).

Aerial view of Wembley Stadium as the two teams line up for the traditional prematch presentation to the watching dignitaries.

GENOA WIN SUCCESSIVE TITLES

William Garbutt steered Genoa to successive Italian championships in 1923 and 1924. In the title-deciders, they beat Lazio 6-1 on aggregate in 1923 and Savoia 3-1 the following year. In 1912, at the age of just 29, Garbutt had become the first professional coach in Italy and three years later he was in charge of Genoa's first title-winning side. During his time at the club, which was interrupted by the First World War, the pipe-smoking former Arsenal and Blackburn player introduced new techniques and ideas, while emphasising the importance of team spirit. He also established a reputation as a first-class man-manager.

SEE ALSO 'GENOA EMPLOY 'MISTER GARBUTT' (page 72).

Garbutt had gone to Genoa to find work on the city's docks in order to support his family. The turnaround in his fortunes was amazing.

GOALS DIRECT FROM CORNER KICKS ALLOWED

For the 1923-24 season, the Football Association decreed that goals could now be scored direct from corner-kicks and experts on Scottish football believe that the first goal ever to be scored in this way was by Alston of St Bernard's against Albion Rovers on 21 August 1924. Five years later, in May 1929, Scotland's Alec Cheyne scored the winner against England at Hampden Park direct from a corner, and the celebrations around the ground were so loud that the legendary 'Hampden roar' was born. Famous goals direct from corners also include Artim Sakiri's effort for Macedonia against England at St Mary's Stadium, Southampton, in October 2002.

SEE ALSO **'CHEDGZOY'S CHUTZPAH'** (page 98).

A swirling Manchester City corner spells panic in the opposition's penalty box. A goal direct from a corner is unusual – but now legal.

ARGENTINA PUTS UP A FENCE

After their stunning performances at the Paris Olympics, Uruguay were the undisputed Kings of World Football – a fact that their neighbours Argentina found especially difficult to bear. A friendly between the two took place at the 30,000 capacity Estadio Sportivo Barracas in Buenos Aires on 28th September. It was suspended after only four minutes. Four days later the teams met again, only this time a twelve metre high fence was positioned around the perimeter to keep the spectators from encroaching onto the pitch. Argentina recorded a 2-1 victory over their rivals and the use of a wire fence to separate players and spectators went on to become commonplace in Latin American football.

SEE ALSO **'TAYLOR REPORT RECOMMENDS ALL-SEATER STADIUMS'** (page 434).

The atmosphere at many football matches in Latin America – let alone a Fla-Flu or Boca-River derby – is fantastic to experience.

CHEDGZOY'S CHUTZPAH

During Everton's 5-2 victory at Tottenham Hotspur on 12 April 1924, winger Sam Chedgzoy exploited the vague wording of the rules to score direct from a corner kick by dribbling from the corner and firing into the net. The opposing team's defenders looked on in disbelief, but Chedgzoy convinced the referee that the goal should stand. That year the Football Association had changed the rules to allow goals to be scored direct from corners without another player touching the ball, but the law did not specify that the corner taker could only take one touch. The FA soon clarified this issue.

SEE ALSO **'DONKEY KICK BOOTED OUT'** (page 311).

Everton's Sam Chedgzoy's inventiveness was matched only by his thorough understanding of the FA's recent rule amendments.

INTERNATIONAL BOARD CHANGES THE OFFSIDE LAW

On 13 June 1925 the International Football Association Board passed a new law stating that a player needed two, not three, opponents between him and the goal to be onside. The change, which was proposed by the Scottish FA, had a dramatic impact on the number of goals scored. In 1924-25, 4700 goals were scored in the Football League. The following season, when the new law was applied, this figure leapt to 6373. Still, not everybody was happy. One football annual reported, 'The change did not improve the quality of first-class football.' However, the publication conceded that spectators were happy because there were more goals.

SEE ALSO **'INTERNATIONAL BOARD AMENDS OFFSIDE RULE'** (page 448).

The offside changes had the desired effect as spectators were treated to much more action inside the penalty box and many more goals.

BARCELONA CROWD WHISTLES DURING ANTHEM

At half-time during a 14 June benefit match between Barcelona and Jupiter, the Spanish national anthem was greeted by whistles from all around the Les Corts Stadium. It was an expression of the anger felt by the people of Catalonia towards the military government in Madrid after dictator General Miguel Primo de Rivera closed down Catalonia's local government and banned the use of the Catalan language. The English Royal Marines band was so surprised by the hostile response that it immediately started playing the English national anthem instead. The crowd responded with applause. Spain's outraged government suspended Barcelona from all football and administrative activities for six months.

SEE ALSO **'BASQUE CLUBS SHOW SOLIDARITY'** (page xx).

The Barca fan's show of disrespect towards the Spanish anthem led to the team being suspended from football for six months.

SAMITIER BECOMES WORLD'S HIGHEST PAID FOOTBALLER

There are no records to reveal how much he earned, though it would have been significantly more than the three-piece suit and watch he was given as a signing-on fee six years earlier – and considerably less than David Beckham is earning in Los Angeles. Dashing Samitier was a true Barcelona hero, nicknamed the 'Lobster' for his overhead kicks and the 'Magician' for his brilliant contribution to the club's success in the 1920s. In fact, he helped Barcelona win ten Catalan Championships, five Spanish Cups and the first ever La Liga.

SEE ALSO **'SUPERSTAR BECKHAM JOINS GALAXY'** (page 608).

Barcelona legend Samitier was nicknamed the 'Lobster' for his overhead kicks and the 'Magician' for his brilliant contribution to the team.

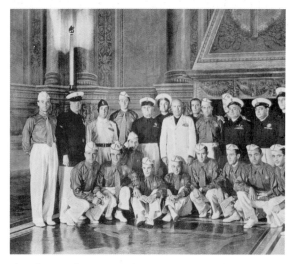

The referees' strike gave Mussolini an opportunity to play a greater role in Italian football – culminating in the 1938 World Cup triumph.

ITALIAN REFEREES GO ON STRIKE

In the early 1920s, Italian referees suffered intimidation and deliberate tarnishing of their reputations by virtually everyone involved in the game. So the president of the Italian referees' association (AIA), Giovanni Mauro, demanded greater protection for match officials. When this was not forthcoming, he called his members to strike action. Strikes were commonplace in Italy during this period – even the priests had gone on strike – but the referees were hardly militant. They didn't organise picket lines or march through city centres, but simply refused to referee matches. Unfortunately, their strike gave Mussolini's fascist regime an excuse to seize greater control of Italian football.

SEE ALSO 'MUSSOLINI EXPLOITS WORLD CUP FOR HIS OWN ENDS' (page 121).

Herbert Chapman was the undoubted mastermind behind Arsenal's startling emergence as a true force in English football.

HERBERT CHAPMAN TRANSFORMS ARSENAL

After guiding Huddersfield Town to three trophies in three seasons, Herbert Chapman was lured to North London by Arsenal chairman Henry Norris. Over the next nine years Chapman transformed a club that had never won significant silverware into one of the powerhouses of English football. Under Chapman Arsenal lifted their first ever trophy, the 1930 FA Cup. That was followed by title triumphs in 1931 and 1933. Chapman was a canny operator in the transfer market, bringing famous players like Charlie Buchan, Alex James and Cliff Bastin to the club. He died suddenly of pneumonia in January 1934, aged 55, while still Arsenal manager.

SEE ALSO 'ARSENAL SIGN CHARLES BUCHAN –£100 A GOAL' (page 101); 'ARSENE WENGER ARRIVES AT HIGHBURY' (page 503);

ARSENAL SIGN CHARLES BUCHAN – £100 A GOAL

When Sunderland demanded £4000 for Charles Buchan, Herbert Chapman found an innovative way of beating down the price he had to pay to bring the 33-year-old back to Arsenal – he persuaded the Wearside club to accept half the amount, plus £100 for every goal Buchan scored in the next season. Sunderland got their second £2000 in the end, since Buchan, who made his debut against Tottenham on 29 August, struck 20 goals that term. Buchan had first played for Arsenal as an amateur, before joining Sunderland in 1911. He captained Arsenal when they lost their first ever Cup final to Cardiff City in 1927.

SEE ALSO **'ARSENAL'S 'WM' FORMATION'** (page 101).

Buchan's return to Arsenal was secured by a novel transfer deal that meant Sunderland received payments on a goal-by-goal basis.

ARSENAL'S 'WM' FORMATION

At the suggestion of forward Charles Buchan, Arsenal manager Herbert Chapman adapted his formation to suit the new offside rule. The attacker was now onside if he had two, not three, opponents between him and the goal, so Buchan's idea was to bring back centre-half Jack Butler from his attacking midfield role to marshal the defence from a central position. It took a 7-0 thrashing by Newcastle United on 3 October 1925 to persuade Chapman this was the way ahead. Arsenal first employed the new formation, known as WM or 3-3-4, in their next match, against West Ham United. They won 4-0.

SEE ALSO **'BELA GUTTMAN AND HIS 4-2-4'** (page 217).

As captain, Charles Buchan was able to offer his manager tactical advice that brought almost instant success for the Gunners.

VIAREGGIO CHARTER SHAPES ITALIAN FOOTBALL

The Carta di Viareggio was a constitution imposed by Mussolini's government to control a game blighted by scandals, crowd violence and suggestions of refereeing bias. Mussolini appointed three supposed football experts to devise the new framework, and they met in the Tuscan coastal resort of Viareggio, which had been the scene of crowd violence in 1920. The most important new rules included the legalisation of professionalism, the banning of foreign players and the creation of a unified national league consisting of Serie A and Serie B. The charter also abolished the referees' association and created a special committee to select officials for specific matches.

SEE ALSO **'ENGLISH REFEREES IN EL DORADO'** (page 165).

Mussolini continually exerted his influence over Italian football. Il Duce was to play a big part when Italy hosted the 1934 World Cup.

356 GOALS IN 357 GAMES

On 5 July 1927, Barcelona played Spain in a match to celebrate the career of the recently retired Paulino Alcantara Riestra, the brilliant forward who remains the Catalan club's leading all-time marksman. Philippines-born Alcantara made his debut in 1912, aged only 15. Over the next 15 years, which were interrupted by a two-year spell back in Manila, he notched an incredible 356 goals in 357 appearances, a feat that will surely never be matched. Alcantara's goals helped propel Barcelona to five Copa del Rey triumphs and ten Catalan Championships. He also scored five goals in six appearances for Spain. After his retirement, Alcantara became a doctor.

SEE ALSO **'BRAZIL HERO ARTUR FRIEDREICH RETIRES'** (page 125).

In his 15 years with Barcelona, the Philippines-born Paulino Alcantara maintained a truly remarkable scoring record with the Catalan team.

FIRST MATCH
BROADCAST ON RADIO

Highbury was the venue for a major landmark in sports broadcasting history when, on 22 January 1927, BBC radio listeners heard commentary on a league match for the first time. So that listeners could picture the action, the commentators divided the pitch into a grid with squares marked one to eight. If listeners imagined they were sitting on the halfway line, square one was the far left-hand corner, while square eight was the near right-hand corner. This gave rise to the expression 'back to square one'. Arsenal's Charlie Buchan scored the first goal to be broadcast, but Sheffield United fought back and the game ended 1-1.

SEE ALSO **'FIRST LIVE TELEVISED CUP FINAL'** (page 135); **'MATCH OF THE DAY GOES ON AIR'** (page 254).

Radio and football's relationship would continue, here Derby County captain Jack Nicholas steps up to the microphone to give his opinion on his team's FA Cup victory in 1946.

CARDIFF CITY TAKE
FA CUP OUT OF ENGLAND

Not for the last time, Arsenal lost a final because of a
goalkeeping blunder. The Gunners dominated their
first ever FA Cup final, on 23 April 1927, with Charlie
Buchan to the fore, but they were unable to break down
Cardiff City's resolute defence. On 73 minutes, disaster
struck for the Gunners, as Cardiff centre-forward Hugh
Ferguson hit a tame shot towards the Arsenal goal. Dan
Lewis lined himself up for a comfortable save, only
for the ball to slide gently under his body, and Cardiff
became the only non-English team to win the FA Cup.
For Lewis, meanwhile, defeat had a painful irony – he
was a Welsh international.

SEE ALSO **'NAYIM SCORES WINNER AGAINST ARSENAL'**
(page 486).

Unfancied Cardiff pose with the FA Cup on Welsh soil. Winning-
goal scorer Hugh Ferguson sits to the right of the trophy.

MEISL CREATES MITROPA CUP...

The Mitropa Cup was the brainchild of Austrian
football administrator Hugo Meisl and can claim to be
the first major international European competition for
club sides. The decision to organize the competition
was taken at a meeting in Venice on 16 and 17 July
1927. Initially, two teams each from Hungary, Austria,
Czechoslovakia and Yugoslavia were invited to enter.
Sparta Prague were the first winners, beating Rapid
Vienna in the final. The competition later welcomed
entrants from Italy and England, among other countries,
but failed to capture the imagination in the same way as
the European Cup would later in the century.

SEE ALSO **'BOLOGNA WIN CUP BY DEFAULT'** (page 121);
'L'EQUIPE ARTICLE SUGGESTS EUROPEAN CUP' (page 199).

Meisl's innovation began European club competition. The Central
European dominance was indicative of the strength of those nations.

... AND DREAMS UP
HOME AND AWAY SYSTEM

When he created the Mitropa Cup, Hugo Meisl devised an excellent way of making sure that neither side benefited unfairly from home advantage, while giving both sets of fans the chance to see their team in European action. Another advantage of his idea of playing ties over two legs, home and away, was that each club would gain revenue from hosting a match. The first final saw Sparta Prague face Rapid Vienna on 30 October and 13 November 1927. Sparta won the first leg 6-2 before going down 2-1 in Vienna, so they won 7-3 on aggregate.

SEE ALSO **'UEFA BAN ENGLISH CLUBS FROM EUROPE'** (page 405).

Meisl's plan laid the foundation for a great tradition of memorable nights of European football and was soon adopted domestically.

HOME NATIONS
WITHDRAW FROM FIFA – AGAIN

This time it was a row over the definition of amateurism, as well as a general feeling that national associations were ceding too much power to a central body, that prompted the home nations to withdraw from FIFA, in February 1928. FIFA was concerned that countries could not field their best teams at the 1928 Olympics if the games' rules on non-professionalism were adhered to strictly, but the British football associations had always been represented by amateurs and refused to accept a FIFA suggestion that players should receive broken-time payments to compensate them for loss of pay and other expenses. The home nations didn't rejoin FIFA until 1946.

SEE ALSO **'ENGLAND GEARS UP FOR INTERNATIONAL COMPETITION'** (page 155).

Whilst the home nations stepped back from international competition, they still played each other in a fiercely competitive spirit.

King George V shakes hands with Scotland's hat-trick hero Jimmy McMullan before the match as the two teams are presented.

SCOTLAND'S WEMBLEY WIZARDS

On 31 March 1928, England were torn apart and suffered their first Wembley defeat on a magical day for the Tartan Army. Observers on both sides of the border expected Scotland to buckle against England's superior skill and physique, but it was England who were outclassed by the pace, movement and clever interplay of the Scotland forward line. Manchester City's brilliant half-back Jimmy McMullan smashed a hat-trick, and Alex James of Preston North End bagged a brace. At the other end, Tom 'Tiny' Bradshaw, making his only Scotland appearance, completely contained Dixie Dean. Scotland celebrated a famous 5-1 victory and avoided the wooden spoon in the Home Championship.

SEE ALSO **'WINGLESS WONDERS FLY IN MADRID'** (page 261).

The contest is considered to owe more to luck than judgement and is a hit with those who don't follow football, as well as fans of the game.

'SPOT THE BALL' LAUNCHED

In April 1928, British periodical *Athletics News* published an innovative competition that featured a photograph from a match, with the ball erased. Competitors had to place a cross where they believed the ball to be. The winner was the person whose cross was nearest to where the ball actually was. Over the years spot-the-ball competitions have become extremely popular because they offer punters the chance to win money, match tickets or other prizes, while testing their football knowledge and instinct. Sometimes the correct answer is decided by a panel of experts and is not where the ball really was. Competitions now appear in print and online.

SEE ALSO **'FOOTBALL POOLS BEGIN'** (page 87); **'FOOTBALL LEAGUE IN DISPUTE WITH POOLS' PROMOTERS'** (page 131).

DIXIE SCORES 60 LEAGUE GOALS

Everton have never spent £3000 more wisely than when they bought 18-year-old Dixie Dean from Tranmere Rovers in 1925. Dean soon established a reputation as England's most dangerous forward as he smashed 32 goals in his first season with the Toffees, but it is for his achievements in Everton's 1927-28 Championship victory that Dean is best remembered.

Despite a serious motorcycle accident in 1926, Dean smashed 60 goals in 39 league appearances, which beat the previous record of 59 goals in 37 games, set by Middlesbrough's George Camsell the season before. Dean's aerial ability was his biggest asset and he headed 40 of those 60 goals. However, perhaps the most remarkable aspect of Dean's record, which still stands, is that to achieve it he needed to score a hat-trick in the last match of the campaign against Arsenal. On 5 May, the Gunners were leading 3-2 with eight minutes left – Dean had struck both Everton goals – when Alec Troup delivered a corner, and Dixie headed home. "Every Arsenal player shook my hand," he recalled, "except Charlie Buchan."

SEE ALSO '356 GOALS IN 357 GAMES' (page 102); 'PELE'S 1000TH GOAL' (page 292).

Strong and powerful, Dixie Dean was the archetypal old fashioned British centre forward.

1928

URUGUAY DEFEND OLYMPIC TITLE

Olympic champions Uruguay won all their matches at the 1924 games in Paris and travelled to Amsterdam determined to once again impose their style of short passing on Europe's more physical teams. Defeats of Holland and Germany set up a tough semi-final showdown with Italy, one of their rivals to host the first World Cup. Uruguay dominated and were not flattered by the 3-2 scoreline. Next up were old rivals Argentina. There was nothing between the sides as they drew 1-1. In the replay on 13 June Uruguay achieved a narrow, hard-fought 2-1 victory in which Hector Scarone struck the second-half winner.

SEE ALSO '... AS URUGUAY STUN BRAZIL' (page 175).

Uruguay's Olympians celebrate another international success – this time at the expense of their neighbours Argentina.

ARSENAL PAY
£10,000 FOR DAVID JACK

Arsenal splashed out the world's first ever five-figure transfer fee to acquire inside-forward David Jack from Bolton. According to legend, during negotiations Gunners boss Herbert Chapman plied the Bolton board with gin, while he himself stuck to tonic water, but however he did it Chapman persuaded Bolton, who were initially reluctant to sell, to drop their asking price from £13,000 to £10,890. Jack had already won the FA Cup twice with Bolton and became a key player at Arsenal, helping them to one Cup success and three League championships in the early 1930s. A prolific goal-scorer, he notched 113 times in 181 League appearances.

SEE ALSO 'FIRST £20,000 TRANSFER' (page 160).

Jack also held the distinction of being the first player to score in a Wembley Cup final. He opened the scoring for Bolton in 1923.

SPANISH FOOTBALL TURNS PRO

The wages paid to stars such as Barcelona's Josep Samitier from 1925 heralded the dawn of the professional era in Spanish football the following year, but the idea of the National Spanish league was not proposed until April 1927, by Maroa Atxa Larrea, a director at Arenas Club de Getxo in the Basque Country. In 1928, the Spanish Football Association (RFEF) finally agreed on the ten teams that would form the first La Liga: Arenas Club de Getxo, Athletic Bilbao, Atletico Madrid, Barcelona, CE Europa, Espanyol, Racing Santander, Real Madrid, Real Sociedad and Real Union. The first champions of Spain were Samitier's Barcelona.

SEE ALSO 'ARGENTINA ACCEPTS PROFESSIONALISM' (page 118).

After the furore surrounding Josep Samitier and others, the widespread adoption of professionalism in the Spanish game was inevitable.

SPAIN'S ZAMORA STOPS ENGLAND

Spain broke England's long-standing record of never having lost to a team from outside the British Isles in a friendly match at the Metropolitano Stadium, Madrid, on 15 May 1929. The outcome was all the more surprising since England made a perfect start, with West Bromwich Albion's Joseph Carter scoring twice in the first 20 minutes, but Gaspar Rubio and Jaime Lazcano also scored to restore parity. After the break, Birmingham City's Joe Bradford put England in front again, before Rubio grabbed his second, and Severino Goiburu struck the winner in the final minutes.

However, Spain's real hero was goalkeeper Ricardo Zamora, of Espanyol, who courageously played on despite suffering a broken sternum. Zamora was an utterly fearless character who loved the high life and his superstar status. He smoked 60 cigarettes a day, supped cognac and beer, and his antics were regularly reported in the Barcelona press, yet Zamora is still regarded as one of the greatest custodians in history. The trophy that bears his name is awarded annually to the best goalkeeper in Spain.

SEE ALSO **'ENGLAND STRIKE BACK AGAINST SPAIN'** (page 119).

Ricardo Zamora, Spain's legendary goalkeeper, broke through the pain barrier to thwart England.

URUGUAY APPOINTED
FIRST WORLD CUP HOSTS

Uruguay's enthusiasm for and commitment to hosting the first World Cup was so impressive that the other bidders – Italy, Spain, Sweden and Holland – withdrew from the running. In fact, the Uruguayan Football Association was so keen it promised to pay all travel and hotel expenses for the visiting teams and construct a brand new stadium in Montevideo, and indeed the Estadio Centenario was completed in just eight months. For a soccer-mad nation, to lay on a festival of world football was the perfect way to celebrate 100 years of independence, but the European countries were unimpressed, and only France, Yugoslavia, Romania and Belgium made the long journey to South America.

SEE ALSO **'FIFA PLANS FOR THE FUTURE'** (page 267).

Aerial view of Montevideo's Estadio Centenario, the impressive and extremely quickly constructed venue for the first ever World Cup final.

FIFA LAYS DOWN
THE FINANCIAL LAW

At its May 1929 congress in Barcelona, FIFA decided on the financial structure of the World Cup and awarded the first tournament to Uruguay. The organising country would cover all costs, including travel, and FIFA would pocket a 10% share of the gross revenue. "Football has already frequently been accused of being led by financial considerations so we must be careful not to give fuel to such ideas," observed Belgium's representative Rodolphe Seeldrayers. The success of Uruguay's bid was partly down to its economic stability at a time when Europe was beset with financial difficulties, a situation that would worsen after the New York stockmarket crash in October 1929.

SEE ALSO **'FIFA VOTE IN FAVOUR OF USA WORLD CUP'** (page 426).

When the FIFA Congress met in 1929, they could have hardly dared to dream how popular the World Cup would become – and how lucrative.

The notion of pre-match team-building was a new one in 1930. The experiment brought instant results and quickly became commonplace.

ENGLAND'S PRE-MATCH GET TOGETHER

In the modern era, international teams spend a few days together at a training camp before a match, but at the beginning of the 1930s it was quite revolutionary of England to have a pre-match get-together the day before their 5 April Home Championship clash with Scotland. The new arrangement obviously worked, though, because England delighted a Wembley crowd of over 87,000 with a convincing victory that clinched the Championship. West Ham's Victor Watson and Ellis Rimmer, of Sheffield Wednesday, each struck twice, and skipper David Jack was also on target for England.

SEE ALSO **'POZZO TAKES PLAYERS TO MOUNTAIN RETREAT'** (page 128); **'IVORY COAST LEADER THREATENS TEAM WITH MILITARY SERVICE'** (page 532).

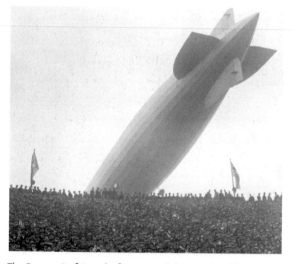

The German Graf Zeppelin flies extremely low over Wembley during the FA Cup final, barely clearing the massed ranks of spectators.

ZEPPELIN SOARS OVER WEMBLEY

During an absorbing FA Cup final on 26 April 1930, the silver German airship Graf Zeppelin appeared over Wembley Stadium and saluted King George V. The craft symbolised the renewed economic and military might of a German nation that had rebuilt itself after the First World War and it hovered for a few minutes before moving slowly on its way, but reports claimed the roar of its engines was deafening and distracted both players and spectators, who were uncertain whether to boo or cheer. Zeppelins or airships are now a common sight above major sporting events and are often used to facilitate breathtaking aerial shots of the arena.

SEE ALSO **'ENGLAND TEAM GIVE NAZI SALUTE'** (page 137).

ARSENAL WIN THEIR FIRST TROPHY

Arsenal finally claimed their first major honour on 26 April 1930 – 37 years after their League debut. This FA Cup final was an especially momentous occasion for their manager, Herbert Chapman, who came face to face with the Huddersfield team with which he had enjoyed so much success. In front of a crowd of over 92,000, forward Alex James gave the Gunners a first-half lead. After the interval, Huddersfield battled in vain to claw their way back into the game, but Arsenal stood firm and they knew the Cup was theirs when Jack Lambert embarked on a long solo run that ended in the second goal.

SEE ALSO **'ALEX JAMES DIES'** (page 184).

Alex James's header finds the net for Arsenal despite the goalkeeper's desperate attempts to scramble across and make a save.

RIMET LEAVES FOR URUGUAY

On 21 June 1930 FIFA president Jules Rimet joined other FIFA officials and the Romanian, Belgian and French teams on the Conte Verde as the liner set sail from the French port of Villefranche-Sur-Mer for South America and the inaugural World Cup. Also on board was the trophy, a four-kilogram, 35-centimetre tall statuette of Nike, the ancient Greek goddess of victory, designed by the French sculptor Abel Lafleur. It was made of gold-plated sterling silver. "We were 15 days on the ship," recalled France's Lucien Laurent. "We did our basic exercises down below and our training on deck. The coach never spoke about tactics at all."

SEE ALSO **'SOUTH AFRICA TO HOST WORLD CUP'** (page 617).

Long-standing FIFA president Jules Rimet presents the World Cup to Dr Paul Jude, president of the Uruguayan Football Association.

LAURENT MAKES HISTORY

Nineteen minutes into the very first World Cup match at the Pocitos Stadium, Montevideo, Lucien Laurent met Ernest Liberati's cross with a precise right-foot volley into the Mexican net. According to Laurent's account of the 13 July match, it was snowing at the time since it was winter in the Southern Hemisphere. "Everyone was pleased, but we didn't all roll around on the ground. Nobody realised that history was being made," he added. Laurent's opener set France on course for a 4-1 victory, in which Marcel Langiller, Andre Maschinot and Mexico's Juan Carreno were also on target. Just a thousand spectators watched the match.

SEE ALSO 'RONALDO RECORDS HIS 15TH WORLD CUP GOAL' (page 601).

The French World Cup squad including their historic goalscorer, Lucien Laurent who sits second from the right on the front row.

ARGENTINA SCRAPE PAST FRANCE

On 15 July, France lost 1-0 to Argentina in a game packed with incident. Luisito Monti's 20-yard free-kick gave the South Americans the advantage nine minutes from the end, but then, on 84 minutes, France's Marcel Langiller dribbled the length of the field, only to hear the final whistle just as he was bearing down on goal. As Argentina followers ran onto the pitch, closely followed by mounted police, the French surrounded Brazilian referee Almeida Rego. The man in black consulted his fellow officials before admitting the error and restarting the match. France still lost, but were saluted as winners by the watching Uruguay players.

SEE ALSO 'REFEREE BLOWS FULL-TIME EARLY' (page 357).

France goalkeeper Alexis Thepot catches the ball under pressure from the onrushing Argentinian striker, as well as his own centre back.

Guillermo Stabile slots home one of his two goals as Argentina run the USA team ragged to reach the first ever World Cup final.

ARGENTINA THRASH USA

Attendances soared for the semi-finals of the first World Cup, and on 26 July a crowd of 80,000 watched powerful Argentina demolish the USA 6-1 at the Centenario. Monti grabbed the only goal of the first period, before Alejandro Scopelli's 57th-minute strike completely broke the North Americans' resistance. In the remaining 21 minutes, Guillermo Stabile, who would be crowned the tournament's top scorer, struck a double. Speedy right-winger Carlos Peucelle also bagged a brace, while James Brown scored the USA's consolation goal. The game was refereed by Belgian Jan Langenus, who was not required to issue any cautions. His performance earned him the coveted job of refereeing the final.

SEE ALSO 'GAETJENS SCORES FOR USA AGAINST ENGLAND' (page 173).

The two teams take to the pitch and wave to the spectators before the match. Argentina are on the left and Uruguay on the right.

WHOSE BALL FOR FINAL?

Amid a cacophony of firecrackers, on 30 July referee Jan Langenus tossed a coin to decide which ball would be used in the first ever World Cup final. Both participants, Argentina and hosts Uruguay, 6-1 winners over Yugoslavia in their semi-final, had insisted a ball made in their own country should be used. Since this issue was not addressed in the tournament's regulations, it was agreed that the decision would be left to chance. Argentina won the toss, so their ball would be used. However, unconfirmed reports suggest that Uruguay's ball was used in the second half.

SEE ALSO 'BURST BALL LIVENS UP FINAL' (page 158); 'WHITE BALL INTRODUCED' (page 179).

1930

ONE-ARMED FORWARD SEALS FINAL

The 20,000 Argentinian supporters who travelled across the River Plate to Montevideo on specially chartered boats were greeted by police who frisked them for firearms, but nobody wanted trouble – they were only there to see the match. When the gates of the Centenario opened at 8am on 30 July, fans began to flood in. Several hours before the 3.30pm kick-off, the stadium reached its capacity of 90,000.

The home supporters soon had something to cheer about as winger Pablo Dorado gave Uruguay the lead on 12 minutes, his fierce shot flying between the legs of goalkeeper Juan Botasso. But Carlos Peucelle soon levelled and Argentina went ahead seven minutes before the break through Guillermo Stabile. Referee Jan Langenus, sporting a jacket and tie, turned down Uruguay's offside appeals.

Uruguay's coach Alberto Suppici must have said something inspirational at the break because his team discovered new belief in the second half. Ten minutes in, Pedro Cea equalised after a storming run. Another ten minutes and Uruguay were ahead through Santos Iriarte's stunning strike.

Argentina advanced, but dogged defending kept them out. Then, in the dying seconds, Héctor Castro, the one-armed forward, headed home to seal Uruguay's triumph, 4-2. He had lost his right forearm at the age of 13, after an accident with an electric saw. Nicknamed 'El Divino Manco', the 'One-Armed God', he had also scored Uruguay's first World Cup goal, against Peru.

SEE ALSO '... AS URUGUAY STUN BRAZIL' (page 175).

Uruguay's Héctor Castro scores his team's fourth goal past Argentina's Juan Botasso.

Uruguay's team and officials celebrate winning the first World Cup final and launch a party that would last for several days across the nation.

Francisco Varallo was a star Argentinian forward who played in the 1930 World Cup final. He is the all-time top scorer for Boca Juniors.

ARGENTINIAN FOOTBALL GOES PROFESSIONAL

Argentina had a national league for four decades before leading clubs, including Boca Juniors, River Plate and Independiente, realised it was time to follow the European model, especially since several clubs were already paying players unofficially, and formed the 18-team Liga Argentina de Football, South America's first professional league. The first title was won by Boca and the second by River, as the Buenos Aires heavyweights began their domination of Argentinian football. The League's top scorer in 1931 was Alberto Zozaya of Estudiantes de la Plata, with 33 goals. The following year that honour went to River's Bernabe Ferreyra, who struck 43 times.

SEE ALSO **'BUENOS AIRES FORMED'** (page 16); **'RIVER PLATE BECOME 'THE MILLIONAIRES''** (page 137).

Jimmy McStay leads Celtic onto the pitch where a two minutes' silence was observed in memory of Thomson, who died the previous week.

GOALKEEPER DIES AFTER GOALMOUTH COLLISION

Shortly after half-time in a 5 September goalless Old Firm clash at Ibrox, Celtic custodian John Thomson and Sam English of Rangers challenged for the ball, but, in a tragic accident, Thomson's skull was fractured as it crashed against English's knee. The 22-year-old was stretchered from the field and died later that evening in the Victoria Infirmary. "His merit as a goalkeeper shone superbly in his play," said Celtic manager Willie Maley. "Never was there a keeper who caught and held the fastest shots with such grace and ease." Thomson's grave in Fife is still a place of pilgrimage for Celtic fans.

SEE ALSO **'ALEX JAMES DIES'** (page 185); **'DUNCAN EDWARDS DIES'** (page 214).

ENGLAND STRIKE BACK AGAINST SPAIN

On 9 December 1931, England exacted revenge for
their defeat in Madrid two and a half years earlier by
annihilating Spain 7-1 in front of a crowd of 55,000
at Highbury. Ricardo Zamora, Spain's celebrated
goalkeeper, was humiliated as England raced to a 3-0
half-time lead thanks to John Smith's double and
Thomas Johnson's strike. Zamora was reputed to be one
of world football's top wage earners, but was powerless
to stop second-half goals from Samuel Crooks (two),
Dixie Dean and Johnson. Even Spain's legendary
forward Josep Samitier was unable to influence the
game, although Guillermo Gorostiza bagged the visitors'
consolation goal three minutes from time.

SEE ALSO **'SPAIN'S ZAMORA STOPS ENGLAND'** (page 110);
'SPAIN PROVE THEIR METTLE IN EUROPE' (page 253).

Spain's goalkeeper Zamora saves a close-range shot from England's
prolific Dixie Dean during the international match at Highbury.

CHAPMAN'S PUBLICITY DRIVE BRINGS RESULTS

Herbert Chapman did everything in his power to raise
standards on the field and increase Arsenal's profile,
and his influence in North London even spread to the
underground system. Chapman persuaded the London
Electric Railway to change the name of the closest tube
station to Highbury from Gillespie Road to Arsenal.
He argued that nobody knew where Gillespie Road
was, but that everybody wanted to go to Arsenal, and
the LER agreed, despite the cost of reprinting tickets,
maps and timetables. A great innovator, Chapman was
also instrumental in improving spectator facilities at
Highbury, realising that this would attract larger crowds.

SEE ALSO **'HIGHBURY – THE FILM STAR'** (page 143).

Fans flock to the newly-renamed tube station after a match at nearby
Highbury. An upsurge in attendances vindicated Chapman's efforts.

'BALL OVER THE LINE' CUP FINAL CONTROVERSY

'Cup final goal was not a goal' roared the *Daily Herald* after Newcastle's controversial 2-1 Cup final defeat of Arsenal on 23 April 1932. The Gunners were leading 1-0 when Newcastle's Jimmy Richardson chased a pass through the inside-right channel and hooked the ball back from just behind the byline for Jack Allen to score. Film and photographs proved that the ball had crossed the line, but referee WP Harper and his linesmen were poorly positioned and allowed the goal. Allen struck the winner on 71 minutes, and Arsenal claimed the unwanted distinction of being the first side to score first in a Wembley final and lose.

SEE ALSO **'GOAL LINE CONTROVERSY ENRAGES GERMANS'** (page 277).

Newcastle United's Jack Allen fires the controversial equalizer past Arsenal goalkeeper Frank Moss.

BOLOGNA WIN CUP BY DEFAULT

Bologna FC 1909 became the first Italian club to win the Mitropa Cup in bizarre circumstances. Having beaten First Vienna FC in the semi-finals, Bologna were awarded the trophy when the semi-final between Slavia Prague and Juventus was abandoned because of time-wasting and crowd trouble. Many of Bologna's players hailed from South America, including Uruguayans Francesco Fedullo, Raffaele Sansone and Michele Andreolo. Italian clubs were banned from fielding foreign players, so they tracked down players with Italian blood in other countries. Such players were known as 'oriundi', meaning they were of Italian extraction but had been born or brought up outside Italy.

SEE ALSO **'ITALY SCRAPS BAN ON FOREIGN PLAYERS'** (page 369).

The Stadio Renato Dall'ara, home of Bologna FC, is crafted out of the red stone for which the city's architecture is famous.

MUSSOLINI EXPLOITS WORLD CUP FOR HIS OWN ENDS

Italy had been the European front-runner to host the 1930 World Cup, but it took FIFA eight meetings to agree, at its Stockholm congress of 1932, that the Italians should get the next tournament, so some administrators may have realised that Benito Mussolini would exploit the competition for political gain. From the moment when Italian Black Shirts were seen guarding the trophy at the draw, fascism cast a long and sustained shadow over the tournament. 'Il Duce' certainly used it to promote his right-wing doctrines, but what he really needed was for Italy to triumph, and this they duly did, thanks in part to some dubious refereeing.

SEE ALSO **'NORWAY EMBARRASS OLYMPIC HOSTS GERMANY'** (page 132).

By 1932, Mussolini's grip on Italian football was absolute. As Prime Minister and fascist leader he was determined Italy should be the hosts.

AUSTRIA'S 'WUNDERTEAM'

In the modern era, friendlies are rarely more than a training exercise, but there was a time when they were as hard-fought and exciting as any competitive match. Indeed, on 7 December 1932 Stamford Bridge played host to a mouth-watering encounter between the mighty England and an Austria side that had hit such heights it was dubbed the 'Wunderteam'.

Under Hugo Meisl's impressive management, the visitors were unbeaten in 14 matches during the previous 18 months. They had scored 11 goals and conceded none in two recent clashes with Germany, and their star player was the free-scoring Matthias Sindelar. However, cheered on by a crowd of 72,000, England overwhelmed Austria 4-3. James Hampson struck twice to give England a 2-0 lead at the interval, before Austria's Karl Zischek netted on 51 minutes. William Houghton then restored the Three Lions' two-goal cushion, only for Sindelar to strike back a minute later. Samuel Crooks's 82nd-minute effort seemed to have made England safe, but Zischek scored again, leaving the home side to hang on for a nerve-jangling last five minutes.

Matthias Sindelar was a potent goal-scoring threat in the Austrian 'Wunderteam'.

NUMBERED SHIRTS WORN FOR THE FIRST TIME

Numbered shirts were worn for the first time on 29 April 1933, when Everton defeated Manchester City 3-0 in the Cup final, watched by a crowd of 92,950. Everton wore numbers 1 to 11 and City sported 12 to 22. The Toffees were formidable: Ted Sagar was a fine goalkeeper, Warney Cresswell provided an immovable force in defence, and Dixie Dean led the attack with phenomenal strength and predatory brilliance, also getting on the scoresheet, his goal sandwiched between strikes from Jimmy Stein and Jimmy Dunn. City would return to Wembley the following year and triumph over Portsmouth, by which time numbered shirts were compulsory in the Football League.

SEE ALSO **'BRAZIL'S SHIRT DESIGN COMPETITION'** (page 188).

The Duke of York looks on as the Duchess of York presents the FA Cup to the winning captain and Everton number 9, Bill 'Dixie' Dean.

PROFESSIONAL LEAGUES IN RIO AND SAO PAULO KICK OFF

Arguments over professionalism had caused divisions in Brazilian soccer for several years and during the 1920s many leading clubs made unofficial payments to players. The state federations of Rio de Janeiro and São Paulo were strongly in favour of professionalism and, because of the disagreements, players from these two great cities were not allowed to represent Brazil at the 1930 World Cup. Consequently, on 23 January 1933, the Rio Federation founded its own professional Liga Carioca de Futebol and almost simultaneously the São Paulo Federation created the Bandeirante Football League, also professional. However, the Confederacao Brasileira de Futebol did not endorse professionalism until 1937.

SEE ALSO **'THE FLA-FLU SETS ATTENDANCE RECORD'** (page 251).

The two states followed Argentina's lead as they saw that the development of a professional league was inevitable in Brazil.

HERBERT CHAPMAN PUT IN CHARGE OF ENGLAND

England did not have an official team manager until 1946, when the FA appointed Walter Winterbottom, so the FA's International Selection Committee chose the team and then asked one of the club managers to take charge on a game-by-game basis. In May 1933, Arsenal's successful boss Herbert Chapman was an obvious choice to guide England through a summer tour of Europe, which began with a 1-1 draw against Italy in Rome, in which Arsenal's Cliff Bastin equalised Giovanni Ferrari's strike. The tour concluded with the 4-0 thrashing of Switzerland in Berne a week later, with both Bastin and Newcastle's Jimmy Richardson bagging a brace.

SEE ALSO **'ENGLAND RECRUIT WINTERBOTTOM'** (page 155); **'ALF RAMSEY TAKES OVER ENGLAND REIGNS'** (page 247).

Herbert Chapman had proved his managerial capabilities over time at Arsenal – now the FA turned to him to help the national side.

DFB: JEWS ARE 'UNACCEPTABLE'

When Adolf Hitler came to power, the Deutscher Fußball-Bund (DFB) shamefully excluded all Jewish players, club owners, sponsors and journalists from German football. Many German Jews, including former national team hero Julius Hirsch, later perished in Nazi death camps. Historians cannot agree on whether the DFB was eager to actively pursue the Nazis' agenda of hatred and genocide, but it is clear that, at the very least, the federation mirrored public support for the regime. In 1933, around 40,000 Jews were involved in German sports clubs, about a tenth of the country's pre-war Jewish population. By 1945, there were only a few thousand Jews alive in Germany.

SEE ALSO **'AUSTRIAN FA COMES UNDER GERMAN CONTROL'** (page 135).

The DFB's shameful stance was sadly reflected in all areas of German state-controlled society during the build up to War in the 1930s.

Arthur Friedenreich was an early poster boy for the Brazilian national team. His goal-scoring exploits are comparable to those of Pelé.

BRAZIL HERO ARTHUR FRIEDENREICH RETIRES

Arthur Friedenreich was Brazilian football's original goal-scoring maestro years before anybody had heard of Pelé. Some claim he scored 1239 times in 1329 appearances, others that he smashed 1329 goals in 1239 games, but the consensus is that Friedenreich, who was nicknamed 'The Tiger', was at least as prolific as Pelé, whose record was 1281 goals in 1363 games. Friedenreich, the Brazilian game's first black superstar, was leading scorer in the Liga Paulista nine times between 1912 and 1929. He represented a number of clubs, including Clube Atletico Paulistano, SC Germania and Flamengo, and also scored ten goals in 22 internationals, before retiring in 1934, aged 42.

SEE ALSO 'PELÉ'S 1000TH GOAL' (page 292).

HERBERT CHAPMAN DIES

On 6 January, Arsenal fans arrived at Highbury for a match against Sheffield Wednesday, their team champions of England and top of the league, but on the way to the stadium they were given the shocking news that their manager Herbert Chapman had died. Chapman had caught a bad cold watching a game at Bury and, despite doctor's warnings, just days later he took that fever to an Arsenal reserve match. His hunger for the game brought on pneumonia and, just hours before the fixture with Sheffield Wednesday, the great man passed away.

SEE ALSO 'JOCK STEIN DIES AS HIS TEAM QUALIFY FOR THE WORLD CUP' (page 405).

Chapman's sudden death, right, shocked football. To commemorate the legendary manager a bronze bust stands at Arsenal's Emirates Stadium.

Karel Petru, the Czechoslovakia manager who tried in vain to get striker Raymond Braine to renounce his Belgian citizenship.

RAYMOND BRAINE REFUSES CZECH KRONEN

Striker Raymond Braine became Belgium's first professional when he signed for Sparta Prague in 1930, aged 23. He was highly successful in the Czechoslovakian league, winning two championships and twice finishing top scorer. But as a professional player, Braine was not eligible for Belgium's 1934 World Cup team, which was amateur, so the Czech Football Association offered Braine 100,000 kronen to become a citizen of Czechoslovakia and represent his new country at the tournament. Braine, who was a veteran of Belgium's 1930 campaign, refused. He played again for Belgium later in the decade and finished his career with an excellent record of 26 goals in 54 internationals.

SEE ALSO 'REBEL COLOMBIAN LEAGUE PROVES ATTRACTIVE' (page 169); 'REVIE ABANDONS ENGLAND' (page 350).

Young Frank Swift's collapse on the final whistle, a result of relief mixed with elation, provided one of the great stories of the FA Cup.

FRANK SWIFT FAINTS AT FINAL

City's 19-year-old goalkeeper Frank Swift sat in the Wembley dressing room at half-time on 28 April distraught that his error had allowed Portsmouth to take a 27th minute lead in the Cup final. The young man had only played half the season for City and was seemingly overawed by the occasion. However, centre-forward Fred Tilson sat down next to him and said, "Tha doesn't need to worry. I'll plonk two in the next half" – and that's exactly what he did. Tilson's winner came just four minutes from time and on hearing the whistle Swift collapsed. He was brought round, but was still in a daze when he met the King.

SEE ALSO 'PELE SCORES FIFTH GOAL' (page 223).

Reigning champions Uruguay were not to grace the Stadio del Partito Nazionale Fascista in Rome, the venue for the 1934 World Cup final.

URUGUAY BOYCOTT WORLD CUP

Incensed by European apathy towards the 1930 competition and with their domestic scene in disarray because of player strikes, Uruguay refused to participate in the 1934 World Cup. They remain the only winners not to defend their title at the next tournament. Other South American countries were angered by the arrangements for the early World Cups, but Argentina and Brazil did travel all the way to Italy, only to lose their first matches and have to go straight home again, because the tournament worked on a knockout basis throughout. Argentina later boycotted the 1938 tournament in France because their bid was rejected.

SEE ALSO 'AFRICAN NATIONS BOYCOTT THE WORLD CUP' (page 264).

It is hard to overstate the extent of the rivalry between Montevideo's two oldest teams. This final is an example of their competitiveness.

HARD FOUGHT COPA URUGUAYA FINAL

Passions were running high when bitter Montevideo rivals Penarol and Nacional met to decide the Uruguayan championship. With the score at 0-0, a cross from Penarol's Bahia went into touch, but rebounded in off Nacional's physio's bag, and Braulio Castro fired home. Referee Telesforo Rodriguez appeared to allow the goal and was attacked by furious Nacional players, two of whom were dismissed, so Nacional played the final 25 minutes of the goalless draw with nine men. At the replay, on 9 August, they were only allowed nine players as a punishment, but again the match finished scoreless. Finally, on 18 November, Nacional, now back to 11 men, defeated Penarol 3-2.

SEE ALSO 'THE BATTLE OF BERNE' (page 193).

POZZO TAKES PLAYERS TO MOUNTAIN RETREAT

Legendary Italy coach Vittorio Pozzo was a renowned disciplinarian and, with the support of Italy's fascist government, enjoyed complete control over his players. Before the 1934 World Cup, he whisked them away to a training camp at a mountain retreat, where he focused on tactics for the tournament. Pozzo devised a system based on the 2-3-5 formation that brought back two of his forwards to support the midfield, allowing dominance of this crucial area. The result was a 2-3-2-3 formation known as Sistema. Pozzo's approach took Italy to consecutive World Cup triumphs and Olympic gold – no wonder they called him 'Il Vecchio Maestro' or the 'Old Master'.

SEE ALSO **'BELA GUTTMAN AND HIS 4-2-4'** (page 217).

Pozzo made sure his squad received the perfect preparation, without any distractions, in the build-up to their World Cup campaign.

ITALY FIRE SEVEN PAST USA

Italy opened their World Cup campaign on 27 May with a resounding 7-1 defeat of the United States in Rome. The Azzurri fielded a large number of imported players or 'oriundi', including Luisito Monti, who had played for Argentina at the previous tournament. Italy's scorers were Angelo Schiavio (three), Raimondo Orsi (two), Giovanni Ferrari and Giuseppe Meazza. Orsi was Argentinian, as was unused substitute Enrique Guaita, but coach Pozzo had no qualms about selecting so many players who had only come to Italy for the money. He reportedly said, "If they can die for Italy, they can play football for Italy."

SEE ALSO **'ARGENTINA THRASH USA'** (page 115).

The triumphant Italian team, pictured in front of the PNF Stadium in Rome, the scene of their famous win on home soil.

ITALY FIGHT BACK
TO TAKE WORLD CUP

Italy survived thorough examinations of their character and ability by Spain
and Austria to reach the 1934 World Cup final, where they faced Czechoslovakia,
conquerors of Switzerland and Germany, on 10 June.

The Czechs were a skilful side and started the Rome final in confident fashion,
though Italy once again demonstrated their resilience. The first goal did not
arrive until the 77th minute, when Czech left-winger Antonin Puc struck a long-
range shot past Giampiero Combi in the Italian goal. Italy seemed defeated, but
Czechoslovakia failed to kill them off as Frantisek Svoboda's effort rebounded off
a post and eight minutes from time Orsi, the left-winger, latched onto Guaita's
pass and evaded the Czech defence. His right-foot shot swerved beyond Frantisek
Planicka's fingertips, and Italy were level.

Pozzo wanted forwards Schiavio and Guaita to switch positions for extra-time
and had to run around the edge of the pitch to get himself heard in the excited
din, but Guaita moved into the middle and in the 98th minute collected Meazza's
cross and found Schiavio, who skipped past a defender and fired Italy to World
Cup glory.

Italy's controversial coach
Vittorio Pozzo is carried high
after his tactical experiments and
pre-match build-up had brought
the Italians victory.

SEE ALSO **'ROSSI SCORES IN FINAL AND TAKES THE GOLDEN BOOT'** (page 390-1);
'ITALY WIN WORLD CUP' (page 604).

1934

THE BATTLE OF HIGHBURY

At the end of the match England's treatment room looked more like a casualty ward on a rowdy Saturday night after the Italians had taken offence to a second-minute challenge by Ted Drake that left their centre-half Luisito Monti with a broken foot. The defender had to be carried off and from there the World Champions forgot about football and set about exacting revenge.

The red mist that plagued the Italians on 14 November 1934 at Highbury meant England took a 3-0 lead after just 15 minutes thanks to two goals from Eric Brook and one from Ted Drake. A 19-year-old Stanley Matthews was having a fine game on the wing, but soon any footballing prowess was null and void. England skipper Eddie Hapgood had his nose broken by a stray Italian elbow and Drake needed treatment for a heavy challenge. A strong Italian contingent in the 55,000 crowd meant the referee was put off sending anyone off and while the Italians did improve in the second-half, scoring two goals, the elbowing, pushing and even jumping on players never subsided.

SEE ALSO **'PIOLA'S HANDBALL'** (page 143).

Action from the bruising Battle of Highbury with England firmly on the attack.

LEAGUE'S DISPUTE WITH POOLS PROMOTERS

In the early 1930s a new pastime arose, the football pools. They were an instant hit with families all over the country who enjoyed taking a punt on the upcoming football results, but the Football League itself grew suspicious about the influence the pools could have over the game. Consequently, in February 1936 it took steps and decided to withhold fixtures until the very last moment, hoping to put the coupon distributors out of business. Instead, of course, the game was thrown into disarray and three weeks of frantic discussion saw the League back down. The pools were here to stay.

SEE ALSO **'FOOTBALL POOLS BEGIN'** (page 87);
"SPOT THE BALL' LAUNCHED' (page 106).

The public latched on to the notion of the football pools and the League were powerless in the face of such overwhelming popularity.

LUTON'S JOE PAYNE SCORES 10

He wasn't a goalscorer. He wasn't even in the first team, but this was his day. Joe Payne was given the job of makeshift centre-forward as Luton's first choice strikers were both injured and in the first 20 minutes of the Third Division South match against Bristol Rovers on 13 April it seemed that the 'new' number 9 was out of his depth. Payne, however got his hat-trick before half-time and in the second-half continued where he left off. Every time he received the ball the Luton fans cried for another goal and each time they were satisfied. He got the last of his ten-goal haul on 86 minutes.

SEE ALSO **'... BUT EUSEBIO SCORES FOUR'** (page 273);
'FOG ROBS DENIS LAW OF DOUBLE HAT-TRICK' (page 237).

Joe Payne wasn't even a recognized striker but he quickly got into his stride to score an astonishing ten goals to the delight of the home fans.

The civil war tore Spain apart and football also suffered. The scars of the conflict are still felt by some Spanish clubs to this day.

CIVIL WAR WRECKS SOCCER

The onset of the Spanish Civil War soon divided a nation and one of the first casualties was football. With Franco's nationalists taking great swathes of the country, there was no way an organized league could be maintained and so La Liga was immediately suspended. Atletico Madrid had been the most impressive team prior to the war, but they, along with their neighbours Real Madrid, would be unable to take part in subsequent regional leagues (they applied but were turned down by Barcelona). They would, like the Spanish people, have to wait until 1940 for the action to resume.

SEE ALSO **'WAR SUSPENDS COMPETITIONS'** (page 144).

NORWAY EMBARRASS OLYMPIC HOSTS GERMANY

Germany had won the right to host the 1936 Olympics a year before Adolf Hitler's Nazi party had come to power, but the Berlin event was to be the Fascist regime's crowning glory. Germany, of course, would have a successful Games, but in the football they were embarrassed in the quarter-finals by Norway. At 2-0 a stern-looking Hitler left his seat, leaving his propaganda tsar Goebbels to explain that he was "keen to watch the rowing". Norway went out in the semi-final, but beat Poland in the plays-off for bronze. World Champions Italy took gold.

SEE ALSO **'FOOTBALL REVIVED FOR MORALE'** (page 146).

Hitler enjoying the Olympic swimming. He was less pleased when Germany were eliminated in the football quarter-finals by Norway.

149,547 WATCH SCOTLAND TRIUMPH OVER ENGLAND

The official figure was 149,547, but it's thought that 10,000 more eager fans broke into Hampden Park on 17 April, desperate to see the 'auld enemy' defeated. In terms of that year's Home International Championship the game mattered little. Wales had taken the crown and the match was for second place, but that wasn't the issue when Scotland played England, and the bulging terraces were treated to a fine display. Stoke's Freddie Steele gave the English the lead, but in the second-half the Hampden roar was deafening as Frank O'Donnell equalized, before Bob McPhail got two late goals to seal a famous 3-1 win.

SEE ALSO **'THE FLA-FLU DERBY SETS ATTENDANCE RECORD'** (page 251).

A view of the enormous crowd bound to Hampden Park hoping to cheer Scotland on to a convincing victory. They got their wish.

SCHALKE WIN DOUBLE

Economic conditions in 1930s Germany were harsh and only their football team, Schalke 04, gave the Ruhr Valley's poor mining communities something to smile about. Schalke dominated the German game in the 30s, winning four championships and ending seemingly unbeatable Nuremberg's domination. In 1937 Schalke became the first side to win the German double. Inspired by brothers-in-law Fritz Szepan and Ernst Kuzorra, and a style of play nicknamed 'the spinning top' – the ball was moved from player to player in short, quick bursts – Schalke took the title and in the final, played in January 1938, they beat Fortuna Dusseldorf to win the German cup, the DFB Pokal.

SEE ALSO **'SCHALKE ARE NAZI FAVOURITES'** (page 149).

Schalke's footballing achievements during this time will be forever tarred by Germany's political direction in the 1930's.

NEW GERMAN COACH MAKES AN IMPACT

Hitler hadn't been impressed with the nation's football team at his Olympic Games and so it was no surprise that a new coach was brought in to change German fortunes. Having taken the job in 1923, Otto Nerz had been Germany's first and only manager, but soon after the Berlin Games Sepp Herberger stepped in and immediately had a positive effect. The team's 8-0 win over Denmark on 18 May in the now Polish town of Breslau galvanized the nation, who nicknamed the team the 'Breslau Elf' or Breslau Eleven, and with Otto Siffling leading the attack they looked a potent threat before the following year's World Cup in Italy.

SEE ALSO **'WILLY MEISL'S WHIRLWIND REVOLUTION'** (page 207).

German coach Sepp Herberger keepes a close eye as Helmut Rahn does press ups during training after he took control of the side.

'KEEP STANLEY AT STOKE'

Stanley Matthews was said to have had a financial disagreement with Stoke's board and had put in a transfer request to leave the club he had joined as a boy. When the news went public in February 1938 local pottery manufacturers complained of a drop in production. Something would have to be done. Local industrialists took it in hand and called a meeting at Stoke's town hall at which 3000 locals – 2000 were locked outside with banners begging Matthews not to go – decreed that the club and the player must be made to see sense. Matthews, the wizard of dribble stayed another nine years.

SEE ALSO **'FINNEY OFFERED LIRA LIFESTYLE'** (page 180).

Stanley Matthews proudly wearing the strip of his home-town club. He would make 318 appearances during two spells with the Potters.

AUSTRIAN FA COMES UNDER GERMAN CONTROL

When Adolf Hitler annexed Austria, football was the last thing on his mind. After all, the Nazis had bigger plans, but with the Austrian game coming under the German umbrella the national team gained access to a vast array of Austrian talent. Under their coach Hugo Meisl, Austria's 'Wunderteam' had impressed with a fluent style that saw them beat England in 1936. They had qualified for the World Cup, but after their annexation they would not participate. Instead, Germany could draw upon their resources and, keen to have a team that represented the new Greater German Reich, added a number of Austrians to their squad.

SEE ALSO **'BAYERN TEAM DEFY NAZIS'** (page 145).

The merging of the two FAs meant that the German national team had access to an array of Austrian talent, such as goalkeeper Rudolf Hiden.

FIRST LIVE TELEVISED CUP FINAL

For years FA Cup final day had been the most important date in the English footballing calendar and thanks to the magic of television the action was now to be broadcast live straight into the country's living rooms – well, the living rooms of those lucky enough to have a TV set. Preston and Huddersfield were the stars of the show on 30 April, but couldn't live up to the top billing. The game was a dull affair and as it edged goalless towards the end of extra-time BBC commentator Thomas Woodrooffe declared, "If there's a goal scored now, I'll eat my hat." A minute later he had to do just that.

SEE ALSO **'TELEVISION MAKES HISTORY'** (page 268);
'TELEVISION COMPANY COLLAPSE SPELLS TROUBLE FOR ENGLISH LEAGUE CLUBS' (page 554).

The winning captain, Preston North End's Tom Smith, shows off the Cup as he is chaired around the pitch in triumph after the match.

MUTCH WINS FA CUP WITH LAST MINUTE PENALTY

North End's George Mutch scores the games' only goal from the spot, just 30 seconds from the end of extra time.

Preston North End had almost won the Cup the year before, but lost to Sunderland in the final. They had almost won the league in 1938, but were beaten to the crown by Arsenal. Now, though, they would be triumphant, but only just. The 20 April final against Huddersfield was dull and for the first time went into extra-time. With a minute left and fans already heading home, Preston's Scottish international George Mutch was upended in the box by Huddersfield centre-half Alf Young. The referee's whistle roused the remaining supporters and it was Mutch himself who smashed the first ever penalty in an FA Cup final in off the crossbar.

SEE ALSO **'RAMSEY SAVES THE FA'S 90TH BIRTHDAY BLUSHES'** (page 185); **'LAST KICK EQUALIZER DASHES ENGLAND HOPES'** (page 275);

ENGLAND TEAM GIVE NAZI SALUTE

They did it reluctantly. They didn't want to, but with the atmosphere in Berlin's Olympic Stadium as tense as it was all around Europe, they were told it was for the best and so the England team lined up and offered the 110,000 crowd the Nazi salute. Hitler wasn't present, but his party's hierarchy, including Goebbels and Goerring, were in the crowd. English captain Eddie Hapgood recalled, "We sensed that this wasn't merely a football match, but something deeper, a challenge from Germany that England had to answer."

Prior to the match, secretary of the FA Sir Stanley Rous had been told by his hosts that they would stand to attention for the English anthem, but expected the English to return the courtesy by offering the Nazi salute. Rous was unsure and went to the British Ambassador in Germany, Sir Neville Henderson, who advised it was the right thing to do. He argued that he did it, so why shouldn't the footballers?

After giving the salute the England team gave their hosts a footballing lesson, running out 6-3 winners in a very tense match.

SEE ALSO **'ITALY WEAR BLACK SHIRTS AGAINST FRANCE'** (page 138). **'DI CANIO GIVES NAZI SALUTE TO SUPPORTERS'** (page 586).

RIVER PLATE BECOME THE 'MILLIONAIRES'

Both Boca Juniors and River Plate were based in the La Boca region of Buenos Aries and something had to give. River Plate had been formed in 1901 and already had a 'healthy' rivalry with their neighbours. It is said that the two teams played a match to see who would have to move and River Plate lost. Having already purchased a number of great players in the early part of the decade, the club were already seen as affluent, but once they moved to Nunez, a far smarter suburb, their reputation was set and the nickname 'Los Millionarios' – the Millionaires – has stuck ever since.

SEE ALSO **'DYNAMO DRESDEN RELOCATE'** (page 198).

River Plate's status as the fashionable club in Buenos Aires remains to this day. Their clashes with Boca Juniors are must-see affairs.

Brazilian forward Leonidas da Silva made his mark on the World Cup with a four goal haul that meant Brazil just edged out the Poles.

LEONIDAS DA SILVA SCORES FOUR

Brazil came to France in 1938 eager to impress and on 5 June in a damp Strasbourg they did just that. In their first round match against the Polish, Brazil gave six players their international debuts, but it was their small but ambidextrous centre-forward Leonidas da Silva who was the greatest threat. Playing for some of the match with bare feet due to the mud, he got three goals before half-time and another in the second period, making him the first man to get four goals in the World Cup. Polish striker Ernest Wilimowski matched that feat, but it was the Brazilians who, after extra-time, ran out 6-5 winners.

SEE ALSO '... BUT EUSEBIO SCORES FOUR' (page 273).

The Italian team controversially perform the fascist salute as one before the start of the World Cup final in Colombes Stadium in Paris.

ITALY WEAR BLACK SHIRTS AGAINST FRANCE

Among the 55,000 fans in Paris on 12 June to see hosts France take on holders Italy in the quarter-final of the World Cup were thousands of Italians who had fled Mussolini's Fascist regime. France was now their home, but when it came to football, they supported Italy. Italian coach Vittorio Pozzo had links with the Fascists and those fans would have been saddened to see their team take to the field in a menacing all-black strip. Pozzo had already insisted that players give a Nazi salute before their game against Norway, a move that brought boos from the crowd, and once more he underlined his allegiances.

SEE ALSO 'POZZO'S MOMENT OF TRIUMPH' (page 140).

MEAZZA MAKES BRAZIL PAY PENALTY

Bewitching Brazil were the surprise package of the World Cup, but when they met holders Italy in the semi-final on 16 June they were over-confident and 'rested' Leonidas and his fellow striker Tim. Italy were simply too strong and too organised for them and from the start meant business. Colaussi scored the first and when the great forward Piola was brutally fouled in the box it was up to their captain Meazza to give them an unassailable two-goal cushion with just 14 minutes gone. He made no mistake, but amid the celebrations his shorts were ripped and came clean off. The cheek of it!

SEE ALSO **'LEONIDAS RETURNS HOME'** (page 141).

Italian hero Meazza. The great San Siro stadium in Milan is actually named the Stadio Giuseppe Meazza in honour of the Inter legend.

PIOLA GETS FINAL GOAL

They had dominated the match. They were undoubtedly the stronger, fitter, more modern team, but with just ten minutes remaining in the World Cup final Italy held a tenuous 3-2 lead over a Hungarian side that refused to lie down. The game was incident packed, Italy swept the ball about confidently, taking the lead after just six minutes through Gino Colaussi. Hungary unexpectedly equalized through Titkos, but the Italians scored two more before half-time.

Hungary got back into the match with 20 minutes to go, but the Italians would simply not be deterred. They attacked down the right with Amedeo Biavati and Silvio Piola swapping passes. Biavati played a clever back-heel into the path of Piola, who smashed the ball high into the net.

SEE ALSO **'POZZO'S MOMENT OF TRIUMPH'** (page 140).

Despite Antal Szabo's wonder saves the Hungarian resistance was finished and the Italians could once more hold the World Cup aloft.

1938

POZZO'S MOMENT OF TRIUMPH

While his players and staff embraced and wept, Italian manager Vittorio Pozzo stood with a knowing look upon his face. He had won the World Cup once more, but, never one to show emotion, even a celebratory bucket of water thrown over him failed to get a response. Inside though, he must have been so satisfied. Italy had won the World Cup in 1934, of course, but there they were accused of home favouritism. This team, however, had clearly won on merit. Pozzo's 'metodo' formation (a 2-3-2-3 system) had looked the most competent and Pozzo's men were more than worthy of the title of World Champions.

SEE ALSO **'POZZO STEPS DOWN'** (page 163).

Vittorio Pozzo, left, celebrates with his players after winning his second successive World Cup.

Despite failing to win the World Cup, the Brazil fans were proud of their team and had a new hero in Leonidas (second, left).

LEONIDAS RETURNS HOME

The Brazilian football team – South America's only participants at the World Cup – flew home a little embarrassed not to have done better and to answer questions about why they'd 'rested' their best player. Although he sat out the defeat to Italy, Leonidas was still the tournament's top scorer with eight goals and he returned to Brazil a national hero. The nation's players were starting to become gods and it was the acrobatic centre-forward who first had such acclaim thrust upon him. One chocolate manufacturer even made a new bar and named it 'Diamante Negro' in honour of the man they called the 'Black Diamond'.

SEE ALSO **'BRAZILIAN AIR FORCE ESCORT THEIR HEROES HOME'** (page 225); **'RONALDO IS EUROPEAN PLAYER OF THE YEAR'** (page 507).

POLITICS PREVENTS ENGLAND FROM COMPETING

The build up to the 1938 World Cup was heavily disrupted. The world was on the precipice of war and those tensions had an effect on proceedings that summer in France. Austria, annexed by Germany, pulled out, as did Spain due to its Civil War. In South America Uruguay were still smarting from European apathy towards their inaugural championship eight years before, while Argentina refused to travel as they had hoped to be hosts. There were 15 nations set to play and FIFA pleaded with England to make up the numbers, but the Football Association, still looking down their noses at the tournament, declined.

SEE ALSO **'ENGLAND GEARS UP FOR INTERNATIONAL COMPETITION'** (page 155).

England were still seen as the international team to beat. Their absence at the World Cup deprived the tournament of it's biggest draw.

BRAZILIAN SOCIOLOGIST FOCUSES ON FOOTBALL

In 1933 a young Brazilian sociologist called Gilberto Freyre had written a study that celebrated Brazil's rich ethnic mix and in 1938, with the likes of Leonidas having thrilled the nation at the World Cup, Freyre turned his attention to football and just how the sport best summed up Brazil's marvellous diversity. "Our style of playing football," he wrote, "contrasts with [that of] the Europeans because of a combination of qualities of surprise, malice, astuteness and agility, and at the same time brilliance and individual spontaneity... Our passes, our dummies, our flourishes with the ball, the touch of dance and subversiveness that marks the Brazilian style."

SEE ALSO '*FEVER PITCH* PUBLISHED' (page 463).

Freyre's academic approach explored Brazil's drive and flair for football in sociological terms, long before they go on to would dominate the game.

ARGENTINA PLAY BRAZIL TWICE IN ONE WEEK

By 1939 the time-honoured rivalry between Brazil and Argentina had become a matter of national pride. Incidents in 1920 and 1937 had stoked the fire, but it was during a week in January that tempers really boiled over.

Argentina had won 5-1 in Rio and returned a week later for their second match of the Roca Cup. The atmosphere was electric as Brazil sought revenge and scored first only for the Argentinians to take a 2-1 lead.

It looked as though they had secured a joyous second win in seven days, but with just minutes remaining the referee gave a hugely dubious penalty. The Argentinians were incensed and Arcadio Lopez berated the referee in no uncertain terms. He was asked to leave the field and then made to go by sturdy police. Lopez' treatment was the last straw. His team-mates all vacated the pitch, leaving Brazil to take the penalty with no goalkeeper. A tumultuous game ended 2-2.

The Argentina team knew that national pride was at stake every time they took on Brazil and there was huge pressure on them to win.

SEE ALSO 'BRAZIL, ARGENTINA AND BROKEN BONES' (page 153).

The famous facade of the East Stand at Highbury appeared on the silver screen in 1939 as the scene of a mysterious murder.

'HIGHBURY – THE FILM STAR'

On 6 May Brentford came to Highbury for the last game of the season and for the day took on the mantle of movie stars as well as footballers. The Brentford players were used as fictional characters for a new film called The Arsenal Stadium Mystery, in which an amateur side called the Trojans take on Arsenal, only for their star player to be found dead, casting suspicion on his team-mates, as well as on his mistress. Gunners manager George Allison had a speaking part in the movie, while Arsenal's stars of the time, Eddie Hapgood and Cliff Bastin, could also boast about their cinematic debuts.

SEE ALSO 'STALLONE SAVES THE DAY IN *ESCAPE TO VICTORY*' (page 377).

Italy were fresh from their World Cup win when this grudge match took place. Handball villain Piola is fourth from left on the back row.

PIOLA'S HANDBALL

Billed as 'The masters of association football versus the World Cup holders', the match played in Milan on 13 May 1939 didn't disappoint. The Battle of Highbury was still fresh in the memory, but this time the only fists used were by the Italian centre-forward Piola, who scored a highly controversial goal. Tommy Lawton had given England the lead, but the Italians equalized in the second half though Biavati. Piola was then just five yards out when he clearly fisted the ball into the net. The crowd laughed, Piola looked sheepish, but incredibly the German referee awarded a goal. England got over the shock and equalized through Willie Hall.

SEE ALSO 'THE HAND OF GOD' (page 415).

The continuation of a professional football league was simply impossible as it became clear the threat of war was to become a reality.

WAR SUSPENDS COMPETITIONS

On 2 September 1939 football grounds all over Britain were as packed as ever. The day before Germany had invaded Poland, but, no matter, on the terraces fans could forget about the threat of war. As the punters left the stadiums, talk would have been a mix of what they had just seen and what was happening across the Channel. Little did they know that this would be the last competitive football they would see for six years as the following day Britain declared war on Germany and all organized football (apart from morale-boosting exhibition games) was cancelled.

SEE ALSO 'SOVIET UNION LEFT OUT IN THE WORLD CUP COLD' (page 330).

GERMAN OCCUPATION HALTS NORWEGIAN GAME

Norway were still rejoicing at their nation's efforts in the 1936 Olympics. The achievements of the 'Bronselaget' or 'Bronze Team' were fresh in the memory, they had qualified for the 1938 World Cup and club football was extremely popular. Then on 10 June 1940 came the boom of guns as Germany invaded and ultimately prevailed in the first direct land confrontation between the Allied and German troops of World War Two. As a result of German occupation a nationwide strike amongst athletes and athletic associations was called and football suspended. Norway's star player, Reidar Kvammen, was immediately placed in a concentration camp.

SEE ALSO 'NORWAY EMBARRASS OLYMPIC HOSTS GERMANY' (page 132). 'NORWAY RANKED SECOND IN THE WORLD' (page 469).

Waves of German paratroopers land on snow-covered rock ledges in the Norwegian port and city of Narvik as their invasion begins.

BAYERN TEAM DEFY NAZIS

In 1932 Bayern Munich, under the presidency of Kurt Landauer, won their first German championship and looked set to dominate the national game. Landauer, though, was a Jew and a year later he was placed in a concentration camp, where he remained until in 1939 he escaped and fled to Switzerland. In the interim Bayern's fortunes took a turn for the worse, but those players he had guided to the title hadn't forgotten his input and in 1940 they travelled to Switzerland to visit their exiled former boss. The Nazis, of course, frowned on the visit and immediately shunned Bayern, bestowing financial favours upon 1860 Munich instead.

SEE ALSO **'DFB: JEWS ARE 'UNACCEPTABLE'** (page 124); **'BAYERN MUNICH STEP UP'** (page 258).

1940

Bayern Munich bravely refused to play politics and disown their Jewish president in 1940.

FOOTBALL REVIVED FOR MORALE

Loved ones were being lost, morale was flagging and even Christmas was unable to provide some much needed cheer. Maybe football could help? Brighton and Hove Albion travelled to Norwich on Christmas Day, but with depleted resources they only took five players. It became common practice to recruit more along the way and with the help of Norwich reserves and some soldiers in the 1,419 crowd a match took place. Perhaps the soldiers asked to turn out had been at the Christmas booze, because Norwich ran out emphatic 18-0 winners.

SEE ALSO **'PEACE – AND FOOTBALL – BREAKS OUT IN NO-MANS LAND'** (page 79).

Even football had a role to play in the war effort by providing some much needed cheer on the home front during the Christmas of 1940.

Manchester United's stadium was a target for German bombers raiding the city. Their great rivals Manchester City came to the rescue.

OLD TRAFFORD BOMBED

Given its proximity to the Trafford Park Industrial Estate, Manchester United's stadium was always going to be at risk from eager German bombers on their regular raids. The ground had suffered a hit in 1940 but it was on 11 March 1941 that it was extensively damaged. Two bombs made their mark, one destroying the Main Stand, the other partially destroying the United Road terrace and scorching the pitch. Underlining the neighbourly spirit of the Blitz, Manchester City offered to share Maine Road with United. In 1945 the War Damage Commission awarded the club £4800 to clear away the debris and a further £17, 748 to build the new stands.

SEE ALSO **'FIRST POST-WAR FA CUP FINAL'** (page 154).

Winston Churchill was not a football fan but he recognized the popularity of the game among the British people.

CHURCHILL SUPPORTS FOOTBALL

1941

While Winston Churchill's war cabinet deliberated on how best to repel Adolf Hitler, they also were well aware that the population needed a boost and what better way than through the sport that had become so popular in the years prior to the hostilities? Exhibition games were seen as the perfect means to pump up morale, but seen as ideal ways of funding the war effort and suddenly the Establishment, previously so quick to turn it's nose up at the game of the masses, was taking an interest.

In April 1940 England had played Wales at Wembley and dignitaries such as Princess Alice and Princess Helene Victoria were present to give the punters an extra lift. This didn't go unnoticed by the Arsenal and England captain Eddie Hapgood, who noted, "The Royal Box was always crowded when we played a charity international at Wembley." That fact was underlined on 4 October 1941 when Scotland visited the Imperial Stadium and the Prime Minister, not football's biggest fan, came along with seven of his cabinet to see the English win 2-0.

SEE ALSO **'THE 'KHAKI CUP FINAL'** (page 81).

Fluminense took advantage of the small scale and peculiar geography of the Gavea Stadium. Now Fla-Flu matches take place at the Maracana.

THE FLA-FLU DE LAGOA

In November 1941 eternal rivals Flamengo and Fluminese met in the Carioca decider at Flamengo's Gavea Stadium. Fluminense only needed a draw and were 2-1 ahead when Flamengo grabbed a late equalizer. For the remaining six minutes Fluminense players, one after another, deliberately hoofed the ball out the stadium and into the lagoon next to the Gavea. As the clock ran down, the timekeeper on the touchline was bombarded by both team's irate officials. Fluminense wasted more time when Carreiro was sent off for diving and refused to leave the pitch. They survived to take the championship but the match was forever christened the Fla-Flu de Lagoa.

SEE ALSO **'CHILE'S WORLD CUP 'PLOT' FAILS'** (page 432).

REBELO JUNIOR: 'GOOOOAAAAALLL!'

It was 1942 that Junior first used his trademark "Goooaaaalll!" It was a broadcasting technique that earned Junior the nickname 'The Man of Unconfoundable Goal.' Junior had started out as a horse racing commentator but soon turned his elongated vowels to his nation's favourite pastime. It is a technique that quickly took off and to this day is synonymous with Brazilian football and their commentators One broadcaster Raul Longas would scream Goaaalll for even longer than Junior. Longas though was very shortsighted and needed to bide some time so his colleague could write down the scorers name on a piece of paper.

SEE ALSO **'NORWEGIAN COMMENTATOR'S RANT AGAINST ENGLAND'** (page 378); **'FOOTBALL BECOMES GIRL TALK'** (page 612).

With incident-packed matches, dramatic South American football gave commentators like Rebelo Junior plenty to shout about in the 1940's.

Between 1935 and 1939 Schalke didn't lose a single match. Fritz Szepan and Ernst Kuzorra were two of their Polish immigrant stars.

SCHALKE ARE NAZI FAVOURITES

Schalke 04 had come from obscurity to be hailed as the great team of 1930s Germany and their biggest fans, of course were the Nazi party, who cited the club as a typical example of great German strength. Schalke had taken their first title in 1934 and won their fourth crown in five years in 1939, just months before the onset of war. Naturally the Nazi propaganda machine just had to highlight the team's achievements, although it failed to point out that many of the club's best players were, in fact, Polish immigrants.

SEE ALSO **'DYNAMO DRESDEN RELOCATE'** (page 198).

STAN MORTENSEN PLAYS FOR BOTH ENGLAND AND WALES

Stan Mortensen had signed for Blackpool in 1938 and hoped a career playing the game he loved was about to kick off. However, war curtailed those ambitions and instead Mortensen found himself in the RAF as a wireless operator. War-time appearances did follow and the impressive centre-forward even tasted international football, albeit for the opposition. England played Wales in Cardiff in September 1943 and when the hosts lost Ivor Powell to injury they had no reserves and so called on the young Englishman. Mortensen was just pleased to be on the pitch, as earlier in the war he had been the sole survivor when his Wellington bomber crashed

SEE ALSO **'PROSINECKI SCORES FOR TWO NATIONS'** (page 512).

Mortensen in full flight for Blackpool. The disruption to his career by the War meant he represented both England and Wales.

Real Madrid president Santiago Bernabeu went on to celebrate 25 years in charge of the Spanish giants. Their stadium bears his name.

BERNABEU ELECTED REAL MADRID PRESIDENT

Atletico Madrid may have been the dominant force, but young Santiago Bernabeu only had eyes for Real. He never missed a game as a fan, joined the youth ranks at 14, was the club's centre-forward at 17 and later captained the side, before retiring in 1927. Before the Civil War he had spells as club secretary, coach and manager, and it was Bernabeu who worked tirelessly to rejuvenate post-war Real Madrid. In 1943, after crowd trouble between Real Madrid and Barcelona forced both clubs' presidents to stand down, it was Bernabeu, a director, who was elected president. He held the position until he died in 1978.

SEE ALSO **'REAL MADRID'S BERNABEU STADIUM OPENS'** (page 160).

FANS TURN ON HERO MAZZOLA

Valentino Mazzola had been plucked by Venezia from the Italian Navy during the war and had steered them to an unprecedented Coppa Italia triumph in 1941. With Mazzola controlling games with his high energy and fine touch, Venezia came second in Serie A the following season and suddenly the Milanese wing-half was the hottest property around. Juventus secured a 'gentleman's agreement' with Venezia, but at the last minute it was Torino, Italy's top club, who offered 200,000 lira and the player was theirs. The season was still alive and Venezia fans got wind of the move, chanting 'sell-out' to their departing player.

SEE ALSO **'BAGGIO'S PENALTY PRINCIPLES'** (page 454).

Mazzola, who's move to Torino turned him from fans' hero to villain at his old club Venezia, stands on the far right of the back row.

Malmo went on to become the only Swedish side to reach the final of the European Cup. They were beaten in 1979 by Nottingham Forest.

MALMO WIN THEIR FIRST SWEDISH TITLE

Ever since the Napoleonic Wars, when it came to European hostilities Sweden had enjoyed peaceful neutrality. Its geographical location meant that life could carry on pretty much untouched by the war and so football continued to be played. Since its foundation in 1910 Malmo FF had seen very little success, but in the late 1930s, under the shrewd chairmanship of former manager Eric Persson, the club grew in stature and was able to challenge the big clubs in Gothenburg and Stockholm. The 1943-44 season saw that potential wonderfully realised as the club, nicknamed 'Iff-iff' by its fans, took the first of its 15 titles.

SEE ALSO **'SWEDEN WIN OLYMPIC GOLD'** (page 164).

FRITZ WALTER AVOIDS FORCED MARCH

Fritz Walter, a creative and intelligent inside-forward, had made his international debut for Germany in 1940, scoring two against Romania. More caps and more goals followed, but two years later he found himself in the armed forces and, at the end of the war, in a Hungarian prisoner-of-war camp. Russian troops arrived from the east to march thousands back to the Russian gulags, where life expectancy was under five years, and it was here that Walter's talent saved his life. A Hungarian prison guard who had seen Walter play for Germany and recognised him told the Russians he was, in fact, Austrian and so he avoided the gulags.

SEE ALSO **'TOR... TOR... TOR!'** (page 195).

Fritz Walter went on to captain West Germany in the famous 1954 World Cup final in Berne.

Dynamo Moscow coach Mikhail Yakushin leads his team out at Stamford Bridge to face Chelsea during their successful tour of Britain.

DYNAMO MOSCOW HEAD WEST

When Dynamo Moscow became the first Russian team to visit the west in 1945, it was supposed to be a good-will trip. Instead, as George Orwell wrote, "If such a visit as this had any effect at all on Anglo-Soviet relations, it could only be to make them worse than before." This may have been true, but the British public couldn't get enough. The opening game against Chelsea at Stamford Bridge saw 85,000 people cram in to catch a glimpse of a team that shocked everyone with their fluent and tireless football. The Russians drew 3-3, beat Cardiff 10-1, vanquished Arsenal 4-3 and drew 2-2 at Rangers.

SEE ALSO **'SOVIET UNION WIN FIRST EUROPEAN CHAMPIONSHIP'** (page 234).

RED STAR BELGRADE FORMED

In March 1945 a group of students at Belgrade University decided to form a football club and in honour of the new socialist government called themselves Red Star Belgrade. Just months later an army team, Partizan Belgrade, were formed and a rivalry that flourishes today soon begun. Partizan won the double in their first season in 1947, while Red Star would have to wait until 1951 for their first league title. Red Star, though, are the only Yugoslav team to have won the European Cup, a feat they achieved in 1991.

SEE ALSO **'YUGOSLAVIA REFUSED ENTRY TO THE EUROPEAN CHAMPIONSHIPS'** (page 459).

Red Star Belgrade play in red and white vertical stripped shirts and are the only Yugoslav team to have triumphed in the European Cup.

There is always tension when these two football giants meet. This game of terrible tackles caused a ten-year suspension of the fixture.

BRAZIL, ARGENTINA AND BROKEN BONES

In 1945 Brazil beat Argentina 6-2, but the game left a bad taste in the mouth as Argentina's Batagliero had his leg broken in a tackle with Ademir Menezez. A year later, on 10 February, the two met to decide the winners of the South American championship in Buenos Aries and, once more, the physical and hostile nature of the fixture clouded proceedings. Argentina took an early two-goal lead, but on 26 minutes their captain Jose Salomon had his fibula and tibia shattered in a tackle with Jair. Mayhem ensued, the teams had to be taken off and they refused to play each other again for a full ten years.

SEE ALSO **'VIOLENCE DOGS INTERCONTINENTAL CUP'** (page 283).

THE BURNDEN PARK DISASTER

FA Cup ties that season were fought over two legs and Bolton had won 2-0 at Stoke, so on 9 March Bolton fans came in their thousands to Burnden Park to see their team stroll into the semi-finals. With kick-off fast approaching there were 20,000 still outside the ground and when many of them found a way in, crash barriers behind the goal collapsed. As a result there was a calamitous crush of bodies. The game started, but when it became clear that there were fatalities the players left the field. In all, 33 fans died that day and a further 500 were injured.

SEE ALSO **'STAMPEDE LEADS TO AFRICA'S WORST FOOTBALL DISASTER'** (page 546).

Tragic scenes on the pitch at Burnden Park. 33 fans were killed in a crush caused by overcrowding as fans tried to make their way into the ground.

FIRST POST-WAR FA CUP FINAL

The end of the war had caused much celebration, but hostilities had taken a huge toll on the country and life for many was bleak. What better tonic, then, than an FA Cup final at Wembley? The game itself was a good one. The deadlock wasn't broken until the 80th minute when Charlton's Bert Turner scored an own-goal, but it was Turner himself who equalized, taking the game into extra-time. Derby were always stronger and Jack Stamps, told he would never play again after getting injured at Dunkirk, set up Peter Doherty before scoring two himself to ensure a 4-1 win for the Rams.

SEE ALSO **'PORTSMOUTH WIN WITH EX-SERVICEMEN'** (page 169).

Derby County captain Jack Nicholas hands the FA Cup to goalkeeper Vic Woodley as they celebrate their victory on the lap of honour.

WILF MANNION SUFFERS MALARIA

Wilf Mannion was born in Middlesbrough, a shy boy with an exceptional talent for the game of football. He signed for Boro in 1936 and broke into the team in 1937, but the war meant he missed out on six vital years of league football. Mannion, who would later be described affectionately by Tommy Lawton as "a little ballerina in boots", served his country in France, Africa, Italy and the Middle East. It was in the latter that he experienced severe bouts of jaundice and caught malaria, only to be nursed back to health by a young Bertie Mee, who would later manage Arsenal.

SEE ALSO **'FRITZ WLATER AVOIDS FORCED MARCH'** (page 151); **'PELE DONS UNIFORM'** (page 228).

The War robbed Mannion and so many other great players of the years when they should have been playing at their peak.

ENGLAND GEAR UP FOR INTERNATIONAL COMPETITION

Organized, competitive football returned to Britain and, with the end of the boycott of FIFA by the Football Association (FA), England, along with the other home nations, would be eligible for the next World Cup in Brazil and could at last prove to the world that they were indeed the best on the planet. England's first game back came in September at Windsor Park, where Northern Ireland were beaten 7-2 thanks largely to a hat-trick from Wilf Mannion, plus efforts from Raich Carter, Tom Finney and Tommy Lawton. Those foreign teams had every right to be concerned.

SEE ALSO **'WEST GERMANY READMITTED TO FIFA'** (page 176).

Huge crowds queuing outside Stamford Bridge to witness the long-awaited first match of the first Football League season for seven years.

ENGLAND RECRUIT WINTERBOTTOM

Walter Winterbottom had gone relatively unnoticed during his 27 appearances for pre-war Manchester United before he retired in 1938 due to a spinal injury. His work as a lecturer at Carnegie Physical Education College hadn't gone unnoticed by the Football Association (FA) though, and they invited him to come and work at their summer camp. The Oldham-born coach impressed so much in September 1946 he was asked – aged just 33 –to become the FA's director of coaching. He looked after the senior team with distinction and was given the added responsibility of being first team manager in May 1947.

SEE ALSO **'ENGLAND GO FOR ERIKSSON'** (page 543).

Winterbottom had trained as a teacher before becoming the first FA appointed England coach. The FA were impressed by his coaching ideas.

LEN SHACKLETON MAKES HIS NEWCASTLE DEBUT

He had just become the record Second Division signing. At St James' Park on 3 October 52,000 expectant Geordies strained to catch a glimpse of their new £13,000 striker, so you couldn't blame Len Shackleton, signed from Bradford Park Avenue after an impressive stint of wartime football that had seen him amass 166 goals, for being nervous about his Newcastle debut. "What if I muff chances and things go wrong?" wondered Shackleton. However, the new boy got his first goal after just seven minutes and went on to score five more in an incredible 13-0 win over Newport County. The last of his goals bounced in off his backside. It was his day.

Despite his stunning Newcastle debut Shackleton famously left the Magpies after less than 2 years to join deadly rivals Sunderland.

SEE ALSO 'JACKIE MILBURN SCORES IN FINAL' (page 199).

THE LAUNCH OF SUBBUTEO

In 1947 Subbuteo (Latin for an English bird of prey called the hobby) Table Football was launched by Peter Adolph from Tunbridge Wells in Kent. With materials still at a post-war premium, the format was basic. You cut out the cardboard players, the goals were made from wire and there was no pitch. Instead you were given chalk to mark out the lines on an old blanket. It was sold at that year's Schoolboys' Own Exhibition and was an immediate hit – not just among kids. The night before the following year's FA Cup final, Matt Busby had his United players playing the game in their hotel.

SEE ALSO **'REF GETS IT IN THE NECK FROM THE ITALIANS'** (page 574).

The table football game found favour with fans as well as players and managers. Here, Chelsea manager Tommy Docherty gives a tactics talk to his squad using a Subbuteo set in 1963.

1947

BURST BALL LIVENS UP FINAL

On 26 April the 99,000 fans packed into Wembley must have wished they'd stayed indoors as this FA Cup final tottered towards the awful prospect of a replay. In 90 minutes the only real moment of excitement was when the ball burst for the second year running. Charlton were also making a second successive appearance in the final and it was they who put aside the previous year's disappointment with a late winner against Burnley, thanks to Chris Duffy with good work from Bill Robinson. Duffy was ecstatic and took off, arms aloft, with his team-mates hot in pursuit. The fans were just as pleased. The misery was over.

SEE ALSO **'WHITE BALL INTRODUCED'** (page 179); **'MEXICO AND BULGARIA ALL FALL DOWN'** (page 477).

Burnley goalkeeper Jimmy Strong leaps to intercept a high cross in a rare moment of excitement during the tedious 1947 Cup final.

MANNION'S HAT-TRICK HELPS GREAT BRITAIN BEAT EUROPE

It was billed as 'The match of the century' and attracted 135,000 fans to Hampden Park to celebrate the home nations' post-war return to FIFA, although the hyperbole was understandable as, after several years without international football, British teams could now pit their wits against the best on the continent. Britain ran out 6-1 winners on 10 May, which was hardly surprising considering Europe's players had never played together, and Wilf Mannion was the hero with a hat-trick, while Tommy Lawton got two and Morton's Billy Steel pleased the Scottish fans with a cracker from 35 yards.

SEE ALSO **'GAME OF THE CENTURY'** (page 303).

Rest of Europe captain Johnny Carey shakes hands with referee George Reader, watched by Great Britain captain George Hardwick.

FINNEY RUNS PORTUGAL RAGGED

The big question for post-war English football was how to accommodate both Tom Finney and Stanley Matthews. The latter was regarded as the more skilful, but many saw all-rounder Finney as the better player. At the end of the 1946-47 season England played two internationals. They lost to Switzerland and so, on 25 May travelled to Lisbon, keen to finish the season well. Finney had missed the Swiss game, but due to injury was asked to play on the left-wing against Portugal – where he was immense. He had never played there, but he ran Portugal's right-back and skipper Cadoza ragged and England were 10-0 winners.

SEE ALSO **'GARRINCHA SHOWS HIS CLASS... '** (page 244).

Tom Finney practices before a match for Preston North End. He turned out to be the answer to England's prayers on the left-wing.

MATTHEWS EARNS OVATION

No doubt roused by Tom Finney's remarkable performance in May against Portugal, Stanley Matthews responded with his own master-class in the art of wing play to help England overcome Belgium 5-2 in Brussels on 21 September. The friendly Finney-Matthews rivalry certainly aided England as Blackpool's new wing wizard (he'd signed for the club for £11,500 at the end of the previous season) made every goal, two of which were scored by Finney. "The misery on the Belgian right-back's face became more and more noticeable," remarked England debutant Billy Wright. On the whistle 70,000 Belgians rose to their feet to salute the wonderful Stanley Matthews.

SEE ALSO **'OLD TRAFFORD RISES TO ACKNOWLEDGE A MASTER'** (page 569).

With Finney excelling on the left, Stanley Matthews also starred for England. Against Belgium he created all 5 of England's goals.

Notts County's £20,000 record signing Tommy Lawton climbs high above the challenge of Millwall's Walter McMillen at Meadow Lane.

FIRST £20,000 TRANSFER

He had scored 30 goals in 42 games for Chelsea, he was England's main goal-getter and at 28 he was still in his prime. Tommy Lawton, however, was about to drop two divisions. The fine centre-forward, always a crowd favourite, had failed to settle in London and had fallen out with Blues manager Billy Birrell. Incredibly it was ambitious Notts County of the Third Division who stumped up a record £20,000 (plus wing-half Bill Dickson) to bring Lawton to Nottingham. County were managed by former Chelsea physio Arthur Stollery and despite the possible damage the move would could do to his international career, Lawton became a Meadow Lane hero.

SEE ALSO 'ENGLAND'S FIRST £1 MILLION PLAYER' (page 366); 'MARADONA SIGNS FOR BARCELONA IN RECORD DEAL' (page 378).

REAL MADRID'S BERNABEU STADIUM OPENS

Santiago Bernabeu was keen to develop Real Madrid and, looking around their Estadio de Chamartin, he concluded that they needed a bigger venue. As a boy, Bernabeu had helped paint the seats and lay the pitch at the club's first ground on O'Donnell Street in Madrid. Now he would give them a stadium that would become one of the most famous arenas in the world. It opened on 14 December 1947 with a friendly against Portuguese club OS Belenenses and the same name as the previous venue, but in recognition of his contribution to the club in 1955 it was renamed the Bernabeu.

SEE ALSO 'EULOGIO MARTINEZ RAMIRO SCORES THE NOU CAMP'S FIRST GOAL' (page 210).

The Bernabeu is one of only 4 stadiums to have held the European Cup final, the European Championship final and the World Cup final.

STANLEY MATTHEWS – FOOTBALLER OF THE YEAR

In September 1947 four journalists, including the ex-England international turned writer Charlie Buchan, were travelling by ferry back to England, having seen the national team dissect Belgium 5-2. They agreed that it was about time that the growing band of football writers should form their own association, a body that would argue the case for better press facilities at grounds and maintain communication with the world's governing bodies. They also decided to award an annual trophy to the player they felt embodied, in one season, what they held to be the true virtues of the game – skill, honesty and sportsmanship.

Their first winner was the man who had played so well on that trip to Belgium and Stanley Matthews picked up his trophy at the Hungaria restaurant the night before his first Cup final. The bronze statuette has been a prized award among players ever since.

Matthews, along with his Blackpool team-mate Stan Mortensen, who had come second in the vote, did wonder about the wisdom of staying out so late before the game, but they stuck to the orange juice and both managed to play their part in the following day's final against Manchester United – a game that is still regarded as one of the best in the trophy's illustrious history.

Matt Busby had shaped Manchester United's first great side and, having played top-flight sides in every round, they deserved their victory on 23 April. Blackpool, however, put up a great fight, leading twice before ultimately being denied by four goals to two. Matthews and Mortensen would have to wait for their day in the sun.

SEE ALSO **'MATTHEWS EARNS OVATION'** (page 159); **'LEV YASHIN WINS FOOTBALLER OF THE YEAR'** (page 247).

Matthews played in the English top flight until he was 50 years old and remains the only footballer to have been knighted whilst still playing the game.

In a later friendly played in November 1949, England captain Billy Wright shakes hands with the Italy captain Riccardo Carapellese.

ENGLAND WIN 4-0 IN TURIN

England had enjoyed many great moments. Fans had rejoiced at seeing the Scots put to the sword, but the game was changing and the world was catching up. On 16 May 1948 Italy, still the World Champions after their 1938 triumph, hosted a friendly against England in Turin, hoping to prove this point, but England were magnificent, perhaps even their very best, winning 4-0 on a humid afternoon. Their opening goal summed up their dominance with Stan Mortensen taking a perfect pass from Matthews, striding into the box and unleashing a fire-cracker of a shot which went in at the near post. The World Champions were humbled.

SEE ALSO **'GERMANY 1 ENGLAND 5'** (page 551).

Nereo Rocco helped his home-town club to their highest ever finish in Serie A – a feat which brought him to the attention of Italy's top teams.

ROCCO INVENTS THE 'CATENACCIO'

Nereo Rocco had enjoyed a modest playing career, winning only one cap for Italy, but as a coach he would change the way the game was played in his native country. Born and bred in Trieste, Rocco played for his local club before taking over as coach in 1947. Despite playing as an offensive winger, Rocco preferred stifling tactics that involved three banks of three, while also deploying a sweeper who would nullify attacks and set up breaks, often with long balls. The system would come to be called 'catenaccio' or 'door-bolt' and in 1947-48 it helped Triestina to a runners-up spot in Serie A – their best ever finish.

SEE ALSO **'BELA GUTTMAN AND HIS 4-2-4'** (page 217); **'PARMA RISE TO THE TOP'** (page 437).

International youth tournaments remain a showcase for talents of the future. Those that shine on the international stage attract attention.

INTERNATIONAL YOUTH FOOTBALL LAUNCHED

The Football Association (FA) was at the forefront of a drive to encourage football at youth level, introducing the FA County Youth Cup and producing publications such as the annual FA Book for Boys. So London was the obvious place to host the first FIFA junior tournament, consisting of under-18 teams from England, Wales, Belgium, Northern Ireland, the Netherlands, Ireland, Italy and Austria. England were crowned winners after beating the Dutch 3-2 in the final at White Hart Lane. Seven years later UEFA took over the running of the competition, which is now for under-19s and known as the UEFA European Under-19 Championship.

SEE ALSO **'MARADONA INSPIRES ARGENTINA'** (page 368).

Italy's failure to follow up their recent World Cup wins with an Olympic medal signalled the end of Pozzo's long tenure as national manager.

POZZO STEPS DOWN

Under the watchful eye of Vittorio Pozzo Italian football had grown, blossomed and become the best in the world – twice. Pozzo had first taken charge of the Azzurri for the 1912 Olympics and, in between two famous back-to-back World Cup triumphs, he won gold with them in 1936, so it was fitting that he chose the 1948 Olympics to retire, convinced by the 4-0 defeat to England prior to a 5-3 defeat to Denmark in the second round of the tournament. However, Italians disagreed with his decision and chants of "Pozzo, Pozzo" regularly went up as the national team suffered after his departure.

SEE ALSO **'ALF RAMSEY SACKED'** (page 332).

SWEDEN WIN OLYMPIC GOLD

While local eyes were on the hosts, the discerning football fan couldn't help but notice Sweden's impressive trail through the opening rounds of the Olympic football tournament and by the time they had dispatched Korea with 12 goals in the quarter-finals they were many people's favourites. Sweden's great striking trio of Gunnar Gren, Gunnar Nordahl and Nils Liedholm (nicknamed 'Gre-No-Li') were unplayable at times and a 4-2 semi-final win over the impressive Danes set up a final with Great Britain's victors Yugoslavia. On 13 August there were 60,000 fans at Wembley to see the Swedes outmanoeuvre the Yugoslavs 3-1, thanks to two goals from Gren.

SEE ALSO **'GRE-NO-LI HELP MILAN TO SCUDETTO'** (page 177); **'SWEDEN WIN WOMEN'S EUROPEAN CHAMPIONSHIPS'** (page 378).

Gunnar Gren scores the third goal from the penalty spot, making the final score 3-1 and securing the Olympic gold medal for Sweden.

YEOVIL SLAY THE GIANTS OF SUNDERLAND IN THE FA CUP

Beating Second Division Bury wasn't enough for Southern League Yeovil. The players wanted a bigger scalp and they got it in the next round. On 29 January Yeovil took an early lead, but Sunderland equalized and then, with the fog descending, the hosts went ahead again through Eric Bryant. The second-half was tense and 17,000 fans chewed their nails as the First Division team tried to batter their way through, but to no avail. The whistle went and the party could begin. The next round saw them face Manchester United at Maine Road (Old Trafford was still being rebuilt) where a Cup tie record attendance of 81,000 saw them lose 8-0.

SEE ALSO **'HEREFORD AND RADFORD BOOT NEWCASTLE OUT'** (page 317); **'THE CRAZY GANG STUN LIVERPOOL'** (page 317).

Yeovil Town's non-league players are mobbed by fans after they knocked mighty Sunderland out of the FA Cup in the fourth round.

THE SUPERGA DISASTER

Surprisingly, an official championship in Italy continued throughout World War Two and it was Torino who dominated. After the war they took the 1946-47 title by a luscious ten points from Juventus and were even more rampant the next season, winning Serie A by 16 points from AC Milan. Their team was littered with stars, including a fine forward line of Ezio Liok, Valentino Mazzola and Guglielmo Gabetto, players whom fans all over the country learnt to cherish. That's why, when the plane carrying them back from a friendly in Lisbon crashed into Turin's Superga hills on 4 May 1949, killing everyone on board, a nation mourned as one.

SEE ALSO **'THE MUNICH AIR CRASH'** (page 212-3); **'THE ZAMBIA AIR CRASH'** (page 467).

The aftermath of the aircrash on the mountain of Superga, near the outskirts of Turin, which killed several members of Torino football club.

EL DORADO FOR ENGLISH REFEREES IN COLOMBIA

Between 1949-54 the Colombian League was the strongest in Latin America. Though the country was in the midst of La Violencia, an especially bloody period in the long-running civil war, the domestic league flourished. Yet it was dogged by corruption and ill discipline among players. English officials, seen as firm, fair and above bribery, were actively recruited by Colombia's football authorities to tackle the problem. Arguably the most famous of these refereeing exports was Cyril Jack Barrick who retired from the English game after officiating in the 1948 FA Cup final. During an 8½ month spell in South America, Barrick took charge of 91 games, including 12 of the 29 games in the 1949 Copa America.

SEE ALSO **'REBEL COLOMBIAN LEAGUE PROVES ATTRACTIVE'** (page 169).

Colombian football authorities knew the success of their League was in danger of being undermined by corruption so they imported referees.

PUSKAS –THE 'GALLOPING MAJOR'

Kispest AC were far from Hungary's top post-war club, but they had some fine young talent and so when the new Communist government nationalized football clubs in 1949, the Hungarian national team coach Guzstav Sebes brought them under the rule of the Hungarian army. Sebes had observed the success in the 1930s and wanted to emulate the fact that most of the players had been drawn from just one or two clubs. Kispest then were re-named Budapest Honved (meaning 'Defender of the Homeland') and with youngsters such as Jozsef Bozsik and Ferenc Puskas to mould, the team became the focal point of the Hungarian game.

SEE ALSO **'PUSKAS TEACHES ENGLAND A LESSON'** (page 186); **'PUSKAS JOINS REAL MADRID'** (page 226).

In 349 appearances for Kispest AC/Budapest Honved, Puskas scored 357 goals and was Europe's top scorer in 1947.

Spain was one of the four nations who saw a Latin Cup as a means of increasing their competitiveness and generating extra revenue.

THE LATIN CUP KICKS OFF

Money was tight for many post-war European clubs, but the desire to pit their wits against one another was strong. The innovative French, Spanish, Italian and Portuguese football federations decided to start the Latin Cup, a tournament to be played in one nation at the end of every season (thus saving on travelling costs). The inaugural tournament was held in Spain and it was Barcelona who prevailed, beating Sporting Lisbon in Real Madrid's new Estadio Chamartin 2-1, thanks to goals from Estanisalo Basora and Seguer. Torino, so tragically depleted by the recent Superga air-crash, came a commendable third.

SEE ALSO **'EUROPEAN CUP LAUNCHED'** (page 201).

ENGLAND DEFEATED AT HOME BY THE REPUBLIC OF IRELAND

As ever, England were red-hot favourites to win a football match on home soil, but for the first time they came unstuck at the hands of non-British opponents. Captained by Manchester United's brilliant Johnny Carey, the Republic of Ireland set about England from the off. The hosts may have taken the 21 September game at Goodison Park lightly – the selectors had awarded three new caps – but England still featured Tom Finney and Billy Wright, although neither could quash the eager Irish. A goal in each half from Con Martin and Peter Farrell gave them a famous win, but their hero was part-time carpenter and Shamrock Rovers goalkeeper Tommy Godwin.

SEE ALSO **'NORTHERN IRELAND KNOCK OUT ITALY'** (page 211).

Johnny Carey of Manchester United was the captain of the Republic of Ireland team that inflicted England's first home defeat at Goodison Park.

Neil Franklin at Stoke City. Despite the financial rewards Franklin couldn't settle in Colombia and returned home after just 4 weeks.

REBEL COLOMBIAN LEAGUE PROVES ATTRACTIVE

For too long the suits at the Football League had regarded players, many of whom were going for transfer fees of £20,000, as mere commodities. Neil Franklin, England's brilliant centre-half, was upset with the £20 maximum wage he earned at Stoke, so when an offer from Colombia came in on the eve of the World Cup he told England's selectors to ignore him as he was off to Independiente Santa Fe of Bogota, where he would earn £5,000 a year plus bonuses and luxury accommodation. He wasn't alone. The Colombian net snared other Englishmen as well as a plethora of Argentinian players, including the great Alfredo di Stefano.

SEE ALSO **'ALFREDO DI STEFANO JOINS REAL MADRID'** (page 183).

PORTSMOUTH WIN LEAGUE WITH EX-SERVICEMEN

For the second successive season, the Pompey chimes rang out for the League champions. Fashionable? No. Full of stars? No. But Portsmouth, managed by Bob Jackson, proved once more that honest team-work can prevail. Not that they didn't have real talent. Reg Flewin was a fine captain and centre-half, while young winger Peter Harris had won England caps. On the last day of the 1949-50 season there was all to play for. Pompey led the table on goal average from Wolves, while Sunderland were just a point behind. Portsmouth sealed their title with a 5-1 win over Aston Villa, ensuring the Championship trophy stayed on the south-coast.

SEE ALSO **'HUNGARIAN PLAYERS DISPERSE AFTER UPRISING'** (page 206).

Winger Peter Harris spent 14 years at Fratton Park and is still Portsmouth's record scorer having netted 208 times between 1946-60.

SCOTLAND'S STUBBORNNESS

Overjoyed to have the British federations as members, FIFA offered a generous two places for the 1950 World Cup, but a stubborn Scottish Football Association declared they would only go if they won the Home Nations competition. Scotland only needed to draw with England at Hampden Park on 15 April to take that crown, but a Roy Bentley goal won the match and the championship for England. The offer of a place in Brazil still stood, but Scotland's hierarchy were adamant. The players wanted to travel, the skipper George Young was asked by his England counterpart Billy Wright to plead with his 'superiors', but it was no use.

SEE ALSO **'AUSTRIA SHOW SCOTLAND WHAT THEY HAVE BEEN MISSING'** (page 178).

The Scottish team in 1950 who missed out on the chance to travel to Brazil and take part in a World Cup over a point of principle.

Denis Compton was the original Brylcreem boy. David Beckham also advertised the product – until he famously shaved his head.

COMPTON BECOMES 'BRYLCREEM BOY'

Denis Compton was a man for all seasons. Worshipped in the winter for his ability with a football at Arsenal, he was even more idolised in the summer months for his cricketing prowess with Kent and England. In those innocent days marketing men hadn't quite got their claws into national sport, but Denis Compton changed that. He helped Arsenal win the Cup in 1950 and, the first sportsman to have his own manager, capitalised on his fame by signing up to represent hair product Brylcreem. His face adorned posters everywhere and Compton became known as the 'Brylcreem Boy'.

SEE ALSO **'MANCHESTER UNITED ADVERTISE TONIC WINE'** (page 65); **'EL BEATLE IS BORN'** (page 265).

HUNGARY KICK OFF WINNING RUN

A 5-2 win over Poland hardly had the world's press scribbling frantically, but this was a match that was to kick-start a wonderful winning sequence in which Hungary were victorious for 32 matches in a row. It should have finished with World Cup glory (they had taken the Olympic Gold in 1952), but they came unstuck against the Germans in Berne. Due to financial reasons, Hungary missed the 1950 World Cup, but instead they began to mould their great team and on 4 June it was the Poles who were the first to suffer.

SEE ALSO **' PUSKAS TEACHES ENGLAND A LESSON'** (page 186).

Hungary were building a team who would become one the strongest in the world.

England's Johnny Aston, Jack Rowley and Stanley Matthews jogging during training at home before they made the long trip to Brazil.

MATTHEWS BUYS NEW BOOTS IN BRAZIL

Having played an end-of-season exhibition match for Blackpool in North America, Stanley Matthews travelled to his first World Cup by ferry via Trinidad and arrived in Rio for what he hoped would be the pinnacle of his footballing career. England had a few days to kill before their opening game and so visited the new Maracana Stadium to watch the host nation. Matthews was transfixed by Brazil's inside-left, Didi, who gave England players a glimpse of a bent free-kick. Matthews noticed that the Brazilians wore light-weight boots and immediately bought a pair. "I realized," he said, "that with a pair of these I could be even quicker."

SEE ALSO 'STANLEY MATTHEWS CROWNED 'KING OF FOOTBALL'' (page 209).

IV CAMPEONATO MUNDIAL DE FUTEBOL

·TAÇA JULES RIMET·

JUNHO DE 1950
BRASIL

WORLD CUP KICKS OFF IN BRAZIL

As the crowds milled around outside, the builders frantically tried to get the Maracana Stadium – named after the river on whose banks it was built – finished. The attendance at the opening game of the World Cup was just over 81,000 due to that unfinished work, but with seating for 130,000 and a further 50,000 able to stand, the Maracana was a fitting arena for the competition and a stadium the locals felt keenly would soon house the new World Cup winners. On 24 June Brazil opened the tournament and the stadium by taking Mexico apart, winning 4-0, thanks to two goals from Ademir and one apiece from Jair and Baltazar.

SEE ALSO 'BELLINI LIFTS WORLD CUP' (page 224).

The excitement generated by the World Cup was huge and the home fans were certain that a Brazilian victory was practically inevitable.

GAETJENS'S GOAL
SHOCKS ENGLAND

"Football wouldn't be the same without these results, but that doesn't make them any more palatable when you are the victim." That was England manager Walter Winterbottom's philosophical response to what remains arguably the biggest shock in World Cup history. England had won an uninspiring opening game against Chile and on 29 June travelled north of Rio to Belo Horizonte, to play the part-timers of the United States. However, on a dusty, bumpy pitch England's talented forwards simply couldn't convert superior skill and possession into goals and when a Haitian forward named Larry Gaetjens leapt to head past Bert Williams in goal after 37th minutes it was, staggeringly, enough.

SEE ALSO 'LOWLY CAMEROON BEAT MIGHTY ARGENTINA' (page 439).

Joe Gaetjens is carried off by cheering fans after his team beat England 1-0 at Belo Horizonte.

URUGUAY STUN BRAZIL

It is said that in the stunned silence of the Maracana, as Uruguayan players embraced, there was the sound of a single shot as a distraught Brazilian fan, unable to comprehend what he had just witnessed, turned the gun on himself and finished it there and then. Brazil had done the unthinkable. They had thrown away the World Cup and for some that was too much to bear.

In 1950 FIFA had adopted a new system that saw the final stages of the tournament played out as a round-robin and going into the last match on 16 July Brazil needed only to draw with Uruguay to win the Cup, while a victory for their opponents would deliver a second World Cup triumph. A glut of goals in the final pool stages had seen Brazil go into the game as favourites and the first half promised more goals for the carnival crowd in the region of 200,000.

The deadlock was broken in the 47th minute when the outside-right Friaca smashed the ball into the net and started a party on the terraces that looked capable of going on for months. Uruguay, though, had other plans and were soon relishing their role as the ultimate party-poopers. Brazil's instinct was to continue to attack, but after 66 minutes Schiaffino scored an equalizer and with just ten minutes remaining Ghigga finished off a neat move and won Uruguay the World Cup.

In Montevideo three Uruguayans died of heart failure. Back in Rio it was heart-break. So sure had they been of imminent triumph that the Brazilian Football Association had already had commemorative medals made up.

Ghiggia scores Uruguay's second goal against Brazil, to silence the Maracana Stadium

SEE ALSO '**BRAZIL WAITS TWO DECADES FOR REVENGE**' (page 305).

PELÉ MAKES A PROMISE

Brazil had lost the World Cup to Uruguay and his father was in shock. The boy wanted to help, but his mother suggested he leave his father alone. To the boy, it was just as painful. He lived to play the game, lived to have a ball at his feet and dreamt of one day playing for his country. He was only nine, but already he had plans. He ignored his mother's advice and went to his father, who was by now in tears. "Dad," he said, "one day I will win you the World Cup." His father smiled. That boy would one day go by the name of Pelé.

SEE ALSO '**FUTURE STAR MAKES DEBUT AGED 15**' (page 207).

Uruguay's defeat of home favourites Brazil sent an entire nation into mourning and inspired a young Pelé to win the trophy for his country.

THE ENGLISH FOOTBALL LEAGUE EXPANDS TO 92 CLUBS

The 1948-49 season had seen a record number of fans attend games. In fact, 41,272,424 punters is a record that still stands and will probably never be beaten, and it convinced the Football League that it was time to expand the game and increase the number of clubs playing professional football in England. The third tier of English football was divided into north and south sections, and each was increased to 24 clubs as Football League membership expanded from 72 to 92. From Shrewsbury to Gillingham, the new clubs were now part of a boom in the popularity of English football.

SEE ALSO 'PREMIER LEAGUE LAUNCHED' (page 462).

With attendances going up as more and more people became interested in the game, the Football League saw an opportunity for expansion.

WEST GERMANY READMITTED TO FIFA

It was going to be a long, hard struggle for post-war Germany to get back on its feet after six catastrophic years of war. The country had been divided among its victors, but five years after hostilities ended West Germany were once again allowed back into football's global community – a community they would go on to thrive in. West Germany were managed by Sepp Herberger, their pre-war coach, who would lead them to a famous World Cup triumph just four years later. Such lofty ambitions were a world away in Stuttgart, though, as the new side took to the field on 22 November 1950 and beat Switzerland by a solitary goal.

SEE ALSO 'WEST GERMANY LOSE TO EAST GERMANY' (page 337).

Five years after the end of hostilities FIFA's move to admit West Germany allowed one of football's powerhouses back into the fray.

Tottenham Hotspur manager Arthur Rowe was the architect of Spur's exciting new tactic – however much he derided the name it was given.

'PUSH AND RUN'

On 28 April, while Newcastle were winning the FA Cup, a fixture quirk meant that just a few miles from Wembley, Tottenham were playing to win the title, a feat they duly managed with a 1-0 win over Sheffield Wednesday. It was a nervy performance, but the hard work had already been done. Spurs played a fresh brand of football, nicknamed 'push and run', much to manager Arthur Rowe's annoyance, as he simply told his men to, "Make it simple and make it quick". However you wish to label it, Spurs' brand of quick, one-touch football delighted fans and they were worthy champions of the English game.

SEE ALSO **'RINUS BRINGS 'TOTAL FOOTBALL' TO AJAX'** (page 255).

Having won gold in the 1948 Olympics Milan's trio of Swedes set about bringing the glory days back to the famous old club.

'GRE-NO-LI' HELP MILAN TO THE SCUDETTO

Milan fans had been starved of success or heroes, but in the early 1950s they got both, thanks to three Swedes. Gunnar Gren, Nils Liedholm and Gunnar Nordahl had all signed for the 'Rossoneri' in 1949, having impressed the world at the previous year's Olympics. They immediately settled in – Nordahl scored 35 goals in his first season – and the 1950-51 campaign saw the team's first Scudetto triumph since 1907. The trio were electrifying, aided manfully by the likes of Cesare Maldini and Lorenzo Buffon, and today the 'Gre-No-Li' strike-force at Milan remains an iconic reminder of a golden era.

SEE ALSO **'CESARE MALDINI LEADS HIS SON PAOLO TO FRANCE'** (page 510).

SEE ALSO 'MOROCCO STUN SCOTLAND' (page 513).

1951

AUSTRIA SHOW SCOTLAND WHAT THEY HAVE BEEN MISSING

Scotland's narrow-minded football association had taken a lot of flak for their decision not to travel to the 1950 World Cup. They were adamant that they had done the right thing, but on a cold 13 December at Hampden Park 68,000 fans witnessed first-hand the error of the governing body's ways. Scotland had never lost to an overseas team on home soil and an Austrian side, not quite up to the standards of the 'Wunderteam' of the 1930s, seemed of little threat. Scotland, though, were toothless and a goal from the Austrian outside-right Ernst Melchior sealed an historic victory.

SEE ALSO **'MOROCCO STUN SCOTLAND'** (page 513).

Scotland's Billy Steel tries to burst between Austria's Ernst Happel and Rudolf Rockl.

FLOODLIGHTS FINALLY ADOPTED

Herbert Chapman had been so impressed by the use of floodlights on the continent that he had had them built at Highbury before the war. The Football Association – as ever unable to see the light – banned their use, stating they would cost too much to operate. Floodlights had been used as far back as 1878, but it wasn't until 1951 that the governing body at last plugged into the idea. Israeli club Hapoel Tel Aviv came to London to play Arsenal in a friendly on 19 September and they played at night under brilliant light. As they watched Tom Whittaker's Arsenal stroll to a 6-1 win, 44,000 fans were illuminated

SEE ALSO 'FIRST FLOODLIT MATCH' (page 23).

It took 73 years, but the prospect of watching football under floodlights was now a reality as the FA followed the continental game's lead.

WHITE BALL INTRODUCED

With the advent of floodlights came a problem. Players and fans alike had argued that they too often lost the flight of the ball under the glare of the new lights, but with night games proving so popular it was the ball that would have to change. By 1951 the football had come a long way. The heavy, laced-up rock had evolved, making it less damaging for those brave headers of the ball, and to combat the poor visibility it was decided to make the ball white. Not only that, but an orange ball would also be used in the winter to combat heavy snow.

SEE ALSO 'WHOSE BALL FOR FINAL?' (page 115); "TELSTAR' TAKES FLIGHT' (page 298).

The white ball was the latest innovation as the football authorities could see that games at night were especially popular with spectators.

FINNEY OFFERED LIRA LIFESTYLE

On 18 May mercurial forward Tom Finney had just played another outstanding game in Italy, helping England to a 1-1 draw in Florence. After the game Italian millionaire Prince Roberto Lanza di Trabia visited the England squad and made a beeline for Finney, asking him to play for Palermo for two seasons. Finney, on £14 a week, was offered £10,000 immediately, £130 a month, bonuses, a car and a villa on the Med. It must have been tempting, but Finney took the offer to his club, Preston rejected it and he got on with playing. The next time the hail came crashing down on Deepdale he must have thought again.

SEE ALSO **'JOHN CHARLES TAKES ITALIAN JOB'** (page 211); **'JIMMY GREAVES RETURNS FROM ITALY'** (page 238).

Finney managed to resist the lure of the Italian lira after he was personally targeted by Palermo. Loyally, he left the decision to his club.

THE LION OF VIENNA

Austria had recently bashed eight past Belgium, seven past Yugoslavia and six past the Republic of Ireland, but on 25 May England weren't intimidated, not with Nat Lofthouse leading the line. England took the lead through Lofthouse, but Austria scored a penalty, only for England to re-gain the advantage through Jackie Sewell. The first half finished all square as Dienst scored and a physical second period looked like going either way before Lofthouse raced clear, collided with the keeper and rolled in the ball. The concussed striker – now the 'Lion of Vienna' – knew little of it, but was carried off on the shoulders of delighted British troops from the 65,000 crowd.

SEE ALSO **'AUSTRIA'S SENSATIONAL COMEBACK'** (page 192).

England's Nat Lofthouse, and Austrian Ernst Happel, anxiously watch as the ball goes for a corner kick during the tight 2-2 draw in Vienna.

East Germany goalkeeper Jurgen Croy tries to punch clear from England's Peter Osgood and Geoff Allen during a youth match in 1965.

GDR TEAM FORMED

At the end of World War Two a defeated Germany was divided into four zones, each one to be administered by one of the victors. In October 1949 the Soviet Union took charge of the eastern zone and the German Democratic Republic was born. It, of course, needed a footballing governing body and so a new 'Deutsche Fussballverband' came into existence. This would set up and officiate over a domestic league, a domestic cup and the national team, who played their first game on 21 September 1952 against the Polish in Warsaw, where, managed by Willi Oelgardt, they lost 3-0.

SEE ALSO **'DECLINE OF THE EAST GERMAN STATE CLUB'** (page 450).

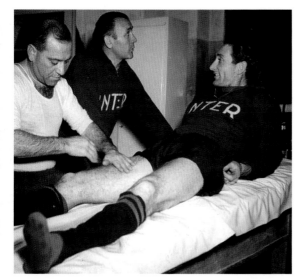

As well as their mean defence Inter also relied on the goals of prolific Dutch centre forward Faas Wilkes, seen here on the treatment table.

INTER'S DEFENCE WINS TITLE

Alfredo Foni was charged with bringing the Serie A crown to Inter Milan for the first time since 1940. He had been a fine centre-half for his country, winning Olympic gold in 1936 and the World Cup two years later, and having arrived as coach he immediately moulded the team into a defensive unit that would stifle their way to glory. Inter had fine forwards in Istvan Nyers and Benito Lorenzi, but they managed only 46 goals, 30 fewer than closest rivals Juventus. Instead it was their defence that held fast, conceding just 24, to bring the title back to Inter.

SEE ALSO **'BARESI BOWS OUT'** (page 506); **'INTER CANTER TO CHAMPIONSHIP'** (page 613).

'THE MATTHEWS FINAL'

Stanley Matthews had reached the FA Cup final twice in recent years and twice he had had to make do with a losers' medal. Time was running out for the 38-year-old Blackpool winger and just a minute into the final on 2 May Bolton took the lead through Nat Lofthouse. Stan Mortensen managed to equalize via a deflection, but the Trotters were the stronger, more capable side. They took a 2-1 lead into the dressing-room thanks to Billy Moir and increased their advantage ten minutes into the second-half through Bell.

That looked to be that, but Matthews had other ideas and slowly the veteran began to get into the game. A deep cross saw Mortensen get his second and Bolton began to wither. Matthews was dazzling, but it was Mortensen, with just three minutes left, who crashed the ball in to equalize. Matthews smelt blood and on receiving the ball once again darted towards the by-line, beat two defenders and centered it for Perry to knock in. Matthews detested it being called his final, but that's exactly what it was – and always will be.

After his stunning performance Stanley Matthews is carried from the Wembley pitch along with team captain Harry Johnson.

SEE ALSO '... AND WINS BRAZIL THE WORLD CUP' (page 245).

DI STEFANO SIGNS FOR REAL MADRID

In September 1953 Alfredo di Stefano arrived in the Spanish capital to sign for Real Madrid. "I went to play for two years, signed for four and stayed all my life," said Di Stefano, who would become known as the club's greatest ever player. The Argentinian had begun his career at River Plate before joining Milonarios in Colombia in 1949. Playing for them in Real Madrid's 50th anniversary tournament in 1952 he impressed Madrid's club president Santiago Bernabeu and, after a long and bitter struggle with Barcelona, Bernabeu got his man.

SEE ALSO **'PUSKAS JOINS REAL MADRID'** (page 226); **'ZIZOU BECOMES A GALACTICO'** (page 549).

Di Stefano's signing, especially given the competition from Barcelona, was a real coup. He scored 216 goals in 282 appearances for Real Madrid.

THE BUSBY BABES ARE BORN

Matt Busby arrived at Old Trafford and quietly went about creating a system that would bring unprecedented success to the club. Busby's scouting system was second to none and soon England schoolboys such as David Pegg and Duncan Edwards were lured to the club. By 1953 the Football Association had decided that an organized Youth Cup was in order and it was Busby's United that won the first five trophies. That first season saw non-league Nantwich beaten 23-0 over two legs, in front of 36,000 fans, Wolves were beaten 9-3 on aggregate in the final.

SEE ALSO **'THE MUNICH AIR CRASH'** (page 212-3); **'THE MUNICH AIR CRASH'** (page 216).

Busby was so thorough that he interviewed prospective landladies to make sure those looking after his new recruits were up to scratch.

NO SUCH THING AS A FRIENDLY

To the hosts it was a famous victory. To England, though, beaten 3-1 by a ram-pant Argentinian side, 14 May 1953 was merely a warm-up. Argentina, they argued, had beaten a Football Association (FA) XI which was far from a full international side, but at the final whistle 120,000 Argentinians, including Juan and Eva Peron, celebrated as if the World Cup had been won. Billy Wright had no doubt about the importance of the game. "We were really angry that the Argentinian press had reported the game as being an official international match, while we regarded it as a practice match."

SEE ALSO 'THE HAND OF GOD' (page 415).

England had played – and beaten – Argentina at Wembley in 1951. The 2-1 defeat strengthened the Argentinian's resolve to chalk up a win.

The Times, never a paper to eulogise much over footballers, gave Arsenal hero Alex James the unusual honour of a full obituary.

ALEX JAMES DIES

Scotsman Alex James was simply the most idolised player of his pre-war generation, but in the early summer of 1953 he died a quiet, unceremonious death. James had arrived at Herbert Chapman's Arsenal keen to earn more than the £8 per week he had been on at Preston and to circumvent the maximum wage rule the London club arranged a supplementary 'sports demonstrator' job at Selfridges department store for him. He repaid them with eight seasons, four championships and two FA Cups. Having served in the armed forces, James became a journalist after the war, but died of cancer on 1 June 1953 aged only 52.

SEE ALSO **'GEORGE BEST LOSES THE BATTLE'** (page 593).

England's Alf Ramsey clears from Rest of Europe's Giampiero Boniperti during the dramatic match to mark the FA' 90th birthday.

RAMSEY SAVES THE FA'S 90TH BIRTHDAY BLUSHES

There were 97,000 fans at Wembley on 21 October to celebrate the 90th birthday of the Football Association (FA) and watch England take on the Rest of Europe, but England looked out of touch at first and it was Europe, buoyed by fine forward play from Spain's Kubala and Yugoslavia's Vukas, who entertained the crowd. The continentals were 3-1 up at one stage, but Stanley Matthews took matters in hand and set up two goals for Mullen. Europe went 4-3 up through Kubala, but there was still time for Mortensen to be brought down in the box and for Alf Ramsey to step up and save the home sides' blushes.

SEE ALSO **'ALF RAMSEY TAKES OVER ENGLAND REIGNS'** (page 247); **'BECKHAM SAVES ENGLAND'** (page 551).

1953

PUSKAS TEACHES ENGLAND A LESSON

Hungary's Magic Magyars came to England on a run of form that had seen them win Olympic gold and go unbeaten prior to the match in 29 successive games. On 25 November England took to the field with their familiar 2-3-5 formation, but it looked almost archaic when compared to the Hungarians' flexible 4-2-4 pattern. Hungary took the lead in the first minute through their fine centre-forward Nandor Hidegkuti, who had been played in by Ferenc Puskas, the captain and main conjuror of this magic side. England did manage an equalizer, but they were taken apart in 13 spell-binding minutes that finally drew a line under any false notion that the English were still the lords of football's manor.

Hidegkuti got another before Puskas produced not only the moment of the match, but also the moment when all English football fans realized that the game had moved onto another level. The stocky number 10 received the ball deep in the England penalty area. He was challenged by England's best defender, Billy Wright, but left the England captain kicking thin air as he dragged the ball back with the sole of his left foot and smashed the ball into the roof of the net. Geoffrey Green of The Times noted that Wright had gone into the challenge "like a fire engine going in the wrong direction to put out the blaze".

Puskas got another before half-time and while Stan Mortenson and Alf Ramsey got second-half goals, Hidegkuti, completing his hat-trick, and Jozef Bozsik completed the rout. The final score was England 3, Hungary 6 and the 100,000 England fans inside Wembley were stunned, but proud to say they were present.

SEE ALSO **'ENGLAND TAKE ANOTHER BEATING FROM HUNGARY'** (page 189).

Ferenc Puskas smashes the ball in for a rampant Hungary.

BRAZIL HOLD SHIRT DESIGN COMPETITION

In the aftermath of Brazil's infamous defeat to Uruguay in the 1950 World Cup in front of nearly 200,000 disbelieving fans at the Maracana Stadium, a distraught nation frantically sought answers.

The all-white kit Brazil wore against Uruguay was blamed for being insufficiently patriotic and so in December 1953, with the support of the Brazilian football authorities, the newspaper *Correio da Manha* launched a competition to design a new kit for the national team based on the colours of the Brazilian flag.

The successful candidate from 301 entries was from Aldyr Garcia Schlee, a 19-year-old illustrator from the Brazilian town Pelotas. He blended the colours of the flag to produce the now renowned strip consisting of a yellow shirt with green collar ands cuffs, blue shorts and white socks. This kit was first worn by Brazil when they played Chile in March 1954.

The away kit dates from the 1958 World Cup final. Brazil faced Sweden, who also wore yellow, so the Brazilians quickly invested in a set of blue shirts and sewed on the emblems from their yellow shirts.

SEE ALSO **'JUVENTUS STRIP FADES IN WASH'** (page 53);
'MANCHESTER UNITED BLAME GREY KIT' (page 493).

The yellow shirts and blue shorts quickly became synonymous with the most flamboyant team in world football.

The North Korea squad were one of the most successful during the early years of the Asian confederation and qualified for World Cup 66.

ASIAN CONFEDERATION FORMED

The Asian Football Confederation (AFC) was founded in Manila in the Philippines during the second Asian Games in May 1954. There were 12 founding members – Afghanistan, Burma, Republic of China, Hong Kong, India, Indonesia, Japan, Korean Republic, Pakistan, Philippines, Singapore and Vietnam – and they chose Sir Man Kam-loh from Hong Kong as the AFC's first president and Lee Wai-thong as the first general secretary. FIFA accepted the AFC as an official confederation on 21 June 1954 and invited AFC representatives to join its executive committee. Today the AFC has 46 members, the most recent being Australia, who joined in 2006.

SEE ALSO **'JAPANESE PLAYER TACKLES EUROPE'** (page 353); **'AUSTRALIA JOINS ASIA CONFERENCE'** (page 594).

With their recent defeat still lingering in the memory England must have approached the second match against Hungary with trepidation.

ENGLAND TAKE ANOTHER BEATING FROM HUNGARY

In November 1953 Hungary had beaten England 6-3 at Wembley to become the first team outside the British Isles to beat England at home. On 23 May 1954 they proved it was no fluke by beating them 7-1 in Budapest, a defeat that in early 2007 was still their largest ever, and inflicted greater damage on England's world-wide reputation. The Hungarians, led by Ferenc Puskas, who scored twice in Budapest, utterly bewildered the jaded English with their attacking formation and tactics. "That defeat remained with me for a long, long time, because they were such a wonderful side," recalled Sir Tom Finney, who was part of the beaten England side.

SEE ALSO **'WEST GERMANY'S TACTICAL LOSS TO HUNGARY'** (page 192).

1954

Adidas have had a long and fruitful association with the German national side.

ADIDAS INNOVATE WITH SCREW-IN STUDS

At the 1954 World Cup German coach Sepp Herberger understood the value of preparation, which is why he recruited founder of Adidas, Adi Dasler, to his support staff. When it began to rain during the final against Hungary in Berne, Dasler introduced his new innovation – screw-in studs of varying lengths for the bottom of football boots. These helped the German players grip the pitch better and overcome Hungary to win the World Cup. "It only took a few seconds to take out the studs and quickly raise the boots," remembered Germany's Ottmar Walter. "Before half-time we were already using the higher studs and that gave us a certain advantage."

SEE ALSO **'EX-FOOTBALLER INVENTS THE 'PREDATOR' BOOT"** (page 472).

UEFA FORMED

On 15 June 1954 Europe created its own governing body, the Union of European Football Associations (UEFA) in Basel, Switzerland. It came 50 years after the foundation of FIFA, at a time when the European nations believed the world was becoming less Euro-centric and so wanted their own voice. The inspiration behind UEFA's creation was the former Italian Football Association secretary and president, Dr Ottorino Barassi, and his counterparts in the French and Belgian football associations, Henri Delaunay and Jose Crahay. They held several meetings across Europe and were given the green light when FIFA approved the creation of continental football confederations at its 1953 extraordinary congress in Paris.

SEE ALSO **'THE FORMATION OF FIFA'** (page 55); **'PLATINI – FROM SOCCER PLAYER TO FOOTBALL POLITICO'** (page 608).

The next UEFA president Austrian Gustav Wiederkehr makes a European draw, with a little help from Jose Crahay in 1964.

SCOTLAND'S WORLD CUP DEBACLE

Scotland's World Cup debut at the 1954 tournament in Switzerland on 19 June swiftly descended into farce and humiliation. The squad was hamstrung before they even arrived as Rangers refused to release their players and the Scottish Football Association decided to send only a 13-man squad. After losing their opening game 1-0 to Austria, the Scottish manager Andrew Beattie resigned. Ahead of their second game against Uruguay in Basel, Italy's double World Cup winning coach Vittorio Pozzo declared, "[Scotland] will die in the sun." He was proved spectacularly right as the reigning world champions ran up a 7-0 victory, which remains Scotland's heaviest ever defeat.

SEE ALSO **'MOROCCO STUN SCOTLAND'** (page 513).

Scotland's Jock Aird loses out to Uruguay's Julio Cesar Abbadie. It set the pattern for the game as Scotland were comprehensively thrashed.

WEST GERMANY'S
TACTICAL LOSS TO HUNGARY

On 20 June in Basel, West German captain Fritz Walter led out a team consisting of up to eight reserves to face the might of Hungary. Unsurprisingly, they were soundly beaten 8-3 with Sandor Kocsis helping himself to four goals. Crucially, Hungary's leading player Ferenc Puskas was injured and forced to miss the next two games after a challenge by Werner Liebrich. After the West Germans had won the tournament a few weeks later their approach to the game, devised by their coach Sepp Herberger, was hailed as inspired, because they hid their best side from Hungary, and avoided Uruguay and Brazil on their way to the final.

SEE ALSO '**NEW GERMAN COACH MAKES AN IMPACT**' (page 134).

West Germany's national manager Sepp Herberger explains his tactical decision to field a weakened team to a radio reporter.

Swiss forward Josef Hugi scores during the quarter-final match. He went on to grab a hat-trick but still ended up on the losing side.

AUSTRIA'S
SENSATIONAL COMEBACK

Hosts Switzerland would have been confident of reaching the last four as they raced to a 3-0 lead in this quarter-final against Austria in Lausanne. But they hadn't reckoned on the most rapid comeback in World Cup history as the Austrians scored five unanswered goals, two each for Theo Wagner and Alfred Korner, in just nine minutes to forge into a 5-3 lead after 34 minutes. The disbelieving Swiss pulled a goal back before half-time, but Wagner completed his hat-trick nine minutes into the second half. Each side scored once more before the Austrians triumphed 7-5 in a game that remains the highest scoring in the tournament's history.

SEE ALSO '**... BUT EUSEBIO SCORES FOUR**' (page 273).

THE BATTLE OF BERNE

A crowd of over 40,000 came to the Wankdorf Stadium in Berne to see what promised to be a classic quarter-final encounter between Brazil and Hungary. The Hungarians took a 2-1 lead at half-time with goals from Sandor Kocsis and Nandor Hidegkuti, before Djalma Santos pulled one back for Brazil. After 61 minutes Mihaly Lantos re-established Hungary's two-goal advantage from the penalty spot, but five minutes later Julinho gave Brazil hope with a goal.

At 3-2, the Brazilians were becoming increasingly frustrated and Nilton Santos ploughed into Jozsef Bozsik. The pair traded blows and were both sent off by English referee Arthur Ellis. Just eight minutes later the Brazilian Humberto was dismissed for a foul on Kocsis, who confirmed Brazil's tournament exit with an 88th minute goal.

At the final whistle fights broke out on the pitch and it has even been alleged, but never proven, that Ferenc Puskas, watching the game injured on the sidelines, hit the Brazilian Pinheiro with a bottle. What is certain is that fighting between the sides continued in the dressing rooms after the game.

SEE ALSO **'THE BATTLE OF SANTIAGO'** (page 243).

Hungary's Sandor Kocsis is challenged by Brazil's Brandaozinho during the physical quarter-final match.

193

1954

WEST GERMANY 2-0 DOWN IN THE WORLD CUP FINAL

Hungary had effortlessly glided to the World Cup final with four resounding victories to take their run of unbeaten games to a record 32. On 4 July 1954 in front of a crowd of 60,000 in Berne they expected to extend that run to 33 against a West German side they had already humiliated 8-3 in the group stage. After only eight minutes Hungary were 2-0 in front, with goals from an unfit Ferenc Puskas and Jozsef Czibor, and seemingly on their way to becoming world champions. But West Germany still had 80 minutes to launch a comeback. "Now let's show them," shouted the Nuremberg inside-right Max Morlock.

SEE ALSO 'RAMSEY'S STIRRING WORDS' (page 278).

After making a terrible start against Hungary, Max Morlock springs into action and pulls one back for the West Germans.

194

"TOR! ...TOR! ...TOR!"

Within two minutes Morlock had put his stirring words into action and pulled a goal back. Hungarian midfielder Jeno Buzansky lost the ball to the West German captain Fritz Walter, who played it to Helmut Rahn on the left wing and a stretching Morlock tipped in his cross. Suddenly the game changed – the West Germans were now in control. They pressed for an equalizer and on 19 minutes Rahn stroked the ball past Gyula Grosics to make it 2-2.

At half-time the West German coach Sepp Herberger implored his players to complete the job. "Go out there and become world champions," he told them, but after the interval Hungary came back hard, with Nandor Hidegkuti first hitting the post and then Sandor Kocsis banging the cross-bar. The scores stayed level until the 85th minute when Rahn received the ball on the edge of the box and powered a left-foot shot past Grosics. As Rahn's shot hit the back of the net, the radio commentator Herbert Zimmerman shouted: "Tor Tor Tor," [Goal Goal Goal] to millions of listening Germans.

Five minutes later the English referee Bill Ling blew his whistle to signal full-time and confirm West German as world champions. At the start of the tournament no one expected to witness the West German captain Fritz Walter being presented with the World Cup and that gave rise to the final becoming known as the 'Miracle of Berne'.

SEE ALSO **'BECKENBAUER OFFERS HIS SYMPATHIES'** (page 447).

Rahn's goal sparks wild West German celebrations and leaves the Hungary players flattened.

PUSKAS' BITTER ACCUSATION

The two captains, West Germany's Fritz Walter and Hungary's Ferenc Puskas shake hands before the match – and before the controversy began.

Two minutes after Rahn's winning goal it appeared as though Puskas had actually saved the Hungarians with a late equalizer. He collected a pass from Mihaly Toth and smartly beat Toni Turek, but as the Hungarians celebrated, over on the side of the pitch the Welsh linesman Mervyn Griffiths stood with his flag raised to signal offside, although television footage suggests it was a harsh decision. Two months after the game a bitter Puskas gave an interview to the magazine *France Football* in which he suggested the West German players might have taken drugs, as several had developed jaundice. Puskas would later withdraw the accusation.

SEE ALSO **'MARADONA ACCUSES FIFA OF FIXING THE WORLD CUP'** (page 449).

DI STEFANO INSPIRES MADRID

"No one believes me when I tell them that Real Madrid, when I joined them in 1953, had gone so many years without winning the league that hardly anyone could remember the last time," said Di Stefano. It was back in 1933 that Madrid had last been champions of Spain and in the two decades since they had been firmly in the shadow of their rivals, Athletico Madrid and Barcelona.

The Madrid president Santiago Bernabeu had signed Di Stefano in September 1953 to return the club to greatness and the Argentinian did not disappoint. He scored on his league debut against Santander in a 4-2 win and two weeks later scored four goals against Barcelona in a 5-0 victory at the Bernabeu. By the end of the season Madrid were La Liga champions.

SEE ALSO 'RONALDINHO WOWS THE NOU CAMP' (page 572).

Such was his impact at the Bernabeu, Alfredo Di Stefano was named Honorary President of Real Madrid in November 2000.

DYNAMO DRESDEN RELOCATE

In the early 1950s the head of the Stasi, the East German secret police, Erich Mielke, became increasingly jealous at being forced to watch the success of the infant club Dynamo Dresden, who won the East German Cup in 1952 and the East German title in 1953. Mielke, who was based in Berlin, a city starved of a successful club side, announced that Dynamo Dresden would leave their home city and move to the East German capital, so as of 21 November 1954 the club became known as Dynamo Berlin.

SEE ALSO 'DECLINE OF THE EAST GERMAN STATE CLUB' (page 450).

The team carried on despite losing its best players and gradually built a new side. Dynamo Berlin won domestic doubles in 1989 and 1990.

GYULA GROSIC ARRESTED

Gyula Grosics, a leading member of the Hungarian side that lost to West Germany in the 1954 World Cup final, knew that defeat would bring dire consequences. In January 1955 his fears were realized when he was arrested on suspicion of spying by the Hungarian Ministry of Defence. For the next year Grosics was held under house arrest. "I was locked from the outside world, my flat under constant police surveillance so nobody could visit me," he said. He was also banned from playing and expelled from the national side. In December 1955 he was told no evidence of spying had been found and he could resume his football career.

SEE ALSO **'STEVE BLOOMER INTERNED'** (page 76); **'FRITZ WALTER AVOIDS FORCED MARCH'** (page 151).

Despite his heroics in goal for his country Gyula Grosics could not escape the politics of Communist Hungary after the war had ended.

WOLVES TAKE ON EUROPEAN TALENT

After Wolves had won the League Championship in 1954 their innovative manager Stan Cullis wanted to set them a greater challenge, so arranged a friendly against the Hungarian champions Honved at Molineux in December of that year. Honved boasted half of the Hungarian national side that had beaten England 6-3 and 7-1 in the previous 12 months and the Hungarians showed their class by taking a 2-0 lead at half-time. However, Wolves staged a come-back in the second half with a penalty from Johnny Hancocks and a double from Roy Swinbourne. Cullis described his side, with some justification, as "the champions of the world".

SEE ALSO **'THE FIRST 'WORLD CHAMPIONS"** (page 32). **'*L'EQUIPE* ARTICLE SUGGESTS EUROPEAN CUP'** (page 199).

The Honved players, wearing striped shirts, raise their arms after scoring their opening goal against Wolves at Molineux Stadium.

L'EQUIPE ARTICLE SUGGESTS EUROPEAN CUP

When Wolverhampton Wanderers beat the renowned Hungarian side Honved 3-2 in a friendly at Molineux in December 1954 their manager Stan Cullis hailed his side as "the champions of the world". Three days later the French sports newspaper *L'Equipe* challenged this assumption in an article by their football editor Gabriel Hanot, who wrote, "We must wait for Wolves to visit Budapest and Moscow before we proclaim their invincibility. There are other clubs of international prowess, like Milan and Real Madrid. There is a strong case for starting a European championship for clubs." Within nine months *L'Equipe's* lobbying helped give birth to the European Cup.

SEE ALSO **'EUROPEAN CUP LAUNCHED'** (page 201).

This match between Wolves and Honved in 1954 sparked the idea of a tournament of European club football.

JACKIE MILBURN SCORES IN FA CUP FINAL

A statue of Jackie Milburn stands outside St James' Park as a fitting tribute to Newcastle United's greatest ever player. A former pit apprentice and the uncle of Bobby and Jack Charlton, Milburn was a powerful and prolific striker who graced the Newcastle team for 15 years between 1943 and 1957, scoring 239 goals in 494 appearances. He had many great moments, but what was probably the finest came in the 1955 FA Cup final, when he scored the opening goal in a 3-1 victory over Manchester City to win the trophy for the third time.

SEE ALSO **'WEMBLEY SHOCK FOR CUP FAVOURITES'** (page 355).

Newcastle United is a club with a history of great centre-forwards. None more so than St James' Park icon 'Wor Jackie' Milburn.

CHELSEA FORCED TO PULL OUT OF EUROPEAN CUP

Twenty-five years after refusing to take part in the first World Cup finals, English football proved it remained as insular as ever when the Football League prevented Chelsea from entering the inaugural European Cup. The London club had won their first ever League Championship in 1955 and so were invited to take part in the European Cup the following season. Chelsea were keen and were drawn to meet Djurgarden of Sweden in the first round. However, the Football League secretary Alan Hardaker, fearing fixture congestion, but also that the new competition would prove successful, advised Chelsea to withdraw. They agreed and their place went to Polish side Gwardia Warsaw.

As Champions, Chelsea had won the right to play in Europe but they withdrew under pressure from the English Football League.

SEE ALSO **'MANCHESTER UNITED WITHDRAW FROM FA CUP'** (page 531).

Real Madrid's Zarraga is the first man to lift the European Cup. The Spaniards have won the trophy nine times more than any other team.

EUROPEAN CUP BECOMES REALITY

After publishing its famous article calling for the creation of a European Cup, Gabriel Hanot and his colleagues at *L'Equipe* decided to put their words into action. In April 1955 they convened a meeting of 18 clubs in Paris to decide on the format for the new competition and a knock-out tournament was devised, consisting of home and away games with aggregate scores and climaxing in a final. It was confirmed the tournament would begin at the start of the 1955-56 season and *L'Equipe* agreed to hand its organization over to UEFA. On 4 September 1955 the European Cup began when Sporting Libson met Partizan Belgrade in Lisbon.

SEE ALSO **'BIRTH OF THE NEWLY BRANDED CHAMPIONS LEAGUE'** (page 454).

Hib's Paterson and Combe defending against Stade de Reims' Leon Glovacki as Hibernian's first European Cup run comes to an end.

HIBS BECOME BRITAIN'S FIRST EUROPEAN CUP REPRESENTATIVES

Hibernian became the first British side to play in the European Cup when they accepted an invitation to play in the inaugural tournament. While they had only finished fifth at home in the previous season, Hibs had a fine reputation after winning the Scottish title in 1948, 1951 and 1952. The club's chairman Harry Swan had organized tours across the world, including Brazil, and eagerly led the Edinburgh side into Europe for the first time. He watched as his team made their way past the Germans Rot Weiss Essen and the Swedes Djurgardens to reach the semi-finals, where they lost over two legs to France's Stade de Reims.

SEE ALSO **'ABERDEEN LIFT CUP WINNERS' CUP'** (page 200).

ROUS PROPOSES INTER-CITIES FAIRS CUP

The general secretary of the English Football Association, Stanley Rous, and the Swiss pools inventor, Ernst Thommen, conceived the European competition called the Inter-Cities Fairs' Cup in 1955. The competition was meant to promote international trade fairs and was initially open only to clubs from cities that hosted trade fairs, but eventually domestic league placings could earn clubs qualification. The first side to win the Inter-Cities Fairs' Cup were Barcelona in 1958 and the final winners were Leeds United in 1971. After that the competition was replaced by the UEFA Cup.

SEE ALSO **'GOTHENBURG WIN UEFA CUP'** (page 381).

After serving as general secretary of the English FA, Sir Stanley Rous went on to be elected by a large majority to be FIFA president in 1961.

GIGI PERONACE SIGNS BRITISH PLAYERS

In the late 1950s and early 1960s the Italian football agent Gigi Peronace was instrumental in the transfer of several British footballers to Italian clubs on lucrative deals. In 1957 he took John Charles to Juventus from Leeds United for £65,000 and in 1961 he brought Jimmy Greaves to AC Milan from Chelsea for £80,000. Greaves said about Peronace, "His knowledge of footballers and the game was profound and matched by his financial acumen." In the same year Denis Law and Joe Baker signed for Torino, where Peronace was also a sporting director, for a combined sum of £185,000.

SEE ALSO **'JOHN CHARLES TAKES ITALIAN JOB'** (page 211); **'JIMMY GREAVES RETURNS FROM ITALY'** (page 238).

One of the earliest football agents Gigi Peronace was instrumental in securing lucrative moves to Italy for several British footballers.

Tempelin hit the cross-bar for Reims in the closing stages but Real Madrid held on and Zarraga lifted the very first European Cup trophy.

MADRID LIFT FIRST EUROPEAN CUP

Real Madrid won the first of their record five consecutive trophies with a dramatic 4-3 victory over Reims in Paris. The French side, orchestrated by the wonderfully talented Raymond Kopa, who joined Madrid immediately after the final, took the lead after six minutes when Michel LeBlond headed in. Four minutes later Jean Templin added another.

Madrid recovered to level after half an hour though their Argentinian pair, Alfredo Di Stefano and Hector Rial. Reims went back in front when Michel Hidalgo turned in Kopa's free-kick, only for Madrid to claw their way back through Marquitos. Madrid finally edged in front for the first time when Rial claimed his second of the game after 79 minutes. It was to prove to be the winner.

SEE ALSO **'BIRTH OF THE NEWLY BRANDED CHAMPIONS LEAGUE'** (page 454).

YUGOSLAV PLAYERS SMUGGLED INTO SPAIN

A major problem presented itself when Real Madrid were drawn to face Partizan Belgrade in the quarter-finals of the first ever European Cup. The Franco regime had severed diplomatic relations with all countries from the Soviet bloc and, as it stood, the Yugoslavians could not enter Spain. Of course, Real Madrid were Franco's team and they found a way around this, so when Partizan's players and officials arrived at Madrid airport they didn't pass through passport control and were instead smuggled through a side entrance. The Yugoslavs were beaten 4-0 by Real in the first leg at the Bernabeu.

SEE ALSO 'HUNGARIAN PLAYERS DISPERSE AFTER UPRISING' (page 206).

Milos Milutinovic was one of the Partizan Belgrade players that had to be sneaked into Franco's Spain to fulfil a European fixture.

NAZI PARATROOPER PROCLAIMED 'FOOTBALLER OF THE YEAR'

In April 1956 German goalkeeper Bert Trautmann became the first foreigner to be voted Footballer of the Year by the Football Writers' Association. Having fought for the Nazis against the British little more than a decade earlier, the award was the ultimate symbol of acceptance.

During the war Trautmann had been one of Hitler's paratroopers on both the Eastern and Western fronts. He was captured by the Americans, French and Russians, but on each occasion managed to escape, before finally taken by the British in Belgium. He was famously greeted with the words, "Hello Fritz, fancy a cup of tea?"

After serving time at a POW camp near Manchester, Trautmann was released at the end of the war. He remained in England and played for St Helens Town before being spotted by Manchester City. At first there were protests about signing a German but Trautmann swiftly won over the Maine Road faithful.

Trautmann became one of the Manchester City's greatest ever servants, playing over 500 matches for the clubs between 1949 and 1964.

SEE ALSO 'TRAUTMAN PLAYS ON WITH BROKEN NECK' (page 204).

Of the moment of impact Trautmann said, "I flew forward and he came into me... I got his thigh in my neck and in that moment I was gone".

TRAUTMANN PLAYS ON WITH BROKEN NECK

After 75 minutes of the 1956 FA Cup final Manchester City were beating Birmingham City 3-1 when their goalkeeper Bert Trautmann dived at the feet of Peter Murphy. "It was like a train crash," recalled the German. Trautmann had broken his neck, but, unaware, played on and made several crucial saves. An X-ray after the game showed he had snapped a vertebra in his neck and was fortunate to be alive. "That was the luckiest time of my life – lucky that I got to play in an FA Cup final and lucky that I could carry on playing after the injury," he recalled.

SEE ALSO **'SPAIN'S ZAMORA STOPS ENGLAND'** (page 110); **'CAR CRASH ROBS ENGLAND OF STAR KEEPER'** (page 332).

Brazil's Nilton Santos and his England counterpart Billy Wright lead the teams out at Wembley for the first match between the two nations.

ENGLAND FINALLY MEET BRAZIL

On 9 May 1956 England played Brazil for the first time in front of a crowd of 100,000 at Wembley Stadium. England were 2-0 in front after only five minutes through Tommy Taylor and Colin Granger, before early in the second half goals from Didi and Paulinho drew Brazil level. But Taylor and Granger each scored another goal to give England a 4-2 win. Their victory would have been a lot more flattering had England not missed two penalties. When the first one was awarded the Brazilian Alvaro grabbed the ball and began walking off with it in protest, before he was persuaded to return.

SEE ALSO **'MUTUAL APPRECIATION SOCIETY'** (page 300); **'RONALDINHO BAMBOOZLES ENGLAND'** (page 562).

ENGLISH CLUB MAKES EUROPEAN CUP DEBUT

After winning the League Championship in 1956 Manchester United manager Matt Busby was determined to enter the fledging European Cup. He wanted a new challenge for his side, known as the Busby Babes as eight were home-grown and had an average age of just 22, and accepted UEFA's invitation to play in the second season of the competition. "This is where the future of the game lies," proclaimed Busby. The Football League forbade Busby from entering, but with the support of Stanley Rous at the Football Association he ignored them. United won their opening tie 12-0 on aggregate against Anderlecht and reached the semi-finals before losing to eventual winners Real Madrid.

English football's European pioneers, Manchester United pose for a picture before boarding their plane to Madrid for the semi-final.

SEE ALSO **'TEARS AS UNITED ARE CROWNED'** (page 286).

DUNCAN EDWARDS 'BOOMS' AT THE GERMANS

"The best player that I've ever seen and the only other player who ever made me feel inferior," said Sir Bobby Charlton about his Manchester United team-mate Duncan Edwards. The Busby Babe became the youngest player in the 20th century to play for England when he made his debut aged just 18 years and 183 days against Scotland in April 1955. A year later he starred in England's 3-1 win over the world champions West Germany at the Olympic Stadium in Berlin, contributing a wonderful goal from 25 yards and earning the nickname 'Boom-boom' from the impressed German fans for the power of his shots.

SEE ALSO **'THE BUSBY BABES ARE BORN'** (page 183); **'THE MUNICH AIR DISASTER'** (page 212-3).

Duncan Edwards' precocious talents marked him out as a great player from a young age.

REAL MADRID TAKE ON RAPID VIENNA IN EUROPEAN PLAY-OFF

1956

While Real Madrid would ultimately defend the European Cup successfully in 1956-57, their bid was very nearly derailed in the first round by Rapid Vienna. The Austrians were trounced 4-2 in the first leg in Madrid, but won the second leg 3-1 in the Prater stadium with a hat-trick from Ernst Happel. The match was tied 5-5 on aggregate. If the away goals rule had applied Madrid would have been out at the first hurdle. However, at that time a play-off was used to determine the winner and it didn't have to be at a neutral stadium. Madrid talked the Austrians into playing the game at the Bernabeu, where they triumphed 2-0, and Rapid Vienna's chance of an upset was gone.

SEE ALSO **'REAL MADRID WIN FIFTH EUROPEAN CUP'** (page 230).

Ernst Happel here on the left trains with the Austrian national side. His goals almost took Rapid Vienna to a momentous win over Madrid.

HUNGARIAN PLAYERS DISPERSE AFTER UPRISING

1956

On 23 October 1956 the Hungarian people took to the streets to overthrow the Soviet-backed communist government. For 12 days it looked as though they had succeeded, but then the Soviet Union sent the tanks in. Honved's great side were in Spain at the time for a European Cup tie against Athletico Bilbao. Honved decided it wasn't safe to return home, summoned their families and embarked on a fundraising tour. Afterwards, some players returned to Hungary, while others defected, including Ferenc Puskas, who went to Real Madrid, and Sandor Kocsis and Zoltan Czibor, who went to Barcelona. The great Hungary side would never play together again.

SEE ALSO **'YUGOSLAV PLAYERS SMUGGLED INTO SPAIN'** (page 203); **'PUSKAS JOINS REAL MADRID'** (page 226).

The brutal crushing of the Hungarian uprising by the Soviets meant many of their great football team would never play in the country again.

FUTURE STAR MAKES DEBUT AGED 15

Pelé started his professional career as he meant to carry on – with a goal. Aged only 15, five feet tall and replacing the rested Del Vecchio, Pelé scored on his debut for Santos against Corinthians. In a sustained run in the first team he scored 15 goals in 11 games that season. He spent 18 years with Santos, resisting overtures from big European clubs to stay in Brazil, only leaving as his career was winding down to play in the MLS.

Throughout his career he hit the net an amazing 1,283 times in 1,365 appearances but of his first professional goal Pelé said: "It was enough to keep me walking on air for a few days".

SEE ALSO **'PELÉ MAKES A PROMISE'** (page 175); **'A LEGEND'S FIRST STEPS INTO THE LIMELIGHT'** (page 309).

Brazil's Pelé follows up as the ball flies loose during his early years at Santos, the club where he established his reputation as a world-beater.

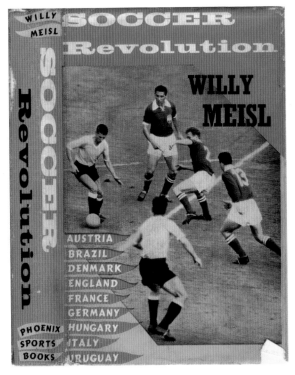

WILLY MEISL'S WHIRLWIND REVOLUTION

Between the wars, under Hugo Meisl, Austria's 'Wunderteam' finished fourth at the 1934 World Cup and were silver medal winners at the 1936 Olympics, playing football with a rare flair and freedom. Two decades later Meisl's sportswriter brother Willy published a book called *The Soccer Revolution* in which he celebrated that Austrian team and hailed a formation called 'The Whirl', an early forerunner of 'Total Football', where players constantly interchange all over the pitch. "We must free our soccer youth from the shackles of playing to order, along rails as it were," he wrote. "We must give them ideas and encourage them to develop their own."

SEE ALSO **'RINUS BRINGS 'TOTAL FOOTBALL' TO AJAX'** (page 255).

The front cover of Willy Meisl's book emphasises its appeal in all the countries across the world where football is followed with passion.

1957

FIRST AFRICAN NATIONS CUP

In February 1957 Egypt became the inaugural winners of the African Nations Cup, although they triumphed in a field of only three teams. The first tournament consisted of the four founding members of the African Football Confederation (CAF) – Sudan, Egypt, Ethiopia and South Africa. However, South Africa were disqualified for their refusal to play a multi-racial team, so Ethiopia were handed a bye straight to the final. There they were joined by Egypt, after they overcame Sudan 2-1 in the only semi-final. In the final in the Sudanese capital Khartoum, Egypt had little trouble getting past the Ethiopians 4-0 to be crowned African champions.

SEE ALSO **'AFRICAN NATIONS BOYCOTT THE WORLD CUP'** (page 264); **'NIGERIA TAKE OLYMPIC GOLD'** (page 500).

Nigeria captain Christian Chukwu is congratulated by Nigeria president Shehu Shagari as he lifts the African Cup of Nations in 1980.

1957

THE TREATY OF ROME

The European Economic Community (EEC) was created when six nations – France, West Germany, Italy, Belgium, Holland and Luxembourg – signed the Treaty of Rome in March 1957. Britain didn't join the EEC until January 1973, but the Treaty aimed to encourage freedom of movement of labour across Europe's borders and more footballers did move across the continent to play for foreign clubs. However, the Treaty's major influence on football came nearly four decades later when the Belgian footballer Jean-Marc Bosman successfully argued that football was contravening it by not allowing players freedom of movement after their contracts had expired.

SEE ALSO **'THE BOSMAN RULING'** (page 491).

The signing of the Treaty of Rome which created the European Economic Community, forerunner of today's European Union.

MANCHESTER UNITED HAVE THE DOUBLE IN THEIR GRASP

Manchester United were confident of becoming the first English side to win the double in the 20th century – they just had to beat Aston Villa in the Cup final. However, on 6 May they were hit by a crucial injury after only six minutes as goalkeeper Ray Wood gathered a header from Villa left-winger Peter McParland and was then knocked to the ground by him. Wood broke his cheekbone and was stretchered off. Today McParland would have been sent off instantly, but instead he remained on the pitch and scored twice past United's stand-in keeper Jackie Blanchflower, to win the game 2-1 and take the Cup back to Villa Park.

SEE ALSO **'SPURS WIN THE DOUBLE'** (page 238).

United goalkeeper Ray Wood receives treatment after having his cheekbone fractured in a clash with Aston Villa's Peter McParland.

STANLEY MATTHEWS CROWNED 'KING OF FOOTBALL'

Many players have been hailed as the King of Football, but only one has actually been given the honour at a special ceremony. This was experienced by Sir Stanley Matthews, who missed a week's training to fly to Ghana, to be made 'King of Football' by a tribe as part of the country's independence day celebrations. Matthews also played in several matches in front of President Nkrumah and large crowds. Such an honour serves to prove the former Stoke and Blackpool winger's global fame. When Matthews died in 2000 Pelé said he was, "the man who taught us how football should be played".

SEE ALSO **'MATTHEWS BUYS NEW BOOTS IN BRAZIL'** (page 172); **'SIR STANLEY BOWS OUT'** (page 257).

Stanley Matthews' Ghanaian adventure is testament to how the Stoke legend had become one of the most famous names in world football.

1957

EULOGIO MARTINEZ RAMIRO SCORES THE NOU CAMP'S FIRST GOAL

For all that Barcelona's magnificent Camp Nou Stadium is a symbol of Catalan identity, the first goal scored there came from a Paraguayan, Eulogio 'Kokito' Martinez Ramiro, who netted in the 11th minute of a 4-2 victory over Select Warszawa. The 24 September match had been specially arranged to mark the opening of Camp Nou and over 90,000 fans packed the new arena, which took three years to build and replaced the old Les Corts Stadium. Goal machine Martinez was Barcelona's top scorer on three occasions and helped the Catalans to two La Liga titles, two Spanish Cups and two European Fairs Cups.

SEE ALSO **'WANTED – A FOOTBALL CLUB!'** (page 44); **'BAYERN MOVE TO A NEW HOME'** (page 223).

FC Barcelona's imposing Camp Nou. The current capacity of the grand stadium is 98,477.

CHARLES ACCEPTS ITALIAN JOB

In the summer of 1957 Welsh striker John Charles of Leeds United became one of the first British players to join a foreign club when he signed for Juventus for a then British record fee of £67,000. Over the following five seasons in Turin Charles proved his worth by scoring 93 goals in 155 games and winning the Scudetto on three occasions. Three decades later Juventus fans voted Charles their greatest ever foreign player. "I had many happy memories playing for Leeds and Wales, but what gave me the most pleasure was winning the Italian championship with Juventus at the end of my first season with them in 1958," said Charles.

SEE ALSO **'GIGI PERONACE SIGNS BRITISH PLAYERS'** (page 202); **'CLOUGH BLASTS JUVENTUS 'CHEATS''** (page 324).

Juventus captain Gianpiero Boniperti sizes up his team's new £67,000 capture John Charles when the Welshman arrived in Turin.

NORTHERN IRELAND KNOCK OUT ITALY

In 1958, for the first and only time in their history, Italy failed to qualify for the World Cup. While the Italians beat both Northern Ireland and Portugal at home in their group, they lost 3-0 to the Portuguese in Lisbon to set up a winner-takes-all match against Northern Ireland in Belfast. After the original December 1957 game was replaced with a 2-2 friendly when the referee's flight was cancelled, the sides met again on 15 January 1958 at Windsor Park. Northern Ireland led 2-0 lead at half-time with goals from Jimmy Mcilroy and Wilbur Cush, but while Dino Da Costa responded for Italy it wasn't enough to take them to Sweden.

SEE ALSO **'ARMSTRONG PUTS NORTHERN IRELAND INTO SECOND ROUND'** (page 384).

Northern Ireland held on to claim the 2-1 victory over Italy that sent them to Sweden and left the Italians disappointed at home.

THE MUNICH AIR DISASTER

On 6 February 1958 the BEA Elizabethan aircraft carrying the reigning English League champions Manchester United back from Yugoslavia after they had claimed a place in the European Cup semi-finals with a 3-3 draw against Red Star Belgrade landed at Munich's Reim airport to refuel.

After a quick stop, the United party reboarded the aircraft, but take-off was twice aborted by the pilots. The tense passengers returned to the airport terminal convinced that ice on the runway would force them to stay overnight in the German city. Duncan Edwards sent a famous telegram to his landlady saying, "All flights cancelled. Flying tomorrow. Duncan."

The aircraft's captain James Thain attempted a third take-off, but once again he had problems getting the plane off the ground and as the Elizabethan left the runway it went through a fence, crossed a road and struck a house. The plane broke up and was scattered over an area of 150 square metres.

The final death toll would reach 23 and include United players Roger Byrne, Geoff Bent, Eddie Colman, Mark Jones, David Pegg, Tommy Taylor and Liam Whelan. The United secretary Walter Crickmer, trainers Tom Curry and Bert Whalley, and eight journalists also perished. The United manager Matt Busby was badly injured and given only a 50-50 chance of survival, while Duncan Edwards was also critically ill.

Among many tributes, goalkeeper Harry Gregg, who saved the lives of his team-mates and other passengers, said, "The most important thing about the Busby Babes… they say they might have been the greatest team, but one thing's very sure, they were the best loved team."

SEE ALSO **'EMPTY SPACES IN UNITED PROGRAMME'** (page 214); **'TEARS AS UNITED ARE CROWNED'** (page 286).

Manchester United line up to face Red Star Belgrade in the European Cup quarter-final.

The mangled wreckage of the plane after the fatal crash.

DUNCAN EDWARDS DIES

Fifteen days after the Munich air disaster Manchester was plunged into further grief with the news that Duncan Edwards had lost his battle to live. Since the crash Edwards, who it was understood would never play football again, had been close to death, but kept alive by a kidney machine. But on 21 February 1958 he passed away aged only 21. Says Paul Hince, then a 13-year old schoolboy, who would later play for Manchester City and write for the Manchester Evening News, "It was hard to accept the news of Duncan's death... he was like Superman or Hercules."

SEE ALSO **'THE BUSBY BABES'** (page 183); **'DUNCAN EDWARDS 'BOOMS' AT GERMANS'** (page 205).

Edward's tragic death deprived England of its most promising football talent. At only 21 he already had 18 caps and 5 goals for his country.

EMPTY SPACES IN UNITED PROGRAMME

Thirteen days after the Munich air disaster Manchester United were back in action for the first time when they faced Sheffield Wednesday in the fifth round of the FA Cup at Old Trafford. Harry Gregg and Bill Foulkes were the only players fit and available from the last game prior to the crash, and, poignantly, the programme had been printed with eleven blanks for the United team. Although essentially a team of strangers, United won the game 3-0. "That game was more important for what it did for the people of Manchester than what it did for me," said Bobby Charlton. "It gave them something to shout for again."

SEE ALSO **'THE MUNICH AIR DISASTER'** (page 212-3); **'TEARS AS UNITED ARE CROWNED'** (page 286).

Manchester United captain Bill Foulkes leads the makeshift United team out for their first match since the tragedy in Munich.

HERRERA 'PSYCHES UP' THE BARCELONA DRESSING ROOM

Herrera's approach to his players may have raised a few eyebrows in 1958 but his innovations are very much a part of today's game.

The modern game features many examples of managers using so-called 'mind games' to influence a football match, and Alex Ferguson and Jose Mourinho may think they have the monopoly on such tactics, but the godfather of football mind games was Helanio Herrera who, throughout the 1950s and 1960s made a habit of psyching his players up for action. French-Argentinian coach Herrera came to Barcelona in 1958, having worked at several clubs in France and Spain, and immediately set about helping his players maximize their efforts. "He who doesn't give it all, gives nothing,' was one of his favourite sayings. He was also a strict disciplinarian who banned players from drinking and smoking.

SEE ALSO **'WEST GERMANY'S TACTICAL LOSS TO HUNGARY'** (page 192); **'ARSENE WENGER ARRIVES AT HIGHBURY'** (page 503).

BOBBY CHARLTON MAKES ENGLAND DEBUT

Charlton was 21 when he made his international bow. He eventually reached 106 caps, averaging almost a goal every other game.

Bobby Charlton scored the first of his record haul of 49 goals on his international debut in a 4-0 victory over Scotland at Hampden Park in April 1958. Only two months after surviving the Munich disaster Charlton opened his account for England with the final goal of the game when, from a Tom Finney cross, he struck a powerful volley past Scottish goalkeeper Tommy Younger on 85 minutes. So impressed by the goal he had just conceded, Younger ran out of his penalty area to congratulate Charlton. "Well done, son, that was a fantastic goal," he told him. Charlton would score another 48 over the next 12 years.

SEE ALSO **'CHARLTON KICK STARTS ENGLAND'S WORLD CUP RUN'** (page 269); **'LOSERS APPLAUD CHARLTON DOUBLE'** (page 274).

Manchester United's Matt Busby watches his Babes take on Bolton Wanderers in the emotional 1958 FA Cup final at Wembley.

BUSBY MAKES EMOTIONAL RETURN

While Manchester United's form in the League Championship inevitably slumped, they were carried to the FA Cup final on a wave of emotion after the Munich disaster. Two weeks before the final Matt Busby travelled home overland and went down to Wembley with his side. Still on crutches, he didn't lead the team out, believing the honour should be his assistant Jimmy Murphy's, but Busby did speak to the players in the dressing room before the game, although he broke down in tears and had to be led away. Sadly United lost for the second successive season as Nat Lofthouse scored twice to lead Bolton to a 2-0 victory.

SEE ALSO **'TEARS AS UNITED ARE CROWNED'** (page 286). **'SIR MATT SAYS GOODBYE – AGAIN'** (page 316).

The reasoning behind Everton's decision was that matches were all too often called off because of a frozen pitch during the British winter.

GOODISON PARK GETS ALL WARM UNDERFOOT

In May 1958 Everton became the first English club to embrace under-soil heating when it was installed at Goodison Park. The hope was that it would help to remove snow and ice, which could often force the cancellation of games during the winter. The under-soil heating was provided by a series of electric wires, but there was a problem because the drains couldn't cope with a lot of water and thus there was presumably a danger of electrocution. In 1960 it was replaced by a new system and then eventually replaced again with a series of hot water pipes.

SEE ALSO **'FLOODLIGHTS FINALLY ADOPTED'** (page 179); **'QPR LAYS ARTIFICIAL PITCH'** (page 377).

BELA GUTTMAN AND HIS 4-2-4

The legendary Hungarian coach Bela Guttman managed 19 different sides over four decades, but arguably made the greatest impact on a side he had nothing to do with. His countrymen, Marton Bukovi and the coach of the great Hungarian side of the 1950s Gusztay Sebes, had helped to develop the attacking 4-2-4 formation, which involved having six players in attack and then in defence. Guttman introduced and popularized this during a season in charge of São Paulo FC, whom he led to the Sao Paulo State Championship in 1957. The Brazilian national team were inspired by the formation and used it to win the World Cup in 1958.

SEE ALSO SEE ALSO **'ROCCO INVENTS THE 'CATENACCIO"** (page 167); **'WILLY MEISL'S 'WHIRLWIND' REVOLUTION'** (page 207).

Guttman's attacking principles were the tactical inspiration behind Brazil's 1958 campaign.

PELÉ AND GARRINCHA TEAM UP

On 15 June 1958 the Ullevi Stadium in Gothenburg witnessed the coming together of two of football's greatest ever players, Pelé and Garrincha, when Brazil faced the Soviet Union in the group stage of the World Cup. By the time the pair were parted eight years later Brazil had won two World Cups and while they played in the same side their country never lost a single game.

The 24-year-old Garrincha, who had won his first cap for Brazil three years earlier, had an unrivalled ability to glide past defenders with his pace and trickery. The Botofogo winger was the king of the dribble, perversely helped by a childhood illness that had left him with curved legs and which made him able to change direction quickly and swerve past opponents at will.

Destined to be recognized as the greatest player of all time, Pelé had made his debut for Brazil at only 16 years old, but before the World Cup in Sweden he wasn't yet a regular in the team. However, his incredible all-round talents effectively forced the Brazilian coach Vicente Feola to throw the Santos man into the action – and he didn't disappoint.

It has long been rumoured that the rest of the squad put pressure on Feola to play Garrincha and Pelé together, but whatever the truth he chose to use both in Brazil's third game of the tournament against the Soviets, despite the objections of the team psychologist, who said that neither was ready for exposure at this level. That match was won 2-0, with both goals coming from Vava, and two weeks later Brazil were world champions.

SEE ALSO **'BRAZIL FLY THE SWEDISH FLAG'** (page 224).

Brazil's Vava fires his team's second goal past USSR goalkeeper Lev Yashin as team-mate Pelé celebrates.

The victorious Brazil side.

THE WELSH BATTLE AGAINST THE HUNGARIANS

On their only appearance at the World Cup finals, Wales stuck around for as long as they could. In group three they drew their games against Hungary, Sweden and Mexico. At this tournament, when teams finished level there was a play-off, so the Welsh met Hungary for a place in the quarter-finals. The Hungarians, stripped of so many great players, were still skilful and combative, and took the lead in the first half through Lajos Tichy. A brilliant volley from Ivor Allchurch, described by Real Madrid club president Santiago Bernabeu as the best inside-forward at the tournament, equalized for Wales, before Terry Medwin grabbed the winner. It finished 2-1.

SEE ALSO 'RAY HOUGHTON SCORES WORLD CUP CRACKER' (page 475).

Ivor Allchurch fires in a shot as Mexico's Del Muro puts in a challenge during another of the Wales' group matches in Sweden.

THE FOUR HOME NATIONS QUALIFY FOR THE WORLD CUP

The 1958 World Cup finals were the first, and so far only, time the four home nations – England, Scotland, Wales and Northern Ireland – have all qualified for the tournament. The Welsh enjoyed the most glory, reaching the quarter-finals before losing 1-0 to a goal scored by Pelé for the eventual winners Brazil. Northern Ireland also made it to the last eight before succumbing to the rampant Just Fontaine, who scored twice, as France triumphed 4-0. Scotland finished bottom of their group without a win, while England drew all three of their group games before losing 1-0 to the Soviet Union in a play-off.

SEE ALSO 'KEEGAN MISSES – AND UNBEATEN ENGLAND HEAD HOME' (page 386).

Wales keeper Kelsey in called into action against Sweden during the World Cup in 1958 in which all four home nations participated.

Don Howe, Bobby Charlton, Peter Brabrook and Peter Broadbent alight from the plane which carried England back from Sweden.

SOVIET UNION KNOCK ENGLAND OUT OF WORLD CUP

Six months before the 1958 World Cup England harboured realistic hopes of winning the tournament, but that all changed at Munich. In the air disaster England tragically lost three world-class talents in Duncan Edwards, Tommy Taylor and Roger Bryne. And so a weakened England travelled to Sweden and drew all three of their group games against the Soviet Union, Brazil and Austria. In a play-off against the Soviets at the Ullevi Stadium in Gothenburg England's Peter Brabrook twice hit the post before Anatoly Ilyin's goal after 69 minutes denied them a place in the quarter-finals.

SEE ALSO **'SOVIET UNION WIN FIRST EUROPEAN CHAMPIONSHIP'** (page 234).

Wowed by the Brazilian's display, French marksman Just Fontaine reportedly said that, "to lose to a team like that wasn't embarrassing".

PELÉ'S SEMI-FINAL HAT-TRICK

The imperious Brazilians of 1958 were known for their attacking brilliance, but they also reached the semis in Sweden without conceding a goal. In the semi-final they expected to be tested by a French side that boasted the prolific Just Fontaine. He scored in the first half, but goals from Vava and Didi gave Brazil a 2-1 lead at the interval. The French, having pierced the Brazilian defence, were confident of doing it again before they were blown away in the second half as a 17-year-old Pelé scored a hat-trick in 23 minutes. The game finished 5-2 after Roger Piatoni scored a late consolation goal for the French.

SEE ALSO **'LUCKY NUMBER 13 FOR JUST FONTAINE'** (page 222). **'HENRY KNOCKS OUT BRAZIL'** (page 602).

LUCKY NUMBER 13 FOR JUST FONTAINE

For over half a century Just Fontaine has held the record for the most goals scored in a single World Cup after registering an incredible 13 for France at the 1958 tournament.

Before travelling to Sweden, the 24-year-old Stade de Reims striker wasn't even certain of a place in the French side, but an ankle injury to his team-mate Rene Bliard gave him his opportunity. With Real Madrid's Raymond Kopa operating behind him, Fontaine thrived and helped himself to goals at will in Sweden.

Fontaine also scored in six consecutive games to set another record. In the group stage he opened his account with a hat-trick against Paraguay, then a double against Yugoslavia and one against Scotland. In the quarter-finals he scored twice in France's 4-0 win over Northern Ireland and in the semi-final he scored once, but it wasn't enough as France crashed out 5-2 to Brazil. In the third/fourth place play-off Fontaine ran riot and scored four in a 6-3 win over West Germany.

SEE ALSO **'BRAZIL AND FRANCE PLAY OUT CLASSIC QUARTER-FINAL'** (page 413); **'RONALDO RECORDS HIS 15TH WORLD CUP GOAL'** (page 601).

France's Just Fontaine is chaired off by his team-mates after scoring four goals in his team's 6-3 third place play-off win to set a new individual scoring record of 13 goals in one World Cup.

Seventeen-year-old Pelé crashes Brazil's third past Sweden's goalkeeper Kalle Svensson. It was the pick of Brazil's five goals.

BRILLIANT VOLLEY SHOWCASES PELÉ'S TALENT

After scoring a hat-trick in the semi-final against France, much was expected of 17-year-old Pelé in the final against Sweden. He didn't disappoint. The Brazilian scored two goals, including one that to this day neatly showcases his youthful brilliance in Sweden. Ten minutes into the second half Pelé took Nilton Santos' cross on his chest to beat Sigge Parling, lifted the ball over Bengt Gustavsson, before volleying the ball past Kalle Svensson. The goal put Brazil out of sight at 3-1 and they would finish the game as 5-2 winners.

SEE ALSO **'PELÉ STARTS THE ROUT'** (page 306).

PELÉ SCORES BRAZIL'S FIFTH GOAL

In the final minute of the 1958 World Cup final Pelé leapt high into the air and met a cross with a header that looped over Kalle Svensson for Brazil's fifth and final goal. When the whistle blew moments later the occasion proved too much for the 17-year-old and he broke down in tears. Sobbing uncontrollably he was propped up and lifted onto the shoulders of his team-mates. "I was so excited, because we had won and I desperately wanted to tell my family," explained Pelé. "I wanted to phone them to find out if they knew we had won, because it was only on the radio back then."

SEE ALSO **'BRAZIL'S PLACE IN HISTORY IS ASSURED'** (page 307).

Overcome, Pelé cries on the shoulder of Didi as team-mates Gilmar and Orlando congratulate him on his fantastic performance.

BRAZIL FLY THE SWEDISH FLAG

It wasn't just Pelé. At the end of the final the whole Brazilian squad were consumed with emotion at winning the World Cup for the first time and banishing the painful memory of losing the trophy in 1950. "You only believe in yourself once you've won," said Nilton Santos, involved in his third World Cup. "I really thought, 'This is a dream. I really am a world champion.'"

The Swedish people had taken the Brazilians to their hearts, thrilled and inspired by the football they had witnessed. To thank the Swedes for their support the Brazilian players took a large Swedish flag, lifted it above their heads and ran around the pitch. The Swedish crowd got to their feet and applauded the Brazilians' gesture.

SEE ALSO **'SWEDEN WIN INAUGURAL WOMEN'S EUROPEAN CHAMPIONSHIPS'** (page 398).

Of Sweden 58 Pelé remembers "It was a very big cultural shock, as this was my first trip abroad... It was a wonderful experience".

Luiz Bellini was about to set an example that all World Cup winning captains have followed since 1958 by lifting the trophy above his head.

BELLINI LIFTS WORLD CUP

At the end of the 1958 World Cup final the Brazilians were presented with the famous Jules Rimet trophy. As a battery of photographers crowded around captain Luiz Bellini they asked him to lift the small trophy high above his head, so they could get a better picture of this historic moment. Bellini duly obliged and ever since that day each successive World Cup-winning captain has copied this gesture as the ultimate symbol of triumph and, of course, to give the photographers and television cameras the iconic image they need.

SEE ALSO **'WORLD CUP STOLEN'** (page 266).

BRAZILIAN AIR FORCE
ESCORT THEIR HEROES HOME

Eight years after having to hastily cancel a World Cup winning party after losing to Uruguay as tournament hosts, Brazil were finally able to celebrate being champions of the world. As soon as the final whistle blew Brazilians flooded into the streets to hail their new heroes and days later the Brazilian team flew home to Rio de Janeiro on the president's plane with their own fighter pilot escort. On arrival they were greeted by the president before parading the trophy in front of the thousands of fans who lined the streets.

SEE ALSO **'WEST GERMANY GROUNDED IN SEVILLE'** (page 389).

Brazil's exuberant football had lit up the World Cup and won them many fans. They returned home feted as heroes by their countrymen.

Joy Beverley, wife of Wolves and England captain Billy Wright, is flanked by her sisters Teddy and Babs in the stands at Molineux.

BILLY WRIGHT AND
JOY BEVERLEY WED

The England captain Billy Wright and Joy Beverley, a member of singing group the Beverley sisters, who had several hits during the 1950s, can claim to be football's first celebrity couple nearly four decades before the Posh and Becks phenomenon. In March 1958 the couple married in Poole, Dorset, and would remain together for 36 years until Wright's death in 1994. They had tried to keep the details of their wedding a secret, but news leaked out and up to 7,000 fans gathered around the Poole register office.

SEE ALSO **'EL BEATLE IS BORN'** (page 265); **'BECKHAM MANIA HITS JAPAN'** (page 557).

Despite his best efforts Henri Delaunay couldn't persuade the home nations to adopt his plan for a pan-European tournament.

COUNTRIES UNDERWHELMED BY PROSPECT OF NATIONS CUP

The Nations Cup, the original name for the European Championships, was the brainchild of French Football Federation secretary Henri Delaunay. In 1958 UEFA asked for countries to enter the new tournament, which would be staged in 1960, but the response wasn't exactly enthusiastic. The four home nations – England, Scotland, Wales and Northern Ireland – collectively rejected the offer and the 1954 World Cup winners West Germany, and the 1934 and 1938 winners Italy, did so too. There were initial fears that the qualifying tournament wouldn't get the 16 countries it needed to function properly, but some late entries saved the day.

SEE ALSO 'THE LATIN CUP KICKS OFF' (page 168).

After 1956 Puskas could not return to Hungary. Despite his visible weight gain, Real Madrid took a chance on the 'Galloping Major'.

PUSKAS JOINS REAL MADRID

After the Hungarian uprising of 1956 Ferenc Puskas decided not to return home and set off on a tour of Europe and South America with his Honved team-mates. However, his refusal to play for Honved in Hungary earned him a two-year ban from UEFA. By the end of this he was 31 and had put on weight, so he found it difficult to find a new club, before Real Madrid decided to take a chance and bring him to the Bernabeu. The gamble paid off immediately with Puskas scoring four hat-tricks in his debut season and helping Madrid to a fourth consecutive European Cup.

SEE ALSO 'REAL MADRID WIN FIFTH EUROPEAN CUP' (page 231).

BECKENBAUER SIGNS FOR BAYERN

The most illustrious career in German football began when 14-year-old Franz Beckenbauer joined Bayern Munich in 1959. Five years later Beckenbauer would make his first-team debut for Bayern and help transform the club, captaining them to four Bundesliga titles, four German Cups and three consecutive European Cups between 1974 and 1976. Always both a dominant and graceful presence on the pitch, Beckenbauer had no equal as an attacking sweeper. On the international stage he captained West Germany to the 1974 World Cup and then managed his country to success in the 1990 tournament, to become the first and so far only man to win the World Cup as player and manager.

SEE ALSO **'MULLER'S SIGNING LIFTS BAYERN MUNICH'** (page 251).

A young Franz Beckenbauer who went on to become the most accomplished player Bayern Munich have ever produced.

BILLY WRIGHT WINS 100TH CAP

When the England captain Billy Wright led his side out at Wembley to face Scotland in April 1959 he became the first ever footballer to win 100 caps for his country. Wright, who played at both wing-half and centre-half, had made his debut 13 years earlier and had captained England in three consecutive World Cups in 1950, 1954 and 1958. After reaching his century, Wright, always a Wolverhampton Wanderers man, played five more times for England before abruptly retiring from the game. "England has had no better or more loyal a servant," said his team-mate Sir Tom Finney. "Billy was as solid as a rock."

SEE ALSO **'TOM FINNEY RETIRES'** (page 229); **'RECORD-BREAKING SAUDI KEEPER RETIRES'** (page 606).

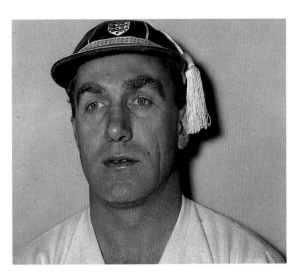

Since 1959 only 3 players have joined Wright in this exclusive club; Bobby Moore, Bobby Charlton, Peter Shilton each passed 100 caps.

FOOTBALL LEAGUE WINS COPYRIGHT CASE

In 1959 the Football League won a landmark legal case in the High Court against pools company Littlewoods, claiming that copyright of the printed fixtures belonged to the clubs. The League were unhappy at how much money the pools companies were making from printing the fixtures each weekend and wanted to share in it. After winning the case the League ploughed their new funds in to redeveloping many of their team's stadiums. By 2004 it was estimated that pools revenue accounted for up to 20% of the Scottish League's income.

SEE ALSO **'FOOTBALL POOLS LAUNCHED'** (page 87).

Sir John Moores, founder of Littlewoods. The Moores family also have a long standing association with Liverpool football club.

Even whilst serving with the military Pelé's rise to greatness was unstoppable as he combined his football career with his national service.

PELÉ SWAPS SHIRT FOR UNIFORM

A year after winning the World Cup Pelé had to serve a year's national service with the Brazilian army. He might have been a national hero, but there was no way of getting out of it. He was stationed with the motorised coast artillery in Santos and, unsurprisingly, picked for the army's football team. Pelé led this side to the 1959 South American Military Championship, scoring 14 goals in ten games. As well as the army side and the barracks team, Pelé continued to play for Santos and Brazil, and also the All-Star São Paulo side, which meant he played an incredible 103 games while doing his national service.

SEE ALSO **'PELÉ'S 30 MINUTE MASTERCLASS'** (page 253).

TOM FINNEY RETIRES

In 1960 a crowd of more than 30,000 flocked to Deepdale to see Tom Finney play his final game for Preston North End – a 2-0 win over Luton Town. Before the game Finney walked through a guard of honour and then stood on a table at the side of the pitch to give a farewell speech to the crowd. Finney, who was born next to the ground, spent his whole career playing for Preston, amassing 433 appearances over 14 years, as well as 76 caps for England, but was forced to retire by a persistent injury.

SEE ALSO **'SIR STANLEY BOWS OUT'** (page 257).

1960

Finney addresses the crowd and watching media. His fellow players also stand and listen to show their respect for the Preston legend.

SPANISH RIVALS CONTEST EUROPEAN CUP SEMI-FINAL

In the 1960 European Cup semi-final it was the Spanish champions Barcelona who stood between Real Madrid, who had been European champions for the previous four years, and a fifth consecutive final. Before the tie Barcelona's manager Helenio Herrera asked his players to place a hand on a football and chant, "The European Cup – we shall have it, we shall have it." It made no difference, however, as Madrid won 3-1 in the Bernabeu with two goals from Alfredo di Stefano and 3-1 in the Nou Camp with two goals from Ferenc Puskas.

SEE ALSO **'AC MILAN WIN ALL-ITALIAN FINAL ON PENALTIES'** (page 570).

1960

Real Madrid's Santamaria, Canario and Vidal in action during training in preparation for the all-important semi-final against Barcelona.

1960

REAL MADRID WIN FIFTH EUROPEAN CUP

In front of an awe-struck record crowd of nearly 128,000 crammed into Hampden Park, Real Madrid produced arguably the greatest ever performance by a club side to win their fifth consecutive European Cup, as they swept aside Eintracht Frankfurt 7-3. "We were aware that the day was something special, even for us," recalled Francisco Gento. "I do not think any of us wanted the referee to end the game and I think that was true for the crowd also. I think it was our best display because of the quality of the goals."

In a repeat of two of their previous four European Cup finals, Madrid actually conceded the first goal when Richard Kress scored from Erwin Stein's cross after 18 minutes. This roused Madrid and they would score an incredible six unanswered goals in the next 55 minutes with a wonderful display of fluid, attacking football. "It was a fantasy staged in heaven," said Celtic's 1967 European Cup winner Jimmy Johnstone, who was in the crowd that night.

Alfredo di Stefano scored twice to put Madrid in front, before Ferenc Puskas powered in a third to give the Spanish club a 3-1 lead at half-time. Nine minutes after the interval Puskas scored again from the penalty spot and soon after he completed his hat-trick with a rare header from a Gento cross.

Greedy for more, the Hungarian became the first, and so far only, player to score four goals in a European Cup final, when he got another on 69 minutes. Stein pulled one back for the Germans, before Di Stefano completed his own hat-trick straight from the restart. Stein scored again after 74 minutes and it ended 7-3.

SEE ALSO '... AND BEAT MILAN ON PENALTIES' (page 591).

Ferenc Puskas sends the Eintracht Frankfurt goalkeeper the wrong way from the penalty spot.

Madrid's heroes, Alfredo di Stefano and Puskas celebrate the win.

PENAROL WIN COPA LIBERTADORES

Penarol in action during a friendly against Celtic. The Copa Libertadores, however, was always fiercely fought with national pride at stake.

In June 1960 the Uruguayan side Penarol became the first winners of the Copa Libertadores, the tournament for the national champions of each of the South American nations. The champions from Argentina, Brazil, Paraguay, Bolivia, Uruguay, Chile and Colombia contested the first tournament. In the first round Penarol beat the Bolivian champions Wilstermann 8-2 before overcoming the Argentinians San Lorenzo 3-2 in the semi-final. In the two-legged final Penarol triumphed 2-1 on aggregate over Olimpia of Paraguay. Penarol would successfully defend their title in 1961 with victory over Palmeiras in the final.

SEE ALSO **'COLO COLO WIN COPA LIBERTADORES'** (page 453).

Rangers captain Eric Caldow exchanges pennants with his Fiorentina counterpart Alberto Orzan before the 1961 Cup Winners final got underway.

EUROPEAN CUP WINNERS' CUP LAUNCHED

Following the success of the first five seasons of the European Cup, a sister competition, the Cup Winners' Cup, was launched for the 1960-61 season. The format was a knock-out competition between the winners of each European nation's domestic cup, but the concept initially received a lukewarm reaction, with Spanish Cup winners Atletico Madrid and French Cup winners AS Monaco turning down invitations to the inaugural tournament. From a field of ten clubs, Fiorentina and Rangers reached the first final. Over two legs the Italians beat Rangers 2-0 in Glasgow and 2-1 in Florence to win 4-1 on aggregate.

SEE ALSO '**LAZIO WIN LAST EVER CUP WINNER'S CUP**' (page 524).

1960

SOVIET UNION WIN FIRST EUROPEAN CHAMPIONSHIPS

While the inaugural European Championships, known originally as the Nations' Cup, was a rather limp and unloved affair, the Soviet Union had few complaints as they became Europe's first national champions. Only 17 teams entered the competition and over the course of a year a series of home and away games were played until they were whittled down to four – France, the Soviet Union, Yugoslavia and Czechoslovakia – who progressed to the final in France. In the semi-finals the Soviets overcame the Czechs 3-0 in Marseille with two goals from Valentin Ivanov and one from Viktor Ponedelnik, while Yugoslavia advanced after fighting out a thrilling 5-4 win over France.

With the hosts out a crowd of only 18,000 bothered to watch the final at the Parc des Princes. Yugoslavia took the lead two minutes before half-time through Milan Galic, before the Soviets replied with two goals. The first was from Slava Metreveli and then in extra-time Ponedelnik scored the winner.

SEE ALSO **'SOVIETS LEFT OUT IN THE WORLD CUP COLD'** (page 330).

Action from the final as the Soviet Union strike force bear down on the Yugoslavian goal.

MAXIMUM WAGE ABOLISHED

PFA secretary Cliff Lloyd with George Eastham outside the High Court after the landmark ruling in the player's favour was announced.

At the start of the 1960s the Football League decreed that the maximum wage a club could pay a player was £20 a week during the season and £17 a week during the summer. In 1961 chairman of the Professional Footballers' Association Jimmy Hill decided to challenge this rule. "The maximum wage had always riled me," said Hill. "There were no other careers, sporting or otherwise, in which you had something like that… We were deadly serious about striking if we didn't get our way." The Football League eventually relented and abolished the maximum wage, and Fulham striker Johnny Haynes became the first footballer to earn £100 a week.

SEE ALSO **'TOTTI HELPS PAY WAGES OF ROMA'S YOUTH PLAYERS'** (page 574).

PELÉ'S 'GOL DE PLACA'

Despite the maddening lack of footage Pelé's wonder strike at the Maracana for Santos in 1961 has firmly entered football folklore.

On 5 March 1961 Pelé was playing for Santos against Fluminense at the Maracana when he collected the ball on the edge of his own penalty area and headed towards goal. On his way he beat six players and the goalkeeper before scoring a goal which would become known as a 'gol de placa', meaning a goal worthy of a plaque. The São Paulo newspaper *O Espore* erected a commemorative plaque at the Maracana Stadium, which reads, 'On this field on 5-3-1961 Pelé scored the most beautiful goal in the history of the Maracana.' Unfortunately, despite many searches, there is no footage of this goal.

SEE ALSO **'MARADONA SCORES INCREDIBLE SECOND'** (page 416).

GREENWOOD GOES TO WEST HAM

West Ham chief Greenwood talks tactics with new charges Malcolm Musgrove, Ken Brown, Bobby Moore, John Dick and John Bond.

In April 1961 West Ham United appointed Ron Greenwood as only the fourth manager in its history. After a playing career largely in London with Chelsea, Fulham and Brentford, Greenwood honed his coaching skills as an assistant at Arsenal, and with the England youth and Under-23 sides. At Upton Park his innovative coaching methods, which Trevor Brooking said, "introduced a continental style of play based around possession and keeping the ball," delivered the FA Cup in 1964 and the European Cup Winners' Cup a year later, as well as grooming Bobby Moore, Geoff Hurst and Martin Peters to win the World Cup in 1966.

SEE ALSO **'BOBBY MOORE APPOINTED ENGLAND CAPTAIN'** (page 249).

ENGLAND THRASH SCOTLAND

Jimmy Greaves makes sure of England's third on their way to a famous thrashing of the 'Auld Enemy' in front of the Wembley faithful.

Since 1872 England have played Scotland on 110 occasions, but never have they handed out such a beating to their neighbours as in April 1961 when they triumphed at Wembley. This was not a poor Scottish side – they had Denis Law, Ian St John and Billy McNeil – but they simply had no answer to the flair of Chelsea's Jimmy Greaves, who scored a hat-trick, and Fulham's Johnny Haynes, who scored twice. England established a 3-0 lead at half-time, Scotland hung in there and after 75 minutes had closed the gap to 5-3, but in the final 15 minutes England heaped on the misery scoring four times to win 9-3.

SEE ALSO **'SCOTS CLAIM 'WORLD CHAMPION' STATUS'** (page 281).

FOG ROBS DENIS LAW
OF DOUBLE HAT-TRICK JOY

On 28 January 1961 Manchester City were leading Luton Town 6-2 in an FA Cup fourth round tie when, with just 20 minutes remaining, the game was abandoned due to heavy fog. This was particularly painful for the Scottish international striker Denis Law, because he had scored all six of City's goals and achieved an incredibly rare double hat-trick. The goals were cruelly wiped from the records due to the game being called off before full-time and to make matters worse City lost the rearranged game 3-1, although Law did score once again.

SEE ALSO **'LUTON TOWN'S JOE PAYNE SCORES 10'** (page 131).

Denis Law trots away after beating Luton goalkeeper Jim Standen to score the first of his soon to be disallowed 6 goals.

SPURS WIN THE DOUBLE

In the 1960-61 season Tottenham Hotspur became the first English side to win the League and Cup double in the 20th century. Boasting such legends as captain Danny Blanchflower, Dave Mackay and Cliff Jones, Spurs always played with flair and won the title by eight points from Sheffield Wednesday. Blanchflower famously said, "The game is about glory… about going out and beating the other lot, not waiting for them to die of boredom." In the FA Cup final Bill Nicholson's side had to work hard against Leicester City, but late goals from Bobby Smith and Terry Dyson proved enough to complete a historic double.

SEE ALSO **'IAN RUSH SCORES TWICE AS LIVERPOOL COMPLETE THE DOUBLE'** (page 410).

Tottenham Hotspur captain Danny Blanchflower shows off the League and FA Cup trophies to a couple of young autograph hunters.

JIMMY GREAVES RETURNS FROM ITALY

In December 1961, only four months after joining AC Milan from Chelsea, Jimmy Greaves arrived back in London to join Tottenham Hotspur for a record £99,999, a fee designed to avoid him becoming England's first £100,000 footballer. "I concede that I made a mistake going to Milan in the first place," said Greaves after arriving at White Hart Lane. "They were employing my feet, but I could not give them my heart." While he never settled in Italy, it didn't affect his form on the pitch and he still managed to score an impressive nine goals in 12 games

SEE ALSO **'GIGI PERONACE SIGNS BRITISH PLAYERS'** (page 202); **'ZBIGNIEW BONIEK TRANSFERS TO JUVENTUS'** (page 393).

Despite finding his feet quickly on the pitch in Italy, Greaves never settled in Italy and was soon rescued by Tottenham Hotspur.

EUSEBIO 'KIDNAPPED'

In the late 1950s the three major Portuguese clubs were all alerted to a talented teenager called Eusebio playing amateur football in the Portuguese colony of Mozambique.

On 17 December 1960, aged 18, Eusebio arrived in Lisbon to sign for Benfica. Legend has it that he came to the Portuguese capital to join Benfica's rivals Sporting Lisbon, who had links to his club in Mozambique, Sporting Club de Lourenco Marquez, but when he arrived in Lisbon he was kidnapped by Benfica at the airport and hidden in an Algarve fishing village.

It's a good story, but Eusebio denies it. "It is a lie," he has said. "Nobody kidnapped me. Benfica never hid me anywhere. What happened was that Benfica signed a contract with me as a professional footballer." Sporting Lisbon did offer substantially more money, but he had already signed for Benfica.

It would prove to be the most important moment in Benfica's history as over the next 15 years Eusebio scored 342 goals in 373 league games, which helped to deliver 11 Portuguese championships and the 1962 European Cup.

SEE ALSO 'DI STEFANO IS KIDNAPPED' (page 250); 'INTER MILAN ROW OVER EUSEBIO' (page 274).

The 17-year old Eusebio's signature was the subject of a fierce battle between Portugal's biggest club sides.

Pelé resisted the offer from Juventus which included a share in Italian car manufacturing giant Fiat in order to stay with Santos in Brazil.

ITALIANS TRY TO SIGN PELÉ

After Brazil's success at the 1958 World Cup it was inevitable Europe's leading teams would come calling for some of their players, but while Didi, Vava, Julinho Botelho and Altafini were lured away, the biggest gem of all – Pelé – proved immune to their charms. Italian giants Juventus were desperate to sign Pelé in the early 1960s and pulled out all the stops. "Giovanni Agnelli wanted to give me a share of Fiat in return for me signing," recalled Pelé. However, he stayed in Brazil with Santos and only moved abroad later in his career, to the New York Cosmos in 1975.

SEE ALSO **'INTER MILAN ROW OVER EUSEBIO'** (page 274).

Benfica's Germano shepherds the ball back to his goalkeeper Pereira to frustrate the Real Madrid attack in a pulsating European Cup final.

BENFICA AND REAL MADRID VIE FOR EUROPEAN GLORY

The Portuguese champions Benfica successfully defended their European crown with victory over Real Madrid in a memorable final on 2 May in Amsterdam. Bela Guttmann's side played nine of the team who won the 1961 final against Barcelona, but they found themselves two goals behind, both scored by Ferenc Puskas, after 23 minutes. Benfica drew level with goals from Jose Aguas and Domiciano Cavem, only for Puskas to complete his hat-trick before half-time. As Madrid tired, the second half was dominated by the Portuguese. Mario Coluna made it 3-3 before Eusebio showed his brilliance with two goals to take the trophy back to Lisbon.

SEE ALSO **'BACK HEEL HELPS PORTO WIN EUROPEAN CUP'** (page 419).

CHILE KICK OFF THEIR WORLD CUP

The 1962 World Cup hosts Chile proved they were going to enjoy their own party by opening the tournament with an impressive 3-1 win over Switzerland. At the national stadium in the capital Santiago, in front of 65,000 fans, Chile were initially shocked by the Swiss and went behind to a Rolf Wuthrich goal after only six minutes. They took some time to regroup, but eventually equalized with a deflected shot from Leonel Sanchez a minute before half-time. In the second half the Chileans really put on a show, with a strike Jaime Ramirez prompting a joyous pitch invasion. Sanchez then made it 3-1 with his second of the game.

SEE ALSO 'CHILE'S WORLD CUP 'PLOT' FAILS' (page 432).

The Chilean team line up before they begin their campaign. Spurred on by fanatical home support they started the tournament brightly.

PELÉ PICKS UP AN INJURY

The 1962 World Cup finals were robbed of one of the world's best players when Pelé injured himself playing against Czechoslovakia in a group game in Vina del Mar. Early on Garrincha had put Pelé through on goal, but as he attempted a shot he pulled a muscle in his groin. Surprisingly, the Czechs refused to exploit this advantage and refrained from forceful tackles on the lame Pelé. "[It is] one of those things I shall always remember with emotion and one of the finest things that happened in my entire football career," said Pelé. Effectively reduced to ten men, Brazil could only manage a goalless draw with Czechoslovakia.

SEE ALSO 'SIMONSEN'S INJURY AGONY' (page 399).

Deprived of their star man after a muscle injury reduced him to a bystander Brazil were unable to break down the Czechs.

THE BATTLE OF SANTIAGO

The infamous Battle of Santiago, fought between Italy and Chile on 2 June in a group game at the 1962 World Cup, was always likely to be a combustible affair once the Italian press had published an article in the build-up to the game depicting Chile as a backward and poverty-stricken country.

The Chileans were desperate to exact their revenge on the field and got stuck into the Italians from the start. After only seven minutes Giorgio Ferrini had been dismissed for retaliating to a brutal tackle from Honorino Landa. The Italian refused to leave the field and the game was held up for ten minutes as police shepherded him to the sideline.

Just before half-time Leonel Sanchez punched Mario David right in front of a linesman, but no action was taken. David responded by kicking Sanchez in the neck and was sent off. Sanchez, the son of a boxer, used his fists to lash out at Humberto Maschio and broke his nose. The game saw several other outbreaks of violence and the English referee Ken Aston would later admit that it was "uncontrollable".

Down to nine men, Italy held out until late in the game, but finally succumbed to two goals, the first scored with a header by Jaime Ramirez after 74 minutes, the second by Jorge Toro, who shot from 25 yards, the ball flying past Carlo Mattrel in the Italian goal, just two minutes from the final whistle. Only days later the Italians were stoned by a group of Chileans at their training base.

SEE ALSO **'THE BATTLE OF HIGHBURY'** (page 130);
'SCHUMACHER'S ASSAULT' (page 387).

Referee Ken Aston argues with Italy's Enzo Robotti and Mario David whilst Leonel Sanchez of Chile lies dazed on the ground.

1962

GARRINCHA SHOWS HIS CLASS...

"At Vina del Mar we lost to one man," remembered England midfielder Bobby Charlton. That man was Garrincha, whom England were powerless to stop as he led Brazil to a 3-1 victory in the quarter-final of the 1962 World Cup. He only stood five feet and seven inches, but Garrincha leapt high to give Brazil the lead with a powerful header in the first half. After Gerry Hitchens equalized for England Garrincha stepped forward and took control. First he fired in a rasping free-kick that Ron Springett could only parry into the path of Vava and then, saving his best for last, curled a stunning shot into the top corner.

SEE ALSO
'RONALDINHO BAMBOOZLES ENGLAND' (page 562).

England's left back Ray Wilson had a torrid time trying to keep Garrincha under control.

... AND WINS BRAZIL
THE WORLD CUP

After losing Pelé for the rest of the tournament, the Brazilian manager Aymore Moreira went to see Garrincha and said "Look, Pelé is not able to play. You have to play good enough for you and Pelé too." Garrincha said, "Yeah, OK. Leave it to me." The 28-year-old winger kept his word and would dominate this tournament with some extraordinary displays. He first inspired his team-mates to a group win over Spain by helping to set up both goals for Pelé's replacement Amarildo in a 2-1 win, and then scored twice against England in a 3-1 quarter-final win.

In the semi-final against Chile Garrincha scored a 20-yard volley and a header to lay the foundation of a 4-2 win. Towards the end of the game he was sent off for responding to the rough treatment dealt out to him, but he escaped a ban for the final. In Santiago, Brazil overcame the Czechs 3-1 with goals from Armarildo, Zito and Vava. There was no goal for Garrincha, but Brazil's success wouldn't have been possible without him.

SEE ALSO **'BRAZIL'S PLACE IN HISTORY IS ASSURED'** (page 307).

Having escaped suspension, Garrincha was in inspirational form during the World Cup final.

Injury brought the curtain down prematurely on Fontaine's career. After his record breaking World Cup exploits this was hard to bear.

FONTAINE RETIRES AT 27

Only four years after setting the record for the most goals scored in a World Cup finals the French striker Just Fontaine was forced to retired aged only 27 years old. A year earlier he had suffered a double fracture of the leg, breaking his tibia and fibula. He had tried to stage a comeback, but was unable to bend his knee and so had to give up football. "It's a shame because I don't think that I had reached my peak," reflected Fontaine. "I could have gone so much further, but I can't complain. It was just a very short career."

SEE ALSO **'GEORGE BEST QUITS AT 26'** (page 319).

An older Moore shows off some of his fashion range. His growing celebrity status didn't affect his form for West Ham.

BOBBY MOORE – FASHION ICON

Footballers weren't considered to be fashionable until the 1960s when the England and West Ham captain Bobby Moore began to change that. Moore's style has been described as mod-ish – he favoured sharp suits, polo necks and drainpipe trousers – and in 1962 the fashion bible Vogue took the unprecedented step of featuring Moore in a shoot alongside a group of models. Fashion photographers were always eager to work with him and Terry O'Neill took a renowned picture in the middle of Epping Forest of Moore in stylish attire with his wife Tina wearing an England shirt as a mini dress.

SEE ALSO **'MOORE ESCAPES JAIL AND TACKLES DOUBTERS'** (page 297); **'SUPERSTAR BECKHAM JOINS GALAXY'** (page 608).

LEV YASHIN WINS
FOOTBALLER OF THE YEAR

"The peerless goalkeeper of the century," is how Eusebio described Lev Yashin, who in 1963 became the first, and so far only, goalkeeper to be voted European Footballer of the Year. Known as the 'Black Panther', Yashin played his club football for Dynamo Moscow between 1949 and 1971 and on the international scene won a record 79 caps for the Soviet Union, playing a major role in their gold medal success at the 1956 Olympics and winning the inaugural European Championships in 1960. He also played in three World Cups, in 1958, 1962 and 1966, and attended the 1970 tournament as a non-playing reserve.

SEE ALSO **'ORDER OF LENIN AWARDED TO 'BLACK SPIDER'** (page 289).

Lev Yashin was a commanding presence in the Soviet Union penalty box and made 78 international appearances between 1954-70.

ALF RAMSEY TAKES
OVER ENGLAND REINS

On 25 October 1962 Sir Alf Ramsey was appointed England manager to succeed Walter Winterbottom. The former Southampton and Tottenham defender, who captained England on three occasions during his 32 international appearances, had won the Football Association's respect by taking Ipswich Town from the Third Division South to the League Championship in 1962. Ramsey immediately began to appreciate the size of his task in February 1963 when England lost his opening game 5-2 to France in Paris in a European Championships qualifier. Even so, Ramsey confidently predicted that he would lead England to the World Cup in 1966.

SEE ALSO **'SCHÖN MAKES GERMANY GREAT'** (page 255).

Bobby Smith, Jimmy Greaves and Maurice Norman pay close attention to the words of their new international manager Alf Ramsey.

SPURS BECOME FIRST ENGLISH CLUB TO WIN IN EUROPE

1963

In May 1963 Tottenham Hotspur became the first English side to claim a European trophy when they brushed aside Atletico Madrid 5-1 in the final of the European Cup Winners' Cup in Rotterdam. The Spurs captain Danny Blanchflower, who needed pain-killing injections in his knee before the game, gave a memorable and rousing speech in the dressing room. Lifted by his words, Tottenham took a 2-0 lead at half-time with goals from Jimmy Greaves and John White. The Spaniards cut the lead with a penalty from Enrique Collar, but the North Londoners pulled out of sight with a brace from Terry Dyson and another from Greaves.

SEE ALSO **'REAL MADRID'S EUROPEAN CUP DOMINANCE ENDS'** (page 267).

Captain Danny Blanchflower lifts the European Cup Winners' Cup aloft as he is carried shoulder-high by his jubilant Spurs team-mates.

MILAN WIN THE EUROPEAN CUP

1963

Benfica's hopes of winning a hat-trick of European Cups were ended by AC Milan at Wembley in May 1963. The Portuguese champions took the lead after 18 minutes through Eusebio and went in at half-time 1-0 ahead. During the interval the Milan coach Nereo Rocco replaced Giovanni Trapattoni with the Peruvian Victor Benitez as Eusebio's man-marker and immediately saw the benefits. With the Milan defence now more protected, the Italians ventured forward and turned the game around with two goals from the Brazilian striker Jose Altafini. Captain Cesare Maldini could now lift the European Cup.

SEE ALSO **'TRIESTE FINISH SECOND IN SERIE A'** (page 162); **'AC MILAN WIN ALL-ITALIAN FINAL ON PENALTIES'** (page 570).

Nereo Rocco's arrival sparked a revival at the San Siro. He went on to guide the Rossoneri to another European Cup victory in 1969.

Moore was permanently appointed England skipper aged just 23 after a series of international friendlies in the summer of 1964.

BOBBY MOORE MADE ENGLAND CAPTAIN

On only his 12th appearance for his country Bobby Moore was handed the captain's armband for England's game against Czechoslovakia in Bratislava on 29 May 1963. The West Ham defender was deputizing for the injured Jimmy Armfield and then replaced him on a permanent basis the following summer. Moore would captain England a total of 90 times, a record he shares with Billy Wright, and then led the team to World Cup glory in 1966. He won 108 caps in all before he retired from international football in November 1973.

SEE ALSO **'MARADONA CAPTAINS ARGENTINA FOR THE WORLD CUP'** (page 411).

Di Stefano and Puskas head the FIFA XI whilst Jimmy Armfield and Bobby Moore are the first men out for England at Wembley.

THE FA CELEBRATES ITS CENTENARY

To commemorate 100 years of the Football Association, the oldest domestic governing body in the world, an exhibition match was staged at Wembley between England and a FIFA World XI. The Rest of the World's team sheet was a roll-call of some of the game's greatest ever players, including Alfredo di Stefano, Denis Law, Raymond Kopa, Eusebio, Franscico Gento and Lev Yashin. Despite facing a team of superstars, England took the lead through Terry Paine in the second half. After 84 minutes Law equalized, but three minutes later Jimmy Greaves scored the winner to send the vast majority of the 100,000 crowd back down Wembley Way happy.

SEE ALSO **'FIFA CELEBRATES CENTENARY'** (page 576).

DI STEFANO IS 'KIDNAPPED'

On 24 August 1963 members of the National Liberation Army Front kidnapped Alfredo di Stefano from a hotel in Caracas during Real Madrid's pre-season tour of South America. "We wanted to do a propaganda operation so the world would hear our demands and to that end we used the most famous player in the world at that time," said the Venezuelan revolutionary Paul del Rio. Di Stefano was held for three days before he was released unharmed and Del Rio revealed he even sent his kidnappers a letter thanking them for their hospitality.

SEE ALSO **'KIDNAPPING THREATENS COPA'** (page 549). **'FOOTBALLER'S MOTHER IS KIDNAPPED'** (page 585).

Di Stefano was Argentinian by birth and a veteran of the Colombian league. A famous name not only in Latin America but across the world.

The Bundesliga, which took so long to come into existence, originally consisted of 16 teams. FC Cologne were the first Bundesliga champions.

BUNDESLIGA FORMED

Seventy-five years after England founded a national professional league, West Germany finally followed suit in July 1962. The impetus for the Bundesliga had been West Germany's embarrassment at their national team's quarter-final exit to Yugoslavia at the World Cup in Chile. Until then football had been largely semi-professional and arranged as regional leagues. The inaugural Bundesliga season consisted of 16 teams chosen on the basis of recent success and an equal representation of the country from the five Oberligas in the North, South, West and Southwest of the country and the capital Berlin. At the end of the inaugural 1963-64 season FC Cologne were the first Bundesliga winners.

SEE ALSO **'THE GREAT BUNDESLIGA SCANDAL'** (page 322); **'J-LEAGUE LAUNCHES'** (page 467).

THE FLA – FLU SETS AN ATTENDANCE RECORD

The derby between Rio de Janeiro teams Flamengo and Fluminense is one of the most hotly contested in world football and is eagerly anticipated by both sets of supporters. Flamengo's official home ground is the Gavea Stadium whilst Fluminense play at the Estádio das Laranjeiras. But the Fla-Flu always takes place at the famous Maracana. In December 1963, 177,020 spectators crammed into the grand old stadium – though some put the figure nearer to 190,000. Ironically the record crowd had little to shout about as they witnessed a nil-nil draw. The outright attendance record is also held by the Maracana – the defeat of Brazil by Uruguay in 1950 was played out in front of 199,854 – mostly shocked – Brazilians.

SEE ALSO **'BENFICA PLAY 89,011 ITALIANS'** (page 260).

Fluminense of Rio de Janeiro arrive at Luton airport ahead of a match against West Ham at Upton Park - a long way from the Maracana.

After Franz Beckenbauer, Bayern's acquisition of Gerd Muller was hugely significant as the club began to assert itself as a European force.

MULLER'S SIGNING LIFTS BAYERN MUNICH

When Gerd Muller joined Bayern Munich from TSV 1861 Nördlingen in 1964, the Bavarians' coach Zlatko Cajkovski was not terribly impressed. Pointing at Muller's stocky build, he asked, "What am I supposed to do with a weightlifter?" But Muller scored twice on his Bayern debut and would prove to be one of football's greatest ever strikers. Muller was incredibly prolific, scoring 401 goals in 459 appearances for Bayern, which helped them to four Bundesliga titles, four German Cups and three European Cups. As Franz Beckenbauer said, "Everything that Bayern has become is due to Gerd Muller."

SEE ALSO **'MULLER'S KILLER GOAL'** (page 303).

A BLACK DAY FOR FOOTBALL

Most reports of the National Stadium disaster in Lima during a Peru versus Argentina Olympic qualifying match on 24 May 1964 are brief – 318 people killed and more than 500 injured when outraged fans rioted after the referee disallowed a Peruvian goal two minutes from time. One eyewitness, though, said that while the decision was unpopular, fans didn't riot. Instead the mayhem was caused when the crowd stampeded for exits to get away from teargas fired into the stands by panicky police. However, as it was a game everyone wanted to see guards had locked the gates and joined the crowds to watch, so the fleeing fans were tragically trapped.

SEE ALSO **'THE HEYSEL STADIUM DISASTER'** (page 404).

Several Peruvian army soldiers stand guard outside the National Stadium in Lima, the scene of the 1964 tragedy.

INTER MILAN WIN EUROPEAN CUP

In May 1964 Inter Milan won their first European Cup with victory over Real Madrid in Vienna. Sandrino Mazzola, the son of the Italian captain Valentino Mazzola who died in the Torino air disaster of 1947, was the star of this side and appropriately gave Inter the lead two minutes before half-time. Auerlio Milani doubled it in the second half before Felo gave Madrid some hope by making the score 2-1 with 21 minutes remaining. Madrid's aging superstars, Di Stefano and Puskas, failed to find a way past Inter's defensive system, famously known as Cantennaccio, and Mazzola put the game beyond doubt with his second of the game after 76 minutes.

SEE ALSO **'INTER'S DEFENCE WINS TITLE'** (page 181).

Picchi looks to surge past Real Madrid's Isidro as Inter Milan carve out their famous victory against Madrid's original *galacticos*.

Pelé's performance was so complete that England were left in no doubt as to who would provide Brazil's biggest threat at the World Cup.

PELÉ'S 30 MINUTE MASTERCLASS

1964

In his long build-up to the 1966 World Cup, England boss Alf Ramsey decided to use the Brazilian Football Association's 50th anniversary Jubilee Tournament as a test of his side against South American opposition. During England's 30 May match against Brazil in Rio's giant Maracana Stadium he was shown the mountain his team had to climb. England played well enough to hold Brazil to one goal in the first half and equalized in the 48th minute, but ten minutes later Pelé stepped up a gear and conjured 30 minutes of football magic that saw the Brazilians put four goals into the England net and run out 5-1 winners.

SEE ALSO **'CRUYFF IN CRUISE CONTROL'** (page 337).

Lev Yashin is powerless to stop Spain's opener finding it's way into the back of the Soviet Union net on their way to a 2-1 victory.

SPAIN PROVE THEIR METTLE IN EUROPE

1964

The 1964 European Nations' Cup, the forerunner to the European Championships, saw politics mar proceedings with Greece refusing to play Albania, a country with which technically they were at war. It was a situation the host nation was only too familiar with. Four years earlier, General Franco had brought Cold War politics onto the pitch by barring the Soviet Union from entering the country to play the away half of a two-game play-off, thus forcing Spain to default from the competition. In 1964, however, politics didn't get in the way when the Spaniards beat the Soviets 2-1 in the Madrid final.

SEE ALSO **'AFRICAN NATIONS BOYCOTT THE WORLD CUP'** (page 246); **'CRUYFF IN WORLD CUP PROTEST '** (page 356).

'MATCH OF THE DAY' GOES ON AIR

The Liverpool versus Arsenal match on 22 August 1964 delivered the right result for the 40,000 fans packed into Anfield – 3-2 in favour of the home side. For 20,000 people in London, the outcome was not so welcome, but at least they had the satisfaction of being the first in the country to have watched their team on Match of the Day.

Football had been shown on television for a number of years on an on-and-off basis before legendary broadcaster Kenneth Wolstenholme stood at pitch side, fixed a camera with a steady gaze and said, "Welcome to Match of the Day, the first of a weekly series on BBC Two. This afternoon we are in Beatleville ..."

The limited TV audience was due to the fact that BBC2 had recently been launched and was only available in London – perhaps one of the factors that persuaded the FA to allow the programme to go out at all considering its paranoia over TV stealing gate-takings. From this low-key start MOTD went on to take the sporting nation by storm.

SEE ALSO **'TELEVISION MAKES HISTORY'** (page 268).

In the background can be seen some of the specially constructed stands for television and newsreel cameramen.

SCHÖN MAKES GERMANY GREAT

It was a happy day for East German-born Helmut Schön when he made it across the border to the West after World War Two and began a flourishing career as a manager that ultimately led to his appointment as assistant coach to the West German national side. It was an even happier day for West Germany in November 1964 when Schön succeeded Sepp Herberger as coach. Under his guidance the national team became runners-up in the 1966 World Cup, took third place in 1970, became European Champions in 1972, World Cup winners in 1974 and European Championship runners-up in 1976.

SEE ALSO **'JOCK STEIN ANSWERS CELTIC PRAYERS'** (page 256).

As an East German Helmut Schön's journey to become coach of the West German national team was even more remarkable.

RINUS BRINGS 'TOTAL FOOTBALL' TO AJAX

Marinus Michels, known as 'Rinus', was an Ajax man through and through. He played his entire career at the Amsterdam club and went on to coach a squad that produced some of the finest football of the time. The style was known as 'total football', a system that allowed any player to fill any position, ensuring that their structure on the pitch was never dragged out of shape. This required supreme fitness and skill, and Michels' exacting training regime not only produced a squad of elite athletes, but also helped players argue for professional status and full-time wages.

SEE ALSO **"TOTAL FOOTBALL DOMINATES'** (page 296).

Rinus Michels was a tactical genius whose football knowledge got the best out of a hugely talented generation of Dutch players at Ajax.

MATCH-FIXING ENDS CAREERS

In 1963, when he left Sheffield Wednesday for Everton, Tony Kay was England's highest paid professional, but a £50 bet when he was still with Wednesday was to end his career and put him behind bars for ten weeks. Kay had bet that his team would lose against Ipswich Town, a wager that entangled him in England's most sensational match-fixing investigation. In 1965 ten League professionals were found guilty, jailed and banned from playing for life. Former Scottish professional Jimmy Gauld was judged to be the ringleader and sentenced to four years, while others received sentences of between four and 15 months.

SEE ALSO **'PAOLO ROSSI IN MATCH-FIXING SCANDAL'** (page 374).

Tony Kay arrives at Mansfield magistrates court to hear his fate. He was to spend ten weeks behind bars for his crime.

JOCK STEIN ANSWERS CELTIC'S PRAYERS

Celtic hadn't been doing well. In fact, they'd gone eight years without a trophy, but just six weeks after Jock Stein became the first Protestant to manage the Catholic club, Celtic won the Scottish Cup. That was in 1965 and in 1967 he took the club to a Scottish domestic treble. Stein's greatest achievement, though, was in Europe and he guided Celtic past the mighty Inter Milan to win the 1967 European Cup and become the first British side to lift the trophy. Astonishing as it may seem, he achieved all this with local talent. All his players were born within 30 miles of Glasgow.

SEE ALSO **'CELTIC'S 'LIONS' ROAR'** (page 282).

Jock Stein meets his new players on his first day in charge. His arrival brought an almost immediate turnaround in Celtic's fortunes.

UNITED THEY FALL

To say the two Uniteds disliked each other would be a massive understatement. Manchester United and Leeds United had already clashed in the 1964-65 season and bad blood was boiling by the time they came to face each other in the sem- final of the FA Cup on 27 March 1965. Fouls flowed from both sides and an hour in all hell broke loose when a clash between Manchester United's Denis Law and Leeds United's Jack Charlton sparked an all-out brawl, leaving Law's shirt in tatters along with the reputation of both teams. The most telling scoreline in the goalless draw was Manchester United 24 fouls, Leeds ten.

SEE ALSO **'CANTONA JOINS MANCHESTER UNITED'** (page 465).

Players anxiously look for the loose ball in the Manchester United box during the FA Cup semi-final replay at Nottingham's City Ground.

SIR STANLEY BOWS OUT

Stanley Matthews played his final professional game on 6 February 1965, five days after his 50th birthday – and the 'Wizard of Dribble' still claimed he had retired too early. That last match was his 710th as a professional in a career that was split between Stoke City and Blackpool. In that time he was voted the Football Writers' Association's Footballer of the Year twice, European Footballer of the Year – and he was never booked. Such was his standing in the game that his testimonial on 28 April drew stars from around the world. Having earned a CBE during his playing career, Matthews was finally knighted in the year of his retirement.

SEE ALSO **'PETER THE GREAT HANGS UP HIS GLOVES'** (page 569).

Matthews hangs up his boots, appearing in an all-star Stoke City team for his testimonial. Changing alongside the old master is Jimmy Greaves.

Sepp Maier was the goalkeeper of the newly successful Bayern Munich team. He also kept goal for the West German national side.

BAYERN MUNICH STEP UP

When the German Football Association decided to establish the Bundesliga as its nation-wide professional football league, Bayern Munich were uncharacteristically in second place in their regional league. Stung by his club's failure to win promotion in the first year, chairman Wilhelm Neudecker drafted in the famed Yugoslavian coach Slatko Cajkovski to build a team that would go up. Enter Sepp Maier, Franz Beckenbauer and Gerd Muller as the axis of a young team that stormed to the Bundesliga in 1965, the second year of the premier division's life. From that point, Bayern Munich went on to become the league's most successful club, winning the championship 13 times.

SEE ALSO 'TASMANIA BERLIN PROVE THEY'RE NOT DEVILS' (page 262).

BLACK POWER EMERGES AT WEMBLEY

South African born Albert Johanneson was not the first black footballer to play in England, but he achieved the distinction of being the first to play at Wembley in an FA Cup final. The skilful left-winger was signed for Second Division Leeds United in 1961 and was a fixture in the side when it won promotion to the First Division in 1964. Johanneson's 1 May 1965 FA Cup final appearance against Liverpool turned out to be the high point of his career, for he was overshadowed over the next two seasons by new signing Eddy Gray and finally left for York City before retiring.

SEE ALSO 'ARTHUR WHARTON TURNS OUT FOR PRESTON' (page 31); 'VIV ANDERSON BECOMES ENGLAND'S FIRST BLACK INTERNATIONAL' (page 365).

Albert Johanneson spent nine years at Elland Road with Leeds United, but his historic Wembley appearance ended in disappointing defeat.

THE KOP'S FAMOUS ANTHEM

Between 1892 and 1965 the Reds had won six First Division titles, but the world's greatest knockout competition, the FA Cup remained elusive. After Liverpool edged out much-fancied Chelsea in the 1965 semi-final, fans were starting to believe, but due to a miserly allocation of just 15,000 final tickets for each club, many of the Kop faithful despaired of getting to Wembley. Although requests were pouring into Anfield from all over the world, legendary manager Bill Shankly declared, "Any tickets I've got are going to the boys on the Kop" – an expression of solidarity with fans who, for their part, had just adopted the Gerry and the Pacemakers hit 'You'll Never Walk Alone' as their terrace anthem. Liverpool beat Leeds United 2-1 to win the FA Cup for the first time in the club's history which was music to the Reds supporter's ears.

SEE ALSO **'LIVERPOOL MARCH ON'** (page 259).
'THREE LIONS ROARS TO NUMBER 1' (page 495).

In the end Liverpool beat Leeds 2-1 after extra-time and the players celebrated lifting the FA Cup for the first time in the club's 73 year history.

LIVERPOOL MARCH INTO INTER

It was only three days since the Reds had brought the FA Cup home from Wembley for the first time and Anfield was a wall of sound when on 4 May Italian champions Inter Milan took to the field for the first leg of the European Cup semi-final. The Kop was singing 'Go Back to Italy' to the tune of 'Santa Lucia' when after just four minutes Roger Hunt put Liverpool ahead. It was a quiet Kop that greeted Allesandro Mazzola's equalizer six minutes later, but goals from Ian Callaghan and Ian St John finally restored Anfield's spirits. Liverpool won 3-1. Liverpool travelled to the San Siro for the return leg in a confident mood but there they found Inter in inspired form. The Italian's triumphed 3-0 and went through to the final.

SEE ALSO **'DALGLISH KEY TO HISTORIC WIN'** (page 355).

Liverpool's Roger Hunt is thwarted by Inter Milan's Guarneri and Luis Suarez on the return leg which Inter triumphed 3-0

With a capacity of nearly 90,000 the San Siro in Milan is one of the most inspiring – and intimidating – theatres in world football.

BENFICA PLAY 89,011 ITALIANS

The San Siro is undoubtedly a great stadium, but for Portugal's Benfica in 1965 it was the lion's den. They had won through all the stages of that season's European Cup and were due to meet the powerful Internazionale in the final on 27 May. The problem was that UEFA had scheduled the final in the San Siro, the home ground shared by Internazionale and AC Milan. The Portuguese were furious at the choice of venue and even threatened to send their youth team unless UEFA relented. The protest was to no avail and despite a heroic performance before 89,000 fanatical Italian fans, they went down 1-0.

SEE ALSO **'ARGENTINA TIED UP IN TICKER TAPE'** (page 357).

Chelsea substitute Bert Murray watches from the sidelines on the first day that substitutes were allowed in the English Football League.

SUBS REDRESS THE BALANCE

There was a time when, once 22 men had been named for a match, come what may they were the only ones allowed to contest the game. If a cold sponge didn't do the trick, a team would battle on with ten players or less. However, when in the 1960s it became clear that results were being unbalanced by the inflexibility of the no-substitute rule the Football Association relented, allowing replacements for injury. History was made on 21 August 1965 when Charlton Athletic's Keith Peacock came on in place of injured goalkeeper Mike Rose 11 minutes into their away match against Bolton Wanderers.

SEE ALSO **"SUBSTITUTES' DENMARK WIN EUROPEAN CHAMPIONSHIP'** (page 460-1); **'MANCHESTER UNITED FIGHT BACK TO WIN TREBLE'** (page 526-7).

'WINGLESS WONDERS' LET FLY IN MADRID

Alf Ramsey was nothing if not a pragmatist, so when he found he had no worthy wingers for an England side in the build-up to the 1966 World Cup he designed a team without them. His innovative 4-3-3 formation was quickly dubbed the 'Wingless Wonders' by the sporting press, who witnessed its first outing during a friendly in Madrid on 8 December 1965. With a rock-solid defence and hard man Nobby Stiles helping to anchor the midfield, England attacked down the centre of the Bernabeu to beat Spain 2-0 with goals from striker Roger Hunt and England's 'Scottish Player', centre forward Joe Baker.

SEE ALSO **'CHARLTON KICK-STARTS ENGLAND'S WORLD CUP RUN'** (page 269).

Nobby Stiles, Manchester United player and member of England's World Cup team played a key role in the 'Wingless Wonders'.

TASMANIA BERLIN
PROVE THEY'RE NOT DEVILS

Unlikely Bundesliga newcomers, Tasmania Berlin, were never likely to do well among Germany's footballing elite. They'd managed to scrape through the promotion process from the regional leagues, but found themselves seriously outgunned in the country's premier league. Despite winning their opening game against Karlsruher SC they were destined to claim the dubious title of worst team in Bundesliga history, with just two wins in 34 games – a campaign during which they scored just eight goals and conceded 108. The lads from Berlin went back down to the Regionalliga Berlin the following season, never to emerge again.

SEE ALSO **'THIRD LANARK DIES'** (page 281).

Tasmania Berlin's Hans-Guenter Becker and Torwart Heinz Rohloff commiserate during a 1-5 defeat to Hamburger SV during 1965.

'RED MOSQUITOES'
MAKE IT TO ENGLAND

North Korea has not been a significant force in World Cup competitions over the years. Even when the tournament was held jointly in Japan and South Korea in 2002, a North Korean team stayed away, but it was not always so for the Red Mosquitoes. They had a brief moment in the sun when they came through the 1965 Asia qualifiers and made it to England for the final stages. Despite howls of protest from the South Koreans, a last-minute compromise by the British Foreign Office at the height of the Cold War cleared the North Koreans to play in England.

SEE ALSO **'ASIAN CONFEDERATION FORMED'** (page 189).
'NORTH KOREA'S 'RED MOSQUITOES' STING PORTUGAL...' (page 272).

North Korea players make their way onto the pitch before their FIFA sanctioned 20 minute training session ahead of their quarter-final.

WORLD CUP WILLIE STARTS A TREND

In the long procession of World Cup mascots, World Cup Willie, the happy little lion with punky red hair, leads the way. Willie was the first mascot to represent a World Cup tournament and many believe he was the best, although purists argue that his Union Jack vest did not accurately represent England's status as the host nation. Still, Willie's arrival on the football radar was remarkable enough to prompt skiffle star Lonnie Donegan to record a pop song in his honour and every host nation since has adopted the concept with a greater or lesser degrees of aesthetic success.

SEE ALSO 'WORLD CHAMPIONS BECOME CHART TOPPERS' (page 296).

1966

As part of the World Cup publicity World Cup Willie poses outside the FA headquarters in London.

FIFA president Sir Stanley Rous and other officials make the draw for the controversial World Cup Finals at the the Royal Garden Hotel.

AFRICAN NATIONS BOYCOTT THE WORLD CUP

North Korea's progress to the final group stages of the 1966 World Cup came as a surprise to most watchers of the game, but their success was due in no small part to a controversial FIFA decision to make teams from three confederations compete for a single place in the finals. Those confederations – Africa, Asia and Australia – branded the decision political discrimination and the Africans promptly withdrew. South Korea also pulled out after FIFA moved the Asian tournament from Japan to Cambodia, leaving only Australia and North Korea in contention. The Red Mosquitoes won the two-leg group play-off convincingly 6-1 and 3-1.

SEE ALSO **'FIRST AFRICAN REPRESENTATIVE IN THE WORLD CUP'** (page 336).

REFEREE ORDERS WALK OFF

Leo Horn was not a referee to trifle with. He was a judo black belt and during World War Two had fought with the Dutch Resistance, so when trouble broke out during the Leeds United versus Valencia Inter Cities Fairs' Cup match on 2 February, he was the man to sort it out. Fifteen minutes from time Jack Charlton had advanced in support of a Leeds attack when he was kicked and then punched by a Valencia player. The free-for-all that ensued brought police onto the field and Horn finally led the players off to let them cool down, while ordering Charlton and two Spaniards not to retake the field.

SEE ALSO **'THE BATTLE OF VALENCIA'** (page 610).

Dutchman Leo Horn ruled his matches with an iron fist and his actions here surely prevented a full-scale riot between both sides.

'EL BEATLE' IS BORN

It was the night that a legend was born. Manchester United had travelled to Lisbon on 9 March with a meticulous game-plan designed to protect their 3-2 first-leg lead against Benfica in the European Cup quarter final. However, within ten minutes a carefree George Best had put United 2-0 up, inspiring Manchester United to go on to win 5-1 – the first defeat Benfica had ever suffered in the European Cup at the Stadium of Light.

With such a result, United boss Sir Matt Busby could not be too upset that his carefully laid plans were ripped up by his mercurial young star. He said wryly afterwards, "Our plan was to be cautious, but somebody must have stuffed cotton wool in George's ears." The next day the newspapers featured Best pictured in a giant sombrero captioned 'El Beatle'– a tag taken up by the British press who fell over themselves to launch him as a style and sporting icon.

Six days after the Benfica match, Best added fuel to the media feeding frenzy when he and close Manchester City friend Mike Summerbee opened Edwardia, a men's fashion boutique in Sale. Such was Best's sex appeal that the opening of the shop drew 400 fans, mainly schoolgirls, who nearly broke the shop window in their eagerness to catch a glimpse of their hero. Best's style and huge public profile led to a modelling contract and a full rock 'n' roll way of life. He became legendary for his partying, but it was a lifestyle that was to quickly undermine his sporting career and ultimately his health.

SEE ALSO **'SENDING OFF IS NO JOKE FOR BEST'** (page 294); **'BEST ADDS CHEEK TO HIS REPERTOIRE'** (page 314).

Best's superlative performances coupled with his female following brought him a huge wave of press attention.

WORLD CUP STOLEN

On 20 March 1966 former soldier Edward Bletchley was jailed for the theft of the gold 12-inch World Cup Jules Rimet Trophy, but he claimed he was just the middle-man for the subsequent £15,000 ransom demand issued to the Football Association. No one witnessed the theft of the £30,000 trophy from the Methodist Central Hall, Westminster, where it was on display with a 'Sports with Stamps' display worth £3 million. The 20 March heist was timed to coincide with a church service in another part of the building, when guards had gone missing.

Bletchley was arrested when he went to pick up the ransom money and, while he claimed he didn't know where the trophy was, it's said he did a deal with police for information about the trophy's whereabouts in return for a prison visit from a lady friend. However, in the end it was four-year-old mongrel Pickles who sniffed out the statuette, wrapped in newspaper and lying in the street outside owner David Corbett's home in South Norwood. The trophy had been missing for just over a week.

SEE ALSO **'FA CUP STOLEN'** (page 39).

Pickles who discovered the lost trophy under a holly bush outside his owner's house, wearing the silver medal presented to him by the National Canine League.

REAL MADRID'S EUROPEAN CUP DOMINANCE ENDS

Real Madrid's decision in 1953 to begin signing international stars set the foundation for the club's success in both domestic and European competition. They won La Liga for the first time in 1954 and on many occasions after. This form was also transferred to European Cup competitions and an outstanding run between 1956 and 1960 saw the club win the European Cup five times, earning them the right to wear the UEFA Badge of Honour. Real's 2-1 win over Partizan Belgrade won them the competition for a sixth time in 1966, a feat they were not to achieve again for another 22 years.

SEE ALSO **'ZIDANE'S STUNNER SEALS CHAMPIONS LEAGUE TRIUMPH'** (page 555).

Real Madrid captain Francisco Gento kisses the European Cup after his team won it for the sixth time. And then began the drought.

FIFA PLANS FOR THE FUTURE

The top administrators of world soccer sat around a table to decide the future of the World Cup for the next 16 years. The main item on the agenda of the FIFA Congress was to pick venues for the 1970, 1974, 1978 and 1982 competitions. With the sport becoming more global dozens of countries had expressed an interest in staging a World Cup tournament, but were to be disappointed. In an era prior to mass air travel, FIFA decided to continue alternating between the continents with strong soccer power bases – Europe and South America. Mexico was picked for 1970, West Germany for 1974, Argentina for 1978 and Spain for 1982.

SEE ALSO **'FIRST WORLD CUP ON AFRICAN SOIL'** (page 617).

MEXICO 70

IX football world championship

may 31 – june 21

FIFA's long-term plan ensured that the World Cup would not become an event always held in Europe but one which would reflect its global reach.

TELEVISION MAKES HISTORY

England's match against Uruguay in front of 87,000 World Cup fans at Wembley Stadium on 11 July 1966 marked the start of a history-making tournament. It was the year the World Cup trophy was stolen; it was the year that England won the title for the first and so far only time; and it was the first time that television coverage featured action-replays. This revolutionary technique was the brainchild of Bryan Cowgill, the head of BBC Sport who was responsible for bringing sporting programmes Grandstand and Match of the Day to a grateful nation. Unfortunately, there were no goal replays in that England match as it ended 0-0.

SEE ALSO **'FOOTBALL ENTERS SPACE'** (page 299);
'FIRST LIVE LEAGUE MATCH IS TELEVISED' (page 395).

The new technology enhanced the game's TV appeal though debate still rages about whether replays should be used during the game.

BRAZIL SURVIVE BULGARIA ASSAULT

It was a great year for England, but a miserable one for World Cup-holders Brazil. They arrived for their opening match at Everton's Goodison Park on 12 July having had a build-up disrupted by internal team politics and met Bulgaria, who seemed more interested in inflicting pain than playing football. Pelé was a particular target, although two fouls on him resulted in the game's two goals – one by Pelé himself and the other from 'Little Bird' Garrincha. It was the last time the two Brazilian stars played together, ending a run of 40 winning matches for Brazil whenever the two teamed up.

SEE ALSO **'GARRINCHA AND PELÉ TEAM UP'** (page 219).

Pelé receives treatment from the Brazilian trainer as referee Kurt Tschenscher warns Bulgaria's hatchet men to watch their tackles.

BOBBY CHARLTON
KICK-STARTS WORLD CUP RUN

Mexico goalkeeper Ignacio Calderon is beaten by Bobby Charlton's thundering shot for the goal that set England on their way in 1966.

Manager Alf Ramsey had unshackled Bobby Charlton for England's second game in the 1966 World Cup tournament. In the 16 July match against Mexico he gave the Manchester United star a free-ranging role behind strikers Geoff Hurst and Roger Hunt – much deeper than in the disappointing first match against Uruguay – and Charlton responded. Picking up the ball deep in the 37th minute he ran 30 yards before unleashing a long-range screamer into the Mexicans' net. Hunt capped the day with a second goal 15 minutes from time, but it was Bobby's goal that convinced a hopeful nation that England could emerge as ultimate victors.

SEE ALSO **'RAY HOUGHTON SCORES WORLD CUP CRACKER'** (page 474).

NORTH KOREA MUG ITALY

North Korea goalkeeper Li Chan-myung is put under heavy pressure by the Italian centre forward but he managed to keep a clean sheet.

World Cup minnows North Korea were an unknown quantity when they arrived for their group four campaign in Middlesbrough, but a joyous attacking style soon won the crowds' hearts. They'd won one and lost one by the time they faced mighty Italy on 19 July and were riding high with chants of "Korea! Korea!" blasting from the stands. In the 33rd minute a powerful header bounced over a flat-footed Italian defence allowing striker Pak Doo-Ik to pounce and drive a half-volley low into the net. Chances of an unlikely Korean win improved further when injury reduced the Italians to ten men and they hung on for an historic victory.

SEE ALSO **'SOUTH KOREA SURPRISE ITALY'** (page 561).

Pelé looks accusingly at Portugal's Jose Augusto after being hacked down once more by a Portugal team intent on nullfying his threat.

PELÉ AND BRAZIL CHOPPED DOWN

By the time Brazil came to play their final World Cup group game, they had been rocked by a loss to Hungary and badly needed a win. On 19 July Pelé was thrown into the fray, even though he was still carrying injuries from his brutal encounter with Bulgaria, and from the start Portugal set out to make sure his threat was neutralised. Close marking did part of the job and gruesome tackles did the rest. English referee George McCabe failed to protect Pelé from punishment that included two particularly murderous fouls by Joao Morais, who many believed should have been sent off. Brazil collapsed to a 3-1 defeat.

SEE ALSO 'MARADONA MARKED OUT OF THE GAME AGAINST ITALY' (page 385).

The Italian team could not escape the wave of public criticism that followed their weak showing and early exit from the World Cup.

AZZURRI RETURN RED-FACED

North Korea's Red Mosquitoes had dumped them out in the first group stage of the 1966 World Cup and the Italian stars were understandably nervous about their reception back home. Hoping to sneak back unnoticed, on 20 July the disgraced Azzurri persuaded the authorities to divert their charter flight to Genoa instead of Milan, but the subterfuge was to no avail. News of their rescheduled arrival plans was leaked to the local Genoese fans by a mysterious character going under the nom de guerrre of 'Christoforo Colombo' and the footballers got their airport reception after all. It consisted of enthusiastic jeering and a hail of tomatoes and eggs.

SEE ALSO 'SORRY ARGENTINA CRASH OUT IN FIRST ROUND' (page 560).

GREEN LIGHT FOR RED AND YELLOW CARDS

Referee Konstantin Zecevic sends off Argentina's Jorge Albrecht as his team-mates complain about the decision by surrounding the official.

England's bad-tempered quarter-final with Argentina in the 1996 World Cup quarter-finals was historic in more ways than one. On the surface, England's win allowed the host nation to proceed to ultimate victory, but behind the scenes it sparked an idea for language-neutral symbol cards. Referees' commissioner Ken Aston had become aware of the language difficulties that had caused so much trouble during the game and was mulling over the problem on his drive home. The stop-start journey through a succession of traffic lights provided him with the inspiration for a warning yellow card and the final red, although the idea wasn't actually adopted for another ten years.

SEE ALSO 'RED CARD FOR PROFESSIONAL FOUL' (page 438).

JACK CHARLTON'S SURPRISE BOOKING

Charlton was as surprised as anyone to find out that he had received a booking during the grudge match between England and Argentina.

The 1996 World Cup quarter-final between England and Argentina was the footballing equivalent of the Falklands War conducted in the Tower of Babel. Neither side understood what the other was saying and with little or no command of either language German referee Rudolf Kretlein was no better off. He did his best to maintain control, but such was the fast and furious engagement that confusion reigned. Jack Charlton was astonished to read in the next morning's newspapers that he had been booked during the game and had to phone the tournament press office to find out whether it was true or not. It was.

SEE ALSO 'CHARLTON'S 'LITTLE BLACK BOOK' OF REVELATIONS' (page 310); 'THREE YELLOWS FOR GRAHAM POLL' (page 601).

1966

RATTIN'S RANT ROW

England's quarter-final clash with Argentina in the 1966 World Cup took on the flavour of a diplomatic incident when Argentina's captain Antonio Rattin was banished from the pitch ten minutes before the end of the first half. German referee Rudolf Kretlein cited "violence of the tongue" as the reason for the dismissal, following a sustained haranguing by Rattin who was demanding explanations for decisions, despite the fact that neither man understood a word the other was saying. England manager Alf Ramsey was so disgusted with the spectacle he refused to allow his players to swap shirts and branded the Argentinians "animals".

SEE ALSO 'BUTCHER AND MARADONA MEET FOR DRUGS TEST' (page 417).

Antonio Rattin gets his marching orders from Rudolf Kretlein after strongly disputing a decision that had gone against his side.

1966

NORTH KOREA'S 'RED MOSQUITOES' STING PORTUGAL...

On 23 July nobody believed North Korea could beat Portugal in the 1966 World Cup quarter-finals – except the North Koreans. Self-belief and a high-energy attacking style saw the Asian side rock the Portuguese with a goal after just one minute. After twenty minutes the 41,780 fans at Goodison Park, Liverpool, were convinced they were witnessing soccer history. The scoreboard read 1000-1 outsiders North Korea 3, Portugal 0. The 'Red Mosquitoes' of Communist Korea had the tournament third favourites rocking with their thrilling series of 'lightning horse' attacks and clinical finishing.

SEE ALSO "RED MOSQUITOES' MAKE IT TO ENGLAND' (page 262); 'TURKEY SCORE FASTEST GOAL IN WORLD CUP HISTORY' (page 564).

A North Korea player celebrates after his side scored their second goal to go 2-0 up. An historic World Cup shock was on the cards.

... BUT EUSEBIO SCORES FOUR

However, Portugal's brilliant and inspirational Eusebio kept his head and launched a one-man rescue act, which saw him exploiting North Korea's defensive frailties. With half an hour gone the Portuguese young gun had had enough. Within two minutes he'd scored one, then a second with a penalty just before half-time. In the second half he took his hat-trick in the 56th minute and a final fourth from the penalty spot. Jose Augusto completed Portugal's great escape with a fifth goal 12 minutes before the whistle.

Despite losing their commanding lead the 'Red Mosquitoes' left the ground as heroic underdogs and returned to Pyongyang to delirious celebrations and a special commendation from President Kim Il-sung. According to conspiracy theorists the players then 'disappeared' because their collapse against Portugal was blamed on a pre-match night of partying – an act deemed 'bourgeois' and 'symbolic of corrupt western imperialism'. The government has denied that many of the squad spent 20 years in an internment camp.

Eusebio claws a goal back for Portugal. At 1-3 the stage was set for a stirring comeback.

SEE ALSO **'IVORY COAST LEADER THREATENS NATIONAL TEAM WITH MILITARY SERVICE'** (page 532).

Eusebio's strong performances and one-man rescue act against North Korea had made him a transfer target for Europe's biggest clubs.

INTER MILAN ROW OVER EUSEBIO

His position as top scorer at the 1966 World Cup and his four-goal rescue act against North Korea brought Portugal's Eusebio to the attention of top Italian clubs. Accusations of 'tapping up' flew from the striker's club, Benfica of Lisbon, and although nothing was ever proved, at the time the Italians were famous for the amounts of money they had available to attract top international stars. The spat obviously didn't unsettle Eusebio, who stayed at Benfica for 16 years, making 301 appearances and scoring 317 goals. He spent his later years in the North America League with a number of US and Canadian clubs

SEE ALSO **'FOOTBALL'S GREATEST STAR LANDS STATESIDE'** (page 344-5).

Charlton strikes home the winner that signalled the end of Portugal's participation in the World Cup and won England a place in the final.

LOSERS APPLAUD CHARLTON'S DOUBLE

Professional appreciation of a fine performance was behind the post-match hands proffered to Bobby Charlton by Portugal's players, because the goals of the midfielder/striker with the famous and ferocious rocket shot had ensured England a place in the World Cup final at Wembley. Charlton opened the scoring against Portugal on 26 July with a crisp side-footed finish after a run by Roger Hunt had forced the Portuguese goalkeeper to come out of his goal. Charlton's winner – after Eusebio had equalized – was a sweetly-struck shot created by a run and pull-back from Geoff Hurst.

SEE ALSO **'OLD TRAFFORD RISES TO ACKNOWLEDGE A MASTER'** (page 569).

LAST KICK EQUALIZER
DASHES ENGLAND HOPES

A collective "Oh no!" could be heard over England. It was 30 July and with just
15 seconds of the World Cup final to go the England team stood crestfallen as
West Germany's Wolfgang Weber snatched away the Jules Rimet trophy. Stealthy
Weber had equalized to send the 1966 World Cup final into extra-time. England,
overcoming an early 13th-minute West Germany goal by Haller, has fought back
to lead 2-1 through goals by Hurst and Peters, and appeared to have their hands
on the trophy for the first time. Weber, if only temporarily, broke their hearts with
his last-minute strike.

SEE ALSO 'FRANCE FIGHT BACK WITH TWO INJURY-TIME GOALS' (page 580).

Wolfgang Weber guides the
equalizing goal past England's
Gordon Banks to take the final
into extra-time.

GOAL LINE CONTROVERSY ENRAGES GERMANS

At the height of the Cold War, it was somewhat unusual to have a kind word for a Russian, but the England team did in a goal controversy that was to rage into the 21st century. On 30 July in the 100th minute of the 1966 World Cup final, and with the scores at 2-2, England midfielder Alan Ball crossed for striker Geoff Hurst, homing in on the near post, to hammer a shot towards the West German goal. It struck the underside of the bar, bounced down and then out of the goal – but on which side of the chalk line did it land? The nearest England player to the ball was Roger Hunt who, believing it to be a goal, wheeled away in celebration, but many thought that he should have stayed to tap the ball back over the line. The furious Germans were adamant it was no goal and Swiss referee Gottfried Dienst was unsure. Enter Soviet linesman Tofik Bakhramov, who was very sure, and the goal was awarded, giving England a 3-2 lead to defend for the next 20 minutes. With television coverage in its relative infancy the action replays of the day failed to prove if the ball had crossed the line or not and even in the computer age 40 years on attempts to ascertain if the ball did indeed cross the line have failed to be conclusive and it remains a major talking point.

SEE ALSO **"BALL OVER THE LINE' CUP FINAL CONTROVERSY'** (page 102); **'TELEVISION MAKES HISTORY'** (page 268).

Geoff Hurst lashes the ball past Willi Schulz to score England's highly controversial third goal.

RAMSEY'S STIRRING WORDS

England's controversial third goal was 100% proof of manager Alf Ramsey's inspirational powers. Striker Geoff Hurst was just one England player to have taken Ramsey's motivational words to heart and his goal set deflated English players back on a World Cup-winning path after German Wolfgang Weber had equalized with just 15 seconds of the first 90 minutes to go. With 30 minutes of extra time looming, and with the calm demeanour of an English gentleman, Ramsey prepared his team for more effort in a game they thought they had won. He firmly told them they had already won it once; but they had the skills to go out and do it again. He is quoted as saying, "You let it slip. Now start again."

SEE ALSO **'AT 2-0 IN THE WORLD CUP FINAL'** (page 194).

After conceding such a late equalizer Ramsey had his work cut out to motivate players who thought they had the match won in normal time.

AND THEN IT WAS ALL OVER

BBC commentator Kenneth Wolstenhome could not have imagined that an off-the-cuff comment would become part of soccer folklore. England striker Geoff Hurst's hat-trick finale to the 1966 World Cup final inspired one of the most famous pieces of commentary. As the West Ham player raced clear of the chasing West German defence some fans thought the final whistle had gone and dashed onto the pitch to celebrate a 3-2 England win. Wolstenhome reported, "Some people are on the pitch. They think it's all over." Then, after pausing as Hurst blasted the ball home again for a 4-2 win, Wolstenhome confirmed it with the words, "It is now."

SEE ALSO **'WEST GERMANY'S SWEET REVENGE'** (page 287).

There were no complaints about Geoff Hurst's emphatic finish to seal his hat-trick. The fourth England goal ended the German challenge.

DORTMUND RESTORE GERMAN PRIDE

A 2-1 win in extra-time at Hampden Park, Glasgow, did more than take the 1966 European Cup Winners' Cup for Borussia Dortmund. The victory over Liverpool gave a West German team a major European trophy for the first time and also restored German pride after TSV 1860 Munich had lost in the previous year's final to West Ham. German teams were major players in the European Cup Winners' Cup every year between 1965 and 1968 with varying degrees of success. Bayern Munich retained it in 1967, but Hamburger SV lost in the 1968 final.

SEE ALSO **'DORTMUND BEAT JUVENTUS'** (page 505).

Jubilant Borussia Dortmund celebrate. Holding the cup aloft is captain Wolfgang Paul. Standing next to him is manager Herr Multhaup.

AJAX WRECK LIVERPOOL'S EUROPEAN DREAM

In the 1966-67 season a 19-year-old Johann Cruyff gave a clue as to his future influence in football when his contribution to a European Cup second round match helped to destroy Liverpool. Cruyff's Ajax side overwhelmed English champions Liverpool in a 5-1 first-round win played in foggy weather conditions at the Olympic Stadium, Amsterdam, on 7 December. Liverpool, were unable to haul back the deficit in the second leg at their home ground and could only manage a 2-2 draw, so their European Cup debut ended with a defeat on a 3-7 aggregate.

In 1966 Cruyff, who was later to play a pivotal part in the Dutch 'total football' system of the 1970s, already had a Dutch championship medal and Holland international caps to his name.

SEE ALSO **'AJAX'S FIRST STEP TO EUROPEAN DOMINATION'** (page 315).

Inspired by the young Johan Cruyff Ajax were just embarking on their most successful period in the club's long history.

SCOTS CLAIM 'WORLD CHAMPION' STATUS

Fanatical Scotland supporters claimed unofficial world champion status for their country when they humiliated the 'Auld Enemy' England in a 3-2 win at Wembley on 15 March. England was on a high after winning the World Cup in 1966 and the Scotland setback was their first defeat since becoming world champions. The Scots' hero was midfielder Jim Baxter who ran the show, mocking the English team with all manner of trickery and cheeky moves. Scotland scored through Denis Law, Bobby Lennox and Jim McCalliog in front of a crowd of 99,063, swelled by a big and vociferous 'Tartan Army' which had travelled from north of the border.

SEE ALSO **'SCOTS INVADE WEMBLEY PITCH'** (page 450).

Scotland's Denis Law is congratulated by an ecstatic Scotland fan after his team's 3-2 victory over the reigning World Champions.

THIRD LANARK DIES

Two events in the month of April fatally injured Scottish Second Division side Third Lanark. Its Cathkin Park ground in Glasgow recorded its lowest ever attendance – 297 people in a game against Clydebank – before a 5-1 defeat to Dumbarton ended the involvement in soccer of the club nicknamed the 'Hi Hi' as a senior professional outfit. Ironically the Thirds were just five years short of their centenary. A subsequent Board of Trade investigation revealed core problems, such as constant player squabbles and bitter internal wrangles for power among board members. A liquidator was appointed and a club which never really made the big time in Scottish football was no more.

SEE ALSO **'LEEDS UNITED – THE RISE BEFORE THE FALL'** (page 547).

Third Lanark chairman James Reilly welcomes new manager Bobby Shearer in 1967. It wasn't enough to save the club from going under.

1967

Celtic's Stevie Chalmers turns away after scoring the winning goal past Inter goalkeeper Sarti.

Captain Billy McNeill lifts the Cup on a famous night in Lisbon.

CELTIC'S 'LIONS' ROAR

A shot deflected home by Steve Chalmers claimed the European Cup for a Scottish side for the first and, to date, only time on 25 May 1967. Celtic became the first British side to win the trophy when they beat Inter Milan 2-1 in front of 45,000 people in Lisbon. The narrow margin of the win disguised the attacking supremacy of the Celtic team, a performance which won them the title 'Lions of Lisbon'.

Celtic, whose players all came from within a 30-mile radius of Glasgow, were a goal down to a penalty inside eight minutes, but manager Jock Stein ordered an all-out attack. The Italians went into familiar deep defensive mode and were saved by the heroics of goalkeeper Sarti and the woodwork. The breakthrough came with a goal by rampaging full-back Tommy Gemmell, before Chalmers' touching-in of Bobby Murdoch's long-range shot won the match. Delirious Celtic fans invaded the pitch and many players lost their shirts to souvenir hunters.

SEE ALSO 'NEW BOY O'NEILL INSPIRES CELTIC' (page 537).

GOALKEEPER TURNS GOALSCORER

Northern Ireland international goalkeeper Pat Jennings could not have picked a better stage to open his goal-scoring account. He chose the traditional season-opening showpiece Charity Shield match to score a historic goal for his FA Cup-winning team Tottenham Hotspur against League champions Manchester United. Jennings' amazing kick upfield from his own goal area gave Spurs a 3-3 draw, but, although he was a powerful kicker, his punt was grabbed by a strong wind. This bamboozled the Manchester United defence and left United goalkeeper Alex Stepney embarrassed as the ball eluded his grasp and dropped into the net 80 yards from where Jennings had launched it.

Alan Gilzean of Tottenham celebrates as United goalkeeper Alex Stepney looks dejected at being beaten by Jenning's speculative punt.

SEE ALSO 'HIGUITA'S SCORPIAN KICK' (page 490); 'JIMMY GLASS – ZERO TO HERO IN 12 MONTHS' (page 525).

VIOLENCE DOGS INTERCONTINENTAL CUP

International soccer relations hit a new low with five players sent off in an Intercontinental Cup match between European Cup winners Celtic and South American champions Racing Club of Argentina. In a torrid night at Hampden Park, Glasgow, on 18 October foul tackles flew and tempers flared in a volatile night that showed the seamier side of football. The Argentinians won 1-0 over two legs. The match had further ramifications as the competition became dogged by foul play throughout the late 1960s and indeed the reputation of the world club championship became so tarnished that by the 1970s some European teams refused to take part.

Celtic's Jimmy Johnstone receives attention from trainer Neil Mochan as Celtic players surround the referee during the ill-tempered game.

SEE ALSO 'ANGLO-ITALIAN ANIMOSITY SPILLS OVER' (page 310).

Jimmy Greaves strike ratio was enviable. He turned out 321 times for Tottenham Hotspur between 1961-1970 and scored 220 goals.

GREAVES IS TOPS – YET AGAIN

In 1966-67 Jimmy Greaves, one of English football's most naturally gifted strikers, was once again the English Football League's leading goal scorer with 25 strikes in 38 matches. Ironically Greaves' sparkling form for his club Tottenham Hotspur coincided with his final appearance in an England shirt, in a narrow win over Austria. However, Greaves' goal-scoring prowess did not propel Spurs to an all-conquering season. With Greaves and fellow striker Alan Gilzean in form Spurs were favourites for a repeat of the 1961 League and Cup double season and although they won the FA Cup in 1967, the team came only third in the League and didn't make an impression in the European Cup Winners' Cup.

SEE ALSO **'UWE SEELER RETIRES FROM HAMBURG'** (page 318).

Josef Masopust of Czechoslovakia. In the same year that he reached the World Cup final, he was named European Footballer of the Year.

CZECH STAR MOVES ON

Handshakes signalled the winding down of the glittering playing career of one of Czechoslovakia's greatest players. Josef Masopust was leaving the country where he had been the midfield general at club and international level for almost two decades. After handshakes all round, Masopust, who fans said "slalomed" through defences, settled in Belgium as the player-coach of Molenbeek. He quickly established his coaching credentials by taking the team into the Belgian First Division. Masopust had previously spent his club career with Dukla Prague and played 63 times for his country, including the 1962 World Cup final defeat to Brazil.

SEE ALSO **'PANENKA – THE SHOOT-OUT HERO'** (page 348).

'BIG BILL' SAVES UNITED

The big occasion needed a big man and Manchester United had just the guy. Bill Foulkes, a six-foot tall ex-miner, left the United defence dubbed the 'wall of steel' to score a goal against Real Madrid. It could not have been more vital as it gave United a 3-3 draw in Spain and, having won the first leg of the European Cup semi-final 1-0 at Old Trafford, a place in the final. Foulkes had been a rock at the heart of Manchester United defence for 18 years and had survived the Munich air crash in 1958.

SEE ALSO **'TEARS AS UNITED ARE CROWNED'** (page 286),

Foulkes played 566 times for Manchester United but was only capped once by England.

TEARS AS UNITED ARE CROWNED

Two men who had been through so much together wept as, on 29 May 1968, Manchester United became champions of Europe. This tearful moment for United manager Matt Busby and player Bobby Charlton was all the more poignant for them because they had survived the Munich air crash that, ten years before, had wiped out the famous Busby Babes.

The English champions had swept aside Benfica 4-1 in a match watched by 100,000 at Wembley and approximately 250 million on TV worldwide. Fittingly, Charlton set United on the road to victory with a first-half goal, but a Eusebio equalizer saved Benfica and took the game forward into extra-time. The mercurial George Best was literally at his 'best' on this occasion and tormented Benfica's defenders with his runs. He put United in front by cheekily rounding the goalkeeper and tapping the ball over the line. Then 19-year-old Brian Kidd and, appropriately, Charlton, scored to clinch an English side's first European Cup success.

SEE ALSO **'THE MUNICH AIR CRASH'** (page 212).

Matt Busby celebrates with Brian Kidd and Bill Foulkes on a night of high emotion at Wembley.

Three England players are unable to prevent Franz Beckenbauer's strike that gave West Germany their first ever victory over an England side.

WEST GERMANY'S SWEET REVENGE

It might have taken them a year and it may have been a friendly, but West Germany finally gained revenge for their 1966 World Cup final defeat to England. When, on 1 June 1968, the Germans claimed their first win over England after 38 years of trying, both teams featured only a handful of players from the 1966 encounter, though, and ironically it was ironically it was a defensive player who settled the game. Franz Beckenbauer scored the only goal of the game in front of a 79,208 crowd in Hanover.

SEE ALSO **'MULLER WINS WORLD CUP AND RETIRES WITH 68 GOALS'** (page 341).

England midfielder Alan Mullery trudges back to the dressing room after being sent off in the final minute of England's 1-0 defeat

MULLERY'S UNWELCOME RECORD

A moment of madness in Italy put a major stain on the footballing CV of England's Alan Mullery – and England's international record. The no-nonsense midfielder boiled over in a European Championship semi-final against Yugoslavia on 5 June and he became the first England player to be sent off in a full international. A kick by Trivic was the final straw after Mullery had endured 89 minutes of persistent fouling. He retaliated and was sent off a minute from the end of the game. Yugoslavia won 1-0, ending the World Cup winners' bid for a second major title in two years, and England had to be satisfied with third place in the tournament.

SEE ALSO **'BECKHAM SEES RED'** (page 515).

The Italy squad of 1968 was talented but had to rely on a very unorthodox means of breaking the deadlock to reach the final.

LUCK FLIPS ITALY INTO FINAL

Italy needed Lady Luck to stay on the path to their first major soccer title for 30 years in the newly- named European Championships. The Azzurris' 5 June semi-final against the Soviet Union was decided on the toss of a coin after the two sides were deadlocked at 0-0. Luck certainly didn't favour the Soviet team, despite the fact that they had their talismanic keeper Lev Yashin in goal. They went on to lose the third and fourth-place decider to England 2-0. The 1968 tournament was also unusual in having two-legged quarter-finals with the semi-finals held in the host country, Italy.

SEE ALSO 'REPLAY CLINCHES EUROPEAN CROWN' (page 288); 'SOVIET UNION WIN FIRST EUROPEAN CHAMPIONSHIPS' page 234).

Italy's Luigi Riva opens the scoring beating Yugoslavia goalkeeper Pantelic with a fierce drive to set Italy on the way to victory in Rome.

REPLAY CLINCHES EUROPEAN CROWN

Jubilant Italy needed a second attempt to win the 1968 European Championship and the game went into the history books as the only international final ever to be decided on a replay. Italy, desperate to end their 30-year gap between major international titles, had frustrated a dominant Yugoslavia in the first match in Rome on 8 June, which ended 1-1. The teams returned to the same stadium two days later where the hosts took advantage of a tired Yugoslavian side and strolled to a 2-0 win with a goal from Luigi Riva in 12 minutes – the fastest goal of the tournament – and Pietro Anastasi on 31 minutes.

SEE ALSO 'ITALIAN WOMEN TAKE THE LEAD' (page 295).

ORDER OF LENIN
AWARDED TO 'BLACK SPIDER'

In 1968 Lev Yashin, the man credited with bringing a new dominance to the penalty area, received his country's highest honour, the Order of Lenin, for his services to Soviet football from Soviet leader Leonid Brezhnev. He played for Dynamo Moscow, his only club, for 22 seasons and in winning 78 caps for his country played in three World Cups. A great ambassador for Russian soccer, he won a football gold medal at the 1956 Olympics and remains the only goalkeeper named European Player of the Year – in 1963. In 1999, nine years after his death, he was voted Russia's athlete of the century.

SEE ALSO **'SOVIETS LEFT OUT IN THE COLD'** (page 330).

Yashin was nicknamed the 'Black Spider' due to his distinctive all-black kit and the belief that he must have eight arms to make so many incredible saves.

PASS MASTER
RIVERA DESTROYS AJAX

A bravura performance by midfielder Gianni Rivera inspired AC Milan to their second European Cup on 28 May 1968. Pass after pass from the talented playmaker found its mark as the Italian champions overwhelmed an Ajax side which boasted the legendary Johan Cruyff in its line-up. On a warm night in Madrid, the Italians romped to a 4-1 win, with Rivera setting up two of his side's four goals. In fact, Rivera's masterful performance against the Dutch champions proved to be a high-water mark for him and he was voted the European Footballer of the Year – only the second Italian player to achieve this accolade.

SEE ALSO '**PASS MASTER MARADONA SHOWS THE BRAZILIANS**' (page 443).

Gianni Rivera stands second on the left of the back row. His accurate and lethal passing allowed Milan to tear apart the Dutch champions.

PENALTY SHOOT-OUTS
MAKE THEIR DEBUT

George Best's low shot to the right heralded a controversial change in English soccer. The penalty shoot-out had arrived and it was apt that one of the game's most colourful characters should strike home the first one. Best converted the first penalty as Manchester United beat Hull City in a Watney Cup semi-final on 5 August, a month after FIFA had sanctioned shoot-out deciders to games. Brian Kidd and Bobby Charlton also scored, but the normally deadly striker Denis Law became the first player to miss in a shoot-out. In another first, the Hull goalkeeper became the first custodian to take a penalty in a shoot-out, but he missed.

SEE ALSO '**FIRST EVER WORLD CUP PENALTY SHOOT-OUT**' (page 388).

Denis Law holds the unwelcome distinction of being the first player to experience the heartbreak of failing to convert in a shoot-out.

FOOTBALL MATCH SPARKS WAR

It all began innocuously enough with Honduran fans throwing stones at the hotel windows of the El Salvadoran national team on the night before their countries met in Tegucigalpa. The El Salvadorans slept badly and lost 1-0 on 8 June, causing distraught fan Amelia Bolanios to shoot herself. In their quest to reach the 1970 World Cup finals the teams met again in San Salvador, and this time the Hondurans were harassed and lost 3-0. Honduran fans raced for the border, but several died. The ensuing war lasted only 100 hours, but left over 6000 dead, 15,000 injured and thousands homeless. A peace treaty was finally signed 11 years later.

SEE ALSO **'WAR SUSPENDS FOOTBALL'** (page 81);
'WHEN FOOTBALL BECAME PURE MURDER' (page 433).

Soldiers point their machine guns towards Honduras from a frontier post near El Poy, El Salvador during the conflict.

1969

PELÉ'S 1000TH GOAL

Who knows how many of the thousands in the crowd realized it at the time, but when the great Pelé struck a 77th-minute goal in Rio de Janeiro's magnificent Maracana Stadium on 19 November he was notching up yet another career high. The strike for his Santos team was Pelé's thousandth in all competitions, national and international. Fittingly, it sealed a 2-1 win over his club's arch rivals Vasco de Gama, but it was not the end of the Brazilian's scoring prowess and he continued scoring for Santos and after that the New York Cosmos.

At club level Pelé was a lethal predator and scored prolifically from all areas of the pitch. He missed few penalties and no goalkeeper relished the one-to-one confrontation with him. Many of Pelé's greatest goals were captured by the world's TV cameras on the international stage and he scored 78 for his country in 91 international appearances. Both his goals and his general vision brought success for the teams he played within, culminating in the World Cup triumphs for Brazil in 1958, 1962 and 1970.

SEE ALSO **'BRAZIL HERO FRIEDENREICH RETIRES'** (page 125); **'FOOTBALL'S GREATEST STAR LANDS STATESIDE'** (page 344-5).

Pelé's 1000th goal – a penalty kick – was captured in this photographic sequence.

1969

SENDING OFF NO JOKE FOR BEST

With a flick of the wrist George Best landed himself in trouble – once again – with the football authorities. As the Manchester United player walked off the pitch after a frustrating 3 December League Cup semi-final against Manchester City, he flipped the ball out of referee Jack Taylor's hands. Best, who had been booked in the game, claimed it was a playful gesture, but the ref reported the player's action to the Football Association. The result was a four-week suspension and a £100 fine. Lowly Northampton Town were the victims of Best's enforced rest when, on his return, he scored a record-equalling six goals in an 8-2 FA Cup win.

SEE ALSO **'BEST ADDS CHEEK TO HIS REPERTOIRE'** (page 314); **'DI CANIO BANNED FOR PUSH'** (page 520).

Best flanked by team mates argues his case but referee Taylor is in no mood to show leniency.

FOXED BY A DUCK

The outsize gloves of Sepp Maier grasped arguably more silverware than most goalkeepers could hope for in a playing career. Regarded by critics as clown-like with his large gloves and over-long shorts, Maier was a legend in West Germany during the 1970s, when he played 437 times for Bayern Munich and 95 for his country. He won World Cup, European Championship and three successive European Cup medals for club or country, but the giant gloves were no match for a duck which wandered onto the pitch during a Bayern game. Maier went duck-hunting, but the bird eluded the keeper's every dive and provided some much-needed entertainment in a dull game.

SEE ALSO **'SEAGULL MEETS ITS MATCH'** (page 312).

Sepp Maier was a formidable and easily recognisable figure in the Bayern Munich and West Germany goalmouth during the 1970's.

ITALIAN WOMEN TAKE THE LEAD

Enlightened authorities in Italy were the first to sanction women being paid to play football and it was a major landmark for the women's game when female part-time professionals were allowed. Women's football had been played for a long time, with records of matches in Scotland in 1892 and England in 1895, and although it was frowned upon by football associations in many countries it continued without their support. However, despite the Italian breakthrough, progress was slow for women in soccer and the USA only formed a full-time national squad in 1984, with Japan the first country to have a professional women's league in 1992.

SEE ALSO **'THE WOMEN'S WORLD CUP ARRIVES'** (page 455); **'WOMEN'S FIRST PROFESSIONAL LEAGUE'** (page 445).

Women's football has a long history in many countries but Italy was the first to allow professionalism – albeit in a part-time fashion.

WORLD CHAMPIONS BECOME CHART TOPPERS

"Back home, they'll be thinking about us when we are far away. Back home, they'll be really behind us in every game we play..." sang the 1970 England World Cup squad on the popular music programme Top of the Pops prior to their departure for Mexico. The squad, many of them from the side that won the World Cup in 1966, had been invited, some reluctantly, into the recording studios to record 'Back Home', a two minutes and two seconds song which turned into a phenomenon by becoming the first football song to make number one in the British pop charts. It stayed in the hit parade for 17 weeks.

SEE ALSO **'THREE LIONS ROARS TO NUMBER ONE'** (page 495); **'GAZZAMANIA'** (page 447).

Companion album 'The World Beaters Sing World Beaters' reached number 4 in the charts. It included contemporary hits like 'Sugar Sugar'.

'TOTAL FOOTBALL' ARRIVES

The wall of cheers that greeted a lobbed shot by Ove Kindvall into the Celtic net signalled the arrival of Dutch supremacy. 'Total football', the concept conceived in Holland which means all ten outfield players are comfortable in any position, was poised to revolutionise the game. Kindvall's winning goal in extra-time on 6 May 1970 in Milan's San Siro Stadium gave his side Feyenoord a 2-1 victory and brought the European Cup to a Dutch club for the first time. With rival Ajax waiting in the wings to win the trophy for the next three years, the future was definitely orange.

SEE ALSO **'HOLLAND SHOW THEIR PEDIGREE'** (page 425).

Feyenoord players celebrate with the European Cup after their 2-1 victory which proved Ajax weren't the only top side in Holland.

Yellow and red cards made their debut in the 1970 World Cup tournament and quickly became a fixture of the modern game.

MEN IN BLACK GO FOR COLOUR

Traffic lights provided the inspiration for a change in the rules that transformed football. The red and yellow card system for disciplining players was introduced at the 1970 World Cup – and all because English referee Ken Aston had been stuck at traffic lights in his car. As he waited, it dawned on him that the sequence from red to amber could be a simple way of conveying a ref's decision to crowds. Along with allowing substitutions for the first time, the cards – yellow for a caution and red for dismissal – made their debut in Mexico and, while a few yellows were brandished, no one was sent off

SEE ALSO **'RED CARD FOR A PROFESSIONAL FOUL'** (page 438).

Despite being embroiled in an off-pitch scandal, Bobby Moore proved his reputation as a world class defender was justified in Mexico.

MOORE ESCAPES JAIL AND TACKLES DOUBTERS

A precision tackle on one of the world's most lethal strikers showed England fans at the Mexico World Cup that captain Booby Moore was back. Only days before, the man who led England to the 1966 World Cup had been languishing in a police cell in Colombia, accused of stealing a bracelet. Freed by a judge to play pending further investigation, Moore joined up with the England squad and, looking fit despite his worries, led them to a win over Romania. The precision tackle on eventual tournament top-scorer Jairzinho proved not only his physical strength but also his mental resilience had not suffered.

SEE ALSO **'BLOODIED KEEGAN GETS HIS REVENGE – ON THE PITCH'** (page 333).

RALLYING CALL FOR GREAVES

Former England goal poacher Jimmy Greaves' first sight of World Cup host country Mexico was through the visor of a crash helmet and a cloud of dust. Greaves, his international career over and club prospects waning, was a participant in the first World Cup Rally. In the drive from London to Mexico he finished sixth in a Ford Escort. Driving on several continents, the rally was more gruelling than rallies had been up to this point and it included long, timed sections of up to 650 miles. Greaves' verdict? "Harder than any football match."

SEE ALSO 'ELECTRONIC BUGGIES BECOME A WORLD CUP FEATURE' (page 474).

Jimmy Greaves tries his hand at rally driving in Surrey before setting off on his mammoth trip across six continents to Mexico City.

'TELSTAR' TAKES FLIGHT

The kick-off in the opening match of the 1970 World Cup hastened in a new era in match balls. As Mexico faced the USSR, out went the old brown and misshapen balls, which were heavy and painful to head when wet. In came the Adidas Telstar, light and almost perfectly round. The Telstar – 32 hand-stitched panels of 12 black pentagons and 20 white hexagons – also became the World Cup official match ball for TV reasons. Mexico 1970 was the first live televised World Cup and the revolutionary design of Telstar – the name contrived from 'star of television' – made the ball far more visible on screen.

SEE ALSO 'WHOSE BALL FOR THE FINAL?' (page 115); 'WHITE BALL INTRODUCED' (page 179).

Italy's Alessandro Mazzola and Brazil's Brito and Gerson all tangle for the new Telstar ball with it's distinctive panels clearly visible.

FOOTBALL ENTERS SPACE

Football fans glued, beer in hand, to England's quarter-final defeat by West Germany could probably not have cared less that the pictures arriving on their TV screens had come via space. The 1970 World Cup was the first to be beamed from Mexico to millions of fans worldwide via satellite. It was a logistical nightmare for the TV companies, but, when Brazil hammered Italy 4-1 in the final to take the Jules Rimet trophy for the third time, it was the first time that the yellow and green strip of the World Cup victors had been seen on TV in all its colourful glory.

SEE ALSO **'FIRST LIVE LEAGUE MATCH IS TELEVISED'** (page 395); **'FIFA VOTE IN FAVOUR OF USA WORLD CUP'** (page 426).

The dawn of satellite technology reinforced the World Cup's reputation as a truly global event, watched in all corners of the world.

Pelé scores the second goal against Czechoslovakia, beating goalkeeper Ivo Viktor with a deft finish in the second half.

PELÉ'S LONG DISTANCE SHOT

Few football moments are chronicled if the player doesn't hit the back of the net, but, although he scored one of Brazil's goals against Czechoslovakia in their 4-1 opening match of the 1970 World Cup, it was a spectacular near miss by Pelé that grabbed the headlines. Fired up by Czech manager Joseph Marko's pre-match comments that Pelé was a "spent force", the 'Black Pearl' then attempted an audacious goal. Seeing Czech goalkeeper Ivo Viktor off his line, Pelé tried a 50-yard lob from inside the Brazilian half. The shot beat Viktor, but, with the crowd gasping, went narrowly wide.

SEE ALSO **'GOALKEEPER TURNS GOALSCORER'** (page 283); **'DAVID BECKHAM SCORES FROM THE HALF WAY LINE'** (page 501).

ITALIAN RENAISSANCE

The boos that ushered the Uruguayan and Italian teams off the Puebla pitch brought the curtain down on a dour 0-0 draw. Group B of the 1970 World Cup was the antithesis to the free-flowing football of the South Americans. Defensive Italy cancelled out negative Uruguay and the spectators were vocal in their disapproval. Italy had, in an earlier game against Sweden, scored the one goal that would put them top of their group. However, in the later rounds an Italian renaissance led to buccaneering displays against Mexico and West Germany which saw them score four times in both matches.

SEE ALSO **'GAME OF THE CENTURY'** (page 303).

Italy players run to celebrate after Gianni Rivera scores the winning goal past West Germany's Sepp Maier in their thrilling 4-3 encounter.

MUTUAL ADMIRATION SOCIETY

It was the photograph that the footballing world had been waiting for: England's Bobby Moore, arguably the best defender in the world, embracing Brazil legend Pelé in friendship. Two of the knights of the football world, famed for their sportsmanship, swapped shirts after doing battle in the 1970 World Cup in Mexico. Victory in Guadalajara went to the Brazilian, who supplied the final assist for the winning goal. Pelé turned down swap offers from other England players so that he could exchange shirts with the man he rated "the greatest defender I ever played against".

SEE ALSO **'AJAX VERSUS BAYERN, CRUYFF VERSUS BECKENBAUER'** (page 324).

The picture of two of the game's legends after a bruising match remains one of the most iconic shots in World Cup history.

BANKS' 'SAVE OF THE CENTURY'

This was the save that produced a gasp that reverberated around the planet. England goalkeeper Gordon Banks underlined his claim to the tag of 'world's best goalkeeper' with what was hailed as the greatest save of all time – and has arguably remained so since. Brazil's Pelé was so convinced his tenth minute downward header in the 1970 World Cup group match was destined for the net that he shouted "Golo!" But he reckoned without the agility of Banks as he dived, and angled backwards and to his right, to scoop the ball one-handed over the bar.

Banks recalled, "Pelé met the ball with the meat of his head. Textbook stuff. I found myself at a 40-degree angle with my right hand stretching out towards the post. I knew if I made contact, I'd have to get it up in the air. I made contact with one finger and rolled my hand, using the third and fourth fingers as leverage." Ironically, Banks' heroics could not stop Brazil's ultimate 1-0 win in Guadalajara.

Banks' acrobatic save stunned Pelé and is generally considered to be the finest save ever seen at the World Cup.

SEE ALSO **'HIGUITA'S SCORPIAN KICK'** (page 490);
'KAHN THE HERO AS BAYERN WIN CHAMPIONS LEAGUE' (page 548).

At every World Cup one Brazilian player seems to showcase their own individual brilliance. In 1970 in Mexico it was Jairzinho's turn to shine.

JAIRZINHO THE HEARTBREAKER

The 1970 World Cup heroics of Bobby Moore and Gordon Banks against Brazil were not enough to save England in the heat of the Guadalajara Stadium. It was fitting that the final blow of the winning goal should be struck by Brazil striker Jairzinho, a player who went on to score in every round of the finals in Mexico. Moore had earlier spectacularly robbed the Brazilian poacher when he looked odds-on to score, but in the 59th minute Jairzinho had the final word and scored the only goal of the game between the World Champions of 1962 and 1966.

SEE ALSO **'RONALDINHO BAMBOOZLES ENGLAND'** (page 562).

England's Bobby Charlton launches an attack on West Germany's goal as England take control early on in the quarter-final match.

ENGLAND'S HIGH HOPES

The end of the first half of England's World Cup quarter-final against West Germany gave the world champions and their fans hope that they might retain their big-occasion power over the Germans. On the hot afternoon of 14 June in the Mexican city of Leon, the packed stadium was treated to a lively exchange, with the England team, much changed from the tournament-winning side of 1966, holding a slight advantage. It came in the 31st minute when midfielder Alan Mullery of Tottenham Hotspur scored. Four minutes after half-time Martin Peters made it 2-0 to send English hopes soaring skywards.

SEE ALSO **'TEARS FOR SOUVENIRS'** (page 444).

Showing a striker's instinct for any opportunity West Germany's Gerd Muller smashes the winner past Peter Bonetti from close range.

MULLER'S KILLER GOAL

Countless heads sank into hands across England as millions of armchair fans witnessed one of the great World Cup comebacks of all time. In this 1970 quarter-final West Germany came from 2-0 down to beat one of the tournament favourites, England. With just 12 minutes of extra-time left and at 2-2, German striker Gerd Muller destroyed the World Champions' hopes with a volley past goalkeeper Peter Bonetti to make it 3-2. Muller, nicknamed 'Der Bomber', went on to be the 1970 tournament top scorer with ten goals, despite West Germany being beaten by Italy in the semi-final.

SEE ALSO **'MIROSLAV KLOSE WINS GOLDEN BOOT'** (page 605).

Ultimately the West German resistance – inspired by Beckenbauer – took it's toll on Italy who were through to face Brazil in the Final.

GAME OF THE CENTURY

The heat of battle matched the 100-degree conditions in the most absorbing clash of the 1970 World Cup. The semi-final would ensure a European finalist in Mexico City, and free-flowing West Germany met a resurgent Italy who had shown signs of an attacking renaissance.

Boninsegna cashed in on two fortunate rebounds to put Italy ahead on nine minutes, then misery piled up for the Germans when a tackle on Franz Beckenbauer left their talismanic captain with a dislocated shoulder, although he stayed on with his shoulder strapped to inspire an equaliser from Schnellinger.

In extra-time Muller put the Germans ahead, but Italy replied through Burgnich and Riva. In a pulsating finish Muller scored again, but at 3-3 West Germany learnt that a minute can be a long time in football, for that was all Rivera needed to finish it for Italy.

SEE ALSO **'BANKS' SAVE OF THE CENTURY'** (page 301).

BRAZIL WAIT TWO DECADES FOR REVENGE

The crowds waving their partisan national colours sensed that this Brazil v Uruguay match was much more than a semi-final tie in the 1970 World Cup. The pride of South America was at stake and for the Uruguayans it was their big chance to emulate their achievement when they won the inaugural World Cup back in 1930. For Brazil, winners in 1958 and 1962 and hot favourites at this stage of the 1970 tournament, it was the opportunity to rid their country of the humiliating 1966 stain of submission.

On a hot day in Guadalajara, Brazil also had the opportunity to erase all memories of the last time these two South American neighbours had met in a World Cup final match, almost 20 years to the day, back in 1950. Played then on a league system, the host country Brazil needed only a draw to become World Champions. A world record 200,000 spectators watched the game and they could not believe the outcome – Uruguay won 2-1 after coming from behind. With West Germany playing Italy in the other semi-final the 1970 final would be South America v Europe and both Uruguay and Brazil also wanted the honour of representing their region.

In Mexico two decades later Uruguay, who had not sparkled in their qualifying group, met an exciting and adventurous Brazil, which included Pelé and Jairzinho in scintillating form. This time it was Brazil who came from behind. Uruguay's Luis Cubilla scored in the 19th minute before Clodoaldo, Jairzinho and Rivelino completed a 3-1 win and booked their place against Italy in the final.

SEE ALSO **'PELÉ MAKES A PROMISE'** (page 174).

Pelé could finally celebrate along with the rest of the Brazil side after finally laying the ghost of 1950 to rest once and for all.

PELÉ STARTS THE ROUT

A majestic leap by arguably the world's most complete footballer put in place the first piece of a historic jigsaw when Brazil met Italy on 21 June in the 1970 World Cup final. The outcome of a titanic battle between two Latin sides – one from Europe, the other from the Americas – would be permanent possession of the Jules Rimet trophy. Italy and Brazil had each won it twice; victory in Mexico City entitled them to keep it. In the 18th minute Italy's hopes nosedived when Rivelino crossed from the left. Pelé rose to head downwards and this time there was no Gordon Banks to make a near-impossible save.

SEE ALSO **'ROSSI GETS A HAT-TRICK AGAINST BRAZIL'** (page 387).

There have been many great Brazil teams through the years. The group that travelled to Mexico in 1970 was one of the very best.

ZAGALO'S INNER CIRCLE

The meetings of Mario Lobo Zagalo's 'Cobras' were never quiet affairs, but they were always passionate and well informed. As the new manager of Brazil preparing for the 1970 World Cup, Zagalo, a 1958 and 1962 winner as a player, relied on his inner circle of Cobras. With captain Carlos Alberto and star players Pelé and Gerson, Zagalo plotted an historic third World Cup win. Gerson said, "We tried to help Zagalo to solve the problems he had selecting the best team or the one that could become the best one." New roles the Cobras formulated for Tostao, Rivelino and Clodoaldo proved vital to their tournament success.

SEE ALSO **'MENOTTI OMITS MARADONA'** (page 354).

Mario Zagalo knew what it took to be a World Cup winner and he imparted that knowledge onto his hugely talented 1970 squad.

BRAZIL'S PLACE IN HISTORY IS ASSURED

The Brazilian contingent in the 100,000 crowd in Mexico City rose as one to acclaim Brazil as epoch-making World Champions – and the 1970 World Cup final was not even over. By scoring Brazil's third goal against Italy, prolific striker Jairzinho claimed his own personal record by becoming the first player to score in every round of a World Cup tournament. A Gerson free-kick was headed by Pelé into Jairzinho's path and he simply guided himself and the ball between the goalposts. It put Brazil 3-1 up – a deficit from which Italy would not recover as Brazil went on to win 4-1.

SEE ALSO **'JAIRZINHO THE HEARTBREAKER'** (page 302).

Jairzinho celebrates not only helping Brazil to a World Cup win, but cementing his own place in history by scoring in every round.

BRAZIL DELIVERS COUP DE GRACE

The bulging of the Italian net in the 86th minute of their 1970 World Cup final performance capped an imperious Brazilian victory. The Jules Rimet trophy – the World Cup itself – became a permanent possession of the Brazilian Football Federation the moment another Brazilian move of flair and skill was launched, appropriately enough, by captain Carlos Alberto.

His run towards the Italian penalty area from the right had alerted Pelé, who with consummate precision placed the ball in his path. All the Brazilian skipper had to do was shoot accurately and hard, and the ball flashed inside the far post past a beaten Italian goalkeeper.

In defeating Italy so impressively 4-1 in Mexico City, Brazil had won not only the World Cup, but possibly also one of the finest finals ever. What's more, the Brazilian squad had endured, despite pre-tournament organisational difficulties, having new manager Mario Zagalo appointed at short notice, the high altitude conditions of Mexico and searing summer temperatures.

SEE ALSO **'RONALDO REIGNS AS BRAZIL RULE'** (page 565).

Fittingly, captain Carlos Alberto rounded off the emphatic win with a memorable finish.

A LEGEND'S FIRST STEPS INTO THE LIMELIGHT

A diminutive figure was dwarfed by the giant Argentinos Juniors Stadium in Buenos Aires as a boy who was to light up – and darken – football made his first public appearance. Diego Armando Maradona, a factory worker's son, was just ten when he demonstrated his brilliant ball-juggling skills in front of thousands at half-time on a match day. Five years later Maradona's precocious talents were recognized as he made his domestic debut for the famous Buenos Aires club ten days before his 16th birthday and went on to take the club to the league title in his first season.

SEE ALSO **'MARADONA INSPIRES ARGENTINA'** (page 368).

Maradona's superlative skills were honed from a young age. Those fortunate enough to witness this appearance knew he had great talent.

ALAN BALL WEARS WHITE BOOTS

The World Cup winner Alan Ball became the first footballer to wear white boots in England when he played for Everton against Chelsea in the 1970 Charity Shield at Wembley. He had been made aware that the boot supplier Hummel wanted a high profile player to wear their white boots for a fee of £2000. "To be honest they were crap, like cardboard," said Ball, "so I got the young apprentices to paint my Adidas football boots white. It was great, until one day it rained and the black came through. A not too happy watching Hummel rep saw what I'd done so I said goodbye to the two grand."

SEE ALSO **'BOWLES' ODD BOOTS'** (page 349);
'EX-FOOTBALLER INVENTS THE 'PREDATOR' BOOT' (page 472).

After taking the money, Ball realized that his white boots were no match for his regular pair and turned to painting his old ones instead.

ANGLO-ITALIAN ANIMOSITY SPILLS OVER

Flailing fists replaced dessert as two footballing sides took to fighting in the streets of Rome in September 1970. FIFA president Sir Stanley Rous was prompted to demand a report after an off-field clash between Lazio and Arsenal players and officials. Ill feeling from a drawn Fairs Cup game spilled over at a post-match banquet. It never emerged which remark started the melee, but dozens were involved. Onlookers alleged even mild-mannered Arsenal manager Bertie Mee grabbed his Italian counterpart by the lapels and threw a punch. Arsenal went on to progress in the competition with a 2-0 home win.

SEE ALSO **'THE BATTLE OF HIGHBURY'** (page 130).

Arsenal's John Roberts challenges Lazio's Giorgio Chinaglia during the extremely heated tussle between the two teams.

CHARLTON'S 'LITTLE BLACK BOOK' OF REVELATIONS

Jack Charlton was never afraid to speak his mind, but it was a throwaway line during a television football programme on 4 October 1970 that got him into trouble with the Football Association (FA). During the chat Charlton said he'd once had a "little black book" of names of players he'd marked out for retribution when he encountered them again future matches. He was threatened with a joint FA and League enquiry, but later explained that he was just using a figure of speech and that no such book existed.

SEE ALSO **'ROY KEANE'S MALICIOUS INTENT'** (page 545).

Jack Charlton was forced to quickly back-track once he made his ill-advised comments about a 'Little Black Book' of scores to settle.

'DONKEY KICK' BOOTED OUT

With a deft flick of heels the 'donkey kick' became part of British football folklore. The BBC's Match of the Day programme cameras were at Highfield Road, Coventry, to capture an outrageously taken free-kick. Midfielder Willie Carr used both feet to flick the ball up behind him, where team-mate Ernie Hunt was lurking. Hunt, a proven striker, hammered the ball home from 25 yards past the Everton goalkeeper. Despite the unusual circumstances, the goal was given, to the delight of the Coventry crowd. However, the football authorities took a dim view and later scrutiny of the rule book showed that it should never have been allowed.

SEE ALSO **'HIGUITA'S SCORPION KICK'** (page 490).

Ernie Hunt, above, and Willie Carr's cheeky free kick move was a training ground routine too far and was swiftly banned by the authorities.

EUROPEAN PENALTY 'CIRCUS'

English side Everton became the first club to win a European Cup tie through the ordeal of a penalty shoot-out. Paired with German club Borussia Monchengladbach in the competition's second round, Everton drew the first leg in Germany 1-1. At Everton's Goodison Park Stadium on 4 November the second-leg result was a similar stalemate score and the penalty shoot-out rule, brought in at the start of the 1970 season, was invoked for Everton to prevail four penalties to three. Everton's manager Harry Catterick, while pleased to go through to the quarter-finals, had yet to be convinced about shoot-outs, describing them as a "circus act".

SEE ALSO **'BARCELONA LOSE EUROPEAN CUP ON PENALTIES'** (page 409).

Harry Catterick was manager at Goodison Park for 12 years. Though his side came out on top, he wasn't a fan of the drama of penalties.

Treytel's bizarre achievement won him a place in Feyenoord football club's folklore – and the seagull remains in their trophy room, too.

SEAGULL MEETS ITS MATCH

One of the more bizarre mementoes in any football club's trophy cabinet is in the Netherlands, and it's a stuffed seagull. On 15 November 1970 thousands witnessed a once-in-a-lifetime event as a goalkeeper's kick blasted a passing seagull out of the sky at the Feyenoord Stadium in Rotterdam. Home keeper Eddy Treytel, a Dutch international, was the man who entered football folklore as he booted the ball high upfield in a Dutch First Division match against local rivals Sparta Rotterdam. Treytel's unusual feat is commemorated by the stuffed bird, which stands alongside Feyenoord's many domestic and European trophies.

SEE ALSO **'TREVOR BROOKING'S SHOT GETS STUCK IN WITH FREAK GOAL'** (page 376).

The grim sight of bodies laid out at Ibrox – the second time the ground had witnessed a major disaster in the twentieth century.

TRAGEDY RETURNS TO IBROX

The number 13 lived up to its grim reputation as 66 people were killed at the home of Glasgow Rangers. As departing fans packed stairway 13 at the end of a match with city rival Celtic, barriers collapsed leading to an appalling death toll. A fan caught up in the crush said, "Around me I could hear shouting and cries, but as time went on – I was trapped for at least 45 minutes – these decreased until it was almost silent." The 2 January 1971 disaster remains the worst in the history of Scottish football and a later inquiry blamed crowd momentum for the tragedy.

SEE ALSO **'THE IBROX DISASTER KILLS 25'** (page 51); **'THE HILLSBOROUGH DISASTER'** (page 428).

CHARLIE TAKES HIS ADULATION LYING DOWN

Talented Arsenal striker Charlie George claims, rather over-modestly, that he is more famous, certainly among supporters of other teams, for lying down on the celebrated turf of Wembley Stadium than for anything else. The iconic photograph of his goal celebration in the 1971 FA Cup final was flashed around the world and over 30 years on the mere mention of George's name can still conjure up the image. Lying down, arms outstretched on the green turf, George was ecstatic at scoring the winning goal in a 2-1 extra-time Cup final win against Liverpool. Pictured soaking up the elation of the fans and his team-mates alike, his heartfelt expression of joy has become part of football folklore.

George had recovered from a broken ankle to play a significant part in Arsenal's 1970-71 Football League championship success and helped clinch Arsenal's first League and FA Cup double. George went on to make 179 appearances for Arsenal and scored 49 goals for the Gunners.

Frank McLintock, George Graham and Charlie George milk the applause from the Arsenal faithful.

SEE ALSO
'GASCOIGNE VOLLEY STUNS SCOTLAND'
(page 496).

Though he was never to grace the world stage with his country, Best proved his international class – as well as his cheek – against England.

BEST ADDS CHEEK TO HIS REPERTOIRE

George Best won the biggest ovation of an unexciting May 1971 Northern Ireland v England international for a cheeky trick that was to cement further his 'Will of the Wisp' reputation. Best, always trying to innovate, pulled a fast one on Gordon Banks as the legendary England goalkeeper was about to punt upfield from his penalty area. In the split second the ball was between Banks' hand and foot, Best nipped in and flicked it over the keeper's head. In a flash he skirted the keeper and popped the ball into the net, only for the referee to disallow the goal, citing "dangerous play". England won 1-0.

SEE ALSO **'THE 'CRUYFF TURN' IS BORN'** (page 335).

Though Gento ended his career on the losing side in a major final his achievements at Real Madrid from 1953-71 were truly remarkable.

GENTO ENDS ON A LOSING NOTE

Even the most fanatical Chelsea fan was able to spare a thought for the lonely figure of Francisco Gento disappearing down the tunnel as he left the football stage for the last time. After two decades as a legendary figure in international football he walked into retirement a defeated man. The fast, skilful Real Madrid winger with six 1950s and 1960s European Cup medals to his name left Athens' Stadium Karaiskaki empty-handed after British club Chelsea beat Real Madrid in the European Cup Winners' Cup final. In a two-legged final, the teams first drew 1-1 before Chelsea claimed their first European trophy with a 2-1 win in the second leg.

SEE ALSO **'PELÉ RETIRES FOR GOOD'** (page 352).

AJAX'S FIRST STEPS TO EUROPEAN DOMINATION

Dick van Dijk's goal after just five minutes in the 1971 European Cup final put Dutch champions Ajax on the road to establishing a European supremacy that was to last until 1973. On 2 June 1971, before a capacity 80,000 at London's Wembley Stadium, van Dijk's strike and a second from Arie Haan after 87 minutes put the Amsterdam club's hands on the European Cup for the first time. It would be another two years – and two more European Cup wins – before their grip on it was broken. A five-year dynasty of Dutch 'total football' had been hastened in the year before when rivals Feyenoord had won the coveted trophy. Sandwiched between the goals at the two extremes of the game, Ajax dazzled to show their commitment to exciting football. Under the midfield generalship and flair of Johan Cruyff, Ajax set their stall out for future seasons and assured him a place among the best European players of the era.

SEE ALSO **'AJAX WIN CHAMPIONS LEAGUE'** (page 487).

Ajax captain Velibor Vasovic
holds up the European Cup.

EUROPE'S LAST LOOK AT THE WORLD CUP

Brazilian superstar Pelé gave adoring soccer crowds in Europe a last look at the original Jules Rimet trophy before Brazil kept it for good. The summer of 1970 had seen Brazil beat Italy to become world champions for the third time and world governing body FIFA gave the trophy in perpetuity in recognition of this incredible feat. The dazzling style of the South Americans – epitomized by the talents of Pelé, Gerson, Vava, Garrincha, Jaizinho and Rivelino – won the cup in 1958 in Sweden, 1962 in Chile and 1970 in Mexico, a winning run interrupted only by England's 1966 win.

SEE ALSO **'CHARLES MILLER 'GIVES' FOOTBALL TO BRAZIL'** (page 40).

Pelé in Paris as part of Brazil's whirlwind European tour before this particular Jules Rimet trophy returned to South America for good.

SIR MATT SAYS GOODBYE – AGAIN

With a wave and to the deafening cheers of the adoring faithful, Sir Matt Busby stepped down for the last time as Manchester United manager. It was a case of déjà vu for Busby as two years earlier – after 23 eventful years that included the Munich air crash and the 1968 European Cup win – he had handed coaching duties to Wilf McGuinness. His retirement was brief as in December 1970, with McGuinness sacked, United's directors invited him to take over again until the end of the season. After his second retirement Busby was a club director until 1982. He died in 1994.

SEE ALSO **'LIVERPOOL'S BILL SHANKLY QUITS AT THE TOP'** (page 342); **'BOB PAISLEY LEAVES LIVERPOOL WITH A TROPHY'** (page 393).

Sir Matt had seen it all with United – tragedy at Munich to triumph in Lisbon. The road leading to Old Trafford is named in his honour.

Hereford United players, including Ronnie Radford, top left, celebrate their giantkilling exploits with a drink or two in the dressing room.

HEREFORD AND RADFORD BOOT OUT NEWCASTLE

A 40-yard rocket-shot stunned English football as the boot of forward Ronnie Radford propelled mighty Newcastle United out of the FA Cup at the hands of non-league side Hereford United. In a giant-killing feat not achieved since Yeovil's 2-1 win over Sunderland in 1949, Hereford qualified for the fifth round of the Cup with a 2-1 win courtesy of Radford's high-velocity drive – just four minutes from time – after a determined run from the half-way line. Hereford had previously earned this 5 February home replay with a 2-2 draw against a Newcastle side packed with star players and internationals.

SEE ALSO **'YEOVIL BEAT GIANTS OF SUNDERLAND'** (page 164); **'THE CRAZY GANG STUN LIVERPOOL'** (page 422).

Playing in all-white like Real Madrid, Leeds turned in a performance the Spaniards would have been proud of against Southampton.

LEEDS UNITED BLITZ THE SAINTS

The Leeds United contingent in the 34,275 crowd chanted "Ole!" as pass after accurate pass found its mark and Leeds' opponents, Southampton, failed to get near the ball. This stunning 4 March demonstration of team arrogance was probably the only time that Leeds truly emulated Real Madrid on the pitch, even though the two clubs shared an all-white strip. The Southampton players ran themselves ragged, not only through the longest 27-pass sequence, but also throughout the match. It was all to no avail, though, as Leeds delighted their home fans at Elland Road with a 7-0 trouncing.

SEE ALSO **"TOTAL FOOTBALL' – ALMOST TOTAL DOMINATION'** (page 326); **'CLOUGH'S 44 DAY REIGN AT LEEDS'** (page 343).

NETZER'S MASTERCLASS

Midfield maestro Gunther Netzer laid to rest England's dominance over West Germany with a masterclass at Wembley. He engineered Germany's first victory on English soil and a 3-1 win in this European Nations Cup quarter-final on 29 April. His midfield generalship was the significant factor and the inspired Netzer was always ready to explode from a strolling gait into a penetrating run for goal. After Hoeness put the Germans ahead and Lee equalized, Netzer got on the scoresheet with a penalty – and even that was exceptional. England keeper Banks pushed Netzer's shot on to the post, but it spun back behind him into the net. Muller made it 3-1.

SEE ALSO **'LIAM BRADY INSPIRES ARSENAL IN 'FIVE-MINUTE FINAL"** (page 366).

Gunter Netzer was in inspirational form, beating England goalkeeper Gordon Banks from the penalty spot to make the score 2-1.

UWE SEELER
RETIRES FROM HAMBURG

Hailed as one of the most consistent and best forwards in the world in the 1950s and 1960s, Uwe Seeler spent his entire career at his home town club Hamburg SV, scoring over 550 goals in some 700 senior appearances. The stocky Seeler possessed a fierce shot that left goalkeepers floundering, a talent he put to good use in four World Cup campaigns, scoring in each to equal Pelé's record. At home he was voted Germany's Footballer of the Year three times. When he retired his reputation was underlined by the benefit match appearance of stars such as Geoff Hurst, George Best, Bobby Charlton, Franz Beckenbauer and Gerd Muller.

SEE ALSO **'MULLER WINS WORLD CUP AND RETIRES WITH 68 GOALS'** (page 341).

His burly physique was deceiving, for Uwe Seeler was a deadly finisher with a ferocious shot who delivered for both club and country.

GEORGE BEST QUITS AT 26

It was unthinkable that a player who could win a place in any World XI should quit aged only 26, but George Best did. Disillusioned and feeling the effects of his fast living, Manchester United player Best flew to Spain after problems at Old Trafford and quit soccer at an impromptu press conference – just days short of his 26th birthday.

Newspapers quoted Best, who had played 466 times for United and scored 178 goals, as saying, "I am no longer a footballer – and that's final." History tells that his decision was not final. The Northern Ireland international returned to the club which nurtured his brilliance, but there were more problems over his pop star lifestyle. After quitting United again he wandered the world to play in countries as far apart as Scotland and Australia. He had lower league spells with Stockport, Fulham and Bournemouth in England, Hibernian in Scotland, and Los Angeles Aztecs and San Jose Earthquakes in California, before finally retiring in 1983.

SEE ALSO **'GEORGE BEST LOSES THE BATTLE'**
(page 593).

On the pitch Best was a genius but off-the-pitch problems continually threatened to overshadow his undoubted talent.

FANS SPOIL RANGERS' BIG DAY

On 24 May 1972 Glasgow Rangers reached the pinnacle of European football without one of their thousands of fans witnessing it. Rangers were presented with the European Cup Winners' Cup in a back room of Barcelona's Nou Camp Stadium while on the pitch drink-fuelled fans clashed with baton-wielding police. As Rangers raced to an early 3-0 lead over Moscow Dynamo their fans broke onto the pitch several times before Dynamo's two-goal fightback led to a mass invasion. As the battle raged, Rangers were quietly handed the trophy followed by a two-year ban by UEFA for their fans' appalling behaviour.

SEE ALSO **'LEEDS UNITED'S FANS NIGHT OF VIOLENCE IN PARIS'** (page 343); **'UEFA BAN ENGLISH CLUBS FROM EUROPEAN COMPETITION'** (page 405).

Rangers players hold somewhat subdued celebrations in their dressing room after their fans' behaviour had incited crowd trouble.

BECKENBAUER THE ELEGANT DEFENDER

Franz Beckenbauer embued the sweeper position in football with class and made this very specialised role glamorous. It brought him accolades as one of the finest defenders in soccer history and saw him lead his club Bayern Munich and his country West Germany to the pinnacles of success. Sweeping behind the defence, 'Der Kaiser' with his extraordinary football vision could read the game, adding extra security and improving the passing out of defence. Unusual in a defender of the 1970s, Beckenbauer was calm and confident with the ball at his feet, yet steely and accurate in his tackling.

SEE ALSO **'BECKENBAUER WINS BUNDESLIGA WITH HAMBURG'** (page 380).

Beckenbauer redefined the role of the sweeper and was a ball-playing defender of the highest order who could also perform in midfield.

MULLER'S GOLDEN GOALS

1972

West Germany's 'Der Bomber' certainly wiped out the Soviet Union's hopes of another European Nations title as he scored two goals in a 3-0 final tie win on 18 June 1972. In the European competition, prolific striker Gerd Muller was reprising the top-scoring role he had played for West Germany just two years earlier with his similar feat in the 1970 World Cup in Mexico. The Bayern Munich player, who had scored 42 goals for his club during the previous league season, also provided much of the artillery for West Germany's World Cup win two years later in 1974 – including the winning goal in the 2-1 final defeat of Holland.

Muller's heroics for his country coincided with a purple patch at club level, too, as he was Bayern Munich's top scorer for three seasons from 1970-71 through to 1973-74, with more than 30 goals in each successive season. Unsurprisingly, this period also coincided with Bayern's three-year domination of the European Cup competition.

In typical predatory fashion Gerd Muller stabs the opening goal past goalkeeper Yevgeny Rudakov.

SEE ALSO 'MULLER WINS WORLD CUP AND RETIRES WITH 68 GOALS' (page 341); 'OLIVER BIERHOFF'S GOLDEN GOAL WINS FINAL' (page 499).

Banks later had a brief career in the NASL with the Cleveland Strikers, part of a sporting franchise that included an American football team.

CAR CRASH ROBS ENGLAND OF STAR KEEPER

A car plunging into a ditch robbed England of the man rated the best goalkeeper they ever had. When Gordon Banks lost control of his car on 22 October 1972 he sustained no life-threatening injuries, but, in a distressing irony for a goalkeeper, he lost the sight in his right eye. It tragically brought down the curtain on an England career of 73 caps in which his country lost only nine matches with him between the sticks. Banks considered trying to resume his playing career, but went into scouting, non-league football management and celebrity speaking.

SEE ALSO **'BANKS' 'SAVE OF THE CENTURY'** (page 303).

The Bundesliga Scandal was far-reaching with all clubs either implicated or viewed with suspicion.

THE GREAT BUNDESLIGA SCANDAL

On 6 June 1971 Kickers Offenbach president Horst Gregorio Canellas celebrated his 50th birthday with a party. Despite Kickers having been relegated the day before, Canellas was in buoyant mood, which made a number of his well-wishers feel a little uneasy. Their concerns would prove correct as with the press of the play button on a tape recorder he blew open The Bundesliga Scandal.

The tape contained secret recordings revealing a litany of offers to be paid-off in return for assisting Kickers Offenbach with their league survival. The repercussions of Canellas's exposé would be far-reaching with two thirds of the league drawn into the corruption scandal.

SEE ALSO **'GERMAN CORRUPTION SCANDAL'** (page 586).

BAYERN MOVE TO NEW STADIUM

Stars such as Franz Beckenbauer and Gerd Muller had played internationals at such a magnificent venue, but might have needed to pinch themselves in 1972 because this was now 'home'. Their club Bayern Munich had taken over Munich's 80,000-seat Olympiastadion with its lightweight, tensile roofs. Built for the 1972 Olympic Games, the stadium was associated with horror and bloodshed when 11 Israeli athletes were murdered there during a terrorist attack. However, the Olympic Stadium move, doubling the capacity of the club's former ground, was to be auspicious for Bayern as it heralded a period of unprecedented supremacy that culminated in three European Cup wins.

SEE ALSO **'BAYERN'S DISTINCTIVE MODERN STADIUM OPENS'** (page 592).

A view from an airship flying
over the Olympiastadion.

AJAX VERSUS BAYERN, CRUYFF VERSUS BECKENBAUER

Ajax's Johan Cruyff was still riding high in 1973 when his club met Franz Beckenbauer and Bayern Munich in the European Cup quarter-final. Billed as the ultimate gladiators' duel, the game ended in a rout with the Dutch putting four goals past the shell-shocked Germans in the first leg and winning 1-2 in the return leg. This victory helped Ajax on their way to their third consecutive European Cup final. Later that year Cruyff transferred to Barcelona where he won European Footballer of the Year. Bayern, however, would bounce back and they won three European Cups from 1974-76, with Beckenbauer being crowned European Footballer of the Year in 1976.

Two of Europe's greatest players, Beckenbauer and Cruyff, meet as captains of two of the continent's most famous clubs.

SEE ALSO **'BECKENBAUER SIGNS FOR BAYERN'** (page 227); **'BARCELONA SNAP UP CRUYFF'** (page 329).

Brian Clough and his forthright views were a regular feature on British television screens in the 1970s and 1980s.

CLOUGH BLASTS JUVENTUS "CHEATS"

It was not the quote that journalists were expecting, but "I will not talk to any cheating bastards" was just part of a tirade from outspoken English club manager Brian Clough. The Derby County boss was seething over Italian tactics after his side's 11 April 3-1 European Cup semi-final defeat to Juventus in Turin. Clough, confrontational at the best of times, emerged from the dressing room to tell Italian reporters: "No cheating bastards do I talk to…" before slamming shut the dressing room door. There was poetic justice for Clough when Juventus lost the final 1-0 to an all-conquering Ajax side from Holland.

SEE ALSO **'CLOUGH CLIPS FOREST FANS AROUND THE EAR'** (page 427). **'MARADONA ACCUSES FIFA OF FIXING WORLD CUP'** (page 449).

CHARLTON FAMILY FAREWELL

Britain's most famous footballing brothers simultaneously said goodbye to their playing careers. Bobby and Jack Charlton never played together for the same club side, but they reached the summit of the game as World Cup winners with England in 1966. 'Big Jack' was a tall uncompromising defender with Leeds United and scored 70 goals – usually because of his height, with his head. Bobby, two years younger, spent his whole career with Manchester United where he won European Cup and English League and cup medals. A goalscorer with a thunderbolt shot, Bobby scored 245 goals in 751 games for United.

SEE ALSO **'BOBBY CHARLTON MAKES ENGLAND DEBUT'** (page 215); **'JACK CHARLTON GIVEN THE FREEDOM OF DUBLIN'** (page 480).

The Charlton brothers on opposing sides. Bobby in the red of Manchester United, Jack in Leeds United's all-white strip.

Montgomery deflects a shot from Peter Lorimer onto the bar, thus completing his famous double save and ensuring a Sunderland victory.

MONTGOMERY BEATS LEEDS – AND THE ODDS

Sunderland goalkeeper Jim Montgomery knew the 1973 FA Cup final would be a big day, but he hadn't anticipated it was one for the history books. However, his spectacular double save was to be the crowning glory at Wembley as his Second Division side Sunderland beat high-flying Leeds United. Ian Porterfield scored for Sunderland on 31 minutes, but it was Montgomery in brilliant form who maintained that lead. Leeds were unremittingly pushing forward for a face-saving equaliser, but Montgomery's wonder saves – firstly from England's Trevor Cherry and then from Scotland's Peter Lorimer – ensured Sunderland became only the second side from Division Two to win the Cup since 1931.

SEE ALSO **'GORDON SMITH MISSES A SITTER'** (page 394).

'TOTAL FOOTBALL' – ALMOST TOTAL DOMINATION

Holland's famed 'Total Football' concept had many high points, but arguably it reached its zenith when a goal from Johnny Rep sealed a 1-0 European Cup win over Juventus for Amsterdam's Ajax. 'Total Football' was to last from 1969–74, a golden age of Dutch football and players. The win over Juventus was Ajax's third European Cup win and, with Feyenoord's victory three years before, confirmed the era of European domination was purely Dutch. Top British, Greek and Italian clubs were steamrollered by the 'Orange revolution' in football as Feyenoord beat Celtic in 1970 and Ajax followed suit against Panathanaikos, Inter Milan and Juventus in the European finals of 1971, 1972 and 1973.

Rinus Michels, the Ajax manager of the era, is credited with developing the successful system of style, grit and determination. It made Cruyff, Muhren, Haan, Neeskens and Rep household names across the world. After so much success the Ajax team slowly disintegrated as players saw more lucrative pay-days in other countries, such as Spain, where Cruyff moved in order to spearhead Barcelona's revival.

The 'Total Football' style was also applied to the international team, but without the same success attained at club level.

SEE ALSO **'RINUS BRINGS 'TOTAL FOOTBALL' TO AJAX'** (page 255); **'AJAX WIN CHAMPIONS LEAGUE'** (page 487).

Ajax's Johan Cruyff, wearing a Juventus shirt, and Barry Hulshoff celebrate with the European Cup after their 1-0 win.

Moore was renowned for his tough-tackling and his sense of fair play. He remains England's most capped outfield player.

ITALIANS SPOIL MOORE'S FAREWELL PARTY

English football rose in acclaim on 6 June 1973 as captain Bobby Moore ended his record-breaking international career after 107 caps. But he didn't bow out in triumph as his final England game was marred by a 0-1 defeat at Wembley Stadium by Italy. Moore, who captained England 90 times, had his fair share of triumphs with England. Indeed, he had stood on top of the world with his country when, as a young 25-year-old at this same Wembley Stadium, he lifted the 1966 World Cup following a thrilling and controversial 4-2 win over West Germany.

SEE ALSO **'BOBBY MOORE MADE ENGLAND CAPTAIN'** (page 249); **'BECKHAM RELINQUISHES ENGLAND CAPTAINCY'** (page 605).

The play-offs provide an incredibly dramatic finish to the season in the lower leagues and are popular with fans and mascots alike.

THE UPS AND DOWNS OF THE FOOTBALL LEAGUE

A majority show of hands signalled a major change to the Football League rules in England. The League committee agreed to a revolutionary three-up, three-down promotion and relegation system – the first big change to movements up and down the four senior soccer divisions for 75 years. The original promotion and relegation system of two up and two down was introduced in 1898. The 1973 rule change was seen as increasing competition for clubs and boosting interest among fans. The next major change was to come thirteen years later when play-offs for promotion places were introduced.

SEE ALSO **'PLAY-OFFS INTRODUCED BY FOOTBALL LEAGUE'** (page 418).

BARCELONA SNAP UP CRUYFF

Dutch international captain Johan Cruyff had a big talent and big reputation and he needed to utilize both when he made a surprise move to Barcelona in September 1973. His mission was to revitalize the domestic fortunes of the Catalan club starved of success and dominated by Real Madrid. It worked, as Cruyff's silky skills and goalscoring ability helped Barcelona to both Spanish League and Cup successes. However, European Cup success with Barcelona eluded him as a player and he would have to wait until 1992, when he was manager, to win that particular title.

SEE ALSO **'CRUYFF SAYS GOODBYE BUT NOT FAREWELL'** (page 365).

A new hero for the Nou Camp. His signing in 1973 was to be the start of Cruyff's long association with Barcelona.

ENGLAND FAIL TO QUALIFY FOR THE WORLD CUP

It was a game England had to win if they were to progress to the World Cup finals – a draw against Poland wasn't enough. In a feverish build-up, Brian Clough branded the Polish goalkeeper a 'clown', but on 17 October 1973 Jan Tomaszewski silenced Wembley by playing the game of his life and frustrating wave upon wave of English attacks. Poland scored in the 55th minute when Grzegorz Lato burst out of defence and crossed to the unmarked Jan Domarski who shot under Peter Shilton's despairing dive. Hope flickered briefly as Allan Clarke took an equalising penalty following a foul on Martin Peters, but it was too little, too late.

SEE ALSO **'ALF RAMSEY SACKED'** (page 332); **'FRANCE FALL APART'** (page 470).

Mick Channon hits the ball past the post in the final minutes against Poland in 1973, typifying England's frustrating evening.

1973

USSR in disarray off and on the pitch. The World Cup was the latest sporting event to suffer from Cold War hostilities.

SOVIETS LEFT OUT IN THE COLD

With the Cold War continuing to sour relations between the Soviet Union and the United States, the 1974 World Cup proved to be a disaster for the USSR team. They were drawn against Chile in the qualifying stages, but refused to play following the bloody overthrow of the Soviet-supported left-wing Allende government in September 1973 by US-backed right-wing army factions led by General Augusto Pinochet. The result was that FIFA was forced to expel the Soviet Union from the following year's World Cup. Chile, incidentally, failed to progress past the first qualifying stage, losing to West Germany and drawing with East Germany and Australia.

SEE ALSO **'YUGOSLAVIA REFUSED ENTRY TO EUROPEAN CHAMPIONSHIPS'** (page 459).

1973

PARIS SAINT-GERMAIN MAKE IT BACK TO THE TOP

Paris Saint-Germain flew the flag for football in Paris for nearly 70 years until the city council began lobbying for the removal of the Saint-Germain reference in the club's name. In 1972 pressure succeeded in splitting the club, with professional players staying on in the top division as Paris FC and amateurs retaining their name, but descending to the third division. PSG clawed their way back to Division Two the following season, turned professional in the 1973-74 season and won promotion to the top division. At the same time, Paris FC were relegated and PSG made their home at the rebuilt Parc des Princes, once Paris FC's ground.

SEE ALSO **'BAYERN MUNICH STEP UP'** (page 258).

The 1973-74 season marked PSG's return to France's premier division and the club they were once linked to, Paris FC's, relegation from it.

CRUYFF DYNASTY CONTINUES IN CATALONIA

Cruyff's decision to call his son Jordi cemented his position as a Barcelona legend. Jordi went on to represent Catalonia at international level.

Johan Cruyff didn't need to do much to be appreciated by the Barcelona fans. Those who crammed into the Nou Camp every other week were well aware of his prowess on the pitch. Having signed for the club in 1973, he stated that he had to choose the Catalan club because he couldn't play for Real Madrid, a club associated with the Franco regime. Months later, the Dutchman went one better, giving his son, born on 9 February 1974, a Catalan name, Jordi, despite the language being banned by the Franco regime. Never mind what Cruyff did with a football, his hero status was confirmed.

SEE ALSO 'CRUYFF IN WORLD CUP PROTEST' (page 356).

DENIS LAW SENDS UNITED DOWN

A statue in Manchester United's Old Trafford Stadium pays tribute to one of the club's greatest stars – Denis Law. Yet on 27 April 1974, at the very end of his career, when playing for Manchester City, an instinctive back-heel in front of the United goal sent the local derby City's way 1-0 and doomed his old club to relegation. The enormity of what he had done hit Law immediately and he asked to be substituted, walking miserably off the field never again to kick a ball in club football. He didn't know that Birmingham City's win on the same day would have sealed United's fate without his intervention.

SEE ALSO 'AC MILAN RELEGATED TO SERIE B' (page 380);

Law is mobbed by jubilant City fans but is in no mood to celebrate as he trudges disconsolately from the pitch.

It was a sad end to the career of the only England manager to win the World Cup only eight years earlier. Sir Alf Ramsey died in 1999.

ALF RAMSEY SACKED

Alf Ramsey took England to World Cup glory in 1966 while also presiding over a record of 69 victories, 27 draws and 17 losses during a 12-year career as England boss. But much of that success came in the 1960s when he created the "wingless wonders", a formation without wings, but with huge attacking force through the centre. However, Ramsey's conservative tactics brought increasing criticism in the 1970s and his fate was sealed following failure to qualify for the 1974 World Cup. He was sacked on 1 May 1974 and it was said the Football Association paid him off with £8,000, seemly confirmed by Ramsey's comment, "It's a tissue handshake."

SEE ALSO **'RAMSEY'S STIRRING WORDS'** (page 278).

Franz Beckenbauer lifts the European Cup as teammates Johnny Hansen and Gerd Muller watch the reaction of the Bayern fans.

SCHWARZENBECK SCORES A SCREAMER

As a tough tackling, physically imposing man-marker, Hans-Georg Schwarzenbeck represented the defensive centre-back bedrock which allowed Bayern Munich team-mate Franz Beckenbauer to shine. But it was Schwarzenbeck who saved the day for Bayern in the 1974 European Cup final against Atlético Madrid. With the seconds ticking down in extra-time and Bayern still trailing 1-0, the unassuming centre-back unleashed a long-range screamer that tied the game and forced the first-ever European Cup final replay. This historic goal allowed Bayern to come back two days later and stroll past the Spanish 4-0.

SEE ALSO **'ZIDANE'S STUNNER SEALS HAMPDEN TRIUMPH'** (page 555).

RIOT IN ROTTERDAM

By the time Feyenoord travelled to White Hart Lane for the first leg of the 1974 UEFA Cup final, English clubs had had six consecutive wins in the European clubs championship – first in the Inter-cities Fairs Cup and then in the renamed UEFA Cup. Spurs took the lead twice only to be pulled back to a 2-2 draw, so emotions were highly charged for the second leg in Rotterdam.

Spurs chairman Sidney Wale appealed for calm before kick-off, but as the game began slipping away, Spurs supporters ran riot, leaving 200 injured. A disgusted Bill Nicholson told fans at half-time, "You hooligans are a disgrace to Tottenham Hotspur and a disgrace to England. This is a football game – not a war." Spurs ended the day 2-0 down, out of the Cup and banned from Europe.

SEE ALSO 'LEEDS UNITED'S FANS NIGHT OF VIOLENCE IN PARIS' (page 343).

A Tottenham Hotspur fan on his way back from Rotterdam, where both sets of fans fought running battles with the police.

BLOODIED KEEGAN GETS HIS REVENGE – ON THE PITCH

In June England's friendly match in Belgrade turned nasty the moment the team touched down in Yugoslavia. As a world-class striker England's Kevin Keegan was used to being clattered and kicked by defenders, but he didn't expect a beating at the airport. As the England team waited for their baggage, a tired Keegan sat on the luggage carousel. Customs officials, not recognising the curly-haired Liverpool striker, had him arrested, taken to a back room and beaten. After intense negotiations Keegan was released, very shaken and sporting a bloody nose. The game was a 2-2 draw and Keegan took his revenge by scoring.

SEE ALSO 'KEEGAN MISSES AND UNBEATEN ENGLAND HEAD HOME' (page 386).

Kevin Keegan turns out for England before his bruising encounter with the Yugoslavian customs officials.

HAVELANGE ELECTED FIFA PRESIDENT

Born in Brazil, the son of a Belgian ex-patriot, Dr Jean-Marie Faustin Goedefroid de Havelange, grew into a man who knew what he wanted and usually got it. Better known as Joao Havelange, the former Olympic swimmer and water polo player became a successful entrepreneur before taking the top job in Brazil's football federation in time to preside over his country's World Cup triple. He then set his sights on the FIFA Presidency and won the 1974 election. "When I arrived, I found an old house and $20 in the kitty," he recalled. "On the day I departed, 24 years later, I left property and contracts worth over $4 billion."

SEE ALSO **'BLATTER ELECTED TO FIFA TOP JOB'** (page 510).

The long-term FIFA President could not be accused of showing false modesty when taking credit for transforming FIFA's finances.

CRUYFF'S TWO STRIPE STAND

Johan Cruyff, the skinny lad from Amsterdam, was described by an early coach as "God's gift to football" and is considered pivotal in the Netherlands' blossoming as a football nation. But while his dazzling skills on the field were courted by club and country, his negotiating skills as a professional player often put him at odds with authority. He challenged the Dutch football establishment over many issues, including, famously, Holland's Adidas sponsorship of the 1974 World Cup side. Having struck a deal to wear Puma boots, Cruyff refused to wear the orange national shirt with the three Adidas stripes and successfully insisted that his own bare only two stripes.

SEE ALSO **'BOWLES ODD BOOTS'** (page 349).

Cruyff's statement of his kit only having two Adidas stripes, instead of the usual three, can be seen here alongside team mate Wim van Hanegem.

THE 'CRUYFF TURN' IS BORN

It was a World Cup finals match and the goalless draw between Holland and Sweden was lacklustre and going nowhere, with the Dutch failing to capitalise on their talent against their much taller opponents. But in one second of brilliance the great Johan Cruyff executed a move that has spawned a thousand training videos.

The 'Cruyff Turn' was born in somewhat unpromising circumstances. The Dutch striker was attempting to attack down the left, just outside the penalty area. He was hounded by Swedish right-back Janne Olsson who was between him and the goal. The striker still had his back to the goal as Olsson nibbled and hacked in an attempt to get a foot to the ball. Cruyff and Olsson were almost shoulder-to-shoulder with their backs to the Swedish goal line when Cruyff looked up as if to pass the ball back infield with his right foot and Olsson lunged to block the line of the imagined pass. However, instead of sending the ball infield, Cruyff caressed it back past his planted left foot and swivelled with astonishing poise to set off towards the Swedish line with the ball at his feet, leaving the bemused Olsson staggering to retain his balance.

The dazzling move brought the crowd to its feet and in living rooms around the world football fans of every nationality gasped in recognition of the genius of Johan Cruyff. The fact that the move came to nothing was completely beside the point – the 'Cruyff Turn' would become a feature of play on football fields around the world.

SEE ALSO **'CRUYFF IN CRUISE CONTROL'** (page 337).

Schoolboys the world over have spent hours trying to perfect the Dutch star's trademark move.

1974

ZAIRE KICK UP A STORM AT THEIR FIRST WORLD CUP

The Leopards of Zaire, now the Democratic Republic of Congo, made World Cup history when they became the first sub-Saharan country to qualify for the finals. But they were thrashed 9-0 by Yugoslavia, possibly due to low morale over a pay dispute. They were consequently warned they would be exiled if they didn't make a game of it against Brazil, which could have prompted defender Mwepu Llunga to sprint out of a Zaire wall during a Brazilian free-kick and boot the ball away – a red-mist moment that earned him a yellow card. Zaire conceded fourteen goals in their shambolic World Cup debut and shared the unwelcome distinction of being the only teams who failed to find the net with fellow first-time qualifier Australia.

Brazil's Edu takes on Zaire's Boba Lobilo as Mwepu Llunga looks on.

SEE ALSO 'LOWLY CAMEROON STUN MIGHTY ARGENTINA' (page 439); 'SENEGAL STUN FRANCE' (page 558).

WEST GERMANY LOSE TO EAST GERMANY

With East German sporting resources channelled into Olympic disciplines such as sprinting and weight lifting, national coach Georg Buschner did well to get his team to the 1974 World Cup finals. In a politically charged first-round match on 22 June 1974, East Germany met West Germany and, for the first and only time, won 1-0. Success was short-lived as East Germany went out in the second phase while West Germany went on to beat Holland 2-1 in the final. On 8 May 1974 Magdeburg also became the first East German club to win a major European trophy, defeating AC Milan 2-0 in the European Cup Winners' Cup.

SEE ALSO **'FIRST INTERNATIONAL AFTER GERMAN REUNIFICATION'** (page 451).

In an incredible upset, East Germany's Jurgen Sparwasser scores the winning goal, beating West Germany's Sepp Maier.

CRUYFF IN CRUISE CONTROL

Holland were at their brilliant best when faced with Argentina in the second phase of the World Cup on 26 June 1974. Johan Cruyff was the 'total' captain of a team playing 'total football' and it's not surprising that he opened the Netherlands' account with super skill. Darting across the Argentinian back line, Cruyff pulled a weighted chip from Wille Van Hanegem under perfect control with his right foot, rounded the advancing goalkeeper and finished with his left foot from an acute angle. Following his performance in the World Cup, Cruyff was voted European Footballer of the Year for the third consecutive time.

SEE ALSO **'GULLIT VOTED EUROPEAN AND DUTCH FOOTBALLER OF THE YEAR'** (page 421).

Cruyff at the peak of his powers torments the Argentinian goalkeeper. He was later voted European Footballer of the Year for the third time.

NEESKENS BREAKS DEADLOCK AGAINST BRAZIL

The Dutch goal that finally unlocked Brazil's defence in the crucial second group stage of the 1974 World Cup began with a Wim Rijsbergen tackle on Jairzinho early in the second half. The tackle caught the Brazilian's ankle and he wasn't pleased. A minute later, Jairzinho went in on Rijsbergen with only one thought in mind – an act of retribution that the referee judged worthy of a free-kick.

With some of the Brazilians still arguing, Wille Van Hanegem, deep inside his own half, took the kick quickly and found Johan Cruyff patrolling out on the right wing. With a chip measured to perfection, Cruyff landed the ball in the path of the flying Johan Neeskens who still had much to do to beat the Brazilian goalkeeper Emerson Leao. With remarkable presence of mind and skill, Neeskens met Cruyff's cross with exactly the right weight and angle to float the ball over the advancing Brazilian goalkeeper. The goal broke the deadlock and gave Holland the boost they needed to go on and score again for a 2-0 win.

SEE ALSO **'HENRY KNOCKS OUT BRAZIL'** (page 602).

With exquisite timing Neeskens opens the scoring.

NO CORNER FLAGS FOR FINAL

Jack Taylor, the referee from England, was on the pitch. The linesmen, Uruguay's Ramón Barreto and Mexico's Archundia González were all keyed up and ready to go. The teams, Holland and West Germany, were assembled and waiting, and so were 80,000 football fans packed into Munich's Olympic Stadium. Yet the 1974 World Cup final, on 7 July 1974, couldn't get underway until someone had found the corner flags. In an unaccountable lapse in organisation, the normally faultless West German hosts had overlooked the final dressing of the pitch and the culminating match of the championships had to be delayed for several minutes while flags were located and placed.

SEE ALSO **'MEXICO AND BULGARIA ALL FALL DOWN'** (page 477).

The captains exchange pennants before the game which was delayed on account of there being no corner flags in position.

The day after the night before. Allegedly. The Dutch team line-up after the damaging revelations were made public in the German press.

'CRUYFF, CHAMPAGNE AND NAKED GIRLS'

The 1974 World Cup final between Holland and West Germany was not only controversial because of its penalties, but also for the below-par performance the Dutch – the exponents of "Total Football" – turned in. Many blamed national gamesmanship when West German tabloid *Bild* ran a story headlined 'Cruyff, champagne and naked girls', which alleged that on the eve of the match the Dutch players had frolicked with a bevy of beauties in the swimming pool of their Hiltrup hotel. Although never substantiated, the story prompted a barrage of phone calls from wives and girlfriends that lasted late into the night, with the team's lynchpin player and captain Johan Cruyff particularly affected.

SEE ALSO **'EL BEATLE IS BORN'** (page 265).

PENALTY – WITHOUT A GERMAN TOUCHING THE BALL

It took only a minute for Johan Cruyff to force a penalty to open the scoring for Holland in the 1974 World Cup final. From the kick-off, the ball was knocked back to Cruyff, who began strolling upfield, before accelerating rapidly, pursued by West Germany's Berti Vogts. With Vogts failing to make ground on the flying Dutchman, Ulrich Hoeness was forced into making a despairing tackle as Cruyff burst into the penalty area looking odds-on to score. Johan Neeskens made sure of the resulting penalty with a central shot as Germany's Sepp Maier dived hopefully to the right. It was 1-0 and no German player had yet touched the ball.

SEE ALSO **'BRYAN ROBSON SCORES AFTER 27 SECONDS'** (page 382).

West Germany's Hoeness brings down Holland's Cruyff to concede a penalty in the first minute and give the Dutch a dream start.

West Germany's Bernd Holzenbein falls to the ground under the challenge of Holland's Wim Jansen. The decision was given.

GERMANY DRAW LEVEL FROM THE SPOT

A niggling first half in the Holland v West Germany 1974 World Cup final saw tempers becoming frayed and the referee under pressure to mete out retribution for alleged foul play. Against this background, Bernd Holzenbein cut into the Dutch penalty area before going down like a poleaxed steer over the outstretched leg of Wim Jansen. Debate raged over whether it was a dive or foul, but referee Jack Taylor awarded the penalty, which was dispatched in the 25th minute by Paul Breitner past an undecided Jan Jongbloed, who was perhaps distracted by Johan Cruyff pointing to the left. Breitner shot right. West Germany went on to win 2-1.

SEE ALSO **'WEST GERMANY WIN SECOND EUROPEAN CHAMPIONSHIPS'** (page 373).

Muller shapes to shoot in the final. His goals brought victory for his team and personal glory as he won the Golden Boot.

MULLER WINS WORLD CUP AND RETIRES WITH 68 GOALS

In a controversial 1974 World Cup final of two penalties, it was somehow extremely fitting that West Germany's great Gerd Muller scored the only clean goal to seal Holland's fate and give Germany the Cup. At the start of the second half the score was tied 1-1, but within minutes Rainer Bonhof had broken down the right with Holland's midfielder Arie Haan in hot pursuit. Bonhof cut the ball back into the box, taking Wim Rijsbergen out of play and finding Muller poised, as ever, in the right place at the right time. Muller swivelled away from the isolated last defender Rudi Krol and poked the ball past Holland's keeper Jan Jongbloed, who was rooted to the spot.

That World Cup final was a fitting stage for Muller's 67th and last game for his country and his 68th goal in a West German shirt. This amazing tally was par for the course for the stocky striker, who had teamed up with Franz Beckenbauer at Bayern Munich to help take the team from the Regional South League into the Bundesliga and onwards to a sustained period of glory.

With his club, Muller won the German championship four times, the German Cup four times, the European Champions Cup three times, the Intercontinental Cup once and the European Cup Winners' Cup once. Oddly, his only individual title was European Footballer of the Year in 1970. A powerful striker with blazing acceleration over short distances, he amassed 628 goals in first class football, including 365 for Bayern during his 14-year career with the club.

SEE ALSO 'MIROSLAV KLOSE WINS GOLDEN BOOT' (page 605).

Newly-retired Bill Shankly acknowledges the fans before his former club Liverpool play Leeds United in the FA Charity Shield.

LIVERPOOL'S BILL SHANKLY QUITS AT THE TOP

In the late 1950s, Liverpool were a failing second division club going nowhere until, in December 1959, they were hit by a Scottish whirlwind in the form of Bill Shankly, who had been a distinguished player in the English First Division and a Scottish international. In nearly 15 years at Anfield he masterminded campaigns that resulted in First Division Championship wins in 1964, 1966 and 1973, and the collection of the FA Cup in 1965 and UEFA Cup in 1973. Citing the strain of a long career, he retired to leave the club to walk on with hope in its heart with former reserve team coach Bob Paisley as boss.

SEE ALSO **'DALGLISH RESIGNS AS LIVERPOOL MANAGER'** (page 451).

SPURS LEGEND NICHOLSON LEAVES THE LANE

"Players have become impossible," said legendary Tottenham Hotspur manager Bill Nicholson when he resigned in July 1974, "There is no longer respect." Thirty years later, on 23 October 2004, Spurs fans stood in silence at White Hart Lane. They were honouring Nicholson, who had died aged 85 after a career that took the club from the lower reaches of the First Division in 1958 to the century's first Football League and FA Cup double in 1960-61 and the FA Cup again a year later. He went on to win the 1963 European Cup Winners' Cup, a third FA Cup in 1967, the 1971 and 1973 League Cups, and the 1972 UEFA Cup.

SEE ALSO **'SPURS WIN THE DOUBLE'** (page 238).

Bill Nicholson – the most successful manager in Tottenham's history. He led the team to the century's first league and cup double in 1960-61.

The vocal Leeds United manager Brian Clough climbs out of the dugout early in his turbulent 44-day reign as manager.

CLOUGH'S 44 DAY REIGN AT LEEDS

Outspoken Brian Clough was universally seen as a hard but fair manager, who insisted on clean play from his players and was outraged at perceived unsporting behaviour by opposition players. As the highly successful Derby County manager in the early 1970s he often criticised arch rivals Leeds United, so it was surprising that he took the Leeds manager's job when Don Revie was called up by England. It was not a good move and he lasted just 44 days before being sacked on 13 September 1974 for upsetting too many players, starting with the advice that they should bin their medals because they had won them unfairly.

SEE ALSO **'CLOUGH AND NOTTINGHAM FOREST WIN EUROPEAN CUP'** (page 367).

LEEDS UNITED'S FANS NIGHT OF VIOLENCE IN PARIS

Leeds fans had had a difficult few months. Their club had finished ninth in the league after Don Revie had left to be replaced by Brian Clough for 44 stormy days. However, new manager Jimmy Armfield had settled the players down and taken the club to the European Cup final against Bayern Munich, but the 28 May game was marred by controversial refereeing that saw winger Peter Lorimer denied a goal through a dubious offside decision and two clear penalty appeals turned down. Fans responded to their team's 2-0 defeat by ripping out seats at the Parc des Princes Stadium, resulting in Leeds being banned from Europe for three years.

SEE ALSO **'LEEDS UNITED – THE RISE BEFORE THE FALL'** (page 547).

Leeds fans look on as trouble erupts below them in Parc des Princes, Paris, following a game marred by controversial refereeing decisions.

FOOTBALL'S GREATEST STAR LANDS STATESIDE

The New York Cosmos' capture of Pelé was a real coup. It seemed to be the moment when football – or 'soccer' as it was branded, to avoid a clash with American football – would finally explode in the States. The game took almost a century to cross the Atlantic, but after NBC covered the 1966 World Cup final two rival US leagues were launched and in 1968 they merged into the North American Soccer League (NASL).

For stars in the twilights of illustrious careers, the NASL provided a lucrative pension. Pelé spent three seasons with the Cosmos leading them to the NASL Championship in his final season. Though his arrival, together with other famous names like Best and Beckenbauer, helped the league expand to 24 teams and boost attendances it was not enough to match players' salaries and in 1984 the NASL folded.

SEE ALSO **'SUPERSTAR BECKHAM JOINS GALAXY'** (page 608).

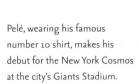

Pelé, wearing his famous number 10 shirt, makes his debut for the New York Cosmos at the city's Giants Stadium.

Bayern Munich's Uli Hoeness and Johnny Hansen parade the European Cup around Hampden Park after their 1-0 win over Atletico Madrid.

BAYERN'S EUROPEAN CUP HAT-TRICK

After winning controversial European Champions Cup finals against Atletico Madrid in 1974 and Leeds United in 1975, Bayern Munich enjoyed considerable luck to win the trophy for a third consecutive time against St Etienne on 12 May 1976. Although the French club's star Dominique Rocheteau was off the field injured for all but eight minutes of the match, St. Etienne rattled the German crossbar twice. The final was decided in the 57th minute with a Franz Roth free-kick after a push on Dieter Muller and, while the French created two more chances before the final whistle, Bayern held on to equal the great Ajax treble of the early 1970s.

SEE ALSO **'LIVERPOOL WIN THIRD EUROPEAN CUP'** (page 376).

Under-fire England manager Don Revie looks pensive as he faces the notoriously critical British media to explain his team's early exit.

EUROPE'S SUPERPOWERS GO OUT IN FIRST ROUND

It was a bleak June for England, France and Italy when they tumbled out in the first round of the 1976 European Championships. England started brightly enough with a 3-0 win over Czechoslovakia, but went on to win just one more game, while losing two and drawing two to end runners-up in their group. France and Italy did even worse, both ending up third in their respective groups. At least England had the consolation of being beaten in their group by the championship's final winner, Czechoslovakia. France's group winners, Belgium, were knocked out in the quarter-finals while the Netherlands, who won Italy's group, survived until the semis.

SEE ALSO **'SWEDES 2 TURNIPS 1'** (page 459).

WEST GERMANY AND CZECHOSLOVAKIA CONTEST FINAL

1976

West Germany and Czechoslovakia arrived in the 1976 European Championships final in nail-biting fashion, with both teams having had to survive extra-time in their semis. After 25 minutes of the 20 June final, a shell-shocked West German team found themselves trailing 2-0 after goals by Jan Svehlik and Karol Dobias. A player with the famous name of Muller fired the Germans back into contention before half-time, but it was Dieter, not the legendary goalscorer Gerd, who gave the Germans hope. Still, West Germany had to wait until literally the last minute before Bernd Holzenbein saved the day with a headed equaliser. The 2-2 deadlock was not broken in extra-time.

SEE ALSO **'CZECH REPUBLIC BEAT GERMANY'** (page 581).

SEE ALSO **'CZECH REPUBLIC BEAT GERMANY'** (page 581).

Czechoslovakia's Jan Svehlik fires home his side's opening goal despite the efforts of West Germany's Erich Beer.

347

PANENKA – THE SHOOT OUT HERO

A penalty shoot-out came to a major competition for the first time in the 1976 European Championships final. Tied at 2-2 after extra-time, West Germany and Czechoslovakia made history when they lined up for spot-kicks. Never before had a major competition been decided by penalties and, unusually in the light of subsequent history, it was the Germans who cracked. During the first seven penalties the great West German keeper Sepp Maier came closest to deflecting a shot, but by the time Uli Hoeness stepped up for West Germany his team were 4-3 down. From a short run-up Hoeness swung his right boot, but clutched his head as the ball cleared the crossbar. It was still 4-3 when Czechoslovakia's Antonin Panenka faced Maier and the tension in the stadium was almost unbearable. Time seemed to slow down as he ran in to strike the ball and Maier dived to the left, but instead of a powerful shot Panenka played a delicate chip that floated almost dead centre into the top of the net. It was 5-3 to Czechoslovakia. Game over.

SEE ALSO **'KAREL POBORSKY'S LOB'** (page 497).

Antonin Panenka chips home the decisive penalty in the shoot- out win over West Germany.

BASQUE CLUBS SHOW SOLIDARITY

To a tumultuous reception the captains of Real
Sociedad and Athletico Bilbao walked onto the pitch
carrying the Basque flag. Politics are never far below
the surface in Spain and as soon as dictator General
Franco died the Basque people in the north began
to campaign to assert their individuality and for the
right to fly their own flag. What is claimed to be the
first public display of the flag after Franco's death
came during this local derby between the two leading
Basque football teams and some 20,000 spectators
cheered wildly when captains Jose Angel Iribar and
Inaxio Kortabarria ceremoniously placed the banned
ensign on the centre circle.

SEE ALSO **'BARCELONA CROWD WHISTLES DURING
ANTHEM'** (page 99); **'CRUYFF IN WORLD CUP PROTEST'**
(page 356).

The Ikurriña flag is a Basque symbol and the official flag
of the Basque Country Autonomous Community of Spain.

1976

BOWLES' ODD BOOTS

The 2-0 Dutch victory over England in a Wembley
friendly on 9 February was memorable for a couple
of reasons. The first was when the Queens Park
Rangers maverick Stan Bowles trotted out onto the
hallowed turf with an Adidas boot on his left foot
and a Gola one on the right. He was honouring two
separate boot sponsorship deals for the international
showpiece in his own eccentric way. The match was
also unusual for Holland's two first-half goals, which
were scored by Jan Peters. Normally a substitute for
his country, this was the first time Peters had been
selected to start the game.

SEE ALSO **'MATTHEWS BUYS NEW BOOTS IN BRAZIL'**
(page 172); **'LIVERPOOL GET A SHIRT SPONSOR'** (page 367).

The eccentric Stan Bowles in full flight against the Dutch. He
doesn't seem to be hampered by his 'odd' choice of footwear.

1977

Ecstatic Scottish fans mount the sagging crossbar as thousands went wild after Scotland's 2-1 victory over England at Wembley.

SCOTS INVADE WEMBLEY PITCH

It was like a children's party that got out of hand. The whistle had just blown on a historic 2-1 Scotland win over England when, unable to contain their happiness, Scottish fans burst onto the pitch to cavort, swing on the goalposts and dig up turf for souvenirs. It was reported in England as an act of outrageous hooliganism causing £15,000 damage, but from the Scots' point of view it was a moment of joyful madness to celebrate a rare victory over the 'Auld Enemy' on their home ground. The trouble, though, hastened the demise of the Home International Championships, which had traditonally involved England, Scotland, Wales and Northern Ireland.

SEE ALSO **'GASCOIGNE VOLLEY STUNS SCOTLAND'** (page 496).

Revie at Heathrow preparing to board a flight to Dubai to take up his controversial new post as the United Arab Emirates's football supremo.

REVIE ABANDONS ENGLAND

As football scandals go, Don Revie's resignation as England boss ranks among the greatest. He was plotting a deal with the United Arab Emirates (UAE) even as his England side struggled – and failed – to qualify for the 1978 World Cup. He was convinced the FA was about to sack him, but got his retaliation in first by signing up as the UAE football supremo for a huge tax-free £65,000 a year salary – and announcing his England resignation in the *Daily Mail*. A furious FA banned him from football for a decade and he was savaged in the press. He never returned to English football.

SEE ALSO **'ENGLAND GO FOR ERIKSSON'** (page 543).

The star player for Borussia Monchengladbach and the Danish national team, Allan Simonsen paved the way for future heroes like Michael Laudrup and Peter Schmeichel.

SIMONSEN NAMED EUROPEAN FOOTBALLER OF THE YEAR

Allan Simonsen became the first Dane to be named European Footballer of the Year, ahead of big names such as Englishman Kevin Keegan and French star Michel Platini. The honour was all the more notable considering that, at the time, Denmark was not a footballing power, so Simonsen had little opportunity to impress on the international stage. His reputation was rooted in West Germany where he played his football for Borussia Monchengladbach and had made a significant contribution toward the club's 1976 German League Cup victory and Bundesliga Championship wins in 1976 and 1977. His success on the European stage and the ease with which he adapted to a foreign league made him Denmark's finest footballing export.

SEE ALSO **'SIMONSEN'S INJURY AGONY'** (page 399).

LIVERPOOL WIN THE LEAGUE AND THEIR FIRST EUROPEAN CUP

Liverpool's 3-1 European Cup win against Borussia Monchengladbach in Rome on 25 May looks, on paper, to have been a comfortable stroll. But without the woodwork saving Ray Clemence's blushes in the first half and the goalkeeper's three world-class saves in the second, Liverpool could have been overwhelmed. This was also the year that Liverpool nearly hit a famous treble. As well as winning the European Cup they won the English League Championship. The Reds also came close to lifting the FA Cup in England, but failed to get past Manchester United in the final, in spite of going into the match as clear favourites.

SEE ALSO **'MANCHESTER UNITED FIGHT BACK TO WIN CHAMPIONS LEAGUE'** (pages 526-7).

Liverpool's Phil Neal, Emlyn Hughes and Jimmy Case show the European Cup to their jubilant fans after their 3-1 victory.

Pelé's superstar status drew huge crowds and is credited with significantly increasing American public awareness of football or 'soccer'.

PELÉ RETIRES FOR GOOD

By the time Pelé waved farewell to Brazilian football in 1972 he was known as the 'King of Football' and had achieved about as much as any player could expect in a lifetime. Yet in 1975 he was persuaded to move from South to North America and sign with New York Cosmos. Aided by the imports of Italian star Giorgio Chinaglia, Germany's Franz Beckenbauer and fellow Brazilian Carlos Alberto, Pelé took Cosmos to its second North America Soccer League Championship. His swansong was a friendly against old club Santos at New York's Giants Stadium. In front of a capacity crowd he played the first half for Cosmos, showing the old magic by scoring a goal from 30 yards out, but in the second spell he came out for Santos. Cosmos won 2-1.

SEE ALSO **'FAREWELL TO A FLAWED TALENT'** (page 508).

JAPANESE PLAYER TACKLES EUROPE

A new page was written in the history of Japanese football when Yasuhiko Okudera emerged from the tunnel with his team-mates to make his first-team debut with FC Cologne in Germany's Bundesliga. That away game against MSV Duisburg paved the way for future generations of Japanese footballers to play in Europe and join a league of world-class players. Okudera had learned his footballing trade as an employee of Furukawa Electric Co, whose team played in the corporate Japan Soccer League, the top flight league in Japan at the time. It was by chance that he was spotted by FC Cologne coach Hennes Weisweiler when the Japanese team toured Germany.

SEE ALSO **'J-LEAGUE LAUNCHED'** (page 467).

Yasuhiko Okudera takes to the pitch for FC Cologne. He was spotted by their coach when his Japanese team toured Germany.

Scotland striker Joe Jordan handles the ball in the Wales penalty area, for which the referee inexplicably awarded Scotland a vital penalty.

JORDAN HANDS SCOTS A WORLD CUP PLACE

Wales had high hopes of making it to the 1978 World Cup in Argentina when they met Scotland at Anfield. Wales were the home team and had requested a larger stadium. It was an open game full of chances, but it was still 0-0 as time began running out. In the 78th minute Scotland striker Joe Jordan challenged with Welsh defender David Jones for a long throw into the box and in doing so flicked the ball with his hand. To Welsh fury, referee Robert Wurtz awarded a penalty against Wales, which Scotland midfielder Don Masson slotted home. Ten minutes later Kenny Dalglish finally crushed the Welsh dream with a second Scotland goal.

SEE ALSO **'PIOLA'S HANDBALL'** (pages 143); **'THE HAND OF GOD'** (pages 414-5).

Menotti dragged Argentinian football into the modern age tranforming them into a major force in the big tournaments.

MENOTTI OMITS MARADONA

Unthinkable as it is today, there was a time when Argentina could do without Maradona in the national side. Argentinian football owes its lofty standing in no small measure to Cesar Luis Menotti, under whose direction the team won their first World Cup, in 1978, while hosting the touranment. Menotti's big gamble for that competition was to prefer veteran striker Mario Kempes to promising youngster Diego Maradona. Standing firm in the face of furious national debate, Menotti was vindicated when Kempes proved to be the team's inspirational leader and goalscorer. The following year, Maradona starred in FIFA's World Youth Championship in Japan, which Argentina also won under Menotti's guidance.

SEE ALSO **'KEMPES STRIKES IN EXTRA TIME'** (page 362).

BLACK PLAYERS UNITE AGAINST PREJUDICE

Black footballers are rightly feted in football leagues throughout the world for their skill, but in England, the so called 'Three Degrees' – Laurie Cunningham, Cyrille Regis and Brendan Batson – are credited with breaking down prejudice and racism in the game. As lynch-pins in an exciting West Bromwich Albion side created by Ron Atkinson in the 1970s, the trio endured unprecedented racist taunts to deliver some of the most memorable soccer in football's flair era. Such was their impact on the game and public consciousness that their legacy is regarded by many as being as important as that left by boxing's great Muhammad Ali.

SEE ALSO **'ANDERSON BECOMES ENGLAND'S FIRST BLACK INTERNATIONAL'** (page 365).

The inspirational Regis, Cunningham and Batson can all be seen here in this West Bromwich Albion team photograph for the 1978-79 season.

Ipswich Town's Roger Osborne's cup-winning strike and the following elation left him shattered, so much so that he had to be substituted.

WEMBLEY SHOCK FOR CUP FAVOURITES

On 6 May Arsenal went into the 50th FA Cup final at Wembley as clear favourites after finishing fifth in Division One, 13 places above opponents Ipswich Town. Yet it was Bobby Robson's Ipswich underdogs who shone and, in the 77th minute, local Ipswich boy, midfielder Roger Osborne, who broke the deadlock. Arsenal's Willie Young half-stifled a cross from David Geddis, but the ball fell for Osborne who drove a low shot beyond goalkeeper Jennings. The elation proved too much for Osborne, who was substituted almost immediately due to exhaustion, leaving his team-mates to hold on for the 1-0 victory.

SEE ALSO **'THE CRAZY GANG STUN LIVERPOOL'** (page 422).

DALGLISH KEY TO HISTORIC WIN

Liverpool became the first British team to win successive European Cups despite a massive rearguard action by their opponents. With two key Club Brugge players injured for the final at Wembley, coach Ernst Happel massed his defence. The ploy worked until the 75th minute when Liverpool substitute Steve Heighway combined with Terry McDermott to find Graeme Souness on the edge of the penalty area. Souness chested the ball down and found Kenny Dalglish free on the right of the box. The Scot waited for the goalkeeper to commit himself and then lifted the ball over his head and into the net.

SEE ALSO **'NOTTINGHAM FOREST WIN A SUCCESSIVE EUROPEAN CUP'** (page 371).

Kenny Dalglish slots the ball passed the advancing Bruges keeper Jensen to put Liverpool ahead in the European Cup final.

Johan Cruyff's political stance deprived the 1978 World Cup and Holland of one of football's most brilliant talents.

CRUYFF IN WORLD CUP PROTEST

Before an ecstatic home crowd at the Estadio Monumental in Buenos Aires, Argentina lifted the World Cup for the first time after beating Holland 3-1. But one player was sensationally absent that day. Holland star Johan Cruyff had refused to take part in the tournament as a personal protest against the military dictatorship of General Jorge Videla, which had ruled Argentina since 1976. Before the event there had been massive controversy over the decision to allow the country to host it and several countries had threatened a boycott. In the end only Cruyff stayed away despite intense pressure at home for him to set aside his principles and play.

SEE ALSO **'DUTCH PLAYERS REFUSE TO COLLECT THEIR MEDALS'** (page 364).

Osvaldo Ardilles was one of the chief beneficiaries of Cesar Menotti's uncompromising approach to team selection.

HOME-GROWN WINNING POLICY

Argentina's policy was to use players who played in Argentina to secure a World Cup win, but ironically the team's success turned on the goal-scoring ability of its one foreign-based star. The team's most sparkling form was shown by 23-year-old striker Mario Kempes, a hit in Spain with Valencia. Kempes later attributed Argentina's World Cup victory to coach Cesar Menotti's emphasis on home-based players, but without doubt it was Kempes who proved to be the star of the World Cup. He coped best with uneven pitches, slaloming through defences, finishing with cool precision and taking the tournament's Golden Boot prize for the top scorer.

SEE ALSO **'VILLA AND ARDILES SPEARHEAD BRITAIN'S FOREIGN LEGION'** (page 364).

A wave of confetti and toilet paper streamers welcomed the home favourites to the pitch in every round of the tournament.

ARGENTINA TIED UP IN TICKER TAPE

The slogan promoted by Argentina's military junta when the country hosted the 1978 World cup was '25 million Argentinians will play in the World Cup'. And for the Hungarian team lining up on 2 June against the host nation's side in the capital's Estadio Monumental it must have felt as though they were facing the entire country. With the vast majority of the 75,000 fans inside the imposing stadium passionately partisan, the noise and atmosphere was intense. The Hungarians were also the first to experience the ticker tape blizzard that was to be a feature of the tournament every time the home team appeared on the pitch.

SEE ALSO **'THE ARRIVAL OF THE MEXICAN WAVE'** (page 410).

Welsh referee Clive Thomas' decision to blow for full-time early caused uproar. He was never again to officiate at a World Cup.

REFEREE BLOWS FULL-TIME EARLY

Brazil weren't the Brazil of old when they went a goal behind to Sweden in their first round World Cup match, but they equalized just before half-time and went on to dominate in the second half. However, the game was deadlocked when, on the stroke of 90 minutes, the linesman flagged for a Brazilian corner. Welsh referee Clive Thomas allowed them to take it, but with the ball in flight he blew for full-time, a fraction of a second before Brazilian star Zico rose to head into the back of the net. Despite furious protests Thomas refused to let the goal stand and the result was Sweden 1, Brazil 1.

SEE ALSO **'REFEREE SHOWS THREE YELLOW CARDS TO ONE PLAYER'** (page 601).

GEMMILL'S MAZY
GOAL STUNS THE DUTCH

In 1978 Scotland's manager Ally MacLeod took his team to Argentina promising to bring back the World Cup. He didn't, of course, but his little midfielder Archie Gemmill did give the Tartan army a moment to take home and cherish forever. Scotland as ever had made hard work of their task, losing to a good Peru side and drawing with Iran. Come 11 June they had to beat the Dutch by three clear goals to progress, but found themselves a goal down to an early Johnny Rep effort. As the Tartan Army thought about packing their kilts, a Kenny Dalglish equalizer and a Gemmill penalty suddenly gave them faint hope. In the 68th minute that hope turned into delirium as Gemmill picked up possession in the inside-right position. He beat one desperate lunge and calmly side-stepped another before deftly lifting the ball with his left foot over the on-rushing keeper Jan Jongbloed. A simple clenched fist said it all, but, alas, the Dutch scored a second and the Scots were going home, empty-handed but with an experience they'd never forget.

SEE ALSO **'MARADONA SCORES INCREDIBLE SECOND'** (page 416);
'CAMBIASSO FINISHES OFF GOAL OF THE WORLD CUP' (page 600).

Archie Gemmill looks up to pick his spot before bending in his team's third goal.

HOLLAND STRIKE DOWN ITALY

On 21 June Holland were a goal down to Italy thanks to an own goal by defender Erny Brandts. Italy held that lead at half-time, but were later undone by two sublime strikes. On 50 minutes it was Brandts again who picked the ball up in a melee of Italian defenders, swung at it with his 'weak' right foot and sent it screaming past Dino Zoff from 25 yards. "What luck!" bemoaned Italian defender Claudio Gentile, but there was no doubt about Arie Haan's winner. The Dutch midfielder received the ball a good 40 yards out, took two strides forward and unleashed a crashing shot into Zoff's left-hand top corner.

SEE ALSO **'BAGGIO WINS SEMI-FINAL FOR ITALY'** (page 479).

Holland's Arie Haan skips
past two Italian defenders.
He won the game with a
stunning 40-yard strike.

ARGENTINA PROGRESS TO FINAL AMID CONTROVERSY

Controversy had surrounded the 1978 World Cup long before a ball had been kicked in anger. In 1976 Argentina, the host country had been the subject of a military junta led by General Jorge Videla. The regime's suspected violation of human rights caused much soul-searching in Europe. There were rumours that the competition would be moved to Holland and Belgium, and that the Dutch would withdraw if it wasn't. This didn't happen, but the Dutch talisman Johan Cruyff refused to travel. The tournament had lost its most famous player and so it was with trepidation that the games got started in Buenos Aires.

By the time the final group stages came along, suspicion still reigned. The final eight teams were split into two groups, Argentina being paired with rivals Brazil. They drew their game 0-0, but other results meant that on 21 June Argentina had to beat Peru by at least four goals. It looked like a tall order. The stench of foul play had been heightened by reports that General Videla had been into the Peruvian dressing room prior to kick-off. Fears were slightly allayed by a good Peru start, but it didn't last. After 20 minutes Mario Kempes scored and the floodgates opened. The hosts scored their vital fourth, again through Kempes, within the hour and managed two more without reply.

The Brazilian manager Claudio Coutinho was apoplectic; the Argentinian press countered global scepticism by stating that it was, in fact, Brazil who had bribed Peru to try harder while the Peruvian keeper Quirgora – notably born in Argentina – had to publish an open letter defending his and his team's action. Tongues are still wagging 30 years later.

SEE ALSO **'SOUTH KOREA MARCH ON AMID CONTROVERSY'** (page 564).

Argentine President Jorge Videla after he had presented the World Cup Trophy to Argentina's captain Daniel Passarella.

Peru's Teofilo Cubillas runs at the Argentina defence.

Referee Sergio Gonella and his linesmen before the final. The Dutch team protested that he was too weak to control the high profile game.

ARGENTINA'S BANDAGE PROTEST

Italian Sergio Gonella was charged with refereeing the final on 25 June, but the Dutch feared he was too weak to control what was bound to be a competitive encounter. That fear soon proved very real as the hosts protested about the heavily bandaged wrist of Holland's Rene Van de Kerkhof. It was strange that Van de Kerkof had worn it for the five preceding games, but, no matter, Gonella made the Dutch winger amend the bandage. "We could not allow ourselves to concede any advantage," said Argentinian skipper Daniel Passarella. "Luque [the Argentinian striker] saw the danger the bandage could be and I as captain had the obligation to protest."

SEE ALSO 'REFEREE GETS IT IN THE NECK FROM ITALIANS' (page 574).

KEMPES STRIKES IN EXTRA-TIME

With his swashbuckling style and flowing dark hair, Mario Kempes had become the idol of an expectant nation. His form from midfield had taken Argentina to the final and now the 78,000 fans packed into the River Plate Stadium eagerly awaited his every move. Those same fans may well have feared the opposition as, only four years earlier, the Dutch had mesmerised the world beating Argentina 4-0 along the way.

Seven of that mighty Dutch team took to the field, but it was Argentina and Kempes who struck first. Holland equalised and looked the stronger unit going into extra-time, but, galvanised by a raucous crowd, the hosts raised their game and 14 minutes in it was Kempes – who else – who rewarded their fervour. The number 10 received a pass from Bertoni and purposefully rode two challenges before toe-poking the ball against Jongbloed, only to prod in the rebound.

SEE ALSO 'MARADONA ON TOP OF THE WORLD' (page 417).

Argentina's Leopoldo Luque, Daniel Bertoni and scorer Kempes celebrate as the ball bounces into the net for Argentina's second goal.

ARGENTINA WIN PROMPTS 'THE HUG OF THE SOUL'

Five minutes from time, Kempes once more made inroads into the Dutch penalty box and the ball broke to Argentine winger Daniel Bertoni, who slotted in the winner. On hearing the final whistle, Argentina's keeper Ubaldo Fillol was overcome. "My legs gave way," he recalled. "I look up and see the image of God." Left-back Alberto Tarantini joined him in prayer on the hallowed turf and, as the crazed locals celebrated with a blue and white ticker-tape storm, Tarantini and Fillol embraced. Then a young boy – with no arms – rushed onto the pitch and threw himself on his idols. It was an image immediately named 'The hug of the soul'.

SEE ALSO **'MUTUAL ADMIRATION SOCIETY'** (page 300);
'THE TARDELLI SCREAM' (page 392).

Overcome by emotion Tarantini and Fillol are joined by a young fan who rushed onto the pitch at the final whistle to celebrate with his heroes.

Cruyff was not the only Dutchman to make a political protest in Argentina. The defeated finalists also took a stand against Videla.

DUTCH PLAYERS REFUSE TO COLLECT THEIR MEDALS

The Dutch were, for the second World Cup running, beaten finalists. Once again the hosts had got the better of them; once more they had to make do with the world's sympathy rather than glory. In 1978 they were in no mood to play the role of honourable losers and instead of accepting their medals from General Videla they left the field in protest at what they, like many others, felt was an unjust, inhumane regime. It is unknown whether, had the Dutch won, they would have taken the trophy from Videla.

SEE ALSO 'CRUYFF IN WORLD CUP PROTEST' (pages 356); 'ARGENTINA PROGRESS TO FINAL AMID CONTROVERSY' (pages 360-1).

VILLA AND ARDILES SPEARHEAD BRITAIN'S FOREIGN LEGION

In July 1978, just weeks after Argentina's World Cup triumph, Tottenham manager Keith Burkinshaw heard from a contact at Sheffield United that some of that squad were up for sale. The Blades couldn't afford to act on their information, but Burkinshaw was straight on a plane to Buenos Aries to pull off the great coup of signing Ossie Ardiles from Huracan for £325,000 and Ricky Villa from Racing Club for £375,000. The Professional Footballers' Association (PFA) feared an influx of foreign players would hinder English players' chances, but anyone who watched those players will tell you they did English football very little harm at all.

SEE ALSO 'KLINSMANN JOINS THE PREMIERSHIP' (page 480).

Keith Burkinshaw welcomes his two exciting South American signings to north London after stealing a march on Sheffield United.

CRUYFF SAYS GOODBYE BUT NOT FAREWELL

Cruyff revitalized the Catalan giants but by 1978 his influence was on the wane. Despite appearing in 28 of Barca's 34 league matches this, together with the furore over his World Cup boycott led the 31-year-old Cruyff to walk away. His retirement proved short-lived, as he became the latest superstar to head to America with the LA Aztecs and Washington Diplomats before making a surprising return to Ajax and an even more startling move to arch rivals Feyenoord. But he was to renew his association with Barcelona when he returned to the Nou Camp as coach, ten years after he left them as a player.

SEE ALSO 'GEORGE BEST QUITS - AT 26' (page 319).

The body language between the Barcelona coach Rinus Michels and his superstar captain Johan Cruyff tells it's own story.

ANDERSON BECOMES ENGLAND'S FIRST BLACK INTERNATIONAL

By the autumn of 1978 Viv Anderson had turned many heads in English football. Nottingham Forest had won the title in May and their right-back was an integral part of Brian Clough's triumph. Here was a defender, strong in the tackle but comfortable in possession, so a call-up to the England squad shouldn't have raised any eyebrows. However, it was the 1970s and he was a black footballer, so it did. All eyes were on Anderson as he strolled out onto the Wembley pitch on a cold night in October to face Czechoslovakia. Anderson was solid (he would struggle to displace Phil Neal though) and England won 1-0.

SEE ALSO 'BLACK PLAYERS UNITE AGAINST PREJUDICE' (page 354).

Nottingham Forest's Viv Anderson on his debut for the national team, the first black player to represent England in a full international.

BRITAIN'S FIRST
£1 MILLION FOOTBALLER

The 16-year-old Trevor Francis had burst onto the scene in 1970, scoring some wonder goals for Birmingham City and earning a call-up for England along the way. In the late 1970s Birmingham flirted regularly with relegation, so Brian Clough decided to pounce. Forest had become league champions the season before and were pushing for European honours when, on 9 February 1979, Clough agreed the first ever £1 million deal in the English game. Forest had been in the Second Division only 18 months prior to the move, but Clough insisted the club could afford this figure thanks to good management.

Trevor Francis with his wife, Helen, and Forest manager Brian Clough at the City Ground after becoming Britain's most expensive player.

SEE ALSO 'MARADONA SIGNS FOR BARCELONA IN RECORD DEAL' (page 378); 'ZIZOU BECOMES A GALACTICO' (page 549).

BRADY INSPIRES ARSENAL
IN 'FIVE-MINUTE FINAL'

With four minutes to go in the FA Cup final on 12 May 1979 they were 2-0 up, but twice in the last five minutes they slipped up and Manchester United drew level. Thank heavens, then, for Liam Brady. Having set up Arsenal's two earlier goals, he purposefully carried the ball into United's half, his perfect left foot teasing a quickly panicking defence. He exploited a gap between Steve Coppell and Lou Macari, played a simple through ball to Graeme Rix on the left wing and watched as the England man crossed perfectly for Alan Sunderland to slide in at the back post and win the Cup for Arsenal.

SEE ALSO 'LIAM BRADY WINS JUVENTUS A SECOND SUCCESSIVE SERIE A CROWN' (page 379).

The inspirational Brady is on the left of the front row as the Gunners celebrate victory - after so nearly blowing their commanding lead.

CLOUGH AND NOTTINGHAM FOREST WIN EUROPEAN CUP

Liverpool, AK Athens, Zurich Grasshoppers and Cologne had all been beaten along the way to set up a 30 May European Cup final in Munich against Malmo. Forest were without midfielders Archie Gemmill and Martin O'Neil, but Trevor Francis was now eligible to play in Europe and it was the new man who would win the Cup. On the stroke of half-time John Robertson went on a trademark slippery run down the left and curled a wonderful cross to the back post, where Francis was on hand to head past Malmo's Jans Moller. From the Second Division to European Champions in just two years – Brian Clough was a genius.

SEE ALSO **'NOTTINGHAM FOREST WIN A SUCCESSIVE EUROPEAN CUP'** (page 371).

Trevor Francis meets John Robertson's sublime cross to head the winning goal past Malmo goalkeeper Jan Moller's despairing dive.

LIVERPOOL GET A SHIRT SPONSOR

Rather then dampening Liverpool's fortunes, Bill Shankly's departure had ushered in an even brighter era under Bob Paisley. An unassuming footballing man from Durham, Paisley may not have had the oratory skills of his predecessor, but his team were very eloquent indeed and big business had taken note of triumphs at home and abroad. Shirt sponsorship had begun to happen in Europe, but not yet in England. Japanese electrical firm Hitachi already sponsored Hamburg and struck a deal to advertise on the famous red shirts of Liverpool. The purists on the Kop may have had their doubts, but the modern game was taking shape and that was that.

SEE ALSO **'FA CUP SPONSORSHIP PLAN THWARTED'** (page 421); **'BARCELONA ANNOUNCE UNICEF SHIRT SPONSORSHIP'** (page 606).

Liverpool were the first top flight club to accept the shirt sponsorship. Few could have predicted the huge sums generated by today's deals.

Diego Maradona's huge potential was evident in Japan. The world waited to see if he would make the step up to international level?

MARADONA INSPIRES ARGENTINA

A year on from their World Cup triumph, the Argentinian World Cup winners were still heroes, but now everyone was talking about a 16-year-old from Villa Fiorito, a shanty town on the outskirts of Buenos Aires – Diego Maradona. The Boca Juniors' playmaker was the captain of the youngsters who sailed through their World Youth Cup group, outplayed old foes Uruguay in the semis, before beating a strong Soviet Union side 3-1 in the final in Tokyo. The Russians had taken the lead, but Maradona inspired his team-mates and it was he himself who curled an irresistible free-kick into the top corner to seal a famous win.

SEE ALSO 'WAYNE ROONEY MAKES HIS MARK' (page 567).

The Olympic Stadium in Rome saw the city's fiercely fought derby end in unprecedented tragedy with the death of a Lazio supporter.

FIRST ITALIAN FAN FATALITY

The Rome derby has long been a tempestuous affair, and Roma and Lazio have often fought with the kind of passion, intrigue and bitterness which would have made their Roman ancestors, packed into the Coliseum, proud. However, in 1979 what some saw as harmless city rivalry turned into tragedy. Vicenzo Paperelli, a Lazio fan, took his place in the Curva Nord section frequented by Lazio fans, but was struck by a rocket fired from the opposite Curva Sud and killed. It was the first time a fan had been killed at an Italian football match and a nation was shocked.

SEE ALSO 'THE HEYSEL STADIUM DISASTER' (page 404); 'ITALIAN FOOTBALL SUSPENDED' (page 609).

ITALY SCRAPS BAN ON FOREIGN PLAYERS

The Italians had returned home from the 1966 World Cup defeated and humiliated. The team was heavily ridiculed and when the dust had settled the authorities decided to stop the influx of foreigners to Serie A, in order to give Italian players a chance to excel at club, and then hopefully national, levels. The ban permitted Italian clubs one foreigner per squad and this ruling lasted until 1980. However, when it was lifted Juventus quickly swooped for Arsenal's Liam Brady and soon scores of players accepted invitations to move to Serie A.

SEE ALSO **'CHELSEA FIELD NON-BRITISH XI'** (page 531).

Frenchman Platini would become of Juve's rapidly growing foreign legion speedily assembled once the ban was scrapped in Italy.

WORLD CLUB CUP SWITCHED TO TOKYO

By 1980 the supposed world championship of club football was in a very precarious state. Since 1960, Europe's champions had taken on their South American counterparts in what were too often overly physical encounters. In the late 1970s the two-legged games had become increasingly difficult to arrange due to conflicting and busy schedules, and the concept didn't look at all viable until car manufacturer Toyota stepped in and the Japanese offered to host a one-off game. The inaugural final saw Nottingham Forest beaten by Uruguayan club Nacional. A sell-out 62,000 crowd saw Uruguayan striker Waldemar Victorino score the only goal. The fixture has been played in Tokyo ever since.

SEE ALSO **'MANCHESTER UNITED WITHDRAW FROM FA CUP'** (page 531).

Nottingham Forest's tricky winger Ulsterman Martin O'Neill attempts to evade Nacional's defender Denis Milar in the first Tokyo final.

ALLEN ALMOST THE YOUNGEST TO PLAY IN A FA CUP FINAL

In 1980 Paul Allen helped Second Division West Ham reach the FA Cup final against Arsenal. Aged only 17 years and 256 days, Allen could have been the youngest player ever to have appeared in an FA Cup final, but in fact he wasn't. In 1879 James Prinsep, aged 17 years and 245 days, had played for Clapham Rovers against Old Etonians in a Kennington Oval final. Allen (unlike Prinsep) would take home a winners' medal thanks to a Trevor Brooking goal, but the youngster was denied a fairy-tale ending just three minutes from time when, with only Pat Jennings to beat, he was unceremoniously hacked down by Willie Young.

SEE ALSO **'BILLY MEREDITH, AGED 49'** (page 95).

Paul Allen played in the FA Cup final aged 17 and 256 days. He was the latest in a line of players from the famous Allen footballing dynasty.

Valencia celebrate with the European Cup Winners Cup after their penalty shoot-out victory over Arsenal at the Heysel stadium.

EUROPEAN CUP WINNERS' CUP FINAL DECIDED ON PENALTIES

Despite the fine array of talent on show at Brussels' Heysel Stadium on 14 May, Valencia and Arsenal couldn't muster a goal between them in 120 minutes of stagnant football. Arsenal, depleted from losing to West Ham just days before, struggled to break the Spaniards down and so, for the first time, a major European Cup final was decided on penalties. The deadlock remained as the two superstars on show, Valencia's Mario Kempes and Arsenal's Liam Brady, both missed their opening kicks, but order was resumed and the next eight penalties were successful. It was sudden death. Arias scored for Valencia, but Graeme Rix, Arsenal's England international, had his effort saved.

SEE ALSO **'MILAN WIN ALL-ITALIAN FINAL ON PENALTIES'** (page 570).

Zebec was responsible for bringing Kevin Keegan to the German club where he won the European Footballer of the Year award twice.

HAMBURG COACH SLEEPS ON THE JOB

A very good Yugoslavian footballer in his day, Branko Zebec arrived to coach SV Hamburg in 1978. In his first season they won the Bundesliga, but in his next they narrowly lost it to Bayern Munich and were beaten by Nottingham Forest in the European Cup final. Zebec's tough training methods were blamed for both defeats, but it was his off-field habits that caused the real problems. He was known to like a drink, including on the bench, and it wasn't unknown for him to fall asleep during a game. In December 1980 Zebec was finally asked to leave the club.

SEE ALSO **'DAUM AND OUT IN GERMANY'** (page 540).

NOTTINGHAM FOREST MAKE IT SUCCESSIVE EUROPEAN CUPS

Some Forest fans still couldn't quite believe they'd done it once, but on 28 May 1980 Brian Clough led his incredible team to another European Cup triumph. SV Hamburg were the beaten team in Madrid, but it was never as comfortable as the victory 12 months before. Hamburg's Kevin Keegan, the double European Footballer of the Year, was a constant threat, but Kenny Burns, Larry Lloyd and the brilliant Peter Shilton in goal were more than a match for him. Once more Forest won it with a solitary first-half goal, this time provided by John Robertson in the 21st minute with a fine drive that cannoned in off the post.

SEE ALSO **'LIVERPOOL WIN THIRD EUROPEAN CUP'** (page 376); **'ASTON VILLA WIN EUROPEAN CUP'** (page 379).

Nottingham Forest's heroic goalscorer John Robertson tightly clutches his second hard fought European Cup winners medal.

REAL MADRID TROUNCE THEIR RESERVES IN SPANISH CUP FINAL

Real Madrid had already pipped the desperately unlucky Real Sociedad to the La Liga crown on the last day of the season and so went into the Copa Del Rey final feeling especially good about themselves. What's more, their opponents were Castilla, their official nursery club (today they're called Real Madrid Castilla and play in the Spanish second division), and they didn't really have a lot to worry about there. Not one yellow card was shown by a mainly unnecessary referee at the Bernabau as Real took a 2-0 lead before half-time, before running over their 'apprentices' in the second half and finishing 6-1 winners.

SEE ALSO **'VILLARREAL RISE FROM OBSCURITY'** (page 596); **'GETAFE DO THE UNTHINKABLE'** (page 613).

Real Madrid beat their official nursery club Castilla 6-1 in what must have been their easiest Copa Del Rey final.

TEAR GAS IN TURIN

England's first game of the 1980 European Championship was on 12 June against Belgium in Turin. Hooliganism was a term little used across the continent. There had been a few incidents but up until now the English national team had been unscathed by the relatively new phenomenon.

Around 15,000 fans turned up to see England score after 26 minutes through Ray Wilkins. The lead lasted just three minutes when Jan Ceulemans equalized, unwittingly prompting skirmishes amongst the fans which quickly involved the far from tolerant police. Soon tear gas was being deployed and just before half-time the referee had little choice but to take the players off. The game would continue, but the damage was done. England were fined £8,000, but the cost to their follower's reputation was far higher.

SEE ALSO **'UEFA BAN ENGLISH CLUBS FROM EUROPE'** (page 405); **'FIREWORKS AS AC MEET INTER'** (page 588).

Clouds of tear gas rise from behind the England goal as Italian riot police try to control the hooligan element amongst the England following.

BELGIUM OVERCOME EUROPE'S SUPERPOWERS

Ceulemans scores the goal that draws Belgium level against England. Belgium advanced to the final where they would face West Germany.

Under their manager Guy Thys, Belgium were set to enjoy the golden period of their footballing history. Thys had become manager in 1976 and would eventually lead his country to fourth place in the 1986 World Cup. That good form was preceded by a fine showing in the 1980 European Championships, when they took the continent by surprise and reached the final. Spain, England and Italy were in their group but, marshalled brilliantly from midfield by Jan Ceulemans, the Belgians deservedly went through. A 1-1 draw with England, a 2-1 win over Spain and a goalless draw with Italy meant they progressed, thanks to scoring more goals than their hosts.

SEE ALSO **"SUBSTITUTES' DENMARK WIN EUROPEAN CHAMPIONSHIPS'** (pages 460-1); **'OUTSIDERS GREECE WIN EUROPEAN CHAMPIONSHIP'** (pages 583).

WEST GERMANY WIN SECOND EUROPEAN CHAMPIONSHIPS

On a balmy evening in Rome West Germany repeated their 1972 European Championship victory to become the first team to win the competition twice. This time, against Belgium, West Germany took a tenth minute lead through the big Hamburg centre-forward Horst Hrubesch. Newcomer Bernd Schuster was pulling the strings in midfield and the Germans looked well in control until the 70th minute when the Belgians won a dubious penalty, put away by Rene Vandereycken. The Germans were not to be denied, though, and with just two minutes left it was Hrubesch again who rose to head a Hansi Muller corner into the corner of the net.

SEE ALSO **'SCHUSTER'S BIG MONEY DEMAND'** (page 406).

West Germany's Karl-Heinz Forster, Horst Hrubesch and Manny Kaltz parade the trophy around the Olympic Stadium after their 2-1 win.

ROSSI IN MATCH-FIXING SCANDAL

1980

Paolo Rossi had burst onto the scene in the late 1970s, impressing for his club, Lanerossi Vicenza, and his country during the 1978 World Cup. Vicenza had been relegated in 1979 and so Rossi was loaned out to Perugia, a move that would change his life. Perugia played a Serie A match against Avellino, the game finished 2-2 (Rossi got both Perugia goals), but later both teams were implicated in Totonero, a betting scam that included both Milan and Lazio, who were both relegated to Serie B. Rossi protested his innocence, but was banned from the game for three years, a sentence that would later be reduced to two.

SEE ALSO **'ROSSI RETURNS FOR WORLD CUP'** (page 381); **'GROBBELAAR IN MATCH-FIXING SCANDAL'** (page 484).

The disgrace of Rossi's ban was not to be the end of his career.

IT'S THREE POINTS FOR A WIN

1981

On a damp winter's day in Solihull the Football League held a special meeting to go over what they saw as 'a blueprint for the future'. A study group of league secretaries and managers, led as ever by Jimmy Hill, had put together its thoughts on how best to improve the game, the main consideration being whether to change the number of points awarded to the winning team from two to three. That particular amendment was passed and would come into effect the following season. The rationale was that teams would have far more to gain by going out to win games rather than settling for boring draws.

SEE ALSO **'PLAY-OFFS INTRODUCED BY FOOTBALL LEAGUE'** (page 418).

Liverpool were the first beneficiaries of the change in the number of points awarded for a win by claiming the First Division title in the 1981-82 season.

REAL SOCIEDAD PIP MADRID TO THE TITLE

Last season Sociedad had gone agonisingly close to winning a first La Liga title, but were cruelly denied on the final day. This side, though, were stout and talented, and boasted Luis Arconada, Spain's keeper, in goal, with another international, Zamora, the side's creative heartbeat. Sociedad went to Gijon for the last game knowing a draw would win the title, but mid-way through the second half they found themselves 2-1 down. Real Madrid were winning at Valladolid and it seemed history would repeat itself. In the last minute, though, the ball broke in the Gijon box and Zamora was on hand to smash it home – 2-2 and Sociedad were champions!

SEE ALSO **'REAL SOCIEDAD FAIL IN TITLE FIGHT'** (page 576).

Atocha Stadium home of Real Sociedad in the centre of San Sebastian. In 1993 the club moved to a more modern stadium on the outskirts of the city.

Ricky Villa's FA Cup winning goal is regarded as one of the finest ever and it won him a place in the hearts of all Spurs fans.

RICKY VILLA DRIBBLES TO FA CUP VICTORY

Tottenham Hotspur's FA Cup replay against Manchester City on 14 May had already scaled the heights. At 2-2, with 13 minutes remaining, tension filled the North London air. Ricky Villa, who had been disappointing in the first match, picked the ball up deep in the City half and would slalom himself into FA Cup history. Running in from the left, he beat Ray Ransom, cut back and beat Tommy Caton, before once more spinning around Ransom and slipping the ball under the onrushing Joe Corrigan. The 100th FA Cup had been won in truly memorable style.

SEE ALSO **'VILLA AND ARDILES SPEARHEAD BRITAIN'S FOREIGN LEGION'** (page 364); **'GAZZA FELLED BUT SPURS SOAR'** (page 453).

LIVERPOOL WIN
THIRD EUROPEAN CUP

When Liverpool and Real Madrid met in Paris it was far from a football showcase as both teams struggled to break the deadlock. That is until the 82nd minute when left-back Alan Kennedy latched onto a throw-in from his namesake Ray and burst into the box to fire past the Madrid keeper Agustín Rodríguez from a tight angle.

One goal was enough and Liverpool were crowned European Champions for the third time. The victory secured Bob Paisley's place in history as the first manager to win three European Cups and continued English football's stranglehold on the biggest European club competition.

SEE ALSO '... AND BEAT MILAN ON PENALTIES' (page 591).

Captain Phil Thompson lifts the European Cup on a memorable night at the Parc de Princes. This completed the Reds hat-trick of trophies.

TREVOR BROOKING GETS
STUCK IN WITH FREAK GOAL

World Cup qualifier defeats in Romania and Switzerland had brought loud cries for manager Ron Greenwood to be replaced. England's players, though, fully supported their boss and went to Hungary on 6 June keen to put a disappointing campaign back on track. The first half had finished 1-1, but the second half belonged to Trevor Brooking. An hour in, the West Ham man struck an unerring first-time shot, so accurate that the ball managed to get stuck in the top right-hand stanchion of the net. Kevin Keegan sealed the win with a 73rd minute penalty and England were back on the World Cup trail.

SEE ALSO 'SEAGULL MEETS ITS MATCH' (page 312).

Brooking played 47 times for his country, scoring five goals. Today he is one of the most respected figures in the English game.

STALLONE SAVES THE DAY IN *ESCAPE TO VICTORY*

Having graced the silver screen in both Rocky and Rocky II, Hollywood star Sylvester Stallone swapped his boxing gloves for the goalkeeping variety in Escape to Victory, a wartime football film that became a cult classic. Real footballers, including Bobby Moore and Pele, play prisoners of war drafted together to face a German national team in Paris. The Allies are 4-1 down at half-time, but rally to make it 4-4. A dubious penalty in the last minute looks like winning it for the Germans, but Stallone flings himself to his left to make the save and ensure justice prevails. The scoreboard says it's a draw, but victory belongs to the Allies!

SEE ALSO **'HIGHBURY – THE FILM STAR'** (page 143); **'WAR SUSPENDS COMPETITIONS'** (page 144).

Sylvester Stallone plays Captain Robert Hatch in the war movie *Escape to Victory*. His goalkeeping heroics helped the Allies to a deserved 4-4 draw.

QPR striker Clive Allen sweeps up the newly laid artificial pitch at Loftus Road. The surface drew many complaints until it was axed.

ARTIFICIAL PITCHES MAKE DEBUT

Queens Park Rangers became the first club to dig up their grass and lay an artificial surface. Manager Terry Venables sanctioned the controversial move, causing critics to bemoan that a plastic pitch meant plastic football. QPR played their first game on the Loftus Road plastic against Luton on 1 September 1981. The visitors won the game 2-1 and must have enjoyed it as four years later they laid their own artificial pitch. A hugely uneven bounce had the purists scratching their heads and QPR ditched the pitch in 1988, before all non-grass surfaces were banned by Division One clubs in 1991.

SEE ALSO **'FIRST WORLD CUP GAME PLAYED INDOORS'** (page 475).

1981

NORWEGIAN COMMENTATOR'S RANT AGAINST ENGLAND

Norway had done it. On 9 September not only did they beat England 2-1 in Oslo, they also put a huge dent in England's World Cup ambitions. For Norwegian radio commentator Bjørge Lillelien it was all too much. "That's the price you pay for fame," he cried in Norwegian. "We are the best in the world. We are the best in the world. We have beaten England 2-1 in football! It is completely unbelievable! We have beaten England… Maggie Thatcher can you hear me?… [reverts to English] Your boys took a hell of a beating! Your boys took a hell of a beating!"

SEE ALSO **'REBOLA JNR: GOOAAAALLLL'** (page 148); **'FOOTBALL BECOMES GIRL TALK'** (page 612).

"Lord Nelson, Lord Beaverbrook, Sir Winston Churchill, Sir Anthony Eden, Clement Atlee, Henry Cooper, Lady Diana! We have beaten them all!".

1982

After he chose Spain over Italy the transfer that took the young Maradona to Catalonia was completed for a then world record fee.

MARADONA SIGNS FOR BARCELONA IN RECORD DEAL

Boca Juniors were desperate to keep hold of the player who had followed them as a boy and done so much for them as a young man. Money, however, was tight and the club knew that Maradona, heralded as the best player since Pele, was a valuable asset. The 21-year-old was under immense pressure. He had to choose his next career step very carefully, knowing full well it meant leaving his beloved Buenos Aries behind. Juventus were keen, but it was Barcelona and their president Jose Luis Nunez who won his coveted signature in a deal worth £5 million.

SEE ALSO **'ANOTHER RECORD AS BARCELONA SELL MARADONA TO NAPOLI'** (page 402).

Liam Brady's elegant style and technical proficiency meant he was well-suited to the slower-paced Italian league.

BRADY WINS JUVENTUS A SECOND SUCCESSIVE SERIE A CROWN

Liam Brady's last kick for Arsenal had been that missed penalty against Valencia in the final of the Cup Winners' Cup. It was on that European run that the Gunners had beaten Juventus and Brady had stood out, prompting a £500,000 move for the Irishman. It proved an inspired purchase, as Juventus won the title in his first season and repeated the feat the following year. The 1981-82 title was won in the last game at Cantanzaro with Brady scoring the decisive penalty. Again, a spot-kick would be his last contribution as Juventus signed Michel Platini later that summer, with Brady moving on to Sampdoria.

SEE ALSO 'ITALY SCRAPS BAN ON FOREIGN PLAYERS' (page 369).

ASTON VILLA WIN EUROPEAN CUP

For the sixth year in a row, an English club took the title of European Champions. Aston Villa, having previously played just twice in the UEFA Cup, won the famous trophy at the first time of asking, beating German giants Bayern Munich in Rotterdam on 26 May. The game wasn't easy. Bayern poured on the pressure, but were continuously denied by young substitute goalkeeper Nigel Spink, on after only ten minutes. The Germans would rue their uncharacteristic slackness in the 67th minute when Villa winger Tony Morley conjured some magic down the left before crossing low for unmarked centre-forward Peter Withe to blast in past Muller in the Bayern goal.

SEE ALSO 'MANCHESTER UNITED FIGHT BACK TO WIN TREBLE' (pages 526-7).

Peter Withe puts away the most famous goal in Aston Villa's long history. It remains the most glorious night in the club's existence.

After thirteen years in the red of Bayern Munich, Beckenbauers return to Germany in the blue of Hamburg SV shocked the Bundesliga.

BECKENBAUER WINS BUNDESLIGA WITH HAMBURG

In 1980 Franz Beckenbauer lay on a hotel bed in New York wrestling with a dilemma. He was playing for Cosmos, but a call from old German team-mate Guenter Netzer, asking him to play for Hamburg, where he was now coach, had given him pause for thought. Could he play again in the Bundesliga? Did the legs have enough left in them? The answer was yes and in his second season (1981-82) he helped Hamburg to their second title. He didn't play in every game, that wasn't possible, but ask people in the northern German city and they will tell you that every time he did play, 'The Kaiser' ruled.

SEE ALSO **'BECKENBAUER OFFERS HIS SYMPATHIES'** (page 447).

Scottish centre forward Joe Jordan had an unhappy time in Italy, culminating in AC Milan's eventual relegation into Serie B.

AC MILAN RELEGATED TO SERIE B

In 1979 the Rossoneri won the 'stella', a star for teams winning their tenth Scudetto. It was a fine moment for a fine club, but it also heralded the beginning of a tempestuous and damning period in the club's history. First of all they were imbroiled in the shameful match-fixing scandal of 1980 that saw Paolo Rossi banned for two years. Milan, along with Lazio, were also found guilty and relegated to Serie B. They would win immediate promotion, but the 1981-82 season was their worst ever, and it was poor form on the pitch rather than off it that sentenced them to another period in Italy's second tier.

SEE ALSO **'ITALIAN MATCH FIXING SCANDAL'** (page 598).

GOTHENBURG WIN THE UEFA CUP

In 1978 struggling part-timers Gothenburg appointed unknown Sven Goran Eriksson as manager. He introduced a 4-4-2 system and in 1982 they won the Swedish League and Cup, and progressed in the UEFA Cup. The club had financial problems, so fans paid for a quarter-final trip to Valencia, but their loyalty was rewarded with a famous victory over the Spaniards and on 19 May a final against Hamburg. The part-timers won their home leg 1-0 thanks to midfielder Tord Holmgren, a plumber by trade. The second leg should have been tough, but they made it look easy, winning 3-0 and becoming the first Swedish team to bring home a European trophy.

SEE ALSO **'ENGLAND GO FOR ERIKSSON'** (page 543).

IFK Gothenburg coach Sven Goran Eriksson and his team pose in the dressing room after their spectacular showing in the UEFA Cup.

ROSSI RETURNS FOR WORLD CUP

Paolo Rossi had been drafted back into Italy's World Cup squad on the basis of his reputation on the pitch. Rossi had impressed the world in 1978 and now he was back, a disgrace maybe, but he was back. On 14 June Italy's opening game was against Poland – not ideal opposition as it was the Polish who had knocked them out in 1974 amid rumours of bribery. The cloud hung over Rossi as he took to the field in Vigo, north-western Spain. All eyes were on the Juventus man (they'd signed him during his ban), but he looked woefully off the pace and out of sorts. The game was as stale as Rossi's form and finished goalless.

SEE ALSO **'ROSSI MATCH-FIXING SCANDAL'** (page 374).

Rossi's journey towards redemption following his ban for his involvement in a match-fixing scandal begins in Spain.

HUNGARY PUT TEN PAST EL SALVADOR

El Salvador's second World Cup (they also qualified in 1970) brought the humiliation of the largest defeat at a World Cup and, to make matters worse, it was at the hands of one of the weaker sides. No matter, 23,000 people were in Elche in southern Spain on 15 June to watch and within three minutes the Hungarians were ahead through Tibor Nyilasi. The traumatized Central Americans were fortunate to be only three down at half-time. At 5-0 they did manage a consolation, but in half an hour Hungary substitute Lazlo Kiss scored a late hat-trick before Nyliasi finished off the rout he had begun. The final score was 10-1.

SEE ALSO **'SAMOA OUT FOR THE COUNT'** (page 544).

Hungarian team line up in the 1982 World Cup. Their 10-1 victory over El Salvador is the greatest winning margin recorded at the finals.

Captain Marvel Bryan Robson celebrates with the man who laid on his astonishing first minute goal, centre-half Terry Butcher.

ROBSON SCORES AFTER 27 SECONDS

Having got over their qualification jitters, England kicked-off their World Cup campaign in Bilbao on 16 June against a strong French side and made a quite remarkable start. Having won an immediate throw-in down the right, England's players moved tentatively forwards in the scorching Spanish sun. England had been working on throw-ins and so when Coppell threw it in, Terry Butcher's flick was purposeful and Bryan Robson stormed into the box to crash a half-volley past Jean-Luc Ettori in the French goal. Just 27 seconds had elapsed and it was a record that would stand until 2002 when Turkey's Hakan Suker scored after only 11 seconds against South Korea.

SEE ALSO **'TURKEY SCORE FASTEST GOAL IN WORLD CUP HISTORY'** (page 564).

ALGERIA DEFEAT WEST GERMANY

On paper, the group had looked a stroll for European Champions West Germany, but their 16 June World Cup opening game had the world scratching its head. Algeria walked into Gijon's Estadio El Molinon lacking the fear African nations facing European or South American teams were supposed to harbour. The first-half was tight, which clearly buoyed the Algerians, who took the lead through Rabah Madjer after 54 minutes. The Germans were stung into action and Karl Heinz Rummenigge scored after 68 minutes. The Germans strolled back to the kick-off thinking order had been restored but Algeria strode forward and Salah Assad played in Lakhdar Belloumi to score an historic winner.

SEE ALSO 'SENEGAL STUN FRANCE' (page 558).

Algeria coach Mahiedieme Khalef celebrates a shock World Cup victory for the North Africans with his heroic goalkeeper.

Despite feeble claims of offside, Eder chips the ball over Scotland goalkeeper Alan Rough to score his team's third.

BRAZIL DESTROY SCOTLAND

On 18 June, on a very warm night in Seville, Scotland had the barefaced cheek to go one up against Brazil, but Zico equalized and then, at the beginning of the second half, centre-half Oscar gave the delicious Brazilians a 2-1 lead. On 64 minutes left-winger Eder received a pass from Serginho on the corner of the penalty box. He had smashed one home against Russia in the previous game, but showed there was more to his left-foot than sheer power as he deftly chipped the ball over a by now bemused Alan Rough in goal. Falcao got another and it finished 4-1 to Brazil.

SEE ALSO 'SCOTLAND HEAD FOR HOME' (page 440).

KUWAITI PRINCE GETS INVOLVED

Supposed minnows Kuwait had looked competent in their opening draw with Czechoslovakia. France, however, lethargic against England, came to life on 21 June, as did Michel Platini, and were three up within 50 minutes. Kuwait pulled one back, but with just minutes to go confusion reigned. Alain Giresse had scored what he presumed was a perfectly good fourth, but the Kuwaitis complained that they had stopped on hearing a whistle (it had been blown in the crowd). Their prince, Sheikh Al-Sabah, gestured to his players to leave the field, then came down to the pitch and talked them into finishing the game – and the ref into inexplicably disallowing the goal.

SEE ALSO **'LET LJUNGBERG PLAY FORWARD BEHIND HENRIK AND ZLATAN'** (page 580).

Spanish police surround Sheikh Al-Sabah as he makes his bizarre on-pitch appearance but they are powerless to stop the cameras rolling.

Armstrong unleashes his unstoppable volley. He went on to spend two successful seasons in the Spanish league with Real Mallorca.

ARMSTRONG PUTS NORTHERN IRELAND INTO SECOND ROUND

Crammed into Valencia's Estadio Luis Casanova on 25 June were 50,000 fans, there to see a game Northern Ireland had to win if they were to progress. In the 47th minute the hard-working Gerry Armstrong picked the ball up and carried it deep into Spanish territory, before passing it to Billy Hamilton on the right wing. Hamilton beat Spain's Miguel Tendillio before crossing into the box. Luis Arconada in goal could only parry and Armstrong, who had continued his run, smashed the ball under the flailing keeper. Armstrong got a move to Spain on the back of that goal and hasn't bought a Guinness back home ever since!

SEE ALSO **'HEALY'S HAT-TRICK HEROICS'** (page 607).

Maradona briefly eludes his nemesis Gentile , but the defender soon regained the upper hand to successfully stifle the playmaker's genius.

MARADONA MARKED OUT OF GAME AGAINST ITALY

Pre-World Cup talk of Diego Maradona signing for Barcelona had reached fever-pitch and it was in Barcelona on 29 June that Argentina faced Italy in the second round group stages. The game was held at Espanol's smaller Estadio Sarria, where 43,000 expectant locals fixated on the city's star-to-be. However, Italy's over-cautious coach Enzo Bearzot had plans for Maradona in the shape of Juventus defender Claudio Gentile, who used every trick in the book to prevent Maradona from getting into the game. He punched, kicked and chopped, but was only booked, as was Maradona, for daring to retaliate. The tactic worked with Italy winning 2-1.

SEE ALSO **'MARADONA IS 'BUTCHERED"** (page 396).

MARADONA SENT OFF AGAINST BRAZIL

Maradona had been visibly incensed by the close attention the Italians had given him and that frustration bubbled over on 2 July in Argentina's next game, against old enemy Brazil. Zico put Brazil in front after 12 minutes, but just as Argentina looked like getting back into it in the second half, they were caught out by two goals inside ten minutes. Maradona was a beaten man, unable to impose himself on the match or the tournament. With five minutes left, Brazil's midfield once more got the better of the number 10, who this time kicked out at his nearest opponent, Batista. The referee brandished his red card.

SEE ALSO **'BECKHAM SEES RED'** (page 515).

A sad end to Maradona's tournament. "Everyone thought it was going to be my World Cup," said Maradona later. "So did I, but it was over."

Agony for England as Keegan watches as his header drifts wide of the post. His introduction wasn't enough to send England through.

KEEGAN MISSES AND UNBEATEN ENGLAND HEAD HOME

Kevin Keegan had spent the World Cup shuttling between Germany and Spain getting treatment on a back injury. England had looked strong without him in the group stages, but a goalless draw with Germany meant they had to beat the disappointing Spanish by two goals on 5 July. England needed inspiration. Glenn Hoddle was inexplicably left out and, with the game teetering towards another goalless draw, Ron Greenwood went for broke and sent on Keegan and Brooking (also missing through injury). With 20 minutes left Bryan Robson sent in a fine cross, only for the clearly rusty Keegan to glance his header wide. England were out.

SEE ALSO **'SWEDES 2 TURNIPS 1'** (page 459); **'WEMBLEY CLOSES... AND COACH RESIGNS ON TELEVISION'** (page 539)

FALCAO SCORES A SCREAMER TO EQUALIZE AGAINST ITALY

It was their last second round game and at 2-1 Brazil needed a goal or their World Cup dream was over. The best team in the competition were being penned back by the Paolo Rossi-inspired Italians, but with 68 minutes gone Brazil worked the ball out to the wing where the marauding Junior moved inside before finding Falcao on the right-hand corner of the area. Cerezo made a decoy run and Falcao moved into the space before unleashing a shot that left Dino Zoff helpless. The Roma player celebrated, but Paolo Rossi had other ideas...

SEE ALSO **'ROSSI COMPLETES HIS HAT-TRICK AGAINST BRAZIL'** (page 387).

Falcao's stunning strike pulls Brazil level to the delight of the yellow-shirted fans amply represented around the ground.

Rossi slides the ball past Brazil goalkeeper Waldir Peres to score the winning goal as Brazil's defence and Italy's Graziani look on.

ROSSI COMPLETES HIS HAT-TRICK AGAINST BRAZIL

Brazil needed only to draw to go through to the semi-finals, but their game was never compatible with caution and so on 5 July the 44,000 crowd were treated to a truly great World Cup match. Rossi had seemed out of sorts after his two-year ban, but five minutes in he scored with a header from left-back Antonio Cabrini's cross. Brazil equalized, but after 25 minutes Italy were ahead once more after Rossi punished some sloppy Brazilian defending. Brazil kept coming and equalized through Falcao, but with 15 minutes left Rossi completed the most inspiring of hat-tricks, slamming in a loose ball after Marco Tardelli had volleyed towards goal.

SEE ALSO **'ROSSI RETURNS FOR WORLD CUP'** (page 381).

SCHUMACHER'S ASSAULT

After 57 minutes with the score at 1-1 in the France v West Germany semi-final in Seville, begrudging respect was replaced by sheer antipathy after an appalling challenge by German goalkeeper Harald Schumacher on French substitute Patrick Battiston. The Germans had taken the lead after 17 minutes through Pierre Littbarski, but Platini levelled things just after half time from the penalty spot.

Later Platini played a sublime ball to the onrushing Battiston. The Saint Etienne full-back was always likely to get to the ball first, but as he went to shoot he was flattened when Schumacher's hip and elbow met his face. Disgust at the assault was only replaced by disbelief at the decision to award a goal-kick. As Battiston lay helpless – he lost two teeth – Schumacher refused to even apologise and neutrals began to hum La Marseillaise.

SEE ALSO **'ROY KEANE'S MALICIOUS INTENT'** (page 545).

Amazingly, Schumacher's horrific tackle was missed by the Dutch referee Charles Corver who only awarded a German goal kick.

1982

FIRST EVER WORLD CUP PENALTY SHOOT OUT

Just two minutes into extra-time the French went ahead through the unmarked Marius Tresor. When the brilliant Giresse made it 3-1 five minutes later it seemed that the game had been settled, but Germany are never beaten and on 102 minutes Rummenigge, on as a sub, pulled one back and you could sense a French wilt. Fischer acrobatically levelled things and the game, a first for the World Cup, went to penalties. It was a hot, tense night in Seville; socks were rolled around ankles and brows were beaded with sweat. Both teams nervously gathered at the half-way line as the World Cup went into uncharted territory. With both teams missing one it went into sudden death and it was the unfortunate Maxime Bossis who had his effort saved by Schumacher. Hrubesch scored the decisive penalty and the French, on a cruel night were out.

SEE ALSO **'ITALY WIN WORLD CUP'** (page 604).

The France team look on as Alain Giresse converts his penalty, sending West Germany goalkeeper Harald Schumacher the wrong way.

WEST GERMANS GROUNDED IN SEVILLE

After goalkeeper Harald Schumacher's foul on Patrick Battiston it was hard to feel sympathy for West Germany, but as they sat in Seville airport waiting for their flight to the final in Madrid you couldn't help but wonder about a major tournament that treats their finalists this way. Already aggrieved that they had had to play a physically gruelling semi-final hours after Italy's easy stroll against Poland, the Germans were pulling their hair out as flight after flight was cancelled and they were left sitting on their suitcases. Paul Breitner, who had played at Real Madrid and spoke fluent Spanish, disparaged the shoddy organisation. He had a point. It is difficult to imagine a top international team being involved in a similar scenario in today's game.

SEE ALSO **'IVORY COAST LEADER THREATENS TEAM WITH MILITARY SERVICE'** (page 532).

The German team before their transport hiccup. Paul Breitner is on the left of the back row.

ROSSI SCORES IN FINAL AND TAKES THE GOLDEN BOOT

If it had been Claudio Gentile's Italian Job on Diego Maradona in the second round that had poured petrol on the Azzuris apparently stagnant World Cup campaign, it was most definitely the resurgent form of striker Paolo Rossi that was the spark to explode them into life. With Brazil gone Italy moved into the semi-finals with real belief. Poland were beaten 2-0 thanks to two more Rossi goals and suddenly, from nowhere, the Juventus man was the talk of Spain – and for all the right reasons. Rossi was a new man. He had trudged his way through the opening games, like a man trying desperately to re-introduce himself to the game, but now he was back on first-name terms.

Italy started with Gentile, this time keeping his close attentions on Littbarski. Rummenigge missed a good chance early on, yet it was the Italians who should have gone into the half-time break leading, but the usually dependable Cabrini put his penalty wide. This was going to be tight, or at least it looked that way until the 57th minute when Marco Tardelli, the Italians' heartbeat, played a quick free-kick to Gentile. The man-marker proved he could play a bit too, whipping in a cross which beat both Altobelli and Cabrini, and found the head of Rossi, before nestling in the German goal. The deadlock had been broken. For two years Rossi had protested his innocence and now, with the fervour of a prisoner walking free from a life sentence, he had scored the all-important first goal in the World Cup final (his sixth in the tournament) and in turn won the Golden Boot.

SEE ALSO **'TOTO SCHILLACI'S STARE'** (page 444).

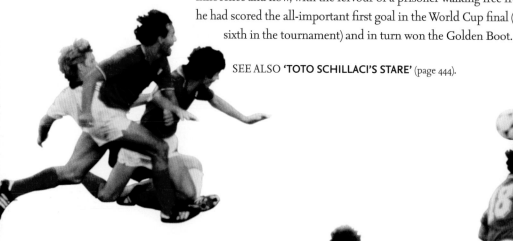

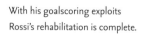

With his goalscoring exploits Rossi's rehabilitation is complete.

THE 'TARDELLI SCREAM'

Having gone 1-0 up against West Germany with half an hour to go, the fear among neutrals was that Italy would go into their defensive shell. As they had shown against Brazil in Barcelona, this Italy were at their best moving forward and, despite it going against their footballing traditions, that's what they would continue to do. Their 40-year-old keeper and captain Dino Zoff had been forced into making a save from Briegel, but on 68 minutes they were 2-0 up through the deserving Marco Tardelli. Scirea played a one-two with Bergomi in the box and laid the ball to the edge of the area where Tardelli waited. The Juventus man's first touch seemed heavy, but he lunged to get his shot away and beat Schumacher. The life had gone from West Germany's challenge and Tardelli knew it. He span away and headed towards his jubilant bench, tears rushing to his eyes, his fists clenched out in front of him, his head shaking in disbelief. They would go onto win 3-1, but Tardelli was the iconic image.

SEE ALSO **'ITALY WIN THE WORLD CUP'** (page 604).

Tardelli's euphoric celebration was mirrored by full-back Fabio Grosso after he scored the decisive penalty in Italy's 2006 World Cup win in Germany.

Boniek played 81 matches and scored 14 times in three years at Juve before moving to AS Roma where he ended his playing career.

ZBIGNIEW BONIEK TRANSFERS TO JUVENTUS

Having missed out on signing Maradona, Juventus had moved swiftly for another talented playmaker, one that had excelled at the World Cup. Zbigniew Boniek had helped Poland reach the semi-finals of the World Cup, scoring four goals along the way and producing some dazzling moments of skill that included one of the all-time great hat-tricks, against Belgium. Juventus, having already nabbed Michel Platini from Saint Etienne and Paolo Rossi, moved quickly once more and when the Old Lady of Italian football comes knocking it is hard for a player or a club like Widzew Lodz to resist.

SEE ALSO 'ITALY SCRAPS BAN ON FOREIGN PLAYERS' (page 369).

BOB PAISLEY LEAVES LIVERPOOL WITH A TROPHY

Under Bob Paisley Wembley had become Liverpool's second home and this was the perfect way for the great man to say goodbye. On 26 March his team came from behind to beat Manchester United and win their third successive League Cup courtesy of Ronnie Whelan, but it was Paisley who was the hero of the hour. His six Championships, three League Cups, three European Cups and UEFA Cup in just nine seasons were an incredible haul, but he was never one for the limelight. His players, though, had other ideas and skipper Graeme Souness ushered him up the famous steps to lift the cup and take his deserved plaudits.

SEE ALSO 'LIVERPOOL'S BILL SHANKLY QUITS AT THE TOP' (page 342).

After being urged on by his players Paisley holds aloft the League Cup at Wembley in a fitting end to his managerial career.

ABERDEEN LIFT CUP WINNERS' CUP

Under the tenacious leadership of Alex Ferguson unfashionable Aberdeen had gate-crashed the Old Firm's dominance of the Scottish game and now they wanted to win abroad. On 11 May they faced the mighty Real Madrid in the Cup Winners' Cup final in Gothenburg and took an early lead through an Alex McLeish header. However, a defensive error led to Madrid's equaliser, a penalty scored by Juanito. The game went into extra-time and under stormy Swedish skies Aberdeen nicked it with a goal in the 112th minute through substitute John Hewitt, who stretched at the back post to knock in a fine cross from Mark McGhee.

SEE ALSO **'ALEX FERGUSON TAKES OVER AT MANCHESTER UNITED'** (page 418).

John Hewitt scores and earns Aberdeen's European victory. The club briefly challenged the Old Firm stranglehold domestically too.

GORDON SMITH MISSES LAST-MINUTE SITTER

"And Smith must score!" cried John Motson, but somehow Brighton's Gordon Smith managed to miss. Brighton had done brilliantly to reach the 21 May FA Cup final, putting their woeful league form aside (they were relegated that season) to beat, among others, Liverpool and Sheffield Wednesday. Manchester United were strong favourites, but Brighton were 1-0 up at half-time, only to be pegged back by two United goals. Gary Stevens equalized in the 87th minute and in the last moments of extra-time Smith had his chance after good work from Michael Robinson. Alas, he snatched at it, Bailey saved and United won the replay 4-0.

SEE ALSO **'THE CRAZY GANG STUN LIVERPOOL'** (page 422).

Gordon Smith completely fluffs his match-winning chance for the south coast team and enters FA Cup folklore – for all the wrong reasons.

TOTTENHAM FLOAT ON THE STOCK EXCHANGE

The FA had long had to deal with clubs wanting to become limited companies. As far back as the 1890s it had allowed them to do so in order to protect members from personal liability for the growing costs. What it didn't allow was directors paying themselves salaries as they feared clubs would become mere money-making vehicles for investors. Tottenham and its chairman Monte Carlo-based tycoon Irving Scholar, though, formed a holding company to bypass the rules and went ahead, floating on the stock exchange and raising funds as a public company. A new era was born.

SEE ALSO **'MURDOCH THWARTED IN BID TO BUY MANCHESTER UNITED'** (page 522); **'GLAZER TAKES OVER MANCHESTER UNITED'** (page 592).

Irving Scholar owned one of football's most famous names but Spurs were struggling financially when he announced they were going public.

FIRST LIVE LEAGUE MATCH IS TELEVISED

Sunday's used to be sacred; a day of rest. Having worshipped on Saturdays at their particular footballing altars, to fans Sunday was a time for reflection, a time to read the papers, to gloat about the win or moan about the loss, but all that was about to change. On Sunday 2 October 1983, television cameras came to White Hart Lane to screen the first ever live showing of a Football League match and Sundays would never be the same again. Brian Clough brought his Nottingham Forest side to the Lane and along with the rest of the country watched his team get beaten 2-1.

SEE ALSO **'PREMIER LEAGUE LAUNCHED'** (page 462).

The television revolution continued apace transforming the modern game beyond recognition with a much needed cash injection.

MARADONA IS 'BUTCHERED'

Fans around the world were united in their condemnation of the cynical – and enforced – removal of one of the game's shining stars. On 24 September 1983 an infamous tackle from behind by Athletic Bilbao's Andoni Goikoetxea Olaskoaga shattered the left ankle of brilliant Argentinian Diego Maradona as he dominated a Spanish La Liga game for Barcelona at the Nou Camp stadium. Goikoetxea's tackle, which left Maradona's leg grotesquely twisted, won him the nickname 'Butcher of Bilbao'. After the event Maradona said, "I felt the axe's blow from behind. I knew that everything was destroyed."

SEE ALSO **'ROY KEANE'S MALICIOUS INTENT'** (page 545).

'The Butcher' also played Athletico Madrid who nicknamed him 'El Gigante de Alonsotegui' (Alonsotegui's Giant) after the place of his birth.

Action from Spain's 12-1 win over Malta. Spain have often turned in impressive one-off performances but have yet to win a major honour.

SPAIN BAG A DOZEN TO QUALIFY FOR EUROPEAN CHAMPIONSHIPS

Even the most optimistic Spanish supporters would have anticipated missing out on the European Championships as they went into their last qualifier against Malta having to win by 11 goals. Spain scored early, but Malta equalized, but then Spain started scoring steadily. It was 3-1 at half-time, then 4-1, then 5-1. Santillana and Rincon got hat-tricks and with each goal came a louder roar. In the 83rd minute at 11-1 Senor collected the ball on the edge of the box and, left-footed, drilled it into the corner of the net. Spain had done it. The Dutch were out and 'the spirit of Malta' is still referred to on Spanish terraces.

SEE ALSO **'SPAIN TRIUMPH IN EURO THRILLER'** (page 534).

VENABLES TAKES BRITISH STYLE TO SPAIN

Few British football coaches had succeeded abroad until Englishman Terry Venables took over at Barcelona in May 1984. Dubbed 'El Tel' by the British press, Venables got the top job at the Nou Camp after leading London club Queens Park Rangers into the English First Division. With Barcelona Venables won La Liga in 1985 and reached the European Cup final in 1986, losing on penalties to Steaua Bucharest. His success was built on a distinctively-English 4-4-2 system and he brought in a trio of British strikers – England's Gary Lineker, Mark Hughes of Wales and Scottish international Steve Archibald. After a poor start to the 1987-88 season, El Tel was sacked.

SEE ALSO **'DAVID BECKHAM JOINS REAL MADRID'** (page 572).

As well as winning La Liga in his first season, Terry Venables took Barca within a penalty shoot out of winning the European Cup.

ELTON JOHN WEEPS FOR WATFORD AT WEMBLEY

Born in Pinner, Elton John was a lifelong Watford supporter. His success in the music industry had earned him millions, so in 1976 he became club chairman and thanks to his cash injection the club rose through the divisions before winning promotion to the top-flight in 1982. They didn't settle for that, though, and having finished second in the League in 1983 they reached the FA Cup final against Everton on 19 May 1984. As his Hornets came out of the Wembley tunnel it proved too much for Mr John and, amid the roars, tears of pride poured down his cheeks. His team went on to lose 2-0.

SEE ALSO **'WORLD CHAMPIONS BECOME CHART-TOPPERS'** (page 296).

Though he resigned as Chairman in 2002, Sir Elton John remains Honorary Life President of the Hornets of Vicarage Road.

SWEDEN WIN WOMEN'S EUROPEAN CHAMPIONSHIPS

The women's game had come along way by the mid-1980s, but when boys' club UEFA gave the go-ahead for a European Championships its original name of UEFA European Competition for Representative Women's Teams suggested they didn't take it that seriously. The championships were not a month-long affair, but a series of matches over two years in which 16 nations competed. England and Sweden earned the right to play in the two-legged final. The Swedes won 1-0 at home, but were pegged back by the same score-line at Luton, so the game was decided by penalties with the Swedish coming out on top 4-3.

SEE ALSO **'FIRST WOMEN'S WORLD CUP'** (page 455).

The Swedish women's team celebrate what remains their only victory in an international tournament after their shoot-out win.

Grobbelaar's mind games work as Conti falters under pressure and blazes the vital penalty over the bar to hand Liverpool the advantage.

JELLY LEGS SERVES UP LIVERPOOL'S FOURTH EUROPEAN CUP

On 30 May 1984 Roma and Liverpool were 1-1 after 120 minutes and for the first time the European Cup would be decided on penalties. Liverpool had done well, but now they'd have to hold their nerve in front of 65,000 Romans baying for blood. And then, amid all the strain, came Bruce Grobbelaar, Liverpool's eccentric goalkeeper. Liverpool had missed their first penalty and were trailing when Bruno Conti, a World Cup winner with Italy, stepped up to be met by Grobbelaar wobbling his legs as if to belittle the seriousness of the occasion, as if mocking the tension. Conti missed and Liverpool went on to win a fourth European Cup.

SEE ALSO **'... AND BEAT MILAN ON PENALTIES'** (page 591).

JOHN BARNES' MARACANA WONDER GOAL

England had failed to qualify for the European Championships in France that summer, so their beleaguered new manager Bobby Robson took them to South America to play three games, the first of which was against Brazil on 10 June. A 2-0 win was one thing, but it was John Barnes' goal that lives in the memory. In the 44th minute the Watford man took a Mark Hately pass on his chest and swept towards goal. Was this really an Englishman? He beat three men, rounded the goalkeeper and put the ball into the empty net. The Brazilian crowd could only gasp. That's how good that goal was.

SEE ALSO **'MESSI'S MARADONA MIRACLE'** (page 612).

The fact that John Barnes's goal was scored in the Maracana, one of the true cathedrals of world football, made it that bit more special.

Simonsen and Le Roux both go for the loose ball. Seconds later Simonsen was stricken and his World Cup dreams shattered.

SIMONSEN'S INJURY AGONY

Great tournaments need great players and the European Championships in France got off to a poor start with one of the most talented around being stretched off with a broken leg. Allan Simonsen had been revered on the continent for a number of years. In 1977 the diminutive Dane had been named European Player of the Year and it had been his form in the qualifiers, as well as his winning penalty at Wembley, that had ensured England would miss out. Denmark's opening game was against the hosts and a minute into the second-half Simonsen clashed with French defender Yvon Le Roux and came off worst. His tournament was over.

SEE ALSO **'ROONEY STRUCK BY CURSE OF THE METATARSAL'** (page 581).

PLATINI SCORES LAST-MINUTE WINNER

Time was running out. European Championships hosts France had twice come from behind to deny Portugal in Marseille, but now the semi-final was teetering towards a penalty shoot-out, which wasn't a welcome option. France had impressed in the group stages, winning all three of their games against Denmark, Belgium and Yugoslavia. They were clearly buoyed by their home support, but there was now a maturity to their play as well. Michel Platini was the best player in Europe. Giresse and Tigana were still brilliant, but now they had Amoros solid in defence and Joel Bats dependable in goal. The French had peaked and this should be their summer.

Much depended on Platini and he had risen to the occasion, scoring in every game and now with the semi-final at loggerheads he would do it again. Jean Tigana wriggled down the right and centred low for Platini, who took a touch. The crowd hushed and he seemed to wait an eternity before caressing the ball into the roof of Bento's net for the winner.

SEE ALSO **'BAGGIO WINS SEMI-FINAL FOR ITALY'** (page 479).

Platini continues his inspirational run as France reach the final with seconds to spare.

FRANCE ARE
EUROPEAN CHAMPIONS

And so to Paris on 27 June for France v Spain. The city of lovers was smitten with its football team and on a dreamy night at the Parc De Princes, 50,000 fans cheered on 'Les Bleus' to a famous victory. The tournament had been a great success, by far the best major competition for years; charisma replacing caution, charm outdoing cynicism. The final itself was less of a spectacle, but the partisan crowd had their victory. Michel Platini opened the scoring with his ninth goal, having scored in every France game of the tournament. His 57th minute free-kick squirmed under Arconada's body and then in the last moments Bruno Bellone raced clear and sealed the 2-0 win.

SEE ALSO **'FRANCE ADD EUROPEAN TITLE TO WORLD CROWN'** (page 535).

Les Bleus celebrate victory over their fierce rivals but their star Platini looks strangely muted.

ANOTHER RECORD AS BARCELONA SELL MARADONA TO NAPOLI

Maradona's move to Barcelona hadn't gone to plan and the Argentinian was desperate to get away. Juventus were once more touted as likely suitors, but their then president Giampero Boniperti joked that Maradona was too small to succeed in Italy.

The other club showing interest were Napoli. Hardly the most fashionable club, but they were clearly keen on Maradona and it wasn't the first time they had shown an interest either. Now, though, Mardona's head had been turned and with Napoli hardly a European rival for Barcelona the move seemed to suit everyone. A deal was brokered, costing a record £5 million. When 80,000 fans turned up at the Stadio Paolo to see their new hero unveiled one flag said it all: 'Maradona Take Charge. If it Doesn't Happen Now, It Will never Happen.'

SEE ALSO **'MARADONA LEADS NAPOLI TO THEIR FIRST SCUDETTO'** (page 420).

The inspirational signing of Maradona put the unfashionable Napoli firmly on the world football map.

Pitched battles between fans and police were all too common in English football during the eighties as hooliganism loomed large.

LUTON RIOT PROMPTS AWAY-FAN BAN

A full-on riot by travelling Millwall fans at Luton Town, caught on television for a disapproving world to see, showed that 'the English disease' had reached epidemic proportions. Luton, hosting Millwall in this 13 March FA Cup quarter-final tie at Kenilworth Road, were leading 1-0 with minutes to go when away fans invaded the pitch. The game was somehow finished, but once the players were off fans ripped up seats and injured scores of bystanders. Luton's chairman David Evans, an MP for a Tory government losing patience with football, would later take steps to ban away fans and introduce an ill-judged identity card scheme to hound out the perpetrators.

SEE ALSO **'UEFA BANS ENGLISH CLUBS FROM EUROPEAN COMPETITION'** (page 405).

THE BRADFORD FIRE DISASTER

It should have been a day of celebration. Local boy and captain Peter Jackson had been awarded the Second Division trophy and a last match against Lincoln City meant the team could relax and turn on the form that had won them the title. That's how 11 May 1985 was supposed to be. Instead just minutes before half-time the linesman noticed smoke coming from the antiquated West Stand. The referee took the players off, but in minutes that smoke was replaced by fierce flames and fleeing supporters. The fire, which took 56 lives, had been started by a stray cigarette that had ignited years of built-up litter under the stand.

SEE ALSO **'THE BASTIA DISASTER'** (page 457).

Smoke can still be seen rising from the charred remains of the main stand at Valley Parade.

1985

THE HEYSEL STADIUM DISASTER

Riots, disasters and mayhem had already stained 1985, but nothing could prepare the football world for what happened in a crazy few hours on a balmy spring evening at the Heysel Stadium in Brussels. Liverpool versus Juventus in the European Cup final on 29 May should have been a momentous occasion. Both sides were packed with massive names, but what happened next rendered the players' superstar status meaningless, as opposing fans, at first just taunting one another, began an ugly riot that saw Liverpool supporters storm their Italian counterparts, who were inexplicably housed in the enclosure next to them, separated only by thin wire. As scores of English fans ran amok in the Juventus section panic ensued and the fleeing fans caused a wall to collapse, leaving hundreds crushed beneath it. The police could do nothing to help as it became clear that people were dying under the pressure. The death toll was 39 and it was the saddest of nights.

SEE ALSO **'UEFA BAN ENGLISH CLUBS FROM EUROPEAN COMPETITION'** (page 405); **'LIVERPOOL AND JUVE LINE UP FOR MINUTE'S SILENCE'** (page 587).

Liverpool fans face a wall of Belgian policemen as one of football's darkest nights unfolds.

UEFA BAN ENGLISH CLUBS FROM EUROPEAN COMPETITION

The scenes that had disgusted not only Europe but the world had to be dealt with and two days before Europe's governing body met to decide England's fate the Football Association announced that they would withdraw their clubs from the following year's European competitions. Uefa, though, went one step further and indefinitely banned English clubs from all competitions, with Liverpool receiving an extra three-year ban on top. There could be no complaints, but you had to feel sorry for Everton, who had won the Cup Winners' Cup just a week before and who were preparing to go into the European Cup for the first time since 1970.

SEE ALSO **'UEFA LIFTS BAN ON ENGLISH CLUBS – BUT NOT LIVERPOOL'** (page 435).

Heysel destroyed relations between two of Europe's giant clubs. Juve fans unfurl a banner decrying Liverpool supporters as 'Animals'.

JOCK STEIN DIES AS HIS TEAM QUALIFY FOR WORLD CUP FINALS

On 10 September Scotland had to avoid defeat in Cardiff to qualify for the World Cup in Mexico, while a Welsh win would ensure their first trip to the finals since 1958. Mark Hughes gave the Welsh the lead, but a late Davie Cooper penalty got the Scots their draw. As the Tartan Army celebrated, their manager Jock Stein had a heart attack pitch-side. The players were in the dark until Alex Ferguson came in to tell them the bad news. Their manager had died. Stein, the man who had led Celtic to European glory in 1967 and a father figure to the Scottish game had gone.

SEE ALSO **'CELTIC'S 'LIONS' ROAR'** (page 282).

Scotland manager Jock Stein, centre, right, pictured minutes before the final whistle, when he suffered a fatal heart attack.

Berlusconi is one of the most colourful and controversial figures Italy has ever seen. His considerable influence extended far beyond football.

SILVIO BERLUSCONI BUYS AC MILAN

AC Milan had endured a torrid start to the 1980s on and off the pitch. Scandal and footballing ineptitude had seen the famous old club spend two seasons in Serie B, with silverware a distant hope. Luther Blissett, Ray Wilkins and Mark Hately had come to the San Siro, but even English grit couldn't cure the troubled club as their time in Serie B had almost crippled them financially. Changes needed to be made if success was to be achieved and up stepped entrepreneur Silvio Berlusconi. The media tycoon invested around £20 million, replacing disgraced Giuseppe Farina, who fled to South Africa, supposedly with much of the club's money.

SEE ALSO **'ARRIGO SACCHI JOINS AC MILAN'** (page 420); **'ROMAN ABRAMOVICH BUYS CHELSEA – AND SUCCESS'** (page 571).

SCHUSTER'S BIG MONEY DEMAND

Mexico '86 could have been Bernd Schuster's tournament. He had become the youngest player ever to represent West Germany in 1979 and had starred in their Euro '80 win. However, arguments with coach Jupp Derwall led to his premature international retirement in 1984. He made several half-hearted attempts at a comeback but he shocked the German public in 1986 when, after new coach Beckenbauer had publicly pleaded with him to reconsider in time for Mexico, Schuster demanded an appearance fee of DM 1 million from the German football authorities. Remarkably, the DFB asked sponsors Adidas to come up with the money but the sportswear giant refused to be held to ransom.

SEE ALSO **'MAXIMUM WAGE ABOLISHED'** (page 235).

Schuster had a successful club career in Spain playing for both Barcelona and Real Madrid but to this day he divides opinion in his homeland.

FANS DESPAIR AT LACK OF FLAIR

Attendances for Bundesliga games had been in steady decline for a decade. In 1985–86 the average gate for a top flight match had plummeted to 17,600.

The reasons for such a fall was in part due to the fear of hooliganism, commonplace across Europe and the dominance of Bayern Munich, but specific to the Bundesliga was the charge of ugly football. Gone were the flair players of Beckenbauer, Overath and Netzer, only to be replaced by more robust and workmanlike footballers, who although effective (no fewer than eight teams played European finals between 1979–1983), had less appeal to spectators.

SEE ALSO 'DECLINE OF THE EAST GERMAN 'STATE CLUB" (page 450).

German footballs robust physical approach won trophies but won few fans, who longed for the stylish, flair game of the 1970s.

DALGLISH BECOMES LIVERPOOL'S FIRST PLAYER/MANAGER

It was an historic moment, but one that couldn't be celebrated, as the actions of a minority of fans just 24 hours before had cast a dark shadow over Liverpool Football Club. Manager Joe Fagan had always planned on retiring after the European Cup final in what he had hoped would be a victorious send-off. Instead a good man who had been involved with the club since Bill Shankly's day arrived back in Liverpool in tears. Liverpool had long promoted from within the heralded boot-room, but this time the new man was from the dressing-room. Kenny Dalglish was given the task of re-building the tarnished club as player-manager.

SEE ALSO "KING KENNY' RESIGNS AS LIVERPOOL MANAGER' (page 451).

After the Heysel tragedy, Liverpool turned to one of Anfield's favourite sons to lead the team through one of its darkest periods.

WERDER BREMEN HAND BAYERN MUNICH THE BUNDESLIGA

For 21 years Werder Bremen had been starved of Bundesliga success, but by the end of the 1985-86 campaign it seemed that at last this homely club would prevail. It was Bayern Munich who were on their heels and by a quirk of the fixture list Bremen would face Munich at home in the penultimate game of the season, knowing a win would take the title. Led upfront by a young Rudi Voller, Bremen were dangerous and in the 86th minute the referee awarded them a penalty. The stadium went deadly quiet as Michael Krutzop stepped up, but agonisingly hit the post. The game was drawn, Bremen lost their final match and the title was Bayern's.

SEE ALSO **'BAYERN WIN GERMAN TITLE – WITH LAST KICK OF SEASON'** (page 547); **'STUTTGART SECURE FIFTH TITLE WIN'** (page 614).

Kutzop puts his penalty against the post as Bayern Munich goalkeeper Jean-Marie Pfaff looks on. It was the only penalty Kutzop ever missed in the Bundesliga.

DYNAMO KIEV WIN CUP WINNERS' CUP

A 50,000 crowd in Lyon on 2 May witnessed a fantastic night of European football as Dynamo Kiev underlined how strong football in Eastern Europe was. Madrid were a decent team, but in Alexandre Zavarov, Oleg Blokhin and Igor Belanov Kiev had three of the best players around. It took just five minutes for Zavarov to give Kiev the lead. Atletico did well to stave off waves of attack, but with five minutes left Kiev swept the ball from left to right with ease before Blokhin nudged the ball past Fillol in goal. Game over. Vadim Evetuchenko sealed a famous win and Kiev had their first European trophy since 1975.

SEE ALSO 'AC MILAN SIGN SUPER STRIKER SHEVCHENKO' (page 529).

Restrained celebrations following Dynamo's win. Their victory underlined how strong football in Eastern Europe was.

BARCELONA LOSE EUROPEAN FINAL ON PENALTIES

Terry Venables' Barcelona were firm favourites against Romania's military side Steaua Bucharest in the European Cup final, a game played on 7 May in Seville. The match was a cagey affair with the Romanians proving they were organised and skilful. After extra-time there were still no goals, so for the second time in three years the final was decided from the spot. Barcelona's keeper Urruti saved the first, but so did Steaua's Helmut Ducadem. The amazing Romanian keeper went on to deny four penalties and with Lacatus and Balint scoring for Steaua the last of those saved brought the trophy – for the first time – to the Eastern Bloc.

SEE ALSO 'VENABLES TAKES BRITISH STYLE TO SPAIN' (page 397).

Ducadern's acrobatics in normal time and during the shoot-out helped Steaua to a shock win over heavy favourites Barcelona.

IAN RUSH SCORES TWICE AS LIVERPOOL WIN THE DOUBLE

After the horrors of Heysel, Kenny Dalglish had managed to bring some pride back to the football club in his very first season in charge. Liverpool had won the title on the last day of the season from their city rivals Everton and on 10 May the two clubs faced each other in the first ever all Merseyside Cup final. The game itself was a classic. Everton took the lead through Gary Lineker, but were once more pegged back by their nemesis Ian Rush whose two goals in the second half ensured a 3-1 victory (Craig Johnston got the other) and an historic double.

SEE ALSO **'IAN RUSH WINS EMOTIONAL FA CUP FINAL AGAINST EVERTON'** (page 430).

Despite Everton scoring first through Gary Lineker, Liverpool fought back through two goals from Man of the Match Ian Rush.

Scientific studies into the phenomenon have shown you need at least two dozen people to start a meaningful Mexican wave.

THE MEXICAN WAVE SAYS HELLO

The 'wave' came to prominence on the first day of the 1986 World Cup, but to say it first appeared in Mexico invites controversy. Many sports and countries have claimed credit for the movement, which sees fans create a wave effect by standing and lifting their arms in unison, one after the other. Hockey teams in America and Canada say they invented it, as do baseball crowds, and it was spotted at the 1984 Olympics in the USA, but not until the World Cup did it enjoy such renown. Today go to any sporting event and a lull in action is sure to bring on the Mexican wave.

SEE ALSO **'BECKHAM MANIA HITS JAPAN'** (page 557).

MARADONA CAPTAINS ARGENTINA FOR THE WORLD CUP

In 1983 Diego Maradona had been preparing to go for a run in Spain. From nowhere his new national team manager Carlos Bilardo appeared and began to run with him. Maradona thought the guy was crazy, but that changed when Bilardo asked him, "Will you be the captain?" Maradona began to cry. It was a massive moment and three years later it would galvanise the Argentinian for the World Cup. The former skipper Passarella had been left out and with that Bilardo opted to play a 3-5-2 formation. It was the perfect way to exploit Maradona's talents and in their opening game South Korea were beaten 3-1.

SEE ALSO **'MARADONA ON TOP OF THE WORLD'** (page 417).

Diego Maradona embraced the responsibility of the captain's armband bestowed upon him by manager Carlos Bilardo.

RAMPANT DENMARK DESTROY URUGUAY

Every now and then a nation puts in a performance in the World Cup that has the whole world drooling. In Neza on 8 June 26,500 fans watched bemused as the Danes ran the Uruguayans ragged. True, the dirty Uruguay team had a player sent-off 19 minutes in, but still they packed their defence and it needed some sparkling football to open them up. Preben Elkjaer and Soren Lerby scored the first two, Uruguay pulled one back, but the second half was a joy. Michael Laudrup waltzed his way through after 52 minutes, underlining his growing potential, while Elkjaer went on to seal a hat-trick and secure a famous 6-1 win.

SEE ALSO **'SUBSTITUTES' DENMARK WIN EUROPEAN CHAMPIONSHIP'** (pages 460-1).

Denmark underline their continued emergence as a growing force in world football with a demolition of a tough-tackling Uruguayan side.

LINEKER HAT-TRICK
SAVES ENGLAND

As ever, England had flown to the World Cup heavy with expectation, a burden that showed in their defeat to Portugal and draw with Morocco. Bobby Robson was under pressure and only a win in their last group game with Poland on 11 June would do. It was a tense start in Monterrey, but Robson and the country could rely on Gary Lineker to rise to the occasion. Lineker had recently been bought by Barcelona, who must have drooled at his predatory instincts when, after just eight minutes, he raced onto a Gary Stevens cross and prodded home. Two more Lineker goals meant the game was won and Robson spared.

SEE ALSO **"THE HAND OF GOD"** (page 414-5); **'SWEDES 2 TURNIPS 1'** (page 459).

Lineker guides home the second of his three goals to the delight of the massed ranks of travelling England fans who made the trip to Mexico.

BATISTA SENT OFF
AFTER 55 SECONDS

By now Uruguay had acquired quite a nasty reputation. They had Bossio sent off against the Danes, kicked their way to a draw with the Germans, and on 13 June Scotland were well aware that they would do whatever was necessary to earn the required draw. With that in mind, Alex Ferguson's decision to leave out his skipper Graeme Souness for a must-win game was baffling and just 55 seconds into the match Uruguay reverted to type when Jose Batista scythed down Gordon Strachan. The referee stood firm and sent off Batista, but no matter, the South Americans also stood firm and battled their way to a 0-0 draw.

SEE ALSO **'RED CARD FOR A PROFESSIONAL FOUL'** (page 438).

Referee Joel Quiniou wastes no time in showing the red card to Uruguay's floored centre-half Batista – despite his protestations.

THE VULTURE DEVOURS DENMARK

Denmark, odds-on favourites having already beaten West Germany 2-0 and annihilated Uruguay 6-1, were actually easy pickings for Spain when they met in the second round of the 1986 World Cup. They were torn apart by Spanish striker Emilio Butragueno, nicknamed The Vulture. Although Jesper Olsen opened the scoring for Denmark, lightning Spanish counter attacking inevitably featuring Butragueno sent the Danes spinning to a 5-1 defeat. Butragueno scored four of Spain's goals and could have had all five had not Andoni Goikoetxea jumped in to take a penalty, given when Butragueno was chopped down in the penalty area.

SEE ALSO **'SPAIN BAG A DOZEN TO QUALIFY FOR EUROPEAN CHAMPIONSHIPS'** (page 396).

Poacher Emilio Butragueno, nicknamed The Vulture, beats the offside trap nipping in to extend Spain's lead and his own goal tally.

BRAZIL AND FRANCE PLAY OUT CLASSIC QUARTER-FINAL

Under the scorching Guadalajara sun in front of 65,000 enraptured fans Brazil began in imperious form. Socrates was strutting his stuff and Careca put them in front with a blistering finish on 18 minutes. France looked like wilting under the pressure, but from nowhere Platini popped up to equalize just before half-time.

The second-half was anyone's. Brazil had the luxury of throwing on their trump card Zico but just three minutes after coming on he stepped up to take a decisive penalty, but opted to use his weaker right foot and Joel Bats made an easy save. France could have nicked it but were denied by cynical goalkeeping and myopic refereeing.

And so to penalties. Socrates missed and he wasn't alone. Another legend, Platini, also failed. Brazil's Cesar hit a post and so it fell to Luiz Fernandez to put France through. He duly obliged, sending Carlos the wrong way. The ghost of 1982 had been laid to rest at last.

France's Luis Fernandez – a new addition to an already formidable French midfield for Mexico '86 – and Michel Platini celebrate.

SEE ALSO **'HENRY KNOCKS OUT BRAZIL'** (page 602).

'THE HAND OF GOD'

Prior to this scintillating World Cup quarter-final Bobby Robson had sat in front of eager journalists and told them, "I've got 24 hours to devise a way to stop Maradona. It won't be easy. Other teams have already tried everything." On 22 June, just over 24 hours later, Robson would have sat in his hotel room and kicked himself for simply not cutting off the Argentinian's left arm.

Strangely, England went into the match not really focusing on Maradona and Robson instead sent his team out to stamp their own authority on the game. In the first half it seemed to work. Argentina had few opportunities to settle into a rhythm and Maradona had very little bearing on the first 45 minutes of action.

The second 45 would be slightly different, though. Five minutes in Maradona turned the game on its head and, for all his incredible skill, altered the way many fans would view him as a player and a man. Maradona forged a path towards goal, but lost the ball on the edge of the box. The ball bounced about before Steve Hodge rushed a clearance and sent the ball back, high into his penalty box. Maradona went after it, but was surely no match for Peter Shilton who came off his line ready to punch the ball clear. In a blur, the ball had ricocheted into the net. How had it happened? Shilton and his defenders were incandescent with rage. They were in no doubt Maradona had punched the ball in, but the officials gave the goal and a new villain was born.

SEE ALSO **'BUTCHER AND MARADONA MEET FOR DRUGS TEST'** (page 417); **"THE HAND OF THE DEVIL"** (page 488).

Unseen by the referee, Diego Maradona punches the ball into the England net.

The Argentinian star reels away in celebration, he later described the goal as 'The Hand of God'.

1986

MARADONA SCORES INCREDIBLE SECOND

If his first goal had been that of a pantomime villain, Maradona's second goal in the Azteca Stadium in Mexico City was pure theatre. It had everything: strength, skill, finesse, and bravery, and coming just four minutes after 'the hand of god' it reminded everyone of the footballing deity they were all so privileged to be witnessing. England lost possession in the Argentine half and the ball broke to Maradona, who spun expertly on it and with that was away. He made Peter Reid look like a Sunday league veteran, then a body swerve saw off Terry Fenwick. Next was Terry Butcher and suddenly he was in the box. Shilton was drawn, the ball never a millimetre from his toes, before he swivelled around the England keeper and dispatched it into the goal. "At the same time Butcher, a big blond guy, caught up with me," recalls Maradona. "He kicked me quite hard, but I didn't care. I'd scored the goal of my life."

Maradona's genius outsmarts Shilton and evades Butcher's last-ditch lunge to score perhaps the greatest goal ever seen.

SEE ALSO 'MARADONA ON TOP OF THE WORLD'
(page 417); 'MESSI'S MARADONA MIRACLE' (page 612).

BUTCHER AND MARADONA MEET FOR DRUGS TEST

It was the last thing he needed. Having just chased Maradona around the pitch for the second half and still smarting from the Argentinian's first handled goal, Terry Butcher, along with Kenny Sansom and Gary Stevens, had been called in for a random drugs test. The authorities had also called in Maradona (no surprise there, if he was on anything then it was worth keeping!) and Butcher for one wasn't pleased to see him. Maradona strolled over and shook their hands, but the big centre-half instead gestured to his hand, informing him of which part of Maradona's anatomy had put the ball in. Maradona just smiled.

SEE ALSO **'MARADONA TESTS POSITIVE'** (page 476).

Maradona and Butcher continued their battle after the match with the England centre half livid over the first goal.

Undisputably the world's best player, Diego Maradona lifts the Jules Rimet trophy at the impressive Azteca Stadium in Mexico City.

MARADONA ON TOP OF THE WORLD

It was easy to forget Argentina had other players. Two more wonderful goals in the semi-final from Maradona had the pundits discussing their 'one-man team', so on 29 June it was timely that Jose Luis Brown and Valdano gave Argentina a 2-0 first-half lead. The Germans came back strongly, equalized through Rummenigge and Voller, and looked in the ascendancy. Maradona, though, a World Cup victory clearly his destiny, once more took control. With six minutes remaining he picked up the ball in his own half, looked up, played a sharp pass that dissected a flat German defence and sent Jorge Burruchaga clear. With his finish the World Cup was won.

SEE ALSO **'FAREWELL TO A FLAWED TALENT'** (page 508).

Alex Ferguson took over a struggling United team and pronounced the level of fitness in his newly inherited squad as 'depressing'.

ALEX FERGUSON TAKES OVER AT MANCHESTER UNITED

It was now nearly 20 years since Manchester United had last won the Championship and with that worrying milestone fast approaching, their manager Ron Atkinson was sacked. Alex Ferguson had turned down big jobs at Arsenal and Tottenham, but was enticed south of the border from Aberdeen for what he saw as the biggest job around. He had already upset the old guard in Scotland; now he was determined to ruin Liverpool's dominance in the English game. It wasn't going to be easy, though. Ferguson's first game was at Oxford United where he saw his somewhat idle squad beaten 2-0 at the Manor Ground. Changes would have to be made.

SEE ALSO 'FERGIE DOESN'T FALTER' (page 434); 'MANCHESTER UNITED WIN THE EUROPEAN CUP WINNERS' CUP' (page 452).

PLAY-OFFS INTRODUCED BY FOOTBALL LEAGUE

English football was in crisis. Attendances and playing standards were falling, while hooligans ran amok. Most fans lost interest well before the season's end since their side had avoided relegation, but had no chance of glory. So the Football League introduced relegation and promotion play-offs to maintain excitement. The original format saw the three teams that finished in the play-off places in the lower division and a relegation-threatened team from the higher division play semi-finals over two legs. Charlton Athletic were the first team promoted to the old First Division this way, beating Leeds United after the two-legged final went to a one-match replay.

SEE ALSO 'IT'S THREE POINTS FOR A WIN' (page 374).

Charlton Athletic's Garth Crooks leaps in front of Leeds United's Jackie Ashurst during the first play-off final.

BACK-HEEL HELPS PORTO
WIN THE EUROPEAN CUP

1987

There were 60,000 fans in Vienna on 27 March to see Porto face favourites Bayern Munich and the Germans took the lead after 24 minutes. Porto, though, were the better side and finally equalized on 77 minutes. When the ball dropped to him in the six-yard box, Rabah Madjer, who had scored against West Germany for Algeria in the 1982 World Cup, coolly back-heeled it into the net. He was injured in his goal celebrations, but recovered to get back on, dribble down the left and cross for Porto's Brazilian substitute Juary to volley the ball into Bayern's net from six yards. Portugal had their first European champions since 1962. The following year Porto added both the European Super Cup and the Intercontinental Cup to their trophy cabinet.

SEE ALSO 'MOURINHO HELPS PORTO BECOME CHAMPIONS OF EUROPE' (page 578).

Ole! Rabah Madjer's audacious backheel brings Porto level.

MARADONA LEADS NAPOLI TO THEIR FIRST SCUDETTO

The natives were getting excited in Naples. Since Maradona's arrival in 1984, Napoli had finished eighth and then third, and they were about to win their first Scudetto. Being a southern club, Napoli didn't enjoy the riches of their Northern rivals, but in Maradona they had a priceless gem whose sheer presence pushed the city towards glory and they took the title on the last day of the season by three points from Juventus. "I was the captain of the ship," said the Argentinian. "I was the flag. They could mess with anyone, but not with me. It was that simple."

"When we started building that team, the results came. Inter came, we thrashed them. Milan came, we beat them. We beat everybody"

SEE ALSO **'SPEZIA ARE FINALLY AWARDED THE 1944 SCUDETTO'** (page 552).

ARRIGO SACCHI JOINS AC MILAN

Berlusconi was an ambitious man. At the end of the 1986-87 season he tried to sign Maradona from Napoli, but was reminded by the Argentinian that neither would be safe in Italy if he did. The San Siro coach was legendary 1950s Swedish midfielder Nils Liedholm, but it was time for a change and in came Arrigo Sacchi. The ex-shoe salesman had done a decent job at Parma, but when he was appointed it hardly had them quaking in their football boots at Juventus, Roma and Napoli. Sacchi was a quiet man, but he had big ideas, the first being to sign Dutch duo Ruud Gullit and Marco Van Basten.

SEE ALSO **'BERLUSCONI RAISES THE EUROPEAN CUP'** (page 430).

A hugely successful coach, Sacchi never played football professionally. He had two spells in charge of the Rossoneri at the San Siro.

Thankfully Keith Houchen's diving header during Coventry City's shock win over Spurs is what the 1987 Cup final is best remembered for.

FA CUP SPONSORSHIP PLAN THWARTED

An Australian lager company sponsoring the most famous knock-out competition in world football? The FA Cup re-named the Fosters Lager Cup? It didn't bear thinking about. When the news leaked that the FA were seriously considering a £20 million deal to sell the name of their flagship competition there was public and press uproar. You couldn't blame the authorities or the clubs for being tempted as a lack of European football was pinching hard, but in the end the FA couldn't bring itself to do the deal. Well not until 1994 at least, when Littlewoods finally put their name to the Cup.

SEE ALSO **'FA'S FIRST COMMERCIAL VENTURE'** (page 15); **'PREMIER LEAGUE LAUNCHED'** (page 462).

GULLIT VOTED EUROPEAN AND DUTCH FOOTBALLER OF THE YEAR

The football world was united in its appreciation of Ruud Gullit's wonderful talent. The Dutchman had started his career as a sweeper, but became a more offensive player after moving to PSV Eindhoven in 1985. There his 46 goals in 68 league appearances helped PSV seal back-to-back Eredivisie titles. Such electric form brought the Dutch and European Footballer of the Year awards, with Gullit dedicating the European gong to Nelson Mandela, who was still a political prisoner in South Africa. That summer Gullit joined compatriots Marco van Basten and Frank Rijkaard at AC Milan for a then world record £6.5 million.

SEE ALSO **'HOLLAND SHOW THEIR PEDIGREE'** (page 424–5).

Gullit went on to spend eight years in the top flight in Italy before finishing his career with Chelsea in the Premiership.

1988

THE CRAZY GANG STUN LIVERPOOL

In the Wembley dressing room, Dennis Wise and Vinnie Jones rallied their team-mates. "Let's try and keep them down to four," they cried, fearing a thrashing from League champions Liverpool in the 107th FA Cup final.

Lowly Wimbledon had been playing non-League football just 11 years before the 14 May match and started the 1988 FA Cup as 33-1 outsiders, so surely they didn't have a prayer against the likes of John Barnes, Peter Beardsley and Alan Hansen? Yet on 37 minutes, Wise curled a free-kick towards Liverpool's near post and midfielder Lawrie Sanchez rose to score his first-ever FA Cup goal with a glancing header and it was 1-0 to Wimbledon.

Goalkeeper Dave Beasant was performing heroically, but on the hour Liverpool won a controversial penalty. John Aldridge, who had not missed in 12 penalty attempts, stepped up, only for the agile Beasant to brilliantly push the kick around his left-hand post. Beasant was the first keeper to save a Cup Final penalty at Wembley and, as Wimbledon skipper, later became the first goalkeeper to receive the famous trophy.

Wimbledon's Lawrie Sanchez rises to score the Crazy Gang's winning goal.

SEE ALSO 'WEMBLEY SHOCK FOR CUP FAVOURITES' (page 355); 'PALACE UPSET FA CUP FAVOURITES' (page 435).

VAN BASTEN PROVES THE DIFFERENCE IN EURO SEMI-FINAL

The Dutch boasted the talents of Ruud Gullit, Frank Rijkaard and Marco van Basten, yet they had never defeated semi-final opponents West Germany in a meaningful encounter. Both sides converted disputed penalties in front of a tense Hamburg crowd and the game appeared to be heading for extra-time until van Basten coolly slotted the winner past goalkeeper Eike Immel. But Holland's Ronald Koeman soured a memorable night by gesturing as if to wipe his bottom with Olaf Thon's shirt after the final whistle. "It was the kind of stupid reaction that follows you for the rest of your life," admitted Koeman.

SEE ALSO **'HOLLAND SHOW THEIR PEDIGREE'** (page 424-5); **'RIJKAARD SPITS ON VOLLER'** (page 442).

Holland's Ruud Gullit celebrates with Ronald Koeman.

HOLLAND SHOW
THEIR PEDIGREE

When Arnold Muhren swung a deep, swirling cross from the Holland left into the Soviet Union penalty area, lesser players would have struggled to even control the ball as it drifted towards the byline. But Marco van Basten was rightly known as Europe's most dangerous and technically gifted striker. Never taking his eye off the ball, the AC Milan forward adjusted the direction of his run, contorted his body and, with perfect timing, swung his right foot through the line of the ball. The resulting volley was executed at the most acute angle, but it harmonised awesome power with pin-point precision, flying beyond the reach of Russian goalkeeper Rinat Dasaev and into the far corner of the net.

The Olympiastadion in Munich erupted in delighted recognition of van Basten's sheer audacity and genius. The goal, one of 24 he scored in 58 internationals, sealed a 2-0 European Championship final victory for the Dutch. It was the first time the Netherlands, coached by the legendary Rinus Michels, had won an international tournament.

SEE ALSO **'VAN BASTEN HOBBLES AWAY FROM FOOTBALL'** (page 489).

The goals of the inspirational Marco van Basten did much to secure Holland's victory.

FIFA VOTE IN FAVOUR OF USA WORLD CUP

Appropriately enough FIFA chose Independence Day to announce that the USA would host the 1994 World Cup. The major figure behind America's successful bid and the tournament's subsequent organisation was Alan I Rothenberg, a Californian lawyer. Rothenberg saw the World Cup as a massive opportunity to boost the sport's profile in the USA and predicted it would bring in $4 billion to the country's economy. A principal source of revenue would be the estimated one million tourists who would visit the US for the tournament. Certainly the World Cup made a $50 million profit, with Rothenberg reportedly receiving a controversial $3 million bonus.

SEE ALSO **'US STARS PERFORM WORLD CUP DRAW'** (page 471).

USA '94 poster seen at the
Stanford Stadium, California
– one of the venues for the
eventual tournament.

CANTONA RECEIVES INTERNATIONAL BAN

Eric Cantona was banned indefinitely from internationals for insulting France coach Henri Michel. On national television a furious Cantona had vented his frustration at not being selected for France, after scoring twice for Olympique Marseille against Strasbourg. "Mickey Rourke referred to the people who awarded the Oscars in Hollywood as shit bags," the 22-year-old exclaimed. "I think Henri Michel is not far from being included in that category." Cantona's subsequent public apology placated nobody at the French Football Federation. "I hadn't told any lies but I had been clumsy," he reflected. "I needed to learn the art of communication."

SEE ALSO **'CANTONA JOINS MANCHESTER UNITED'** (page 465). **'CANTONA'S KUNG-FU FIGHTING'** (page 483).

Eric Cantona strikes a typically rebellious pose. Although a controversial figure throughout his career, his immense talent could not be disputed.

CLOUGH CLIPS FOREST FAN'S ROUND THE EAR

Old Big 'Ead never shied away from physical confrontation as Roy Keane and others would testify. "If a player had said to Bill Shankly 'I've got to speak to my agent,' Bill would have hit him. And I would have held him while he hit him," Clough once said. So Forest supporters who ran onto the pitch to celebrate their 18 January Littlewoods Cup victory over Queens Park Rangers should not have been surprised to receive a clip on the ear from their team's manager. The inevitable media furore ensued and Clough later apologised on TV, kissing two of the fans to show he meant it.

SEE ALSO **'CLOUGH BLASTS JUVENTUS 'CHEATS"** (page 324); **'DI CANIO BANNED FOR PUSH'** (page 520).

Brian Clough is captured on a grainy camera image hurling a Nottingham Forest supporter aside in anger as they invaded the pitch.

THE HILLSBOROUGH DISASTER

The eagerly-awaited FA Cup semi-final between Liverpool and Nottingham Forest at Hillsborough turned into the United Kingdom's worst-ever football tragedy. Sickeningly, 96 Liverpool fans – men, women and children – were killed in a terrible crush in the Leppings Lane end of the ground.

The game would kick off at 3pm on 15 April 1989, but by 2.30pm thousands of Liverpool supporters trying to enter the stadium were caught in a bottleneck. The police outside the ground feared a crush, so they opened a set of gates leading into a narrow tunnel at the rear of the terrace. Fans poured through the tunnel into the already congested central section of the terrace. Those at the front were pushed against the tall anti-hooligan fencing. Many fans tried to escape by climbing over the fence or by being pulled into the upper tier by other supporters.

"The screaming was terrible," one survivor recalled, "the crush awful, but I was still straining to actually see the match. I wasn't interested in the play. I just had to keep my mind on something other than the crush, because there was less and less breath." Liverpool was a city in mourning. People laid flowers on the Kop and across half the Anfield pitch.

The conclusions of Lord Justice Taylor's inquiry into the circumstances surrounding the disaster led to the removal of fences from grounds and the abandonment of terracing in favour of all-seater stadiums. However, families of the victims still believe somebody, notably the South Yorkshire Police, should be made to accept responsibility for a disaster that could have been avoided. Their battle for justice continues.

SEE ALSO **'TAYLOR REPORT RECOMMENDS ALL-SEATER STADIUMS'** (page 434).

Fans carry away the injured on an advertising board being used as a make-shift stretcher.

The Anfield pitch is covered with floral tributes to those who died for a service of remembrance.

IAN RUSH WINS EMOTIONAL FA CUP FINAL

On 20 May Ian Rush's double gave Liverpool fans a fleeting moment of happiness barely a month after the Hillsborough tragedy. The final went into extra-time when Stuart McCall's late goal for Everton cancelled out John Aldridge's fifth-minute strike. But it took just four minutes of extra-time for the Reds to restore their lead when Rush, on as a substitute for Aldridge, produced a typically predatory finish. Back came Everton as McCall grabbed another equaliser. But Rush finally found the knockout blow in the 103rd minute, with a deft touch to beat Neville Southall. The scoreline was 3-2 to Liverpool, but at the final whistle Liverpool's celebrations were understandably tinged with sadness.

SEE ALSO **'THE HILLSBOROUGH DISASTER'** (page 428).

John Barnes celebrates the winning goal with Ian Rush on a bittersweet day for Liverpool Football Club at Wembley.

BERLUSCONI RAISES THE EUROPEAN CUP

AC Milan's beaming president Silvio Berlusconi joined his players on the Nou Camp pitch to raise the trophy as the Rossoneri celebrated their first European Cup triumph for two decades. The future Italian Prime Minister had taken just three years to transform Milan from under-achievers into Europe's top club. Under coach Arrigo Sacchi they fused traditional Italian defensive strengths with the attacking panache of their Dutch imports. Poor Steaua Bucharest had no answer as Milan rampaged to a 3-0 half-time lead, with two goals from Ruud Gullit and one from Marco Van Basten. A minute after the restart, Van Basten completed the rout and it finished 4-0.

SEE ALSO **'SILVIO BERLUSCONI BUYS AC MILAN'** (page 406).

Surrounded by his team of superstars, the controversial Berlusconi sees his substantial investment in AC Milan come to fruition.

THOMAS SCORES
LAST-MINUTE LEAGUE WINNER

"It's up for grabs now," screamed TV commentator Brian Moore as Michael Thomas bore down on goal in the final seconds of a titanic struggle. If the Arsenal midfielder scored past the onrushing Bruce Grobbelaar, the Gunners would snatch the League title on goal difference. If not, Liverpool would be crowned champions and double winners, after winning the FA Cup six days before this 26 May game. In a move started by goalkeeper John Lukic, Thomas latched onto Alan Smith's flick from Lee Dixon's pass and waited for Grobbelaar to commit himself before cunningly poking the ball into the net. "We have the most dramatic finish maybe in the history of the Football League," Moore shouted. The match ended Liverpool 0, Arsenal 2.

Anfield was stunned. Manager Kenny Dalglish stood and stared. Great Liverpool players like John Barnes and Steve McMahon sank to their knees in disbelief as Arsenal celebrated. "People were always writing us off back then, but we loved it," said Thomas. "It was the Arsenal way. It made us stronger."

Michael Thomas scores perhaps the most dramatic goal in the modern English game at Anfield.

SEE ALSO **'RANGERS PIP CELTIC IN LAST DAY FINAL SHOWDOWN'** (page 570).

CHILE'S WORLD CUP 'PLOT' FAILS

The crowd at Brazil's Maracana Stadium might have initially been fooled, but eagle-eyed TV cameramen weren't. On 3 September with Brazil leading in a World Cup qualifier, Chilean goalkeeper Roberto Rojas fell dramatically – apparently bleeding from a wound caused by a thrown firecracker. The Chilean team, needing a win to qualify for the 1990 World Cup, stormed off, but TV replays revealed no flares had landed near Rojas, who had slashed his own scalp with a concealed razor blade. FIFA barred Chile from the 1990 and 1994 tournaments and banned Rojas and some Chilean officials for life. Rojas' ban was lifted in 2001.

SEE ALSO **'KIDNAPPING THREATENS COPA AMERICA'** (page 549).

Roberto Rojas the Chilean goalkeeper didn't count on being caught out by the watching TV cameras. He and his country paid a heavy price.

The image of a bandaged and blood-stained Terry Butcher reflects the courageous way in which he approached the game.

BUTCHER'S BLOOD FLOWS AGAINST SWEDEN

England travelled to Stockholm on 6 September knowing a draw would confirm their place at the 1990 World Cup, but Sweden still hoped to overtake Bobby Robson's men, who might have buckled when defensive linchpin Terry Butcher received a deep gash to the head in an aerial clash with Johnny Ekstrom. Bravely, Butcher refused to be substituted and, after receiving stitches at half-time, he heroically continued to repel the Swedes as they pressed with increasing urgency. Every painful header drew more blood, which seeped through his bandage to leave crimson stains down his jersey, but a goalless draw ensured England's qualification for Italia 90.

SEE ALSO **'BUTCHER AND MARADONA MEET FOR DRUGS TEST'** (page 417); **'... IT GOES TO PENALTIES'** (page 445).

WHEN FOOTBALL BECAME PURE MURDER

The finger of guilt was pointed at organised crime and drug cartels after Colombian League match official Alvaro Ortega was shot dead. He was murdered after running the line during a tense First Division match between Independiente Medellin and America de Cali on 15 November 1989. Although the killer never seems to have been brought to justice, it was widely suspected that the linesman was an incorruptible official who had refused a bribe to try to influence the result between two of the country's major teams. However, the killing led to the suspension of the Colombian League.

SEE ALSO **'ESCOBAR SHOT DEAD AFTER OWN GOAL'** (page 476).

Referees and linesmen in Colombia come under fierce pressure – and not just from the players on the pitch.

RANGERS SIGN A CATHOLIC

Striker Maurice Johnston returned to haunt Celtic by grabbing a late winner at Ibrox on 4 November. Four months earlier, Johnston had become Rangers' first Catholic player for 70 years, a move that angered both sides of the sectarian divide. Johnston was also a former Celtic player and had insisted he would rejoin the Bhoys after his spell with French side Nantes, but Rangers boss Graeme Souness would not let religion decide transfer policy. "I didn't do it to be a revolutionary," Souness said later. "I knew he'd complement what we had at Ibrox." Johnston"s goals helped Rangers to the first three of nine consecutive titles.

SEE ALSO **'DEATH THREATS FORCE INTERNATIONAL RETIREMENT'** (page 566).

Rangers's Mo Johnston fires in the winning goal against his former team Celtic in the always explosive Old Firm derby.

TAYLOR REPORT RECOMMENDS ALL-SEATER STADIUMS

Lord Justice Taylor was appointed by Margaret Thatcher's government to investigate events surrounding the Hillsborough Stadium disaster. The Taylor Report, published in January, concluded that the police, local authorities and football's administrators – not Liverpool fans – were to blame. It made 76 recommendations for improvements in football administration and stadium safety, including the removal of perimeter fencing and that top-flight stadiums should become all-seater. It also addressed the general need to modernise old grounds and improve safety facilities, the prohibition of ticket touting and the need for responsible behaviour by the players and the media.

SEE ALSO **'THE HILLSBOROUGH DISASTER'** (page 428).

Lord Taylor presents the findings of his report into Hillsborough and unveils his recommendations to ensure crowd safety at matches.

Mark Robins wheels away in celebration as Forest captain Stuart Pearce looks on. This goal is often credited with saving his manager's job.

FERGUSON DOESN'T FALTER

Mark Robins is often credited with saving Alex Ferguson's Old Trafford career. Injury-hit United were struggling in the League and a January defeat at the City Ground in the FA Cup third round might have meant the end for Fergie. Left-back Lee Martin won the ball in the Forest half and passed infield to Mark Hughes. The centre-forward flicked a precise cross towards the penalty spot for his strike partner Robins to convert with a simple header and the score was 0-1. The Reds went on to lift the FA Cup, the first of many trophies in the Ferguson era. "I strongly fancied us to beat Forest," Ferguson later insisted.

SEE ALSO **'UNITED ON CLOUD NINE'** (page 614).

PALACE UPSET FA CUP FAVOURITES

Plucky Palace surprisingly won a thrilling FA Cup semi-final at Villa Park on 8 April. Champions-elect Liverpool were firm favourites, having defeated Palace 9-0 earlier in the season, and they led at half-time. But the opportunistic Mark Bright soon equalised and on 69 minutes Gary O'Reilly bundled the ball home from Andy Gray's free-kick. Liverpool struck twice late on to grab a 3-2 lead, before Gray's powerful header took the tie into extra-time. Set-pieces were Palace's main weapon and Alan Pardew's far-post header decided the match in the second period of extra-time. It ended 4-3 in Palace's favour. "They were better organised at set pieces," conceded Liverpool boss Kenny Dalglish.

SEE ALSO **"KING KENNY RESIGNS' AS LIVERPOOL MANAGER'** (page 451).

Alan Pardew celebrates scoring Crystal Palace's extra time winner – the goal that was enough to eliminate the holders Liverpool.

UEFA LIFTS BAN ON ENGLISH CLUBS – BUT NOT LIVERPOOL

After five years in isolation, English clubs were again allowed to participate in European competition. They had been barred since the Heysel Stadium disaster in May 1985, when 39 Italians and Belgians died at the European Cup final between Juventus and Liverpool. Fans of the Merseyside club were widely blamed for the rioting that led to the tragedy, so Liverpool's ban was not lifted for another year. Since Liverpool had won the League in 1989-90, that meant no English side entered the European Cup in 1990-91. Aston Villa didn't survive long in the UEFA Cup, but Manchester United were triumphant in the Cup Winners' Cup.

SEE ALSO 'MANCHESTER UNITED WIN CUP WINNER'S CUP' (page 452).

David Platt leaves Banik Ostrava's Dustan Urto in his wake during Aston Villa's brief UEFA Cup run after English sides returned to Europe.

The World Cup is now one of the most lucrative sporting events in the world second only to the global reach of the Olympics.

WORLD CUP SPONSORS PAY £10 MILLION EACH

The nine official sponsors of the 1982 World Cup paid a combined £10 million for the privilege. Just eight years later, the 11 official sponsors of Italia 90, which included Coca-Cola, Fuji Film and Gillette, reportedly splashed out around £10 million each to be associated with sport's premier tournament. The World Cup is an advertiser's dream because of the global reach provided by blanket television coverage. Extensive stadium signage, in particular, allows advertisers to promote their brands to a worldwide audience of millions. It has been reported that the 15 official partners for the 2006 tournament paid an average of £18 million for their involvement.

SEE ALSO **'NIKE CONTRACT LEAKED'** (page 530).

Bobby Robson at the FA press conference in which the decision to release him from his contract to take over at PSV was announced.

ROBSON PLANS FOR THE FUTURE

Before Italia 90 the FA told Bobby Robson they would not be renewing his contract and permitted him to pursue a post-tournament job, so the England manager agreed to join PSV Eindhoven. Although PSV and Robson decided not to announce the move before the World Cup, the story broke and some newspapers wrongly accused Robson of being a traitor. He sued one and settled out of court. The FA did little to support Robson, but the players were on his side. "They told me, to a man, that I was justified in seeking alternative employment," revealed Robson, who guided PSV to two Dutch titles.

SEE ALSO **'... IT GOES TO PENALTIES'** (page 445).

PARMA PROMOTED TO SERIE A

A 2-0 victory over Reggiana secured Parma's place in Serie A. Newly bankrolled by local dairy giants Parmalat, the small city best known as the birthplace of Verdi suddenly arrived on the football map. An array of stars – Cannavaro, Chiesa, Buffon, Zola, Asprilla and Crespo – were recruited and honours swiftly followed. The 90's brought 2 UEFA cups, one Cup Winner's Cup, one European Super Cup, two Coppa Italias, one Italian Super Cup and in 1997 the club lost out on the Scudetto by a single point to Juventus. However, the dream soon soured in 2003 as Parmalat was embroiled in a scandal leaving the club in financial limbo. Though still in the top-flight, Parma have struggled to recapture the form of their so-called 'Golden Period'.

Nevio Scala was the man in charge as Parma – with the help of their sponsors – began to challenge the tradition hierarchy in Serie A.

SEE ALSO **'ZOLA HELPS CAGLIARI WIN PROMOTION '** (page 579).

Leo Beenhakker's appointment was not universally welcomed by the Dutch squad and he oversaw a disastrous campaign in Italy.

DUTCH PLAYERS WANT CRUYFF

As reigning European champions with a squad full of superstars at their peak the Dutch were considered favourites for Italia 90. Coach Thijs Libregts was axed in 1989 after a player revolt and the KNVB (Dutch FA) consulted the squad before appointing his successor. A vote is said to have resulted with 90% in favour of Johan Cruyff, then manager of Barcelona. The KNVB deferred to Rinus Michels, the man who had masterminded their Euro 88 triumph. Michels had coached Cruyff at Ajax and Barcelona, but instead went for Leo Beenhakker of Ajax. After the players failed to get their man Beenhakker never seemed to have their support and Italia 90 proved to be a tournament the Dutch would rather forget.

SEE ALSO **'DUTCH PLAYERS REVOLT'** (page473).

Once the law was passed the straight red card soon became an all-too-regular sight in world football as referees clamped down.

RED CARD FOR PROFESSIONAL FOUL

The laws of the game were finally changed before the 1990 World Cup so that referees should punish deliberate fouls to prevent a goal-scoring opportunity with a red card. English football had pioneered this change in the domestic game in 1982-83, when Reading's Lawrie Sanchez became the first player to be dismissed for a deliberate handball. Fans, players and officials were fed up with defenders being able to prevent a probable goal through foul play, especially since Arsenal's Willie Young infamously hacked down West Ham's Paul Allen when he was through on goal in the 1980 FA Cup final.

SEE ALSO **'RIKJAARD SPITS ON VOLLER'** (page 442).

LOWLY CAMEROON BEAT MIGHTY ARGENTINA

On 8 June, in the opening match of Italia 90, defending champions Argentina faltered against Cameroon's admirable energy and questionable discipline. Defender Kana Biyik was dismissed on 62 minutes for felling Claudio Cannigia and Benjamin Massing was later red-carded after kicking Maradona throughout. But between the sendings-off Cameroon took a shock lead when goalkeeper Nery Pumpido somehow allowed Omam Biyik's tame header to slip under his body. Maradona blamed the whole team for the defeat at the San Siro, Milan. "Cameroon didn't win, Argentina lost," he insisted. "Cameroon really gave us a kicking, but to talk about that was to make excuses."

SEE ALSO **'ROGER MILLA DANCES TO VICTORY'** (page 441); **'SENEGAL SHOCK FRANCE'** (page 558).

Cameroon celebrate their unlikely victory over Argentina in a group match in Milan.

WEST GERMANY MAKE BRIGHT START

Several of the favourites, including Italy, Holland and Argentina, made disappointing starts to the 1990 World Cup. Not so West Germany, whose dynamic skipper Lothar Matthaus epitomised their intention to assert themselves. Clearly at home on his club ground, the San Siro, the Internazionale midfielder was the catalyst behind a 4-1 thrashing of Yugoslavia on 10 June. His surging run and unstoppable long-range drive opened the scoring on 28 minutes. Matthaus struck again in the second half and still had the energy to nullify Yugoslavia's playmaker Dragan Stojkovic. West Germany's other goals came from Jürgen Klinsmann and Rudi Voeller.

SEE ALSO **'WEST GERMANY WIN FROM THE SPOT'** (page 446).

Lothar Matthaus rides a challenge and breaks free with the ball for West Germany. He was the star performer as Germany progressed.

Scotland's Paul McStay moves across to tackle Costa Rica's Claudio Jara. The Tartan Army were soon heading home to Scotland.

SCOTLAND HEAD FOR HOME

Scotland continued their record of underachieving at World Cups with an embarrassing defeat to Costa Rica in Genoa on 11 June. A team that included Maurice Johnston, Richard Gough, Alex McLeish and Jim Leighton was undone by Juan Cayasso's 50th-minute strike. The Scots laboured throughout and were described by one British sports writer as "moving at a pace that might have been bettered by a woman pushing a pram". Scotland then defeated Sweden, but lost their final group game to Brazil and travelled home after yet another heroic failure. Meanwhile, Costa Rica progressed to the second round where they were humbled by Czechoslovakia.

SEE ALSO **'MOROCCO STUN SCOTLAND'** (page 513).

ROGER MILLA
DANCES TO VICTORY

It was 23 June 1990, Cameroon were playing Colombia and the last-16 clash in Naples was 106 minutes old when the veteran Cameroonian striker finally broke the deadlock. Roger Milla, on as a substitute after 54 minutes, collected Omam Biyik's precise pass and evaded two Colombian challenges before smashing a left-foot shot beyond Rene Higuita. Cue his trademark celebration of dancing around the corner flag, one hand on his stomach, the other pointing to the heavens. Three minutes later, Milla robbed Higuita of possession and rolled the ball into an empty net, before repeating his celebration. Colombia grabbed a late consolation goal, but it was Milla's day. Cameroon were the first African nation to reach the quarter-finals, where they lost to England.

Amazingly, 38-year-old Milla had retired in 1987 and was living on the Indian Ocean island of Reunion before a phone call from the President of Cameroon persuaded him to return for the World Cup. "1990 was my crowning glory," said Milla. "I think the whole world enjoyed seeing a 38-year-old score four goals at the World Cup finals."

SEE ALSO 'AGHAHOWA CELEBRATES IN STYLE' (page 560).

Colombia's Andres Escobar collides with his unconventional keeper Higuita, while the Cameroon's star striker Roger Milla displays his distinctive celebration, one of the most enduring images of Italia 90.

RIJKAARD SPITS ON VOLLER

In the 21st minute of a pulsating World Cup second-round clash, an argument erupted between Holland's Frank Rijkaard and West Germany's Rudi Voller, probably because Rijkaard thought Voeller was guilty of diving. The altercation culminated in Rijkaard spitting at Voeller and the pair almost coming to blows as Argentinian referee Juan Loustau sent them to the San Siro dressing rooms. West Germany went on to win 2-1 with goals from Jürgen Klinsmann and Andreas Brehme. Rijkaard and Voller eventually made up. "Frank told me he had big problems at the time, he was in the middle of a divorce, he wasn't the real Frank Rijkaard," the German revealed sympathetically.

SEE ALSO **'WEST GERMANY WIN FROM THE SPOT'** (page 446).

The culmination of a long-running clash as Rijkaard's spit at Voller is captured on camera.

PASS MASTER MARADONA SHOWS THE BRAZILIANS

Diego Armando Maradona had struggled to influence the last-16 clash in Turin because of an ankle injury that required pre-match painkilling injections and Brazil had dominated. But with eight minutes remaining, Argentina's number 10 received possession in the centre circle, beating two Brazilian challenges as he surged forward. "I ran diagonally towards the right," Maradona recalled, "dragging my markers Ricardo Rocha and Alemao with me, while Caniggia signalled that he was keeping up on the left." Brazil's whole defence followed Maradona, whose perfect right-footed pass left the unmarked Caniggia to dribble around goalkeeper Claudio Taffarel and finish with aplomb. Genius.

SEE ALSO **'MARADONA STIRS IT UP AGAINST THE WEST GERMANS'** (page 445).

Maradona holds off a challenge from Brazil's Ricardo Rocha before playing in Claudio Caniggia to convert the winning goal.

PLATT VOLLEYS ENGLAND THROUGH

"Platt's winning goal… was one of the best by an England player for many years," Bobby Robson purred. England had won their group after hard-fought draws with Ireland and Holland and an unimpressive defeat of Egypt. Belgium were also tough opponents and matched England's every move in Bologna on 26 June until David Platt finally broke their resistance just 60 seconds before a dreaded penalty shoot-out. The irrepressible Paul Gascoigne won a free-kick on the Belgium right and delivered a curling cross towards the far post. There, Platt swivelled and struck an unerring volley past goalkeeper Michel Preudhomme. It was 1-0 and England were through to the quarter-finals.

SEE ALSO **'TEARS FOR SOUVENIRS'** (page 444).

England's David Platt celebrates his last-minute winner with team-mates Mark Wright, Gary Lineker and Terry Butcher.

TOTO SCHILLACI'S STARE

Salvatore 'Toto' Schillaci was Italy's unlikely goalscoring hero, overshadowing such luminaries as Gianluca Vialli and Roberto Baggio. The little-known Juventus striker made his international debut in the group stage, scored a string of decisive goals and was already on course for the Golden Boot when Italy faced the Republic of Ireland in the quarter-finals. The Sicilian pounced on 38 minutes when Pat Bonner parried Roberto Donadoni's fierce drive, calmly guiding the ball beyond the goalkeeper's reach. Schillaci's reaction was from the Marco Tardelli school of goal celebrations: running towards the corner flag, he slid to his knees and, mouth open, stared dementedly into the Rome night. That was the only goal of the match and it ended 1-0 to Italy.

SEE ALSO **'THE TARDELLI SCREAM'** (page 393).

Sicilian-born Schillaci came from nowhere to become Italy's goalscoring hero although they fell short of victory on home soil.

TEARS FOR SOUVENIRS

England were playing West Germany on 4 July in a World Cup semi-final and fans feared the worst when after an hour their side fell behind in Turin to Andreas Brehme's cruelly deflected strike. But Gary Lineker was always a reliable goal-scorer at World Cups and ten minutes from time he capitalised on confusion in the German penalty area and drove home a perfect left-foot strike. In extra-time, both sides hit the woodwork and Paul Gascoigne received a harsh booking that meant he would miss the final should England win. He knew what the caution meant and his face reddened as he wept uncontrollably. The game remained 1-1 and went penalties.

SEE ALSO **'... IT GOES TO PENALTIES'** (page 444); **'GAZZAMANIA'** (page 447).

A star was born that night in Turin. Bobby Robson reflected after the epic encounter, "I don't know anybody who dislikes Paul Gascoigne."

West Germany's captain Lothar Matthaus sportingly consoles Chris Waddle after he had the misfortune to miss the vital penalty.

... IT GOES TO PENALTIES

Sadly, one of the most gripping games of the tournament was decided by penalties. At 3-3 in the shootout, the normally reliable Stuart Pearce smashed his kick against Bodo Ilgner's flying body. Olaf Thon scored for West Germany and Chris Waddle launched his attempt high over the bar. England were out. As true gentlemen, Bobby Robson and West Germany coach Franz Beckenbauer shook hands. Beckenbauer told Robson: "At this level there should never be a loser after a performance like that. You have a nice team, Bobby." However, a disconsolate Robson knew this had been England's best chance of glory since 1966.

SEE ALSO **'MOLLER SCORES WINNING PENALTY'** (page 498).

MARADONA STIRS IT UP AGAINST WEST GERMANY

The Italian crowd favoured West Germany in the World Cup final in Rome since Argentina had eliminated the host nation on penalties five days earlier. Before that match Maradona crudely attempted to exploit traditional rivalry between southern and northern Italy by imploring the Naples public to support Argentina, so during the national anthems in Rome, the Italian crowd let Maradona know precisely what they thought. A cacophony of boos and jeers rang out when Maradona's image appeared on the giant screen. In response, he mouthed a message for the crowd to lip-read: "Hijos de puta, hijos de puta, sons of bitches, sons of bitches."

SEE ALSO **'MARADONA ACCUSES FIFA OF FIXING THE WORLD CUP'** (page449).

Referee Edgardo Codesal Mendez explains the coin toss to the captains, Argentina's Diego Maradona and West Germany's Lothar Matthaus.

WEST GERMANY WIN FROM THE SPOT

A controversial penalty was an apt way to decide a final noted for playacting, diving and cynicism. On 8 July 1990, four years after their memorable encounter in Mexico City, West Germany and Argentina produced the most tedious final in World Cup history. In mitigation, Argentina would surely have been less negative had Claudio Caniggia not been suspended and Maradona not been hampered by injury. In fact, Maradona was jeered throughout by the Roman crowd and West Germany were the better side – which isn't saying much.

The pivotal figure was Mexican referee Edgardo Codesal, who dismissed Argentina's Pedro Monzon and Gustavo Dezotti in the second half and awarded West Germany the decisive penalty after Roberto Sensini brought down Rudi Voeller. Ironically, Codesal had previously turned down better penalty appeals from both sides, but with five minutes remaining, the ever-reliable Andreas Brehme smashed his spot-kick inside Sergio Goycoechea's right-hand post. It was the first time the World Cup final had been decided from 12 yards. Maradona was distraught. "They continued to whistle as my tears appeared on the giant screen," he recalled.

West Germany's Andreas Brehme turns to celebrate after scoring from the penalty spot.

SEE ALSO **'BIERHOFF'S GOLDEN GOAL WINS FINAL'** (page 499).

BECKENBAUER OFFERS HIS SYMPATHIES

After becoming the first man to lift the World Cup as both captain and coach, Franz Beckenbauer admitted he felt sorry for other countries. That was in response to a question in the post-match press conference regarding how football would be affected by the imminent reunification of West and East Germany. "We'll probably be unbeatable for years," Der Kaiser added, inadvertently heaping pressure on his replacement, Berti Vogts. Beckenbauer later admitted it was a rash statement: "Berti Vogts said thanks a lot, but that was in the heat of the moment. Winning the World Cup can make you say things without thinking."

SEE ALSO **'FIRST INTERNATIONAL AFTER GERMAN REUNIFICATION'** (page 451).

With this victory over Argentina, Franz Beckenbauer confirmed his position as the Kaiser – Germany's greatest football legend.

GAZZAMANIA

Paul Gascoigne's scintillating performances – and tears – at Italia 90 captured the hearts of the nation. The Tottenham midfielder could do no wrong and was keen to show off his sense of humour, so the hundreds of England fans who turned up at the airport to welcome their team home were treated to the sight of Gazza wearing a pair of comedy breasts. Still, Gazzamania knew no bounds. Advertising agencies queued up for him to endorse their products; he appeared as a guest on Terry Wogan's chat show; and his truly terrible version of 'Fog on the Tyne' reached number two in the UK charts.

SEE ALSO **'GAZZA'S BURP'** (page 465).

Gazza with Alan Hull of the pop band Lindisfarne who accompanied him on 'Fog on the Tyne'.

1990

INTERNATIONAL BOARD AMENDS OFFSIDE RULE

Explanations of the offside rule have ruined many a social occasion and, for the 1990-91 season, a new point of debate was introduced. Hitherto players were deemed to be offside if they were level with the second last defender or the last two defenders, but the International Football Association Board, which acts as a guardian of the laws of the game, added a new paragraph to Law XI, stating: "A player who is level with the second last opponent or with the last two opponents is not in an off-side position." Importantly, the change gave the advantage to the attacker.

SEE ALSO **'OFFSIDE LAW IS CHANGED'** (page 541).

The familiar sight of a goalkeeper and a defender with his arm raised appealing for offside.

Maradona, seen here protesting at a red card decision against one of his players, was a vocal and always controversial Argentina captain.

MARADONA ACCUSES FIFA OF FIXING WORLD CUP

Maradona believed Italia 90 was fixed for a Germany-Italy final. In his autobiography he claimed the first European team drawn was supposed to play against Argentina and the second against Italy, in order for Colombia and Uruguay to avoid Brazil and Argentina's groups. Czechoslovakia came out first, but went into Italy's group, while Argentina got the Soviet Union. "I asked FIFA to explain… and the shit hit the fan," Maradona said. "I knew from the word go that Italia 90 was going to be difficult for us." Argentina lost the final to a controversial West German penalty. Maradona added, "It felt like the winners had been picked out in advance."

SEE ALSO **'MARADONA TESTS POSITIVE'** (page 476).

BARCELONA SIGN THE 'OTHER CHRIST'

It was love at first sight between the Camp Nou and lightning-fast Bulgarian attacker Hristo Stoichkov, who arrived from CSKA Sofia for £2 million. Stoichkov formed an irresistible partnership with the Brazilian Romario in Johan Cruyff's dream team, scoring 76 goals in 151 appearances as Barcelona dominated Spain and conquered Europe. Stoichkov never lacked confidence. "There are two Christs," he said. "One plays for Barcelona, and the other is in heaven."

He also had a short fuse. Once, he angrily chased a hare around Camp Nou. The poor animal had caused Stoichkov to stumble and miss a chance.

SEE ALSO **'BULGARIA BEAT GERMANY'** (page 478).

Stoichkov was the only Bulgarian in Cruyff's collection of superstars at the Nou Camp.

1990

FAROE ISLANDS SHOCKER

The amateurs of the Faroe Islands stunned the football world by winning their first-ever FIFA-recognised international, against Austria, courtesy of a goal by timber merchant Torkil Nielsen. The European Championship qualifier was played in Landskrona, Sweden, since the Faroe Islands, population 48,000, did not have the facilities to host such a match. The Faroes, a group of islands halfway between Iceland and Norway, had played unofficial matches since the 1930s, mainly against other small islands and Greenland. They then joined FIFA in 1988. The Faroes must have dreamt of going all the way to the European Championship finals, but lost almost all their remaining matches.

Austrian captain Toni Polster seems to sense a shock may be on the cards as the national anthems are played before the match begins.

SEE ALSO **'SAN MARINO RESULT FORCES TAYLOR OUT'** (page 470).

1990

DECLINE OF EAST GERMAN 'STATE' CLUB

Between 1979 and 1988 BFC Dynamo Berlin won ten consecutive East German titles, mainly because the club enjoyed the patronage of Erich Mielke, head of East Germany's notorious secret police. The Stasi ensured the club was able to poach players from other clubs and benefited from the partiality of referees. After reunification in 1990, the club was re-named FC Berlin to distance itself from its unsavoury past. Without powerful patrons, though, its fortunes declined. In 1999, the club reverted to the name BFC Dynamo and it now plays in a regional division of the fourth tier of German football.

SEE ALSO **'DYNAMO DRESDEN RELOCATE'** (page 198).

Erich Mielke headed the fearsome Stasi organisation from 1957 until the Berlin Wall came down in 1989. He died in 2001 aged 92 in Berlin.

FIRST INTERNATIONAL AFTER GERMAN REUNIFICATION

On 19 December 1990 a united German football team took to the field for an international on home soil for the first time in 48 years. Two months after the country's reunification Germany celebrated by beating Switzerland 4-0 at the Gottlieb-Daimler Stadium in Stuttgart, which, appropriately enough, had been the scene of their last international in 1942. In the intervening years West Germany, who had carried off the World Cup in 1954, 1974 and just six months earlier in the tournament in Italy, and East Germany had fielded separate sides in world football.

SEE ALSO **'GERMANY FIELDS TWO NATIONAL SIDES'** (page 66).

Star defender Mattias Sammer was the first player previously capped by East Germany to appear for the newly reunified German side.

'KING KENNY' RESIGNS AS LIVERPOOL MANAGER

A Merseyside derby 4-4 thriller in which his side went ahead four times was Dalglish's last match as Liverpool boss. The Scot announced his shock resignation on 24 February 1991, two days after the drawn FA Cup replay, revealing he felt like his "head would explode". In five years Dalglish led Liverpool to the League and FA Cup double in 1986 and further Championships in 1988 and 1990, but the Hillsborough disaster of 1989 drained him physically and emotionally. Dalglish spent countless hours trying to help those traumatised and bereaved by the tragedy and the pressure became unbearable. He was replaced by former team-mate Graeme Souness.

SEE ALSO **'DALGLISH BECOMES LIVERPOOL'S FIRST PLAYER/MANAGER'** (page 407).

As well as the tragedy at Hillsborough Dalglish also witnessed the shocking scenes at Heysel while he was a Liverpool player.

GAZZA SENDS SPURS TO WEMBLEY

Gazza lit up the first FA Cup semi-final to be played at Wembley with a stunning 35-yard free-kick that flew into the top left-hand corner of David Seaman's net, giving the Arsenal custodian no chance. "Schoolboy's-own stuff," exclaimed BBC TV commentator Barry Davies as Gascoigne celebrated a set-piece of raw power and perfect precision, just five minutes into the tie. Spurs dominated their North-London rivals, with Gary Lineker bagging a brace. Arsenal's only response came from Alan Smith, but the real hero was Gascoigne, who inspired Tottenham despite initially being doubtful for the game because of injury.

SEE ALSO **'SPURS SOAR BUT GAZZA IS FELLED'** (page 453).

Paul Gascoigne's free-kick heads unstoppably towards the top corner of David Seaman's goal as Spurs head towards a Wembley Cup final.

MANCHESTER UNITED WIN THE EUROPEAN CUP WINNERS' CUP

United secured their first European trophy for 23 years on an emotional May evening in Rotterdam. Alex Ferguson's men were regarded as underdogs against the mighty Barcelona of Michael Laudrup and Ronald Koeman, but Mark Hughes gained revenge for a miserable spell with the Catalan club. Sixty-nine minutes into a tight contest, Hughes applied the finishing touch to Steve Bruce's towering goal-bound header. Five minutes later, the Welshman collected a pass from Bryan Robson and rounded goalkeeper Carlos Busquets before smashing the ball home from an acute angle. Though Koeman scored with a late free kick, United held on for a well-deserved 2-1 triumph

SEE ALSO **'MANCHESTER UNITED COME BACK TO WIN THE CHAMPIONS LEAGUE'** (pages 526-7).

Manchester United's Mark Hughes celebrates beating his former team-mates as he holds aloft the European Cup Winners' Cup trophy.

Gascoigne hacks down Nottingham Forest's Gary Charles. The reckless challenge brings his final to a sadly premature end.

SPURS SOAR BUT GAZZA IS FELLED

When Spurs faced Forest in the FA Cup final, Gascoigne was overanxious for his first major honour and was lucky not to be booked early on for a chest-high challenge on Garry Parker. Then he recklessly pole-axed Gary Charles on the edge of the Spurs penalty area and received a yellow card. From the resulting free-kick, Stuart Pearce gave Forest a 16th-minute lead, but Gascoigne's final was over. He was stretchered off with torn knee ligaments. Spurs turned the final around through Paul Stewart's strike and the unfortunate Des Walker's own goal. It ended 2-1 to Spurs and goalkeeper Erik Thorstvedt became the first Norwegian to win the FA Cup.

SEE ALSO **'GAZZA'S BURP'** (page 465).

Colo Colo's diehard fans are known as the Garra Blanca (White Claw) and the team remains the only Chilean team to win the Copa Libertadores.

COLO COLO WIN COPA LIBERTADORES

"The whole country is with Colo-Colo," Chilean television declared as the players came out for the biggest match of their lives in front of 66,000 spectators at the Estadio Monumental, Santiago. After a goalless draw in Paraguay, Colo-Colo stormed to a 3-0 victory over Olimpia Asunción and became the only Chilean club to win the Copa Libertadores, South America's Champions League. In 26 frantic first-half minutes striker Luis Pérez scored twice and the visitors were reduced to ten men before substitute Leonel Herrera's tap-in six minutes from time. "I am happy because the people deserve it," said defender Lizardo Garrido as the celebrations began.

SEE ALSO **'CHILEAN WORLD CUP 'PLOT' FAILS'** (page 432).

The decison to rebrand the European Cup was testament to the stength of European football and it's considerable financial muscle.

BIRTH OF THE NEWLY BRANDED CHAMPIONS LEAGUE

For the 1991-92 season, the European Cup was renamed the UEFA Champions League and its format was changed so that the knockout quarter-finals and semi-finals were replaced with two mini-leagues. The shake-up came in response to pressure from Europe's bigger clubs who were keen on the formation of a European Super League, with more games and greater revenue. Arsenal were England's first entrants to the competition, but they were knocked out in just the second round by Benfica. Barcelona and Sampdoria won the groups that replaced the later knockout rounds and met in the final, at Wembley, where the Catalans lifted the trophy.

SEE ALSO 'MILAN'S PROPOSAL TO UEFA' (page 482).

ROBERTO BAGGIO'S PENALTY PRINCIPLES

Roberto Baggio's £8 million transfer to Juventus in May 1990 sparked rioting by incensed Fiorentina fans. Baggio adored Fiorentina, so when Juventus next visited Florence he refused to take a spot-kick against them. "I just wasn't feeling right," he explained later. "Suppose I miss the penalty kick? People would say I did it on purpose." His stand-in did miss and Baggio was substituted as a punishment by coach Luigi Maifredi. As he headed for the changing room, Baggio was thrown a violet Fiorentina scarf, which he picked up and kept. Juve lost the match 1-0, but Baggio had said goodbye to Florence.

SEE ALSO 'HONESTY IS THE BEST POLICY FOR FOWLER' (page 504).

Baggio was known as 'The Divine Ponytail' by his legion of fans – a reference not only to his hairstyle but also to his Buddhist faith.

THE WOMEN'S WORLD CUP ARRIVES

Twelve teams travelled to China hoping to win the inaugural Women's World Cup. The host nation topped a group that also featured Denmark, Norway and New Zealand, while Germany defeated Italy, Chinese Taipei and Nigeria. A USA team featuring 19-year-old Mia Hamm crushed Sweden, Brazil and Japan.

Bizarrely, eight of the 12 teams progressed to the next round where Germany beat Denmark, Sweden accounted for China, Norway defeated Italy and the USA thrashed Chinese Taipei.

Both semi-finals were high-scoring affairs, with Norway overcoming Sweden 4-1 and the USA recording a 5-2 triumph over Germany. A crowd of 63,000 in Guangzhou then watched Michelle Akers score twice in a 2-1 triumph for the Americans, the first-ever women's world champions. US coach Anson Dorrance summed up the tension of the final when he admitted, "I felt like I was creating diamonds in my lower intestines from the pressure."

The tournament, which is now played every four years, like its male counterpart, marked a crucial milestone in the development of the women's game.

SEE ALSO **'THE FIRST WOMEN'S EUROPEAN CLUB COMPETITION'** (page 532).

The United States hero Michelle Akers powered her team on to win the distinctive Women's World Cup trophy.

455

DAVID GINOLA CAUSES A STIR ON THE CATWALK

In the 1990s many of football's highly-paid stars landed lucrative deals to model for designer fashion labels. One of the first to strut down the catwalk was skilful winger David Ginola, who moved to Paris St Germain in 1992 and signed a modelling contract with Italian designer Nino Cerruti during his three years with the Parisian side. "I admit to feeling more nervous before this fashion parade than before a football match," the skilful winger revealed. "Fear not, I am not going to embark on a new career!" During his time in England Ginola appeared in a TV advert for shampoo in which he asserted, "I'm a footballer, not a movie star."

SEE ALSO 'COMPTON BECOMES 'BRYLCREEM BOY" (page 170); 'BECKHAM MANIA HITS JAPAN' (page 557).

Ginola looks at home on the catwalks of Paris, though within three years he would find himself in the less glamorous North East of England.

A minute's silence to remember the Bastia dead is held before a match between Monaco and Werder Bremen.

THE BASTIA DISASTER

Eighteen fans were killed and over 1500 injured when a temporary metal stand collapsed at the Armand Césari Stadium, Corsica, on 5 May 1992. Demand for match tickets for the French Cup semi-final between tiny Bastia and the mighty Olympique Marseille was huge, so the Bastia board and the local authorities agreed to temporarily increase capacity, but the stand was not strong enough to support an estimated 10,000 spectators. "It was supposed to be a night of celebration," wrote one survivor, "but it was a night without a moon. And in our heads we will always hear the silence of those who died." The French Cup was cancelled.

SEE ALSO **'THE SUPERGA DISASTER'** (page 165); **'THE ZAMBIA AIR CRASH TRAGEDY'** (page 467).

Howard Wilkinson's Leeds United celebrate with the Championship trophy after they had seen off the challenge of Manchester United.

LEEDS WIN THE LAST FIRST DIVISION TITLE

Howard Wilkinson's Leeds side overcame the challenge of Manchester United to win the last-ever First Division title in just their second season back in the top flight. A side that included Gary Speed, David Batty, Lee Chapman and loan signing Eric Cantona sat two points behind the Manchester club on 18 April and had played a game more. However, a dramatic turnaround ensued, with Leeds beating Coventry City and Sheffield United while Alex Ferguson's men lost to Nottingham Forest, West Ham and Liverpool. The delighted Leeds players watched Manchester United's defeat at Anfield on television, having defeated Sheffield United earlier in the day.

SEE ALSO **'LEEDS UNITED BLITZ THE SAINTS'** (page 317); **'LEEDS UNITED – THE RISE BEFORE THE FALL'** (page 547).

1992

KOEMAN FREE-KICK WINS EUROPEAN CUP FINAL

A moment of brilliance from defender Ronald Koeman finally delivered Barcelona's first European Cup after more than three decades of waiting. Their opponents were Sampdoria and in May 1992, seven minutes before the end of extra-time, Hristo Stoichkov and José Mari Bakero teed up a 25-yard free-kick for Koeman to drive a fierce 70-mph strike over the wall and beyond Gianluca Pagliuca's right hand.

While other European giants like Real Madrid, Bayern Munich and AC Milan had racked up numerous European Cup successes, somehow Barcelona always failed. Most notably, in 1986, Terry Venables' Barcelona lost to Steaua Bucharest on penalties in Seville. At last, though, Johan Cruyff's so-called Dream Team was able to exorcise the ghosts of so many failed campaigns. "When we scored that goal," Cruyff recalled, "all I remember thinking was, please, please, Barcelona, don't lose your mind. I knew that if my players hung onto theirs we would win."

Koeman makes sure his free-kick has beaten the keeper before launching his celebrations.

As Catalonia celebrated the Barcelona players swapped the orange shirts they had been wearing for their traditional 'azulgrana' and climbed Wembley's 39 steps to lift the trophy.

SEE ALSO '... BUT BARCELONA COME BACK TO WIN' (page 599).

Dragan Stojkovic, one of Yugoslavian football's stars in 1992. He did represent FR Yugoslavia in other international tournaments.

YUGOSLAVIA REFUSED ENTRY INTO EUROPEAN CHAMPIONSHIP

The former Yugoslavia qualified for the 1992 European Championship, but UEFA disqualified them from the tournament because of the wars that were raging in the Balkans. The conflicts involved the six countries that made up the former Yugoslavia and many were civil wars that included atrocious fighting between different ethnic groups. When the United Nations imposed sanctions on Yugoslavia because of war crimes committed in Belgrade, UEFA had little choice but to hand out its own punishment. Yugoslavia's place went instead to Denmark, the runners-up in Yugoslavia's qualifying group. Yugoslavia were banned from all major tournaments between 1992 and 1996, before returning for the 1998 World Cup.

SEE ALSO **'SUBSTITUTES DENMARK WIN EUROPEAN CHAMPIONSHIP'** (page 461).

Lineker's forlorn expression mirrors the disappointment felt by England fans everywhere. The record remained out of reach.

SWEDES 2 TURNIPS 1

On 17 June Graham Taylor's men needed to beat Sweden to progress to the semi-finals of Euro 92. They took the lead through David Platt's third-minute strike, but the tournament hosts mounted a successful second-half comeback with goals from Lars Eriksson and Tomas Brolin. England were out and Taylor was lampooned by the press. The Sun nicknamed him "Turnip Head" and the newspaper's headline screamed, "Swedes 2 Turnips 1." Taylor also made himself unpopular by substituting prolific goal-scorer and captain Gary Lineker in the 64th minute. Lineker, in his last international, was just one goal away from equalling Bobby Charlton's record of 49 England goals.

SEE ALSO **'SAN MARINO RESULT FORCES TAYLOR OUT'** (page 470).

'SUBSTITUTES' DENMARK WIN EUROPEAN CHAMPIONSHIP

Euro 92 became known as the tournament when Denmark's players came off the beaches and marched to unexpected glory. Just ten days before the start of the tournament, the Danes were enjoying their summer holidays when it was suddenly announced they would be given a place at the tournament because the former Yugoslavia had been disqualified due to the war in the Balkans. Denmark coach Richard Moeller-Nielsen hurriedly assembled his squad and took them to Sweden, where their campaign began on 11 June with a creditable draw against England. After defeat to the hosts, Denmark's energy and purpose earned them a deserved 2-1 victory over France, thanks to goals from Henrik Larsen and Lars Elstrup.

That set up a semi-final against champions Holland. Twice Larsen gave Denmark the lead, but a Dennis Bergkamp strike cancelled out the first goal and Frank Rijkaard's late equaliser took the match to extra-time. Goalkeeper Peter Schmeichel performed heroics in the ensuing penalty shoot-out, crucially saving from Marco van Basten, as Denmark booked their place in the final.

They continued to play with belief and freedom when they met world champions Germany in Gothenburg. Midfielder John Jensen produced the goal of his life to put Denmark ahead on 18 minutes. The Germans attacked persistently, but could not beat Schmeichel, who produced a stunning save to deny Jürgen Klinsmann. With 12 minutes left, Kim Vilfort sealed Denmark's triumph. "Everything had come together for the team during the competition," reflected Schmeichel, "but I still felt bemused as to how and why it had all worked out in our favour."

SEE ALSO 'YUGOSLAVIA REFUSED ENTRY INTO EUROPEAN CHAMPIONSHIP' (page 459).

The Danish players mob Kim Vilfort as they realise they are about to become champions. An incredible outcome considering that they qualified through a technicality.

GHANA WIN OLYMPIC BRONZE

Ghana became the first African nation to win an Olympic medal when they claimed bronze at the 1992 games in Spain. Despite fielding the youngest team at the tournament with an average age of just 18, the Ghanaians finished top of their first-round group with a win over Australia and draws against Mexico and Denmark. In the quarter-finals they overcame Paraguay 4-2, courtesy of a hat-trick from Kwame Ayew, but in the semi-finals suffered a 2-0 defeat to Spain in Valencia. In the third/fourth play-off game Ghana won their historic bronze medal with a 1-0 victory over Australia in Barcelona.

SEE ALSO **'NIGERIA TAKE OLYMPIC GOLD'** (page 500).

Ghana substitute goalkeeper Simon Addo wearing a hastily customized number twelve shirt in Olympic bronze play-off match.

PREMIER LEAGUE LAUNCHED

England's heroic failure at Italia 90 restored the public's appetite for football at a time when the top clubs were considering forming a breakaway super league. It was agreed that the old First Division would become the FA Premier League in 1992-93.

However, the most important change was revenue from the sale of TV rights. The 1988 deal between the TV companies and the Football League brought in £44 million over four years. Rupert Murdoch's Sky TV network recognised the market potential for screening live football and agreed to pay a whopping £191 million over five seasons.

SEE ALSO **'NIKE CONTRACT LEAKED'** (page 530).

Sky injected glamour into the English game. The latest TV rights deal, which runs for three seasons from August 2004 is worth £1.024 billion.

FEVER PITCH PUBLISHED

Nick Hornby's Fever Pitch sold over a million copies in the UK and helped transform public perception of our national sport, which was tarnished by hooliganism in the 1970s and 1980s. The book is autobiographical and details Hornby's passion for football, especially his beloved Arsenal. Each section covers a single match between 1968 and 1992, and Hornby skilfully links the ups and downs of following a football club with his eventful personal life. "When I was talking to publishers and agents about it [Fever Pitch] they told me no chance, trying to sell a football book," Hornby once revealed.

Author Nick Hornby with his unlikely football-based bestseller fictionalising his own life-long obsession with Arsenal to great effect.

SEE ALSO **'SYLVESTER STALLONE SAVES THE DAY IN *ESCAPE TO VICTORY'*** (page 377).

ATLETICO MADRID LET YOUNG RAUL GO

Jesus Gregorio Gil y Gil committed a real howler during his eventful 16-year presidency of Atletico Madrid when he scrapped the club's youth system to save money, letting teenage striking prodigy Raul move to bitter rivals Real Madrid. Raul, who joined Atletico aged 13, broke into the Santiago Bernabeu first team at just 17 and became one of Spanish football's great heroes. He has won domestic and European trophies aplenty, is one of Real's leading all-time scorers and nobody has scored more goals for Spain. Unsurprisingly Gil, who died in 2004, described Raul as his "bestia negra" or bête noire.

Raul could so easily have turned out in the red and white stripes of the other big team in Madrid. He went on to become a Real hero.

SEE ALSO **'MADRID CLAIM EIGHTH EUROPEAN CROWN'** (page 533).

BACK-PASSES TO GOALKEEPERS OUTLAWED

For the 1992-93 season FIFA finally eradicated one of football's worst forms of time-wasting by changing the back-pass rule. Hitherto, teams wanting to run down the clock had been able to return the ball to the safety of their goalkeeper's hands. Now, all deliberate back-passes handled by the keeper would be penalised by an indirect free-kick to the opposition from the place where the infringement occurred. At first, there were some farcical situations, with indirect free-kicks virtually on the defending team's goal line, but the rule has made for far more positive play and encouraged goalkeepers to develop all-round skills.

SEE ALSO **'LAWS AMENDED TO INCLUDE GOALKEEPERS'** (page 18); **'OFFSIDE LAW IS CHANGED'** (page 541).

Southampton goalkeeper Tim Flowers discusses the finer points of the back-pass rule with the referee.

Hamm was one of only two women to make Pele's list of 125 greatest living players. The other was Michelle Akers, also from the US.

MIA HAMM SIGNS WITH NIKE

Nineteen-year-old Mia Hamm was the star of the United States side that won the inaugural Women's World Cup in 1991. A year later sports footwear giant Nike identified the striker as one of the USA's most marketable sportswomen and signed her up on a lucrative long-term contract. Such was Hamm's success that in 1999 Nike named one of the largest buildings at its world headquarters in Beaverton, Oregon, in her honour. During her illustrious 17-year career with the USA, Hamm scored 158 times in 275 appearances, making her the world's leading goal-getter in international competitions, male or female.

SEE ALSO **'BRANDI CHASTIAN STRIPS IN TRIUMPH'** (page 528).

CANTONA JOINS MANCHESTER UNITED

One wet afternoon Alex Ferguson was discussing transfer targets with Manchester United chairman Martin Edwards when the phone rang. It was the Elland Road chief executive Bill Fotherby wanting to buy full-back Denis Irwin. The approach was immediately rejected, but Ferguson scribbled "ask him about Cantona" on some paper. Half an hour later, Fotherby called back to finalise the £1.2 million transfer of Eric Cantona to Old Trafford from champions Leeds. The following day, 27 November, the Frenchman was unveiled as the Reds' new striker. "The French and the Scots have great old alliances," Ferguson smiled, though not even he could have imagined what lay ahead.

SEE ALSO **'CANTONA WINS THE DOUBLE'** (page 494); **'CANTONA'S KUNG-FU ATTACK'** (page 483).

Alex Ferguson welcomes his transfer coup Cantona to Old Trafford after his brief journey across the Pennines from Leeds United.

GAZZA'S 'BURP'

When asked by an Italian TV reporter for his reaction to being dropped from the Lazio side, Paul Gascoigne responded by belching into the microphone. It was an incident that polarised Italian opinion on Gazza, whose three-year stay in Italy was spoiled by injury. Many were appalled, but others, even some Roma fans, adored him and saw the incident as typical of Gascoigne's lovable roguishness. "He embodied what they liked about English football," said Football Italia presenter James Richardson. "There is even a section of Italian fans that wave Union Jacks and talk about how much beer they drink. Very un-Italian."

SEE ALSO **'GAZZAMANIA'** (page 447); **'ENGLAND'S TRIP TO THE HONG KONG DENTIST'** (page 495).

A sunburnt Gascoigne salutes his new adoring fans in the Olympic Stadium. Though a fans' favourite he was beset with injuries in Italy.

After his two goals snatched victory from the jaws of defeat at Hillsborough Bruce said, "I'll never forget the raw emotion of that day."

LAST-GASP WINNER MAINTAINS UNITED'S TITLE CHALLENGE

With only four minutes remaining of this crucial April 1993 Premiership clash Manchester United were losing 1-0 to Sheffield Wednesday at Old Trafford and on the brink of throwing away their best chance of winning the title for 26 years. Enter Steve Bruce. At that moment the United captain secured a draw with a firm header, but United knew this wasn't enough. They kept coming forward and deep into injury time a deflected cross from Gary Pallister looped into the penalty area and Bruce once again headed the ball past Chris Woods. The crowd of 40,102 went delirious. Three weeks later United were champions.

SEE ALSO 'THOMAS SCORES LAST-MINUTE LEAGUE WINNER' (page 431).

STEVE MORROW BREAKS ARM

One moment you've scored the winning goal in a Cup final and the next you find yourself being rushed to hospital in an ambulance. This was the experience of the Northern Ireland international Steve Morrow at the 1993 League Cup final at Wembley. After scoring the goal, his only one for the club, that secured a 2-1 win for Arsenal over Sheffield Wednesday, his jubilant captain Tony Adams attempted to lift him up, but only succeeded in dropping him on the ground. Morrow broke his arm and missed the trophy presentation and lap of honour. "Accidents can happen in moments of ecstasy," said Adams years later.

SEE ALSO 'GAZZA FELLED AS SPURS SOAR' (page 453).

Shortly after the most important goal of his career, Morrow's face is contorted with pain as he is treated on the Wembley turf.

The air crash off the Gabon coast wiped out Zambia's entire international football team. The players are remembered as heroes.

ZAMBIA AIR CRASH TRAGEDY

On the evening of 27 April 1993 the Zambian national football team were on their way to Senegal to play a qualifier for the 1994 World Cup finals when the plane in which they were travelling crashed into the sea shortly after taking off from a refueling stop in the Western African state of Gabon. All 30 people on board were killed, including 18 players, their coach Godfrey Chitalu, his entire support staff and the plane's pilot and crew. The dead are buried outside Independence Stadium in the Zambian capital Lusaka at a special monument called 'Heroes Acre'.

SEE ALSO **'THE SUPERGA DISASTER'** (page 165); **'THE MUNICH AIR CRASH'** (page 212).

J-LEAGUE LAUNCHES

The Japanese Football Association (JFA) decided to revolutionise the game in Japan with a complete overhaul of its league system. Since 1965, the Japan Soccer League (JSL) was the highest level of club soccer in the country, but consisted only of amateur teams. Consequently, facilities were poor, few Japanese sports fans were interested in their domestic league and the national team struggled to compete with neighbouring countries. So the JFA created Japan's first professional competition, the J-League, which comprised 10 clubs from the JSL. The J-League was officially launched in 1993 and has proved immensely popular with Japanese fans.

SEE ALSO **'BECKHAM MANIA HITS JAPAN'** (page 557).

Nagoya Grampus Eight's new signing Gary Lineker meets an expectant media. The new league drew many ageing superstars.

The Olympique Marseille team celebrate with the European Cup becoming the first French side to win the trophy.

MARSEILLE WIN EUROPEAN CUP

Marseille became the first French side to be crowned champions of Europe when they defeated AC Milan in the 1993 Champions League final at the Olympic Stadium in Munich. After winning all ten games en route to the final, it was the Italians, boasting such talents as Paolo Maldini, Frank Rijkaard and Marco van Basten, who started the game as overwhelming favourites. It was Marseille, however, who scored the only goal of the final when the French international defender Basile Boli headed Abedi Pele's corner past a motionless Sebastian Rossi in the Milan goal.

SEE ALSO 'MARSEILLE BRIBERY SCANDAL' (page 568); "MINNOWS' MONACO REACH CHAMPIONS LEAGUE FINAL' (page 577).

MARSEILLE BRIBERY SCANDAL

In May 1993, only 24 hours after winning the Champions League, euphoria was replaced by shame as Marseille became embroiled in a match-fixing scandal. It was revealed that the Marseille club president Bernard Tapie, had been involved in bribing opposition players. The Marseille midfielder Jean Jacques Eydelie had offered large amounts of money to three Valenciennes players to take it easy against Marseille when they met in a French league game just six days before the Champions League final. Marseille won that game 1-0.

While Marseille were allowed to retain their Champions League triumph, they were stripped of the 1993 French title. The club would subsequently be relegated and be declared bankrupt, while Tapie served seven months in prison after being found guilty of corruption and match-fixing charges in 1997.

SEE ALSO 'JESUS GIL BANNED FOR EIGHT MONTHS' (page 486).

The controversial Marseille club president, Bernard Tapie, would later serve seven months in prison for his part in match-fixing scandal.

Gorlan Sorloth celebrates after Norway defeat England during their sensational run of results in the World Cup qualifying tournament.

NORWAY RANKED SECOND IN THE WORLD

It might be difficult to believe, but in October 1993 Norway were ranked by FIFA as the second best national side in the world – behind Brazil. This was achieved through their remarkable form in qualifying for the 1994 World Cup, which, with seven wins from ten games, saw them top a group containing Holland and England to reach their first World Cup since 1938. But it wasn't to last and Egil Olsen's side failed to live up to this ranking in the USA, where they were knocked out at the group stage.

SEE ALSO **'NORWAY'S WOMEN BECOME WORLD CHAMPIONS'** (page 487).

FRANCE FALL APART

After winning six of their first eight qualifying games for the 1994 World Cup finals France simply needed a draw from their final two games, first against Israel and then Bulgaria, to book their place in the USA. The Israelis were bottom of the group, having conceded 22 goals, including a 4-0 defeat to France in Tel Aviv, and had failed to record a single win, so another French win appeared a formality. With seven minutes remaining France were holding a 2-1 lead, but they suddenly imploded, allowing the Israelis to grasp two late goals and threaten Les Bleus' hopes of reaching the USA.

SEE ALSO **'FRANCE FAIL AT HOME TO BULGARIA'** (page 470).

Israel's Ronny Rosenthal puts France's goalkeeper, and centre-half Marcel Desailly under pressure on a tense night in Tel Aviv.

FRANCE FAIL AT HOME TO BULGARIA

After their shock defeat to Israel, France still required only a point to qualify for the 1994 World Cup. So at 1-1 in the dying minutes of the November game against Bulgaria all was going to plan at the Parc des Princes in Paris until David Ginola over-hit a cross, which was intercepted by the Bulgarians, who ran up the other end and scored through Emil Kostadinov. A highly talented Les Bleus side were out. The French manager Gerard Houllier publicly blamed Ginola for France's dramatic exit. "It is something which will haunt me for the rest of my life," Ginola reflected. "I believe a weaker person would have been destroyed."

SEE ALSO **'DAVID GINOLA CAUSES A STIR ON THE CATWALK'** (page 456); **'FRENCH YOUTH SYSTEM ESTABLISHED'** (page 472).

Jean-Pierre Papin collapses on the turf after David Ginola's costly mistake meant France failed to qualify for the World Cup.

SAN MARINO RESULT FORCES ENGLAND MANAGER OUT

It was November and a month after losing to Holland in a crucial World Cup qualifier the England manager Graham Taylor probably thought it couldn't get any worse. However, eight seconds into the final game of the qualifying campaign San Marino, ranked 118th in the world, took the lead against England when Davide Gaultieri pounced on an under-hit back pass from Stuart Pearce and knocked the ball past David Seaman. England would recover to win the game 7-1, but it was all in vain, they failed to reach the 1994 tournament and Taylor resigned. He admitted: "I can see the funny side of that goal now, but it hurt at the time."

SEE ALSO **'COACH SACKED FOR RELIGIOUS VIEWS'** (page 521).

San Marino players get the rare chance to celebrate a goal after taking a shock early lead against England. It helped seal Taylor's fate.

BOLIVIA REACH WORLD CUP

After spending 44 years watching their more illustrious South American neighbours qualify for the World Cup, Bolivia finally rejoined the party at the 1994 tournament in the USA. The Bolivians, who had featured in the 1930 and 1950 tournaments, finally returned by taking advantage of the high altitude – 3,600 metres above sea level – of the stadiums in which their home games in the qualifying campaign were played. This helped them to several victories, including a 2-0 triumph over Brazil. In the USA, however, they failed to win a game and finished bottom of their group.

SEE ALSO 'HIGH-HANDED FIFA?' (page 491).

A proud moment for the tiny land-locked Andean nation as Bolivia finally return to the World Cup stage after a 44 year absence.

STARS PERFORM WORLD CUP DRAW

The first World Cup finals ever to be hosted in the USA always promised to be a little bit different and so it proved right from the start with the draw for the tournament, which took place in December in Las Vegas. For instance, the American comedian and actor Robin Williams called the FIFA secretary general and current president Sepp Blatter "Sepp Bladder" in front of an audience of 4,500, which featured a collection of celebrities not exactly known for their love of 'soccer', including James Brown, Stevie Wonder, Evander Holyfield, Barry Manilow and Willie Nelson.

SEE ALSO 'FIFA VOTE IN FAVOUR OF USA WORLD CUP' (page 426); 'FIRST WORLD CUP GAME PLAYED INDOORS' (page 475).

Actor Robin Williams adds a touch of Hollywood glamour to the draw for USA '94 – even though it took place in Las Vegas, Nevada.

Gerard Houllier who used to be a schoolteacher was instrumental in improving French football's youth system to ensure success.

FRENCH YOUTH SYSTEM ESTABLISHED

After a disastrous Euro 92 and failure to qualify for USA 94, the French FA built firm foundations for future success, and Gerard Houllier did much of the groundwork for France's 1998 World Cup and Euro 2000 triumphs. The focus was placed on youth development at the national football centre in Clairefontaine-en-Yvelines, where Houllier was based as coach of France's under-18 (1994-96) and under-20 sides (1996-97). As senior team coach Houllier had failed to take a side that included Eric Cantona and Laurent Blanc to the World Cup, but he made amends by overseeing the development of, among others, 1998 World Cup winner Thierry Henry.

SEE ALSO **'FRANCE FAIL AT HOME TO BULGARIA'** (pages 5470); **'FRANCE WIN WORLD CUP'** (pages 518-19).

EX-FOOTBALLER INVENTS THE PREDATOR BOOT

After a stellar career with Middlesbrough and Liverpool in the 1970s and 1980s, Craig Johnston returned to his native Australia and stumbled upon the idea for the Predator football boot. "I was coaching kids and I was telling them that they had to grip the ball like a table tennis bat to swerve it. 'But our boots are made of leather, its raining and they are slippery,' the kids told me. So I went home and took the rubber off a table tennis bat and stuck it on my boots with superglue." The Predator boot, with its rubber ridges on the toe, was developed by Adidas and became the world's best-selling football boot.

SEE ALSO **'BOWLES ODD BOOTS'** (page 349).

In the words of Craig Johnston, "Once I had identified the importance of the rubber grip on the ball... I knew I had something special."

DUTCH PLAYERS REVOLT

Holland's hopes of winning their first-ever World Cup were dealt a serious blow before the tournament had begun when Ruud Gullit walked out of the squad on the eve of their departure for the USA. Gullit had fallen out with the Dutch coach Dick Advocaat a year earlier ,when he substituted him in a qualifying game against England, but the pair had appeared to resolve their differences, only for Gullit to leave once again complaining about Advocaat's tactics. The fragile spirit in the Dutch camp was further hurt when they experienced a bomb scare on an internal flight in the US, an experience which stopped Dennis Bergkamp from flying.

SEE ALSO **'DUTCH PLAYERS WANT CRUYFF'** (page 438).

Under Advocaat the Dutch national team was riven with internal strife. Team spirit was further damaged by a bomb scare on a US internal flight.

Eric Cantona turns away after scoring Manchester United's goal as team-mate Roy Keane jumps on his back. Manchester United won 4-0.

MANCHESTER UNITED COMPLETE THE DOUBLE

On a rainy day in May at Wembley Manchester United won their first ever domestic double by overcoming Chelsea 4-0 in the FA Cup final. The southwest Londoners, coached by Glenn Hoddle, had actually beaten United twice in the Premiership during the 1993-94 season, but they couldn't repeat the trick beneath the twin towers. Sir Alex Ferguson's side, who had comfortably retained the Premiership title that season, scored all their goals in the second half. Eric Cantona gave United a 2-0 lead with two goals from the penalty spot before Mark Hughes and Brian McClair completed the rout.

SEE ALSO **'CANTONA WINS THE DOUBLE'** (page 494); **'MANCHESTER UNITED WIN THIRD DOUBLE'** (page 525).

SAVICEVIC LOB SEALS CHAMPIONS LEAGUE WIN FOR MILAN

The 1994 Champions League final in Athens in May, between Fabio Capello's AC Milan, winners in 1989 and 1991, and Johan Cruyff's Barcelona, winners in 1992, should have been one of the greatest games in the competition's history. The sheer brilliance, however, of Milan overwhelmed the Catalans and the Italian team ran out 4-0 winners. The pick of the goals, and a symbol of Milan's utter dominance, was scored by the Yugoslavian Dejan Savicevic when he won a bouncing ball on the edge of the area and lobbed Andoni Zubizarretta in the Barcelona goal from 30 yards.

SEE ALSO **'GOALKEEPER HITS HAT-TRICK'** (page 530).

Mercurial striker Dejan Savicevic celebrates his exquisite lob, the pick of Milan's four goals as they demolished Cruyff's Barcelona.

ELECTRONIC BUGGIES BECOME A WORLD CUP FEATURE

The opening game of the 1994 World Cup in the USA took place on 17 June and featured the defending champions Germany against Bolivia at Soldier Field Stadium in Chicago. A largely uneventful clash was settled by Jürgen Klinsmann, who scored the winning goal for the Germans after 61 minutes, but this game is more likely to be remembered as being the first time in the World Cup that electronic buggies, which, somewhat comically, looked like large golf carts, were used to transport injured players from the field of play.

SEE ALSO **'MEXICO AND BULGARIA ALL FALL DOWN'** (page 477).

The medical team is called onto the pitch as a Romanian player waits for treatment. The buggy was felt to slow the game down.

RAY HOUGHTON SCORES WORLD CUP CRACKER

On 18 June 1994 in front of a sea of Irish green at Giants Stadium in New York Ray Houghton produced the greatest moment in the Republic of Ireland's football history. In the 11th minute of their opening group game against Italy, the Aston Villa midfielder controlled a poor clearance from Franco Baresi and hit a looping shot from 20 yards over the helpless Gianluca Pagiluca. Ireland held on to claim their most famous ever victory. "It was a very special moment and surpasses all of my playing achievements in terms of emotion," confessed the Ireland manager Jack Charlton.

SEE ALSO **'JACK CHARLTON GIVEN THE FREEDOM OF DUBLIN'** (page 480); **'IRELAND KICK OFF MINUS KEANE'** (page 556).

Ireland's goalscorer, midfielder Ray Houghton, is congratulated by team-mates Steve Staunton and Terry Phelan after his looping shot.

FIRST WORLD CUP GAME PLAYED INDOORS

On 18 June 1994 the World Cup staged its first ever indoor game at the Pontiac Silverdome near Detroit when the USA met Switzerland in front of 73,425 fans. The venue, home to the NFL side the Detroit Lions, lacked a natural grass surface, so a field of grass had to be grown in California and flown to the Silverdome, where it was installed by a team from Michigan State University as a series of grass rectangles on top of wooden pallets. The pitch proved to be a success, but players complained about the lack of space between the touchline and the stands, and crucially, the lack of air conditioning.

The Americans and Swiss sweltered their way through a 1-1 draw in the Silverdome's first of four games in the tournament.

SEE ALSO **'QPR LAYS ARTIFICAL PITCH'** (page 377).

The Pontiac Silverdome Stadium on the outskirts of Detroit. The stadium would play host to four games at the 1994 World Cup.

Maradona leaves the field of play with a nurse for a random drug test at Foxboro Stadium. His positive test stained the tournament.

MARADONA TESTS POSITIVE

Since reaching the 1990 World Cup final with Argentina, Diego Maradona's unique talent had begun to desert him and he had also served a 15-month ban after cocaine traces were found in a dope test. He returned to the 1994 tournament and, after a wonderful solo goal in Argentina's opening game against Greece, it was thought he might be able to conjure up his old genius once again, but his celebratory mad scream directly into a television camera hinted not all was right. Following his next game against Nigeria he tested positive for the banned stimulant ephedrine, was thrown out of the World Cup and given another 15-month ban.

SEE ALSO **'FAREWELL TO A FLAWED TALENT'** (page 508).

ESCOBAR SHOT DEAD AFTER OWN GOAL

Colombia arrived at the 1994 World Cup as one of the favourites and Pelé's tip to win the tournament, but they were knocked out in the group stage after defeats to Romania and the USA. In the 2-1 defeat to the USA the Colombian defender Andreas Escobar scored an own goal that would tragically cost him his life. Ten days after the game he was shot 12 times in a restaurant car park in the Colombian city of Medellin. It is believed he was shot by accomplices of a gambler who had lost a large amount of money due to Colombia's early exit, as after each shot the killers shouted, 'Goal.'

SEE ALSO **'WHEN FOOTBALL BECAME PURE MURDER'** (page 433).

Before his death Escobar was affectionately known by the Colombian fans as "El Caballero del Futbol" ("The Gentleman of Soccer").

Match officials hastily try to erect the replacement goal without causing further embarrassment in front of the world's media.

MEXICO AND BULGARIA ALL FALL DOWN

During this second round match of the 1994 World Cup at Giants Stadium between Mexico and Bulgaria the goal collapsed when a melee of players fell into the net. Fortunately, though, there was a spare goal on hand so the game didn't have to be abandoned. The game was also notable for the performance of the Syrian referee Jamal Al Sharif, who showed ten yellow cards and sent off Mexico's Luis Garcia and Bulgaria's Emil Kremenliev. The Bulgarians fared better amid all the mayhem to win 2-1.

SEE ALSO **'NO CORNER FLAGS FOR FINAL'** (page 339).

Roberto Donadoni of hot favourites Italy and Nigeria's 'Jay Jay' Okocha compete for possession in their tightly fought encounter.

ITALY DENY NIGERIA QUARTER-FINAL PLACE

"It looks like we are slipping out of the World Cup without having left even a trace," proclaimed the Italian television commentator Bruno Pizzul as he watched his nation trail Nigeria 1-0 with only 90 seconds remaining of their second round World Cup clash at Foxboro Stadium. Just seconds later Roberto Baggio rescued Italy by scoring a well-placed shot beyond Peter Rufai in the Nigerian goal to level the game, and in extra-time he scored again, from the penalty spot, to put the Azzuri through to the quarter-finals and on their way to the final.

SEE ALSO **'SOUTH KOREA SURPRISE ITALY'** (page 561).

1994

BEBETO INITIATES ROCKING THE BABY

The Brazilian striker Bebeto played in three World Cups, won it in 1994 and scored a more than respectable 39 goals in 75 international appearances, but he is probably best known for his 'rocking the baby' celebration at the 1994 World Cup in the USA. After scoring against Holland in the quarter-finals in Dallas, Bebeto ran off swinging his arms from side to side, as if he was rocking a baby, as a tribute to his two-day-old son Mattheus. It started a trend for goalscoring new fathers that is still performed today.

SEE ALSO **'KLINSMANN JOINS PREMIERSHIP'** (page 480). **'RAVENNELLI'S SHIRT-PULLING'** (page 500).

Team-mates Mazinho and Romario join in with Bebeto's celebration which is still a favourite with new fathers on the pitch today.

1994

German midfielder Thomas Berthold hides his face as the Bulgarian team celebrate their country's first World Cup victory.

BULGARIA KNOCK OUT GERMANY

Bulgaria condemned Germany to their earliest World Cup exit for 32 years with this shock 2-1 win at Giants Stadium at the 1994 tournament. The reigning world champions, and finalists in 1982 and 1986, were expected to have little problem navigating their way past Bulgaria, who had never won a game at the World Cup prior to this tournament. The German captain Lothar Matthaus gave his side the lead, but the Barcelona striker Hristo Stoichkov equalized for Bulgaria with a free-kick and just two minutes later Yordan Letchcov won the game for Bulgaria and enshrined himself in World Cup history by scoring with a perfectly timed diving header.

SEE ALSO **'SENEGAL STUN FRANCE'** (page 558).

Roberto Baggio almost single-handedly took the Azzurri to the final as he slotted Italy's second goal past Bulgaria's Mihaylov.

BAGGIO WINS SEMI-FINAL FOR ITALY

Each World Cup provides a totemic player, someone who captures the imagination of the tournament. In the USA in 1994 Romario's goals were enjoyed, but above all it was Roberto Baggio who made the biggest impact. The saviour of Italy's slow-starting campaign, his greatest moment came in the semi-finals against Bulgaria. The 'Divine Ponytail' as the Italians called him scored twice in the first half to put Italy into the final. His first goal was a work of genius as he glided past one defender, curled a shot past another defender and the goalkeeper Borislav Mikhailov, while five minutes later he doubled Italy's lead with a low volley.

SEE ALSO 'THURAM FIRES FRANCE TO FINAL' (page 516).

Baggio had been the undoubted star of the tournament but he hangs his head as it is his penalty miss that hands the World Cup to Brazil.

SEE ALSO 'ITALY WIN THE WORLD CUP' (page 604).

SHOOT OUT FOR THE WORLD CUP

For the first time ever the World Cup final was settled by a penalty shoot-out when Brazil met Italy. The two nations, previously world champions three times each, were guilty of playing out a dull game in front of 94,194 at the Rose Bowl in Pasadena.

An injured Roberto Baggio limped through the game, while Romario and Bebeto were expertly marshaled by Franco Baresi, just back from a knee operation. There were few chances and for the first time in the tournament's history the final finished goalless after extra-time.

In the shoot-out, Baresi and Brazil's Marcio Santos both missed each side's opening efforts, but Albertini and Evani for Italy and Romario and Branco for Brazil made amends. However, when Massaro missed and Brazilian captain Dunga scored it meant Roberto Baggio had to convert to keep Italy alive. His shot flew high over the crossbar and Brazil were champions for a record fourth time.

JACK CHARLTON GIVEN THE FREEDOM OF DUBLIN

There seemed to be a mutual indifference between Jack Charlton and the Football Assocation of Ireland when he was appointed in February 1986, but he would leave the post a decade later as by far the most successful coach in the country's history. Before Charlton's arrival the Republic of Ireland had failed to qualify for a major tournament in 63 years of international football, but he took them to Euro 88 in Germany, the quarter-finals of the 1990 World Cup in Italy and the 1994 World Cup in the USA. In April 1994 he was awarded the freedom of Dublin, an honour previously bestowed on Nelson Mandela and Mother Teresa.

SEE ALSO 'STANLEY MATTHEWS CROWNED 'KING OF FOOTBALL'' (page 209).

Jack Charlton in reflective mood at the Republic of Ireland's during USA 94. He is the most successful manager in Ireland's history.

KLINSMANN JOINS PREMIERSHIP

The Tottenham chairman Sir Alan Sugar pulled off one of the Premiership's most impressive transfer coups when he persuaded Jürgen Klinsmann to move to North London in the summer of 1994. The German World Cup-winning striker was not popular in England due to his perceived theatrics and diving, but he immediately diffused this by celebrating his first goal for Spurs, against Sheffield Wednesday, with an exaggerated dive to the turf accompanied by his laughing team-mates. He finished up his first season in England by being voted Footballer of the Year.

SEE ALSO 'HENRY PROVES HIS PREMIERSHIP CLASS' (page 529).

Despite initial scepticism Jürgen Klinsmann was a revelation or Tottenham in the Premiership.

HERTHA BERLIN
RESCUED BY BIG BUSINESS

Since their formation in 1892, Hertha Berlin had endured a turbulent history, full of mergers, financial problems, expulsions, relegations, including a spell in the lowly first federal league, losing fans behind the Berlin Wall and a match-fixing scandal. Early in 1994 it was feared Hertha might go out of existence when it was revealed that they had accrued debts of DM 10 million. However, they were saved by a large investment from the German media giant Bertelsmann and the sale of some properties, including the Hertha villa, and by the end of the decade their revival had taken them into the Champions League for the first time.

SEE ALSO **'DECLINE OF EAST GERMAN STATE CLUB'** (page 450).

Hertha Berlin fans in full voice at their home ground, Berlin's Olympic Stadium.

Raith Rovers goalkeeper, Scott Thomson saves Paul McStay's penalty to win the League Cup and secure a place in Europe.

RAITH ROVERS TAKE ON EUROPE

In a dramatic upset Scottish second division Raith overcame Celtic to win the League Cup and qualify for Europe for the first time in their history.

In the dying minutes with Celtic leading 2-1, Raith's Gordon Dalziel scored the equalizing goal to keep the game alive. The final eventually went penalties and in one of the great cup shocks, Raith triumphed 6-5. The following season Raith made their debut in the UEFA Cup and after putting out both the Faroese and Icelandic champions, the club finally succumbed to eventual UEFA Cup winners Bayern Munich, although not before leading 1-0 at half time in the 2nd leg.

SEE ALSO 'BIRTH OF THE NEWLY BRANDED CHAMPIONS LEAGUE' (page 454); 'CALAIS REACH FRENCH CUP FINAL' (page 533).

PELÉ CLIMBS THE POLITICAL LADDER

When the Brazilian government wanted a figure to take on corruption in sport they turned to their greatest ever footballer, Pelé, who served as Minister for Sport for three years between 1995 and 1998. Before taking the post he famously denounced the Brazilian Football Confederation (CBF) as corrupt and once in government he began preparing legislation he hoped would address this. However, in truth Pelé's impact was limited while in office and in 2001 he publicly backed down and called a truce with the CBF.

SEE ALSO 'PLATINI – FROM SOCCER PLAYER TO FOOTBALL POLITICO' (page 608).

Pelé's status as national hero in Brazil undoubtedly made his a popular political appointment.

CANTONA'S KUNG-FU ATTACK

On a cold night at Selhurst Park in January 1995 Eric Cantona was being constantly kicked by the Crystal Palace defender Richard Shaw. Cantona's manager Alex Ferguson could sense his mounting frustration, so at half-time he warned: "Do not get involved with him." But just four minutes after the interval Cantona lashed out at Shaw and was swiftly shown a red card, the fifth of his United career, by referee Alan Wilkie. On his way back to the dressing room, Cantona reacted to the abuse of a Palace fan, Matthew Simmons, by launching himself at him with a kick and then punching him in the face.

United banned Cantona for the rest of the 1994-95 season, but the Football Association extended the punishment to October 1995. He was also given a two-week jail sentence at Croydon magistrates court, later commuted to 120 hours of community service on appeal.

At the press conference to mark his release Cantona uttered the immortal phrase, "When the seagulls follow the trawler it is because they think sardines will be thrown into the sea."

SEE ALSO 'CANTONA RECEIVES INTERNATIONAL BAN' (page 427); 'DI CANIO BANNED FOR PUSH' (page 520).

Cantona launches the attack which saw him receive a lengthy ban and suspended jail term.

GEORGE GRAHAM BANNED FOR ACCEPTING BUNG

On 21 February 1995 Arsenal sacked their manager George Graham after the club was informed of the results of a Premier League inquiry into alleged financial irregularities in the transfers of certain players; transfers in which Graham had been involved. Five months later Graham was found guilty by the Football Association of illegally taking £425,000 from the Norwegian agent Rune Hauge during the signings of two players, John Jensen and Pal Lyndersen, and punished with a one-year worldwide ban from football. He would return to football with Leeds United at the end of his ban.

SEE ALSO **'MARSEILLE BRIBERY SCANDAL'** (page 468).

Already sacked by his club, Graham leaves the Watford Hilton after he was found guilty of misconduct by the FA disciplinary commission.

Grobbelaar also faced legal proceedings – though he won a libel action against *The Sun* newspaper and walked free from court.

GROBBELAAR IN MATCH-FIXING SCANDAL

In November 1994, *The Sun* newspaper alleged it had evidence that former Liverpool goalkeeper Bruce Grobbelaar had taken money to fix matches. Grobbelaar was accused of taking £40,000 to make sure Liverpool lost to Newcastle in 1993 and of blowing the chance to make £125,000 against Manchester United in 1994 by accidentally making a save. In July 1995 Grobbelaar was charged with conspiracy to corrupt and match-fixing. In January 1997 he stood trial alongside the former Wimbledon players John Fashanu and Hans Segers, but the jury failed to reach a verdict. A retrial started in June 1997, but again a verdict couldn't be reached and the players were acquitted and walked free from court.

SEE ALSO **'GERMAN CORRUPTION SCANDAL'** (page 586).

GEORGE WEAH WINS
WORLD PLAYER OF THE YEAR

In December 1995 the AC Milan striker George Weah became the first African
to be voted FIFA's World Player of the Year. In the same year he was also voted
European Footballer of the Year and African Footballer of the Year. This
wonderfully powerful and graceful striker had started his career in his native
Liberia before moving to Monaco and then Paris Saint Germain. He joined AC
Milan in 1995 and played his best football during his four years at the San Siro.
He later moved on to several other clubs, including Chelsea and Manchester
City. In 2005 he ran for the presidency in Liberia, but was defeated by
Ellen Johnson-Sirleaf.

SEE ALSO **'ZIDANE'S WORLD PLAYER AWARD HAT-TRICK'** (page 573).

Weah poses with the Ballon
D'Or, the culmination of his
most successful season.

NAYIM SCORES LONG-RANGE WINNER AGAINST ARSENAL

The 1995 European Cup Winners' Cup final between Real Zaragoza and Arsenal in Paris appeared to be heading towards a penalty shoot-out when it entered the final minute of extra-time still poised at 1-1. However, with the final kick of the game the Moroccan midfielder Nayim, who had spent five years with Tottenham Hotspur, attempted a speculative shot from almost 40 yards which sailed over an unbalanced David Seaman on the line to claim the trophy for the Spanish club. Ever since Tottenham fans have taunted their North London rivals with the chant, "Nayim from the half-way line."

SEE ALSO **'BECKHAM SCORED FROM HALF-LINE'** (page 501); **'ONE FLEW OVER THE SEAMAN'S HEAD'** (page 563).

Nayim's long range effort eludes Arsenal goalkeeper David Seaman's grasp. It was an error that Tottenham fans would not let him forget.

Jesus Gil became president of Atletico in 1987. He was deeply involved in several separate criminal investigations and died in 2004.

JESUS GIL BANNED FOR EIGHT MONTHS

In May 1995 the Royal Spanish Soccer Federation finally lost patience with the controversial Atletico Madrid President Jesus Gil and banned him from club duties for eight months for insulting referees and football officials. After already being fined for calling a referee a homosexual, Gil continued his tirade by claiming, "There's a mafia in refereeing... Competition is disturbed and prostituted... They rob you and you can't do anything about it." An official for the Spanish football federation described the outburst as, "the most serious example of verbal violence in Spanish sport".

SEE ALSO **'THE GREAT BUNDESLIGA SCANDAL'** (page 322).

AJAX WIN CHAMPIONS LEAGUE

The aristocrats of European football AC Milan were playing in their fifth European Cup final in seven years with the aim of equaling Real Madrid's haul of six trophies and becoming the continent's most successful ever club. But in front of 50,000 at the Ernst Happel Stadium in Vienna the Italians were ambushed by a vibrant young Ajax side who would claim their club's first European Cup since 1973. After 85 minutes the game was still goalless when the Dutch constructed a neat move that allowed Frank Rijkaard to put through on goal the 18-year-old substitute Patrick Kluivert, who held off Franco Baresi before finishing past Sebastian Rossi.

SEE ALSO **'TOTAL FOOTBALL' – ALMOST TOTAL DOMINATION'** (pages 326-27).

Ajax's Frank de Boer, Nwankwo Kanu and Ronald de Boer lead the celebrations with their star stiker Patrick Kluivert trailing behind.

NORWAY'S WOMEN CROWNED WORLD CHAMPIONS

While their male counterparts have never come close, Norway's women's football team were crowned world champions at the second ever World Cup finals in Sweden in the summer of 1995. The Norwegians won all three of their group games before advancing to the final with a 3-1 quarter-final victory over Denmark and a 1-0 semi-final win over the USA. In the final Norway swept aside Germany 2-0 with goals from Hege Riise, who scored five throughout the whole tournament and won the Golden Ball, and Marianne Pettersen, at the Rasunda Stadium in Solna.

SEE ALSO **'NORWAY RANKED SECOND IN THE WORLD'** (page 469).

Marianne Pettersen's goal sealed Norway's final victory over Germany in Sweden after a hugely impressive World Cup campaign.

THE '11-MINUTE' CUP FINAL

The 1995 Copa del Rey final between Deportivo La Coruna and Valencia in Madrid is the only game in the competition's history to be played over two days. On June 24 Deportivo took the lead through Javier Manjarin, only for it to be wiped out by Valencia's Predrag Mijatovic. However, in the 80th minute the game was abandoned due to torrential rain. It was decided to play the remaining 11 minutes of the final three days later and Deportivo claimed the first trophy in their 89-year history with a goal from Alfredo Santaelena.

SEE ALSO **'BRADY INSPIRES ARSENAL IN '5-MINUTE' FINAL'** (page 366).

Due to extreme weather, this Copa del Rey fixture is the only game in the trophy's history to be played over two days. Deportivo stormed to victory.

'THE HAND OF THE DEVIL'

It was the moment of revenge for which English supporters had waited nine long years – and it was handed to them by a Brazilian. Following Diego Maradona's infamous 'hand of God' incident when he punched home a goal against England in 1986, the tables were turned on Argentina in a Copa America quarter-final on 17 July. Argentina were leading 2-1 when Brazilian forward Tulio blatantly controlled the ball with his hand before scoring the equalizer. Brazil's eventual 4-2 win on penalties prompted a melee on the pitch and Argentinian president Carlos Menem declared the result a "monumental robbery". The incident was subsequently labelled the 'hand of the devil' in Argentina.

SEE ALSO **'BRAZIL, ARGENTINA AND BROKEN BONES'** (pages 153); **'THE HAND OF GOD'** (pages 414-5).

As President of football-mad Argentina Carlos Menem no doubt knew his words would unite a country and serve a political purpose.

VAN BASTEN HOBBLES AWAY FROM FOOTBALL

Over two years after his last competitive match, the three times European Footballer of the Year was forced into early retirement by a chronic ankle injury. Marco van Basten was still only 30, but could look back at a phenomenal career. At Ajax he scored 128 goals in just 133 appearances, helping the Amsterdam giants to three Dutch titles, three Dutch Cups and the 1987 UEFA Cup. At Milan, van Basten's 90 goals in 147 games brought three Italian titles and two European Cups. He struck 24 times in 58 outings for Holland, including a breathtaking volley in their 1988 European Championship triumph.

SEE ALSO 'FONTAINE RETIRES AT 27' (page 246); 'PETER THE GREAT HANGS UP HIS GLOVES' (page 569).

Van Basten always seemed to perform when it mattered. His goals helped Holland win what remains their only international honour.

FLAMENGO HAVE TO STOMACH DEFEAT

Belly laughs were the order of the day as Brazilian side Fluminese snatched the Rio State Championship with what was to become known as the 'gol de Barriga'. The championship decider between two deadly rivals stood at 2-2 after Flamengo had battled back from two goals down and seen their opponents' lack of discipline reduce them to eight men. In the dying minutes the 'gol de barriga' or belly goal gave Fluminese a dramatic win as striker Renato Gaucho, a former Flamengo player, stuck out his stomach to deflect the ball past the goalkeeper and into the net.

SEE ALSO 'BACK-HEEL HELPS PORTO WIN THE EUROPEAN CUP' (page 419).

That the goal which denied Flamengo victory and the league title was scored by one of their former players added insult to injury.

HIGUITA'S SCORPION KICK

The Colombian goalkeeper Rene Higuita livened up an otherwise forgettable friendly against England at Wembley in September 1995 with his famous scorpion kick. In the first half Jamie Redknapp floated an aimless cross into the Colombian penalty area. Higuita was expected to simply catch the ball, but instead he allowed it to go over his head before clearing it with an astonishing kick of his legs. "I call it my scorpion kick," he explained. "The idea to do it came to me as an inspiration... I like to make people smile. My philosophy is to send the fans home happy if I can, to enjoy myself and to entertain." England coach Terry Venables said, "I have only one word to describe it – extraordinary. He's the only one I know who could have got away with it. They tell me he does it all the time in his own country, but it's probably the reason why his last three managers have had heart attacks."

Higuita wasn't always a potential liability for his country. In 69 appearances he scored 3 goals.

SEE ALSO **'BANKS' 'SAVE OF THE CENTURY"** (page 301);
'GOALKEEPER HITS A HAT-TRICK' (page 530).

HIGH-HANDED FIFA?

Bolivia's passionate football fans felt singled out when FIFA announced a ban on all international matches at grounds lying more than 3000 metres above sea level. With its capital city La Paz at 3600 metres, Bolivia was the only country affected by the FIFA directive and Bolivian fans noisily took to the streets in protest. FIFA's ban was based on the results of sports medicine research into the effects of playing at high altitudes. Opponents from lower altitudes, at both club and international levels, had long complained about the debilitating effects of playing in thinner air, claiming it was unsporting, inhumane and akin to doping opponents.

SEE ALSO **'BOLIVIA REACH WORLD CUP'** (page 471).

La Paz's peculiar geography, high above sea level, is a problem for any visitor let alone for a football team unused to playing at altitude.

THE BOSMAN RULING

A little known Belgian footballer changed football forever when he challenged his team's refusal to sell him. In 1990 Jean Marc Bosman's contract had expired at Belgian second division side RFC Liege and he wished to move to French club Dunkerque, but the Belgian club prevented him as they couldn't agree a transfer fee. Bosman took his case to the European Court of Justice and after a long battle it declared in December 1995 that players in the European Union could move freely when their contracts expired. The Bosman ruling also prevented UEFA and leagues from imposing a quota on the number of foreign players allowed in teams.

SEE ALSO **'PROFESSIONALISM LEGALIZED'** (page 30); **'THE TREATY OF ROME'** (page 208).

His face may be unfamiliar, but Bosman's battle had repercussions far beyond Brussels and sparked a player power revolution in football.

1995

FEUD BETWEEN KLINSMANN AND MATTHAUS

When Jürgen Klinsmann joined Bayern Munich from Tottenham Hotspur in the summer of 1995 not everyone was overjoyed at his arrival. Certainly, his club captain and international team-mate Lothar Matthaus didn't try too hard too disguise his deep dislike for Klinsmann and even went as far as to suggest that they should settle their feud live on national television. The German national coach Bertie Vogts grew so tired of Matthaus' posturing and goading of Klinsmann that he had no option but to exclude him from his ultimately triumphant Euro 96 squad.

SEE ALSO **'CALIFORNIA RESIDENT APPOINTED GERMAN COACH'** (page 579).

With 258 German international caps between them it seemed crazy that Klinsmann (108) and Matthaus (150) could not get on.

1996

Souness failed to guage how provocative his flag-waving antics would be in Turkey and a full-scale riot was only narrowly averted.

GRAEME SOUNESS LAYS SIEGE

After Galatasaray defeated their fierce city rivals Fenerbahce to win the 1995 Turkish Cup their manager Graeme Souness ran the length of the pitch and planted a huge flag in the centre circle. The act nearly sparked a riot amongst Fenerbahce fans as it was thought Souness was replicating the Turkish hero Ulubatli Hasan, who was killed as he planted the Ottoman flag at the of the Siege of Constantinople. However, Souness' reasons were more personal. "When I joined Galatasaray, one of the directors of Fenerbahce said, 'What are they doing signing a cripple?'" says Souness, who had recently had heart surgery. "I looked into the stand and saw this director and I thought, 'I'll show you who's a cripple'."

SEE ALSO **'DEATH THREATS FORCE INTERNATIONAL RETIREMENT'** (page 566).

MAJOR LEAGUE SOCCER LAUNCHED

After the demise of the National American Soccer League in 1984, FIFA awarded the USA the 1994 World Cup finals on the condition that a professional soccer league was established in the US after the tournament. And so on 6 April 1996, when the San Jose Clash met DC United in its inaugural game at Spartan Stadium, Major League Soccer (MLS) was born. The MLS consisted of ten clubs spread across the country and DC United from the US capital Washington would become the inaugural MLS Champions when they defeated Los Angeles Galaxy in the first final at Foxboro Stadium.

SEE ALSO **'FOOTBALL'S GREATEST STAR LANDS STATESIDE'** (page 344-5); **'SUPERSTAR BECKHAM JOINS GALAXY'** (page 608).

MLS 'Soccer' still remains in fourth place in the pecking order of US sports behind American Football, Baseball and Basketball.

MANCHESTER UNITED BLAME GREY KIT FOR DEFEAT

In April 1996 double-chasing Manchester United trooped in at half-time trailing 3-0 to a rampant Southampton side in this crucial Premiership clash. What was the problem? Defensive errors, a weak midfield or wayward strikers? No, United manager Sir Alex Ferguson blamed the colour of their grey away kit. In four previous games United had failed to win wearing it and Ferguson believed this was due to the inability of his players to see each other. "The manager just stormed in and said, 'Get that kit off, you're getting changed,'" recalled Lee Sharpe. United returned for the second half wearing their third change kit of blue and white stripes and lost the game 3-1. The grey kit was never worn again.

SEE ALSO **'JUVENTUS STRIP FADES IN WASH'** (page 53); **'CAMEROON'S SHIRTS CUT TO SIZE'** (page 553).

Alex Ferguson's anger at their nightmare first half display at the Dell ensured that his Manchester United team never wore grey again.

CANTONA WINS THE DOUBLE

In May 1996, only seven months after returning from his eight-month ban for assaulting a fan, a reformed Eric Cantona led a young Manchester United side to their second double in three years. After holding off Newcastle United to regain the Premiership, United faced Liverpool in an eagerly anticipated Wembley FA Cup final. After 86 dull minutes the game was goalless and heading for extra-time when David Beckham lofted in a corner, which was punched by Liverpool goalkeeper David James straight to Cantona on the edge of the penalty area. The Frenchman hit a volley that sailed to the back of the net to win the Cup for United.

SEE ALSO **'CANTONA RECEIVES INTERNATIONAL BAN'** (page 427).

Even in his subsequent career Cantona can hardly have followed a better script than this.

A bleary eyed Gazza faces the press who quickly dubbed him "Guzzler" and demanded that he be dropped from the squad.

ENGLAND'S TRIP TO THE HONG KONG DENTIST

In the build-up to Euro 96 Terry Venables took his England squad on a ten-day tour of the Far East to play friendlies against China and a Hong Kong XI. While in Hong Kong, several England players, including Paul Gascoigne, Teddy Sheringham, Robbie Fowler and Steve McManaman, spent the night at a bar where they took turns to sit in a dentist's chair while tequila and Drambuie were poured down their throats. Gascoigne subsequently admitted that on the flight back to England he broke two seat-back television screens. While the incidents were inevitably splashed across the English tabloids, the squad used them to foster team spirit for the tournament.

SEE ALSO **'GASCOIGNE'S VOLLEY STUNS SCOTLAND'** (page 496).

Football songs are usually eminently forgettable. 'Three Lions' continues to accompany the England team wherever they go.

THREE LIONS ROARS TO NO 1

Football songs had mostly been considered rather sorry and tacky affairs until the release of 'Three Lions' for Euro 96. Indie band the Lightning Seeds collaborated with comedians Frank Skinner and David Baddiel to produce a song that captured England's imagination with it's lyrics about '30 years of hurt' and the agonising near misses since England's 1966 World Cup win. The song reached number one in the charts and became England fans' anthem in the stands throughout Euro 96 as they watched their side reach the semi-finals and chalk up yet another famous near miss.

SEE ALSO **'WORLD CHAMPIONS BECOME CHART-TOPPERS'** (page 296).

1996

GASCOIGNE'S VOLLEY STUNS SCOTLAND

Paul Gascoigne produced a moment of iconic genius, which he still calls the greatest goal of his career, when he scored a stunning volley in England's 2-0 victory over Scotland at Wembley in Euro 96. The man himself offers the best description of the goal: "I timed that goal so well," he recalled. "I could see Colin Hendry coming in, so I flicked it over his head and volleyed it. You can't teach kids that, it was pure instinct. I trained with Andy Goram every day, so I knew how to beat him. I knew I had to get over the ball and hit it low. The feeling when I scored was magnificent!"

Gascoigne celebrated by lying down next to the goal and having his team-mates squirt water in to his mouth to replicate the infamous dentist chair incident in Hong Kong from the previous month. "On the coach to Wembley I told the lads we should do the dentist chair celebration," said Gascoigne.

The goal reinstated him as a hero and gave Gazza a chance to perform his planned celebration.

SEE ALSO **'ENGLAND'S TRIP TO THE HONG KONG DENTIST'** (page 496).

The Holland squad was full of promise but Guus Hiddink's team was deeply affected by the row that exploded during the tournament.

DUTCH SQUAD IN RACE ROW

A year after Ajax had won the European Cup with an exciting team laden with young Dutch talent, Holland travelled to England confident of winning Euro 96, but a row between the black and white players in the squad ultimately wrecked their hopes. The black players complained Dutch coach Guus Hiddink didn't listen to them and Edgar Davids even claimed on radio that Hiddink he should get his head out of the white players' backsides. Hiddink sent Davids home and a dispirited side were beaten 4-1 by England at Wembley. Despite this they narrowly made it out of the group stage, but were knocked out by France in the next round.

SEE ALSO 'DUTCH PLAYERS REVOLT' (page 473).

Poborksy's time at Old Trafford was spent competing for a place on the right of midfield against a young rising star – David Beckham.

POBORSKY'S MAGICAL LOB

The Czech Republic midfielder Karel Poborsky arrived in England for the 1996 European Championships as something of an unknown quantity, but all that changed with one moment of inspiration at Villa Park. In the 53rd minute of the Czech Republic's quarter-final against Portugal Poborsky broke free along the right side of the pitch and, as he advanced on goal, improvised with a lob that cleared the Portuguese goalkeeper Vitor Baia to win the game 1-0. The Czechs would reach the final against Germany, while Poborsky earned a £3.5 million move to Manchester United after the tournament.

SEE ALSO 'SAVICEVIC LOB SEALS CHAMPIONS LEAGUE WIN FOR MILAN' (page 474).

MOLLER SCORES WINNING PENALTY

Six years after losing a penalty shoot-out to Germany in the World Cup semi-final, England lost to their nemesis in the same manner at the same stage of Euro 96. After 120 minutes the game ended 1-1 at Wembley after Stefan Kuntz had ruled out Alan Shearer's goal. In the ensuing penalty shoot-out England and Germany both scored their first five penalties before Gareth Southgate's limp effort was saved by Andreas Kopke. This allowed the Borussia Dortmund midfielder Andy Moller to step up and put a high shot beyond David Seaman and put Germany in the final.

SEE ALSO '... IT GOES TO PENALTIES' (page 445).

Moller kept his nerve to maintain Germany's 100% record in World Cup shoot outs.

OLIVER BIERHOFF'S GOLDEN GOAL WINS FINAL

After spending most of Euro 96 on the substitutes bench, Udinese striker Oliver Bierhoff rose from it to score two goals in the space of 24 minutes and Germany beat the Czech Republic 2-1 at Wembley.

Germany had begun Euro 96 by defeating the Czechs 2-0 in their opening group game, but they encountered a different team in the final. After an hour the Czechs took the lead through a Patrik Berger penalty after the German captain Mattias Sammer was adjudged to have brought down Karel Poborsky.

Ten minutes later German coach Bertie Vogts threw on Bierhoff in place of Mehmet Scholl to give his side a greater threat up front and within four minutes Bierhoff had equalized by heading in a Christian Ziege cross.

The game was poised at 1-1 after 90 minutes and five minutes into extra-time Bierhoff received the ball in the penalty area, turned and hit a shot that slipped through the grasp of Czech goalkeeper Petr Kouba. The Germans had won the game with a major tournament's first ever golden goal.

SEE ALSO 'LAURENT BLANC SCORES FIRST GOLDEN GOAL' (page 514).

Bierhoff's shot somehow finds it's way past Kouba to spark German jubilation.

Nigeria's 'Golden Generation' lived up to their billing at the Atlanta Olympics but they have failed to sparkle on the world stage since.

NIGERIA TAKE OLYMPIC GOLD

Nigeria surprised the football world by claiming the gold medal at the Atlanta Olympics in the summer of 1996 with an exciting side boasting Nwankwu Kanu, Jay-Jay Okocha, Daniel Amokachi and Taribo West. After emerging from their group as runners-up to Brazil, Nigeria defeated Mexico 2-0 and Brazil 4-3, after coming back from 3-1 down, to reach the final against Argentina. In front of a crowd of over 86,000 at the Sanford Stadium in Athens, Georgia, Nigeria beat a strong Argentinian side featuring Hernan Crespo, Ariel Ortega and Claudio Lopez 3-2, with goals from Celestine Babayaro, Amokachi and a last-minute winner from Emmanuel Amunike.

SEE ALSO **'KANU NAMED AFRICAN FOOTBALLER OF THE YEAR'** (page 502).

The 'White Feather' took his celebration to ten clubs in a career that included spells at Juventus and Lazio, as well as Derby and Dundee.

RAVANELLI'S SHIRT-PULLING

Italian goal machine Fabrizio Ravanelli smashed a dazzling hat-trick on his 17 August Premiership debut and celebrated in trademark fashion by whipping his shirt over his head. Each time Liverpool went in front, the predatory Ravanelli levelled, with a penalty and two tap-ins. The 'White Feather' had developed his famous celebration during a successful spell with Juventus, which culminated in European Cup glory shortly before he joined Middlesbrough for £7 million. "Why did I do it so often? It was just something which happens instinctively," he revealed. However, Ravanelli's 17 League goals were not enough to prevent Middlesbrough from relegation that season.

SEE ALSO **'AGHAHOWA CELEBRATES IN STYLE'** (page 560); **'OTILINO TENORIO, AKA SPIDERMAN'** (page 600).

BECKHAM SCORES
FROM THE HALF-WAY LINE

1996

The greatest player of all time Pelé famously tried and failed to do it at the 1970 World Cup and Manchester United legend George Best said it could never be done, but David Beckham proved it could by scoring a memorable goal from the half-way line.

On the opening day of the 1996-97 Premiership season United were leading Wimbledon 2-0 at Selhurst Park when David Beckham received the ball inside his own half in the final minute of the game. "I thought, 'Why not shoot?'" he recalled. "I hit it and remember looking up at the ball, which seemed to be in the air for ages, sailing towards goal, before it dropped over Neil Sullivan and into the net."

The goal elevated Beckham onto a higher level, where he looked more than comfortable, given that he made his England debut soon after, finished the season with his second Premiership winners medal and won the PFA's Young Player of the Year award.

The audacious effort earned Beckham the Match of the Day 'Goal of the Season' award.

SEE ALSO **'NAYIM SCORES LONG-RANGE WINNER AGAINST ARSENAL'** (page 486).

1996

KANU NAMED AFRICAN FOOTBALLER OF THE YEAR

In the summer of 1996 Nwankwu Kanu joined Inter Milan from Ajax after his starring role in Nigeria's gold medal success at the Atlanta Olympics. He would also be voted as that year's African Footballer of the Year. However, on arriving in Milan his new club discovered he had a heart defect. There were fears he would have to retire from football, but after undergoing surgery to replace an aortic valve he made his comeback in April 1997. He left Inter in 1999 and has since showcased his gangly-legged talent in England with Arsenal, West Brom and Portsmouth.

SEE ALSO **'GEORGE WEAH WINS WORLD PLAYER OF THE YEAR'** (page 485).

Kanu is a UNICEF ambassador and patron of the Kanu Heart Foundation to help children in Africa born with heart defects.

1996

GEORGE WEAH'S LONG-DISTANCE GOAL

In the 88th minute of their 8 September League encounter with Verona, the Rossoneri were clinging on to a 2-1 lead and defending a set-piece. George Weah had come back to help defend and, finding himself in space, controlled Verona's deep corner with a perfect first touch. He then surged forward and was in opposition territory before three Verona players converged on him. Strength, balance and supreme skill took him through the three challenges in one sublime instant. Having done a neat pirouette, he was facing goal again and slid the ball effortlessly past the last defender before racing into the inside-right channel to fire a perfect low shot into the far corner. Since his first touch, he had run 85 metres in 14 seconds. AC Milan won 4-1."

SEE ALSO **'MESSI'S MARADONA MIRACLE'** (page 612).

After running the length of the pitch in 14 seconds, Weah later remarked "What made it a great goal wasn't the run, it was the beautiful finish."

Looking every inch 'The Professor' the impact of Arsene Wenger's arrival and his continental methods were felt far beyond Highbury.

ARSENE WENGER ARRIVES AT HIGHBURY

On the morning of 30 September 1996 Arsene Wenger took charge of his first training session as the new manager of Arsenal. "He arrived unnoticed at the training ground," recalled the former Arsenal defender Lee Dixon. "A meeting was called, the players filed in and in front of us stood this tall, slightly-built man who gave absolutely no impression whatsoever of being a football manager." Club captain Tony Adams remembers: "There was a feeling of who the hell is he and what is he going to do?" Wenger would answer this question with three Premiership titles and four FA Cups in his first decade at Arsenal.

SEE ALSO **'HERBERT CHAPMAN TRANSFORMS ARSENAL'** (page 100); **'ADAMS' FAIRYTALE FAREWELL'** (page 557).

SCOTLAND'S OPPONENTS DON'T SHOW

"There's only one team in Tallinn," sang Scotland's supporters as Billy Dodds and John Collins kicked off in the Estonian capital on 9 October. Their hosts had failed to turn up and the Yugoslav referee Miroslav Radoman immediately blew the final whistle. The Estonians were still at their training camp 60 miles away, claiming they could not change their schedule to accommodate a new kick-off time. The game was brought forward by three hours after Scotland complained the floodlights were inadequate. According to FIFA rules, Scotland should have been awarded the game 3-0, but it was replayed in Monaco and they were held to a goalless draw.

SEE ALSO **'PLAYING TO LOSE'** (page 520).

A Scotland player ironically celebrates his team's victory and salutes the unlucky travelling Tartan Army after a farcical night in Tallinn.

ROSENBORG KNOCK OUT MILAN

AC Milan were expected to get the draw they needed for a place in the Champions League quarter-finals. After all, Milan had just brought back their former coach, the legendary Ariggo Sacchi, while Rosenborg had already lost three of their first five games in this group. Rosenberg began well and took the lead when Harald Brattbakk stroked the ball past the Milan keeper Sebastiano Rossi after 29 minutes. Milan's situation improved though when Christoph Dugarry scrambled the ball over the line for an equaliser, but in the second half Vegard Heggem rose between Maldini and Baresi to head the winning goal. Milan were out. Rosenborg were through.

SEE ALSO 'HELSINGBORG SHOCK INTER IN CHAMPIONS LEAGUE' (page 536).

Maldini who has experienced so many nights of European glory with Milan cannot believe his team have been put out by Rosenborg.

HONESTY IS THE BEST POLICY FOR FOWLER

Robbie Fowler shed his bad boy image by telling referee Gerald Ashby not to award a penalty in his favour in a March 1997 game against Arsenal. Liverpool were leading 1-0 when Fowler went through on goal, only to trip as he rounded David Seaman. Although there was no contact, the referee pointed straight to the spot. "No, no, no, ref, it wasn't a pen," Fowler cried, but the decision stood and Fowler was Liverpool's penalty-taker. His effort was weak and saved by Seaman, but Jason McAteer fired home the rebound. Liverpool won 2-1. Fowler later received a letter from FIFA president Sepp Blatter congratulating him on his "act of sportsmanship".

SEE ALSO 'ROBERTO BAGGIO'S PENALTY PRINCIPLES' (page 454); 'DI CANIO SHOWS HIS SOFTER SIDE' (page 542).

Seaman saves the penalty but McAteer (No. 4) is the first player to react and he forces home the rebound to give Liverpool the lead.

DORTMUND WIN EUROPEAN CUP

For the third consecutive year the defending European champions were beaten in the final. After Milan in 1995 and Ajax in 1996, Juventus suffered the same fate against a supremely talented Borussia Dortmund side at the Olympic Stadium in Munich in May 1997. Marcello Lippi's side started strongly, but it was the Germans who took the lead through Karl Heinz-Riedle, who then doubled it five minutes later to establish a 2-0 lead at half-time. Alessandro Del Piero gave the Italians hope with a wonderful goal in the second half, but within a minute of coming on as a substitute Lars Ricken was brilliantly put through by Andy Moller's pass and calmly chipped Angelo Peruzzi to confirm Dortmund as champions of Europe for the first time.

SEE ALSO **'DORTMUND RESTORE GERMAN PRIDE'** (page 279).

Borussia Dortmund followed up this European triumph with a 2-0 victory over Brazilian side Cruzeiro in the Intercontinental Cup.

BELGIAN INTERMEDIARY ADMITS PAYMENT TO REFEREE

Nottingham Forest players had always had their suspicions about the Spanish referee Emilio Guruceta Muro, after they'd lost 3-0 to Anderlecht in the second leg of the 1984 UEFA Cup semi-final, to be knocked out 3-2 on aggregate. "We were convinced something untoward had happened, that it wasn't just bad refereeing," explained Paul Hart, who had a goal disallowed in the second leg. When Muro died in a car crash in 1987 it was assumed he would take his secrets to the grave, but in 1997 the former Anderlecht president Constant vanden Stock confessed a loan of one million Belgian francs had been given to Muro.

SEE ALSO **'ITALIAN MATCH-FIXING SCANDAL'** (page 598).

The Anderlecht side of 1984. Long-held suspicions over their semi-final win were finally proved to be well-founded in 1997.

RANGERS WIN NINTH CONSECUTIVE TITLE

When Rangers won the 1996-97 Scottish Premier League title they equalled Celtic's record, amassed between 1966 and 1974, of nine consecutive Scottish titles. Rangers had stagnated throughout most of the eighties and failed to win the title between 1978 and 1987. The arrival of new chairman David Murray and new manager Graeme Souness was the catalyst for change and, after winning the title in 1987, their era of complete dominance began in 1989, with Walter Smith continuing the run after Souness' departure for Liverpool in 1991. Inevitably it was Celtic who stopped their Glasgow rivals from surpassing their record by regaining the title in 1998.

SEE ALSO **'NEW BOY O'NEILL INSPIRES CELTIC'** (page 537); **'RANGERS PIP CELTIC IN LAST-DAY TITLE SHOWDOWN'** (page 570).

Celtic and Ranger's dominance in Scotland is so great that Aberdeen were the last side to break the Old Firm stranglehold in 1984-85.

BARESI BOWS OUT

In July 1997 AC Milan announced the permanent retirement of their number 6 shirt in honour of Il Capitano Franco Baresi. Rejected by rivals Inter as a youth, Baresi spent his entire career at the San Siro. From his debut in 1978 he made 716 appearances in all, marshalling the famously mean Milan defence of the 1980's and early 90's and leading the Rossoneri to six league titles and a hat trick of European Cups. He won 81 caps for his country though his last act as an international player was to miss his penalty in the USA '94 final shoot-out. A classy defender in the great Italian tradition he currently works with Milan's young players.

SEE ALSO **'SIR STANLEY BOWS OUT'** (page 257).

Franco Baresi typified Italian defending which is commonly regarded as the best in the world.

RONALDO NAMED EUROPEAN FOOTBALLER OF THE YEAR

After two impressive seasons in Holland with PSV Eindhoven, the 20-year-old Brazilian striker Ronaldo was given the stage to show he was the best footballer in the world with a move to Barcelona. And he proved he was beyond any doubt with probably the greatest season of his career as he scored 47 goals in 49 games to help the Catalan club win the European Cup Winners' Cup, the Copa Del Rey and the European Super Cup. At the end of the year Ronaldo was voted European Footballer of the Year, only the second time a non-European had won the award (the first was George Weah).

SEE ALSO **'GEORGE WEAH WINS WORLD PLAYER OF THE YEAR'** (page 485); **'ZIDANE'S WORLD PLAYER AWARD HAT-TRICK'** (page 573).

Bobby Robson brought Ronaldo to Europe. After Robson left the Nou Camp Ronaldo said, "Today he can enjoy the fruits of his labour."

THE IMPOSSIBLE FREE-KICK

In June 1997 Brazilian left-back Roberto Carlos scored a free-kick against France in the Le Tournoi that defied all laws of football physics. The ball was placed 35 yards from goal when Carlos struck with power with the outside of his left foot after an unusually long run-up. The ball immediately began to veer right, away from the goal and around the French wall, and a ball boy beside the goal ducked before it began to swerve back towards the goal and clipped the post on its way in past a motionless Fabien Barthez.

"How did I do it? I don't know," said Carlos. "There's no explanation... the ball was too light, one of those ones that floats all over the place, and I hit it really hard, really well, with the outside of my foot, but it surprised me when it went in. I thought it was going wide and when it swung back and went in off the post I couldn't believe it. It was an impossible goal. Remember it, because you'll never see one like that again."

Roberto Carlos provided the highlight of an uneventful football summer with a free kick that defied the laws of physics.

SEE ALSO **'KOEMAN FREE KICK WINS EUROPEAN CUP FINAL'** (page 458).

Since his retirement Maradona has continued to grab press attention with his much documented weight and alcohol problems.

FAREWELL TO A FLAWED TALENT

Argentina star Diego Maradona finally bowed out of football on 25 October 1997 – his 37th birthday – after another failed drugs test. Some observers cited his move to Naples from Barcelona in 1984 as the start of his problems with substance abuse and this certainly wasn't the first failed drugs test for the flawed talent. In fact, drugs had got him banned in 1991 and barred from the 1994 USA World Cup. However, despite being a colourful and controversial figure ever since he'd first burst onto the international scene as a teenager, Maradona was undoubtedly the most brilliant player of his generation.

SEE ALSO **'A LEGEND'S FIRST STEPS INTO THE LIMELIGHT'** (page 309).

Iran's comeback at the home of Australian cricket meant they reached their second World cup having first qualified in 1978.

IRAN QUALIFY AT AUSTRALIA'S EXPENSE

Australia approached this two-legged World Cup qualifying play-off against Iran full of confidence, having won 14 consecutive games under Terry Venables, and they held the Iranians to a 1-1 draw in Tehran. The second leg at the Melbourne Cricket Ground was full of fans ready to celebrate and after goals from Aurelio Vidmar and Harry Kewell had given the Socceroos a 2-0 lead the party mood was well under way. However, in the final 19 minutes Karim Bagheri and Khodadad Azizi brought the Iranians level. The game finished 2-2 and, despite not losing a single qualifying game, Australia were out on away goals. Venables described the result as "cruel".

SEE ALSO **'AUSTRALIA'S FIRST WORLD CUP GOAL'** (page 599).

ZOLA WINS EUROPEAN CUP WINNERS' CUP

Only three months after becoming Chelsea manager Gianluca Vialli led his new charges to a 1-0 victory over Stuttgart in the 1998 European Cup Winners' Cup. At the Rasunda Stadium in Solna near Stockholm, Vialli had decided to leave his Italian compatriot Gianfranco Zola on the bench, but with the game still goalless half way through the second half, he agreed, under pressure from his assistant Graeme Rix, to send him on in the 69th minute. Twenty-two seconds later Zola took a pass from Dennis Wise in his stride and struck a half-volley past the German keeper Franz Wohlfahrt to claim Chelsea's first European trophy since 1971.

SEE ALSO **'CHELSEA FIELD A NON-BRITISH XI'** (page 531).

Vialli's decision to replace the conventional target man Tore Andre Flo with the wily Zola paid dividends and brought Chelsea the trophy.

ARSENAL WIN THE DOUBLE

At the beginning of March 1998, with Manchester United holding an 11-point lead over Arsenal in the Premiership and only ten games remaining, the Manchester bookmaker Fred Done decided to pay out on bets placed on United winning their third consecutive title. But two weeks later Arsenal beat United 1-0 at Old Trafford to give them the momentum to eventually overhaul their rivals' lead and win the title by a single point. Arsenal's title was confirmed when they beat Everton 4-0 at Highbury, and two weeks later Arsene Wenger's side completed the double by beating an insipid Newcastle United 2-0 in the FA Cup final at Wembley.

SEE ALSO **'SPURS WIN THE DOUBLE'** (page 238); **'ARSENAL'S UNBEATEN LEAGUE SEASON'** (page 575).

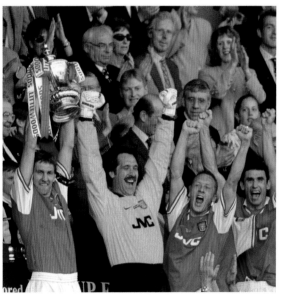

Arsenal's victorious and famously ageing back-line of Adams, Seaman, Dixon and Keown celebrate winning the FA Cup.

LE PEN SPEAKS OUT AGAINST 'FOREIGN PLAYERS'

Instead of beaming with national pride when France won the 1998 World Cup, National Front leader Jean-Marie Le Pen expressed discontentment with the make-up of the side. He complained that the France team was "Black, Blanc, Beur" – Black, White and Arab – and that they did not look sufficiently "French". However, many people recognised that a team which included Marcel Desailly, Emmanuel Petit and Zinedine Zidane was a celebration of modern French multi-culturalism. Besides, a black player, Raoul Diagne, was selected for France as early as 1931, so perhaps Le Pen, who has also criticised French players for not singing the 'Marseillaise', should take some history lessons.

SEE ALSO **'FRENCH PROTEST AT LE PEN'** (page 511).

Jean-Marie Le Pen's distasteful views caused outrage across the world as France were preparing to enter the tournament as hosts.

BLATTER ELECTED TO FIFA TOP JOB

On the eve of the 1998 World Cup finals, which were being held in France, Sepp Blatter was elected as FIFA's eighth president and the successor to the Brazilian Dr Joao Havelange. The 52-year-old Swiss administrator had joined the world football's governing body in 1975 and had made his way up through the ranks to serve as general secretary and chief executive officer. An amateur footballer in his younger days, Blatter had earlier held posts with the Swiss Ice Hockey Federation, as well as helping to organise the 1972 Olympics in Munich and the 1976 Olympics in Montreal.

SEE ALSO **'ISL COLLAPSE IMPACTS ON FIFA'** (page 546).

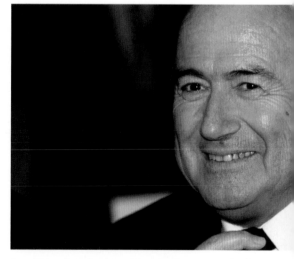

Sepp Blatter has often been the cause of controversy but he remains the man in charge of football's governing body in 2007.

CESARE MALDINI LEADS HIS SON AT WORLD CUP

At the 1998 World Cup the Italian captain Paolo Maldini had a closer than usual relationship with the coach – his boss was his father Cesare. A former AC Milan player and an assistant when Italy won the World Cup in 1982, Maldini senior was promoted from Italy's under-21 coach to the top job in 1996, to succeed Arrigo Sacchi. A proponent of the ultra-defensive catenaccio system, Maldini managed to guide his son and the rest of the squad to the quarter-finals in France before they lost to the hosts and eventual winners in a penalty shoot-out.

SEE ALSO **'CHARLTON FAMILY FAREWELL'** (page 325).

The third generation of Maldinis at Milan is now coming through. Paolo's son Christian is on the books of AC Milan's youth team.

The France team's stand helped generate enthusiasm in the host country which initially seemed remarkably uninterested in France '98.

FRENCH PROTEST AT LE PEN

On the eve of the 1998 World Cup the leader of France's far right National Front party Jean-Marie Le Pen criticised the multi-racial make-up of the French national side. France had several black players, including Marcel Desailly, Thierry Henry and Lilian Thuram, as well players of North African descent, most notably Zinedine Zidane, whose parents were from the former French colony Algeria. As a protest against Le Pen, before France's opening game against South Africa in Marseille the French players sung the national anthem with their arms around each other's shoulders.

SEE ALSO **'FRANCE WIN WORLD CUP'** (pages 518-19).

Prosinecki was a heavy smoker. Whilst at Zagreb he was said to smoke 40 a day. By the time he reached Portsmouth he'd cut down to 20.

PROSINECKI SCORES FOR TWO NATIONS AT WORLD CUP

En route to reaching the semi-finals of the 1998 World Cup Croatia's greatest ever player Robert Prosinecki became the first player in the tournament's history to score for two different nations. In 1990, playing for Yugoslavia before it became fragmented after a long and bloody civil war, the gifted playmaker scored in a 4-1 win over the United Arab Emirates in Bologna. Eight years later Prosinecki was again on the score sheet in a 3-1 group game victory over Jamaica and then again in the 2-1 third-fourth play-off win over Holland.

SEE ALSO 'YUGOSLAVIA REFUSED ENTRY INTO EUROPEAN CHAMPIONSHIPS' (page 459).

JAMAICA PLAY ON WORLD STAGE

In 1998 for the first time in their history the Caribbean nation of Jamaica qualified for the World Cup finals. Bolstered by several English-born players of Jamaican descent, the Brazilian coach Rene Simoes presided over a hard-working group that did not disgrace themselves in France. Jamaica, known by their nickname as the 'Reggae Boyz', lost their opening game 3-1 to Croatia and followed that with a 5-0 thrashing by Argentina, but managed to sign off with their first ever World Cup win over Japan, 2-1, thanks to two goals from Theodore Whitmore.

SEE ALSO 'BOLIVIA REACH WORLD CUP' (page 471).

Jamaica's Robbie Earle marks his goal against Croatia.

MOROCCO STUN SCOTLAND

Scotland had failed to progress past the first round on each of the seven previous occasions they had reached the World Cup. Would their eighth tournament in France be any different? Scotland's official World Cup song was called 'Don't Come Home Too Soon' and once again they didn't follow that advice. After losing to Brazil and drawing with Norway the Scots were confident of winning against Morocco in Saint-Etienne, but Craig Brown's side couldn't shake off the burden of history and endured more World Cup humiliation, losing 3-0 to the skilful Moroccans.

SEE ALSO **'SCOTLAND HEAD FOR HOME'** (page 440).

Morocco's Salaheddine Bassir celebrates as Colin Hendry and Jim Leighton sense Scotland's World Cup dream is finally over.

The Norway team lap up the applause as they celebrate a famous win over the soon-to-be-dethroned World Champions Brazil.

NORWAY DEFEAT CHAMPIONS

"I could coach Brazil better than [Mario] Zagallo does," said the Norwegian coach Egil Olsen ahead of his country's group game with Brazil in Marseille, before adding the Brazilian defence was "as organised as garbage". Bold words, but his team actually backed them up by recording a famous 2-1 victory to take them through to the second round. It was the Brazilians who took the lead through Bebeto, but Norway would not be denied and scored twice in the last eight minutes through Tore Andre Flo and an 88th minute winner from the penalty spot from Kjetil Rekdal.

SEE ALSO **'NORWAY RANKED SECOND IN THE WORLD'** (page 469).

LAURENT BLANC SCORES FIRST GOLDEN GOAL

After winning all three of their group games France ran into a determined Paraguayan side in the second round in Lens. The Paraguayans man-marked the French and kept them away from their goal during regular time. During extra-time France were becoming increasingly concerned until finally, in the 23rd minute of extra-time, Robert Pires crossed for David Trezeguet to cushion the ball with a header into the path of his captain Laurent Blanc, who volleyed the ball past Jose Luis Chilavert to win the game with the World Cup's first ever golden goal.

SEE ALSO 'FRANCE WIN WORLD CUP' (pages 518-19).

Blanc's World Cup was tinged with disappointment. An unwarranted red card in the semi-final meant he missed out on the final triumph.

ROMANIANS' BLOND AMBITION

Having already qualified for the second round of the 1998 World Cup the Romanian squad decided to celebrate by all dying their hair blond for their final group game against Tunisia. The only player not to join in with this was the goalkeeper Bogdan Stelea, but he had a good excuse – he was bald. In the spirit of the act Romanian coach Anghel Iordanescu shaved his head, but kept his baseball cap tightly on his head. On the field at the Stade de France, Tunisia put up a fight and held Romania to a 1-1 draw, but the Romanians still went through as group winners ahead of England.

SEE ALSO 'BARCELONA LOSE EUROPEAN CUP ON PENALTIES' (page 409).

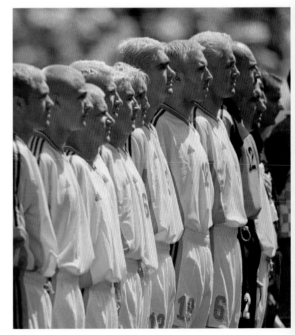

Any good fortune the group hair bleaching brought them had rubbed off by the second round as they were eliminated by Croatia.

OWEN SCORES WONDER STRIKE AGAINST ARGENTINA

In the 15th minute of England's second round clash with Argentina Michael Owen, aged only 18 years old, received a pass from David Beckham in the centre circle and headed towards goal. His pace took him past Jose Chamot and, approaching the penalty box, he dipped his shoulder and beat Roberto Ayala before cutting a shot beyond Carlos Roa into the back of the net to give England a 2-1 lead. The sheer brilliance of the goal introduced Owen to the football world and it remains arguably the greatest goal scored by an Englishman in the World Cup.

SEE ALSO **'ROONEY STRUCK BY CURSE OF THE METATARSAL'** (page 581).

Michael Owen's 16th minute wonder strike lit up St Etiene and shot the 18-year old England striker onto the world stage.

DAVID BECKHAM SEES RED

Early in the second half of this enthralling second round game between England and Argentina, with the score at 2-2, the Argentinian midfielder Diego Simeone barged into the back of David Beckham. As the England midfielder lay on the floor he foolishly flicked his leg at Simeone, who theatrically fell to the ground. First Simeone was shown a yellow card and then Danish referee Kim Milton Nielsen brandished a red card in Beckham's face. The England player trudged off the field like a naughty schoolboy before a ten-man England were knocked out of a major tournament by penalties again.

SEE ALSO **'REVENGE FOR BECKHAM'** (page 560).

"Ten heroes and one stupid boy" proclaimed the front page of the *Daily Mirror* as Beckham returned home to a summer of vilification.

Sublime goals were Bergkamp's speciality. He once took 1st, 2nd and 3rd place in the BBC's Goal of the Month competition.

BERGKAMP'S SUBLIME WINNER

On a hot afternoon at the Velodrome in Marseille Dutch striker Dennis Bergkamp effortlessly conjured up one of the World Cup's greatest ever goals as Holland and Argentina did battle for a place in the semi-finals in France. Patrick Kluivert gave the Dutch the lead after 12 minutes, Claudio Lopez equalized five minutes later and the score remained 1-1 until the final minute of the game. Frank de Boer threw up a long, high pass to Dennis Bergkamp in the Argentine penalty area. The Arsenal man controlled the ball with one touch and then deftly cut inside Roberto Ayala before volleying the bouncing ball high into the top corner.

SEE ALSO **'CAMBIASSO FINISHES OFF GOAL OF THE WORLD CUP'** (page 600).

Lilian Thuram is mobbed by his jubilant team-mates after his unlikely goal scoring exploits had secured France's place in the final.

THURAM FIRES FRANCE TO FINAL

The French were favourites to get past Croatia in this World Cup semi-final at the Stade de France, but a minute into the second half Davor Suker put the Croatians in front. Less than a minute later Lilian Thuram stormed to the other end and equalized for France with his first ever international goal. Thuram quickly developed a taste for this as in the 70th minute he put France into their first ever World Cup final with a wonderful curling left-foot shot. "For one night I think if he had said he wanted to be president of France everyone would have voted for him," said a team-mate Thierry Henry.

SEE ALSO **'LE PEN SPEAKS OUT AGAINST 'FOREIGN PLAYERS"** (page 510).

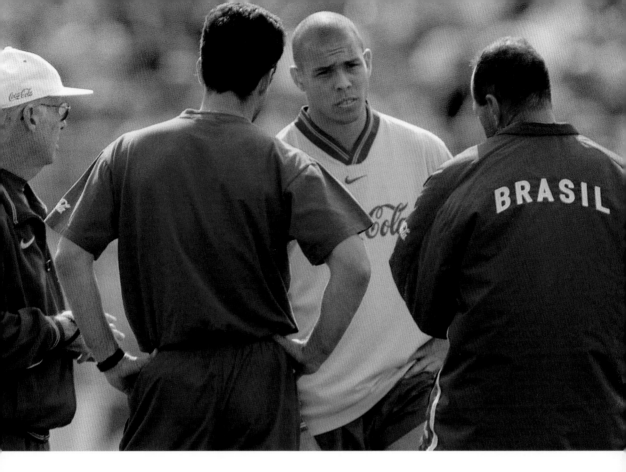

WAS RONALDO FIT?

On the afternoon of the 1998 World Cup final the Brazilian striker Ronaldo suffered a stress-related fit in his hotel room. "I don't know what happened, but I went to sleep and it seems I had a fit for about 40 seconds," said Ronaldo. "The pressure got to him and he couldn't stop crying," explained his room-mate Roberto Carlos. Ronaldo was taken to hospital for tests as the rest of the Brazilian squad travelled to the Stade de France for the final, where the Brazilian coach Mario Zagallo handed in a team sheet before kick-off with Edmundo's name on it instead of Ronaldo's. The striker then turned up at the stadium and declared himself fit, so was reinstated. There were allegations, consistently denied, that the Brazilian Football Conferation or its sponsors Nike put pressure on Zagallo to play Ronaldo. During the game Ronaldo looked a pale shadow of himself out on the pitch and was nothing more than a passenger as Brazil went down to a 3-0 defeat.

Ronaldo's face says it all as he prepares to start a final in which he is a shadow of his former self.

SEE ALSO **'NIKE CONTRACT LEAKED'** (page 530).

FRANCE WIN WORLD CUP

1998

When Emmanuel Petit slipped the ball past Claudio Taffarel in the final minute of the World Cup final to give France a 3-0 lead over Brazil, the French coach Aime Jacquet could finally turn to his bench and shout, "We're world champions." The hosts were worthy winners of the 16th World Cup, despite not having a recognised goal-scorer, they boasted one of the game's finest ever defences, an incredibly solid midfield and flashes of flair from Zinedine Zidane

Already buoyed by the drama surrounding Ronaldo, the French took the lead after 27 minutes in the Stade de France when Zidane scored with a powerful header from a Petit cross. Just before half-time he doubled France's lead with another header, this time from a corner from Youri Djorkaeff. Brazil were a major disappointment, burdened by the ill Ronaldo playing as if he were an impostor. They were given some fleeting hope when Marcel Desailly was sent off at 68 minutes after being shown his second yellow card, but in truth they couldn't get close to the French goal. In the final minute Petit ghosted through onto a pass from his Arsenal team-mate Patrick Vieira to score the decisive goal, France's 1000th in international football. "I don't have many memories of that goal," said Petit. "The only thing I remember is 'It's me!'"

At the whistle the French poured onto the streets all over the country. The epicentre of the party was the Champs Elysees in Paris where over a million people gathered to celebrate as large images of the team were projected onto the Arc de Triomphe. France really were world champions now.

SEE ALSO **'FRANCE ADD EUROPEAN TITLE TO WORLD CROWN'** (page 535).

The three mainstays of the French team – Marcel Desailly, Zinedine Zidane and Youri Djorkaeff celebrate the second crucial goal.

The eventual French victory brings thousands onto the streets – in contrast to the French public's early indifference.

PLAYING TO LOSE ...

When Thailand played Indonesia on 31 August both sides had already qualified for the semi-finals of the Tiger Cup, in which South East Asian nations compete, so each attempted to lose their final group match and avoid hot favourites Vietnam in the next round. After some poor defending, the score was 2-2 in injury time. Then the Indonesians dropped all pretence and turned on their own goal, now defended by Thai players. A deliberate own goal by Indonesia's Mursyid Effendi handed Thailand a 3-2 win, but he was banned from football for life and the teams were each fined $40,000 for "violating the spirit of the game". Ironically, they both lost their semi-finals.

SEE ALSO 'GROBBELAAR IN MATCH-FIXING SCANDAL' (page 485).

Eventual Tiger Cup winners Singapore. The instance of two semi-finalists deliberately trying to lose was described as 'violating the spirit of the game'

DI CANIO BANNED FOR PUSH

After the Sheffield Wednesday striker Paolo Di Canio was shown a red card for getting involved in a brawl with Arsenal's Martin Keown during a Premiership clash at Hillsborough he shoved referee Paul Alcock in the chest and the ref then theatrically fell to the ground. "I've watched the video a million times and still I don't understand how he managed to fall over," recounted Di Canio in his autobiography. Nonetheless, Di Canio was banned for 11 games and fined £10,000 by the Football Association. The Italian never played for Wednesday again and signed for West Ham in January 1998 at the end of his ban.

SEE ALSO 'DI CANIO SHOWS HIS SOFTER SIDE' (page 542); 'DI CANIO GIVES FASCIST SALUTE TO SUPPORTERS' (page 586).

Referee Alcock's fall may have been comical but the severity of his punishment was no laughing matter for Paolo Di Canio.

MIHAJLOVIC'S FREE-KICK HAT-TRICK

In April 2006 Sinisa Mihajlovic scored his record 27th and final free kick in Serie A. A controversial midfielder who latterly switched to defence, Mihajlovic has long been a controversial figure, with questionable politics off the pitch and often too much aggression on it. The Serbian's ability as a free kick taker though is indisputable. His ferocious left foot shot was a deadly weapon that combined power and accuracy. The most stunning example of his dead ball ability came for Lazio in 1998 when he scored a magnificent hat trick of free kicks in a 5-2 victory over his former team Sampdoria.

Mihajlovic once visited a university to understand more about the art of striking a dead ball. "Do you know what I found out? Absolutely nothing."

SEE ALSO **'ROBERTO CARLOS' WONDER FREE KICK'** (page 507).

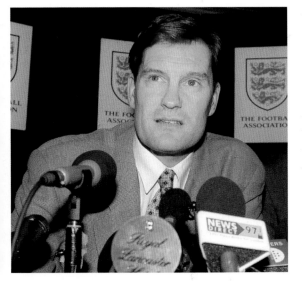

COACH SACKED FOR RELIGIOUS VIEWS

Glenn Hoddle's position as coach had been vulnerable since England's disappointing 1998 World Cup showing, so it probably wasn't wise to expound his views on reincarnation in an interview in *The Times*. "You and I have been physically given two hands and two legs and half-decent brains," he said. "Some people have not been born like that for a reason. The karma is working from another lifetime… It is not only people with disabilities. What you sow you reap." These comments provoked protests and even prime minister Tony Blair called for Hoddle's resignation. Despite saying he had been misrepresented, Hoddle was forced to resign a week later.

Another controversial element of Hoddle's reign was his decision to give faith healer Eileen Drewery a role in the England camp.

SEE ALSO **'HAMBURG COACH SLEEPS ON THE JOB'** (page 371); **'ENGLAND GO FOR ERIKSSON'** (page 543).

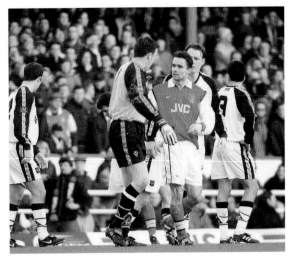

Arsenal's Mark Overmars talks to Sheffield United goalkeeper Alan Kelly after his controversial second goal goes in at Highbury.

ARSENAL AGREE REPLAY

For the first time in 127 years and over 50,000 FA Cup ties the Football Association sanctioned a replay of a game. In February 1999 Arsenal beat Sheffield United 2-1 in an FA Cup fifth round tie at Highbury with a highly contentious winner. With the game poised at 1-1 Sheffield United goalkeeper Alan Kelly kicked the ball into touch to allow team-mate Lee Morris to get treatment. On resumption of play Arsenal's Ray Parlour threw the ball to Kelly, but Kanu stole in and crossed the ball for Marc Overmars to score. United players and manager Steve Bruce protested and Arsenal quickly agreed to a replay.

SEE ALSO 'HONESTY IS THE BEST POLICY FOR FOWLER' (page 504); 'DI CANIO SHOWS HIS SOFTER SIDE' (page 542).

Disgruntled Manchester United fans display their feelings about the takeover of their club by media mogul Rupert Murdoch.

MURDOCH THWARTED IN BID TO BUY MANCHESTER UNITED

On 7 September 1998 Manchester United accepted a takeover offer of £623 million from Rupert Murdoch's BskyB. United fans reacted with anger at the news and an immediate poll in the Manchester Evening News found that 96% of them opposed the deal. United fans, marshalled by the Independent Manchester United Supporters Association and Shareholders United, actively lobbied against the bid throughout the season. The takeover was referred by the government to the Monopolies and Mergers Commission and in April 1999 the secretary for Trade and Industry Stephen Byers rejected it on their recommendation.

SEE ALSO 'GLAZERS TAKE OVER MANCHESTER UNITED' (page 592).

GIGGS' RUN TAKES UNITED TO FINAL

Manchester United kept their hopes of an unprecedented treble alive by overcoming Arsenal 2-1 in an FA Cup semi-final replay of unremitting drama at Villa Park. United took the lead with a wonderful long-range strike from David Beckham in the first-half before Dennis Bergkamp equalised with a deflected shot after the interval.

United had been reduced to ten men following Roy Keane's sending off when Phil Neville brought down Ray Parlour to give Arsenal a penalty in the final minute. Distraught United fans began edging to the exit, only for Peter Schmeichel to save Dennis Bergkamp's penalty.

In extra-time Ryan Giggs, on as a substitute, intercepted a pass from Patrick Vieira and headed towards the Arsenal goal, making his way past Vieira, Lee Dixon and Martin Keown before avoiding Tony Adams and firing the ball high over David Seaman to win. "This was the best goal I've ever scored because of the occasion and how it helped our season," said Giggs. "When I got it there was no way I was passing it. The goal was all about instinct."

SEE ALSO **'MESSI'S MARADONA MIRACLE'** (page 612).

Manchester United's Ryan Giggs leaves Arsenal's Lee Dixon and Patrick Vieira trailing on his way to scoring the winning goal.

1999

Lazio celebrate becoming the holders of the last UEFA Cup Winners Cup after beating Real Mallorca 2-1 in the final at Villa Park in Birmingham.

LAZIO WIN THE LAST EVER EUROPEAN CUP WINNERS' CUP

After 39 seasons and 32 different winners UEFA abolished the European Cup Winners' Cup at the end of the 1998-99 season. The final winners were the Italian side Lazio, managed by Swedish coach Sven Goran Eriksson, and they triumphed over Real Mallorca 2-1 at Villa Park. The Romans took the lead through Christian Vieiri after just seven minutes, only for Dani to equalise for the Spaniards minutes later. The game remained deadlocked at 1-1 until the 81st minute when the Czech playmaker Pavel Nedved's winning goal took the trophy to the Italian capital.

SEE ALSO **'EUROPEAN CUP WINNERS' CUP LAUNCHED'** (page 233).

GOALKEEPER GOES FROM ZERO TO HERO IN 12 MONTHS

It was 12 months of highs and lows for goalkeeper Jimmy Glass. In 1998 he became the first keeper to score an own goal at Wembley, a feat that doomed his team, Bournemouth, to a 2-1 defeat in the Auto Windscreens Shield final. But a year later Jimmy became a hero when, on loan from Swindon, he ran the length of the pitch to score the goal that saved Carlisle United from relegation from the English Football League. With the clock on 94 minutes and the score 1-1, Glass joined his team mates in the Plymouth Argyle penalty box for the last corner of the match. A parry from the Plymouth keeper fell to Glass who, this time, scored in the right net.

SEE ALSO **'GOALKEEPR HITS HAT-TRICK'** (page 530).

Goalkeeper Jimmy Glass celebrates his injury time winning goal which saved Carlisle United from relegation on the last day of the season.

MANCHESTER UNITED WIN THIRD DOUBLE

In the 1998-99 season, for the third time in six years, Manchester United completed the domestic double of the Premiership title and the FA Cup. In the Premiership, United were pursued by defending champions Arsenal until the very last game of the campaign when a wonderful lob from Andy Cole gave United a 2-1 win over Tottenham Hotspur at Old Trafford and the title by a single point. Six days later United had no trouble in beating Newcastle United 2-0 in the FA Cup final at Wembley with goals from Teddy Sheringham and Paul Scholes.

SEE ALSO **'MANCHESTER UNITED WITHDRAW FROM FA CUP'** (page 531); **'MANCHESTER UNITED FIGHT BACK TO WIN TREBLE'** (page 526-7).

Manchester United goalkeeper Peter Schmeichel leads the Premiership title celebrations. Victory in the FA Cup final would follow six days later.

MANCHESTER UNITED FIGHT BACK TO WIN TREBLE

When the fourth official held up his board to show there were only three minutes of added time remaining in the 1999 Champions League final Manchester United were trailing 1-0 to Bayern Munich and about to fall agonisingly short of winning an unprecedented treble. Even Alex Ferguson admitted, "When 90 minutes had been played I started practicing being a good loser."

In the previous ten days United had won the Premiership and the FA Cup, but were apparently about to be denied by the Germans. United had fallen behind after only six minutes when Mario Basler curled a free-kick past Peter Schmeichel and as the game progressed it was Bayern who looked likelier to score, having twice hit the frame of the goal.

When the added time board was displayed the UEFA president Lennart Johansson left his seat to prepare to present the Champions League trophy to Bayern and offered his commiserations to United director Sir Bobby Charlton, while the UEFA chief executive Gerhard Aigner was busy tying Bayern's ribbons onto the trophy.

Twenty two seconds into injury time, United won a corner; David Beckham lofted it into the area, which included his desperate goalkeeper Schmeichel, and the ball pinged around the area before falling to Teddy Sheringham, who steered it into the net. United swiftly won another corner, again Beckham swung the ball in, Sheringham leapt high and glanced it on and there was Ole Gunnar Solskjaer to prod the ball into the roof of the Bayern net. The greatest comeback in the competition's history was complete and United had won the treble.

SEE ALSO 'TEARS AS UNITED ARE CROWNED' (page 286).

From being 1-0 down at the start of injury time, late goals from Teddy Sheringham and Ole Gunnar Solskjaer, celebrating right, transformed the outcome of the 1999 Champions League final.

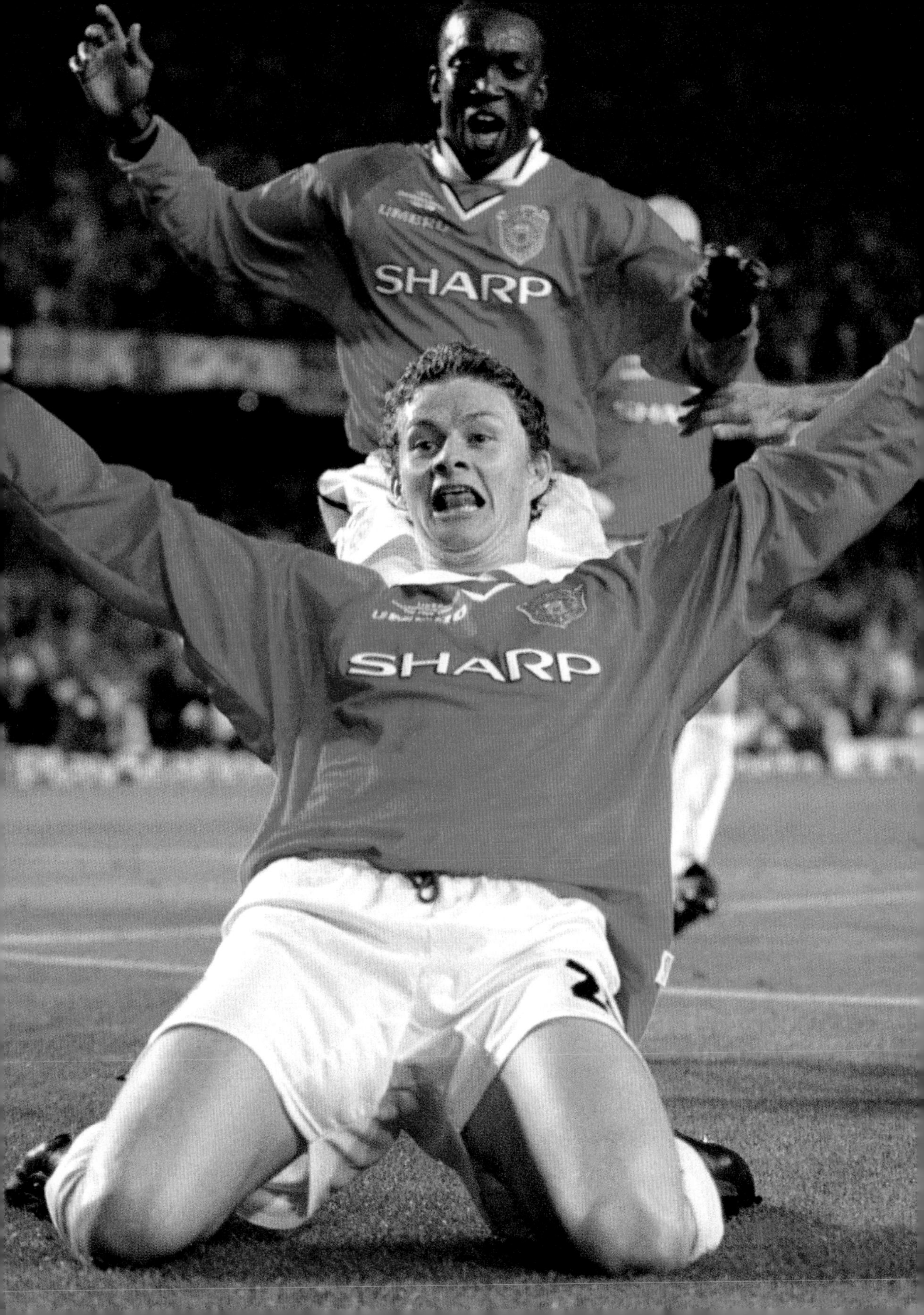
SHARP
SHARP

Martin Palermo shouts in dejection after missing his second penalty kick against Colombia at Feliciano Caceres Stadium in Luque, Paraguay.

MARTIN PALERMO MISSES THREE PENALTIES

Argentinian striker Martin Palermo missed a record three penalties in an international against Colombia at the Copa America in 1999. The first struck the cross bar in the fifth minute. He used the same technique for the second in the 75th minute – leaning back and hitting it with power – but his shot cleared the bar. He finally hit the target with his third effort, only for Colombian goalkeeper Miguel Calero to save it. The misses proved costly as Colombia won 3-0. "It was a disgrace and I have to face the reality of what happened. I hope it never happens to me again, nor to anybody else," said Palermo.

SEE ALSO **'MIHAJLOVIC'S FREE-KICK HAT-TRICK'** (page 521).

BRANDI CHASTIAN STRIPS IN TRIUMPH

The American perception that 'soccer' is a women's sport gained credence when their women's national team won the FIFA Women's World Cup finals at home. The USA met China in the final in front of a crowd of 90,185 at the Rose Bowl and the game went to a shoot-out after the first 120 minutes finished goalless. After China had missed one penalty and the US had scored all of theirs Brandi Chastian stepped forward to score the winning penalty. She celebrated by falling to her knees and removing her jersey to reveal a sports bra. This made her a star and provided the iconic image of the USA's triumph.

SEE ALSO **'MIA HAMM SIGNS WITH NIKE'** (page 464).

Brandi Chastian rips off her shirt in celebration after scoring in the penalty shoot-out against China and securing the Women's World Cup.

HENRY PROVES HIS PREMIERSHIP CLASS

In summer 1999 Arsenal paid an £11 million club record fee to sign Thierry Henry from Juventus. Henry had earned a reputation as a dangerous winger with Monaco and France, but Arsenal manager Arsene Wenger, who had given him his professional debut with Monaco, asked him to play as a striker. He said, "At first, I was worried about playing there, because I'd been playing wide for so long, but Mr Wenger told me I was a better player through the middle than out wide." And so it proved, as Henry went on to score a glut of goals, win five trophies and be voted Footballer of the Year three times.

SEE ALSO **'ARSENAL'S UNBEATEN LEAGUE SEASON'** (page 575).

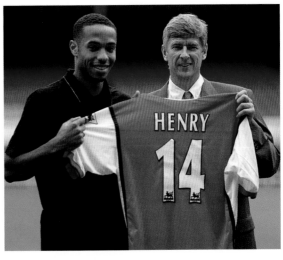

Arsenal's Thierry Henry and his new manager Arsene Wenger hold up his new shirt after he completed his move from Juventus.

AC MILAN SIGN SUPER STRIKER SHEVCHENKO

One of the finest talents to come out of eastern European football, Andriy Shevchenko moved to AC Milan in Italy in August 1999 for a $25 million fee. Shevchenko, who had won the Ukrainian league in each of his five seasons with Dynamo Kiev, seamlessly continued his success as a striker by becoming Serie A's leading scorer with 24 goals in 32 league matches. In the next two seasons with AC Milan a further 51 goals followed for Shevchenko, who as a child had fled the effects of the Chernobyl nuclear disaster in his home country.

SEE ALSO **'ROMAN ABRAMOVICH BUYS CHELSEA – AND SUCCESS'** (page 571).

Andriy Shevchenko stands in his new club strip after transferring from Dynamo Kiev. He scored 24 goals in 32 league matches in his first season.

GOALKEEPER HITS HAT-TRICK

The Paraguayan goalkeeper Jose Luis Chilavert enjoyed an illustrious career, which included being voted World Goalkeeper of the Year on three occasions, captaining his country to the 1998 and 2002 World Cup finals and scoring eight goals for his country. However, he is probably best known for becoming the first, and so far only, goalkeeper to score a hat-trick in professional football. On 28 November 1999 Chilavert scored three goals, all from the penalty spot, for Argentine side Velez Sarsfield against Ferro Carril Oeste as part of a 6-1 win.

SEE ALSO **'GOALKEEPER GOES FROM ZERO TO HERO IN 12 MONTHS'** (page 525).

Goalkeeper Jose Luis Chilavert became Paraguay's first choice free kick taker. Here, he takes a strike against Japan.

NIKE CONTRACT LEAKED

In 1996 Nike signed a £100 million deal with the Brazilian Football Confederation (CBF) to be kit supplier and co-sponsor for Brazil's national team. After the Brazilian debacle at the 1998 World Cup and the mystery surrounding Ronaldo's appearance in the final Nike's involvement came under scrutiny. In 1999 details of their contract with the CBF were leaked, which showed there was a clause stating Nike had a right to organize five international games a year with a minimum of eight high-profile players. However, over the course of an eight-month Congressional commission by the Brazilian government into the CBF, Nike was completely exonerated.

SEE ALSO **'WAS RONALDO FIT?'** (page 517).

The Brazil team's relationship with Nike was heavily scrutinised following the disappointing outcome of the 1998 World Cup final.

CHELSEA FIELD A NON-BRITISH XI

With Graeme Le Saux injured, Chris Sutton suffering from flu and captain Dennis Wise's wife due to give birth, Chelsea manager Gianluca Vialli was 'forced' to field a starting XI made up entirely of overseas players for the Premiership match against Southampton on Boxing Day 1999. The team in full was: De Goey, Ferrer, Babayaro, Thome, Leboeuf, Petrescu, Poyet, Deschamps, Di Matteo, Flo, Ambrosetti. In February 2005, Arsenal manager Arsene Wenger attracted similar criticism when his matchday squad of 16 didn't include a single British player. Blues and Gunners fans weren't complaining too much, though – both teams won convincingly.

SEE ALSO **'CHELSEA END 50-YEAR TITLE DROUGHT'** (page 588).

Chelsea's foreign legion celebrate a goal by Norwegian striker Tore André Flo. Those congratulating him include Roberto Di Matteo and Dan Petrescu.

Manchester United drew against the Mexicans Nexaca, lost 3-1 to Vasco da Gama and chalked up a meaningless win over South Melbourne.

MANCHESTER UNITED WITHDRAW FROM FA CUP

As the reigning European champions Manchester United won a place at the inaugural FIFA World Club Championship in Brazil, but at first the club could see no way of fitting it into an already busy season. United were on the brink of rejecting the invitation until the FA and the British government, in the middle of their bid for the 2006 World Cup, forced them to reconsider. United reluctantly withdrew from the 1999-2000 FA Cup, making it impossible for them to defend their treble. In January they travelled to Rio de Janeiro, but hardly distinguished themselves and were knocked out in the group stage.

SEE ALSO **'LIVERPOOL WIN 'OTHER TREBLE"** (page 550).

IVORY COAST LEADER THREATENS NATIONAL TEAM WITH MILITARY SERVICE

After a 3-0 defeat to Cameroon led to their elimination in the first round of the African Cup of Nations, 'Les Elephants' were taken to the country's capital Abidjan, given a dressing down and held in a military camp for three days by the Ivory Coast's leader General Robert Guei. "You behaved unworthily. You should have avoided us such shame," Guei was quoted as saying. "Next time you will be sent to the barracks until a sense of civic pride gets into your heads." FIFA President Sepp Blatter condemned the actions of Guei, who had come to power in a coup on Christmas Eve 1999. He was deposed in October 2000.

General Robert Guei detained members of the Ivory Coast national team in a military camp following disappointing results.

SEE ALSO **'PELÉ DONS UNIFORM'** (page 229).

FIRST WOMEN'S EUROPEAN CLUB COMPETITION

In May 2000 UEFA approved the introduction of the UEFA Women's Cup. The competition was first played in 2001-02, with 32 teams being divided into eight qualifying groups. The group winners progressed to the two-legged quarter-finals in March 2002, when Umeå IK, HJK Hensinki, Toulouse FC and FFC Frankfurt – the respective champions of Sweden, Finland, France and Germany – won through to the last four. Umeå and Frankfurt advanced to the final after tough home and away ties. They met at the Waldstadion, Frankfurt, on May 23 2002 and the German side lifted the first UEFA Women's Cup after a 2-0 victory.

FCC Frankfurt celebrate winning the first Women's European club competition after a 2-0 victory over their Finnish rivals in Frankfurt.

SEE ALSO **'FIRST WOMEN'S WORLD CUP'** (page 455).

CALAIS REACH FRENCH CUP FINAL

Calais Racing Union Football Club were an amateur team who, through a season of footballing heroics, won the hearts of fans everywhere. With a team of students, decorators and shop assistants, Calais reached the final of the French Cup by beating Strasburg and then champions of France Bordeaux in the quarter and semi-finals respectively. Calais came to the Stade de France to face Nantes in front of 78,000, but the fairy tale wasn't to be and they lost 2-1 to a last-minute penalty. However, in a wonderful sporting gesture Nantes skipper Mickael Landreu asked Calais captain, commercial rep Reginald Becque, to share the honour of lifting the trophy.

SEE ALSO **"MINNOWS' MONACO REACH CHAMPIONS LEAGUE FINAL'** (page 577).

Calais fans rejoice at their team's unlikely cup run to French Cup final, only to be defeated by a last minute penalty.

MADRID CLAIM EUROPEAN CROWN IN ALL-SPANISH FINAL

The first major all-Spanish continental final was memorable for a man-of-the-match display by an Englishman as Steve McManaman inspired Real Madrid to the most convincing European Cup final victory since AC Milan beat Barcelona 4-0 in 1994. Madrid were sensational and their all-round superiority was rewarded with three unanswered goals, although it could have been many more. First Nicolas Anelka rose to head home Michel Salgado's right-wing cross. Then McManaman volleyed in a clearance from the edge of the box. Raul applied the coup de grace, running 70 yards unopposed before rounding Santiago Canizares and finishing coolly. Paris in the spring has rarely looked so beautiful.

SEE ALSO 'ZIDANE'S STUNNER SEALS HAMPDEN TRIUMPH' (page 555).

Real Madrid's Fernando Morientes, Valencia's Miroslav Djukic and Nicolas Anelka in the first all Spanish Champions League final.

SPAIN TRIUMPH IN EURO THRILLER

2000

Crowd trouble, goals, red cards – this game in Bruges had everything. With just five minutes of injury time to play against Yugoslavia, Spain were losing, lying third in group C and on the verge of going out. The ten-man Yugoslavs were finally breached for a third time in the 93rd minute, when Gaizka Mendieta calmly scored from the penalty spot. A draw still wasn't enough for Spain, but with seconds on the clock Alfonso volleyed in spectacularly and both teams reached the quarter-finals. "This shows that in football the difference between heaven and hell is in one minute," said midfielder Josep Guardiola.

SEE ALSO **'SPAIN BAG A DOZEN TO QUALIFY FOR EUROPEAN CHAMPIONSHIPS'** (page 396).

Alfonso scores a spectacular winning goal against Yugoslavia in the last minute of injury time to ensure Spain progress in the tournament.

HOLLAND PAY THE PENALTY IN EURO SEMI-FINAL

2000

The semi-final of the European Championships in 2000 was a game Holland seemed destined not to win. Willed on by a fanatical, orange-clad Amsterdam crowd, they dominated the early exchanges, with Dennis Bergkamp hitting a post. When Italy's Gianluca Zambrotta was dismissed for a second bookable offence in the 33rd minute, the co-hosts seemed certain to progress, but Frank de Boer had a penalty saved minutes later, Patrick Kluivert hit the post from another spot-kick in the second half and several other chances went begging. Three more missed penalties in the shoot out and the Italians were through, but their luck would run out in the final.

SEE ALSO **'HOLLAND SHOW THEIR PEDIGREE'** (pages 424-5).

Jaap Stam holds his head in despair after he blasted the ball over the bar during the penalty shoot out which lead to Holland's elimination.

FRANCE ADD EUROPEAN TITLE TO WORLD CROWN

With Zinedine Zidane and Thierry Henry at their peak, France became the first team to be European and World Champions at the same time with a dramatic extra-time victory. Their opponents Italy had ground their way to the final playing a modern-day form of catenaccio, but produced a much-improved attacking display against a French team that had dazzled on the way to the final.

Preferred to Alessandro Del Piero in the starting line-up, Francesco Totti should have headed Italy in front after just three minutes. The two teams traded half chances until the 52nd minute, when Marco Delvecchio, himself preferred to Filippo Inzaghi in attack, opened the scoring from Gianluca Pessotto's left-wing cross. With France pressing, Italy paid the price for substitute Del Piero missing two great chances when substitute Sylvain Wiltord equalized four minutes into injury time. With Italy tiring in extra-time, it was left to another substitute, David Trezeguet, to score France's golden goal, sweeping home Robert Pires' cross in the 103rd minute.

SEE ALSO **'SENEGAL STUN FRANCE'** (page 558).

Didier Deschamps lifts the European Championship trophy in triumph following France's extra-time victory over Italy.

FC Barcelona's Lionel Messi celebrates after scoring. He made his debut in 2004 and became the third youngest player to line-up for Barcelona.

MESSI SIGNS FOR BARCELONA

In 2000 Argentina was in the grip of a major recession with strikes and fuel protests across the country. Lionel Messi was thirteen and a junior with his hometown team Newell's Old Boys in Rosario. Small for his age he was diagnosed with a deficiency that required expensive hormone treatment to correct. Neither Newell's Old Boys or Buenos Aires super-club River Plate could afford to fund this program and Messi and his family moved to Spain where Barcelona provided the treatment he needed. The gamble paid off in October 2004 when Messi made his debut against Espanyol becoming the third youngest player ever to represent Barcelona.

SEE ALSO **'MESSI'S MARADONA MIRACLE'** (page 612).

Ireland international Robbie Keane is powerless to stop Inter Milan being dumped out of the Champions League by Swedish side Helsingborg.

HELSINGBORG SHOCK INTER IN CHAMPIONS LEAGUE

The Italian giants were expected to qualify comfortably for the first group stage at the expense of the Swedes and dominated the first leg in Helsingborg, but Inter failed to convert any of their chances and were punished eight minutes from time when Nickas Persson crossed for Michael Hansson to volley in the winner. With the second leg in the San Siro a fortnight later, Inter were still strong favourites to progress, but again they squandered several chances, most notably in the 89th minute when Sven Anderson brilliantly saved Alvaro Recoba's penalty. Inter were out and their coach Marcello Lippi was sacked.

SEE ALSO **'ROSENBORG BEAT AC MILAN'** (page 504).

NEW BOY O'NEILL INSPIRES CELTIC

Nothing is guaranteed to bestow hero status on a Celtic manager more than victory over city rivals Rangers. Martin O'Neill achieved it in one Scottish Premier Division match – his first in charge of Celtic. The green half of the Glasgow soccer divide was ecstatic as he inspired Celtic to a 6-2 win over Rangers in the 'Old Firm' derby clash on 27 August 2000. Ulsterman O'Neill instilled a winning mentality into the Celtic players after a decade of dominance by Rangers and led them to a string of domestic successes, cementing his reputation as one of the prime motivators in British soccer.

O'Neill proved an instant hit with the green half of Glasgow by inspiring the team to a 6-2 victory over Rangers on his first game in charge.

SEE ALSO **'CELTIC'S 'LIONS' ROAR'** (page 282).

NORWAY'S GOLDEN GOAL WINS WOMEN'S OLYMPIC FINAL

Norway avenged their 1996 semi-final defeat against the reigning Olympic and World Champions, the USA, in dramatic fashion. Having lost 2-0 to the Americans in a group game just two weeks earlier, Norway led 2-1 in the final until Tiffeny Milbrett struck in the last minute to take the game into extra-time. With 102 minutes on the clock Dagny Mellgren scored the 'golden goal', sparking scenes of unbridled joy. "It was one of the greatest things I've ever experienced," said Mellgren, who became the golden girl of Norwegian football and went on to enjoy a successful club career in the USA before retiring in 2006.

Norway celebrate with their gold medals having fought back in extra-time to overcome USA with a 'golden goal'.

SEE ALSO **'NORWAY'S WOMEN BECOME WORLD CHAMPIONS'** (page 487).

G14 FORMED

Essentially a pressure group of leading European clubs, G14 was founded with the aim of providing a unified voice in negotiations with the football authorities. There were originally 14 members – hence the name – with four more joining by invitation in August 2002. G14 has often been linked with the possible formation of a European super league but its most decisive action to date has involved moves for national associations to pay players' wages when they are on international duty and provide compensation when players are injured on international duty. G14 clubs provided 22% of players at the 2006 FIFA World Cup. The founding members of G14 are Internazionale, Juventus, A.C. Milan, Liverpool, Manchester United, Olympique de Marseille, Paris Saint-Germain, Bayern Munich, Borussia Dortmund, Ajax, PSV, Porto, Barcelona and Real Madrid.

SEE ALSO **'FIFA CELEBRATES CENTENARY'** (page 576).

General manager of the G14, Thomas Kurth, attends a hearing at the European Parliament in Brussels.

WEMBLEY CLOSES... AND COACH RESIGNS ON TELEVISION

The final game staged at the old Wembley Stadium before its demolition and reconstruction also proved to be Kevin Keegan's final game in charge of the England team as he sensationally resigned in a live television interview shortly after England's 1-0 defeat by Germany. A poor game, played in wet, overcast conditions, was settled in the 14th minute. Paul Scholes fouled Mehmet Scholl 35 yards from the England goal, but Dietmar Hamman, who played his club football in England for Liverpool, took the resulting free-kick quickly and it squirmed through the grasp of England goalkeeper David Seaman and into the net. "I probably had a longer run than I could've expected," said Keegan, whose side had beaten the Germans 1-0 in the European Championship finals just two months earlier, prompting the resignation of Germany's coach Eric Ribbeck "I just don't feel I can find that little bit of extra that you need at this level to find that winning formula."

SEE ALSO **'ENGLAND GO FOR ERIKSSON'** (page 543).

SEE ALSO **'ENGLAND GO FOR ERIKSSON'** (page 543).

Kevin Keegan's last game in charge of England was the national team's last match at Wembley before the stadium was redeveloped.

HERO FIGO BECOMES TRAITOR

2000

After telling the Barcelona supporters he wouldn't be joining Real Madrid, Luis Figo's then world-record £38.7 million transfer across one of football's great divides was perhaps the most controversial of all time. Barcelona fans set up anti-Figo websites, Catalan journalists branded him 'Judas' and his return to the Nou Camp four months later saw missiles and abuse rain down from the stands. Worse was to follow in 2002 when the ground was nearly closed after objects such as a whisky bottle and, famously, a pig's head, were launched at the Pesetero (loosely meaning 'mercenary') when he was taking a corner.

SEE ALSO **'ENRIQUE DECLINES INVITATION AND CEMENTS ALLEGIANCE'** (page 553).

The sight of Figo wearing the all-white of their fiercest rivals incensed the Barcelona fans who had so recently regarded him as their hero.

DAUM AND OUT IN GERMANY

2000

Due to take over as German national team coach in June 2001, Christoph Daum was sacked by his club Bayer Leverkusen after failing a drugs test amid rumours he had also hired prostitutes, prompting British newspaper *The Sun*, memorable back-page headline: 'Don't mention the whore!' Daum protested his innocence and supplied a hair sample in an attempt to clear his name, but it tested positive and he lost both jobs. He then fled to Florida for three months before later admitting he had taken cocaine. Daum eventually began rebuilding his career with a second spell in charge of Turkish club Besiktas.

SEE ALSO **'CALIFORNIA RESIDENT APPOINTED GERMAN COACH'** (page 579).

Bayer Leverkusen and future German coach Christoph Daum speaks during a press conference prior to his very public downfall.

KEANE TAKES A BITE AT 'PRAWN SANDWICH BRIGADE'

"Some people come to Old Trafford and I don't think they can spell football, let alone understand it. Away from home our fans are fantastic, but at home they have a few drinks and a prawn sandwich and don't realise what's going on. They want fantasy football and they should stay in the real world," Manchester United's Roy Keane famously pronounced in November 2000. "I'm entitled to my opinion and that's how I felt at the time," he explained six months later. "I wasn't knocking prawn sandwiches themselves. I like the occasional one now and again myself." Proof that the outspoken Irishman also has a sense of humour.

SEE ALSO **'ROY KEANE'S MALICIOUS INTENT'** (page 545); **'IRELAND KICK OFF MINUS KEANE'** (page 556).

Roy Keane, always tough and uncompromising, was highly critical of the atmosphere generated by Manchester United's home fans.

Despite being adjusted to encourage more positive play, the offside law remains open to interpretation and is consistently the source of debate.

OFFSIDE LAW IS CHANGED

The offside law hadn't been amended since 1990, when, as part of a general movement by the game's authorities to make the rules more conducive to attacking play and help the game flow more freely, it was decided that an attacking player would be onside if level with the second-to-last opponent (usually the last defender, after the goalkeeper) when the ball was played forwards. FIFA moved to encourage attacking play still further in 2000 by decreeing that attackers who are on onside when the ball is played forwards should no longer be penalised when a 'passive' team-mate is in an offside position.

SEE ALSO **'OFFSIDE RULE INTRODUCED'** (page 18); **'INTERNATIONAL BOARD CHANGES THE OFFSIDE LAW'** (page 98).

HENRIK LARSSON WINS EUROPEAN GOLDEN BOOT

Signed from Feyenoord for just £650,000, Swedish striker Henrik Larsson went on to become the greatest player in Celtic's recent history. In total he scored 242 goals in 315 games for the club, including 53 in the 2000-01 season, when his 30 league goals made him the top scorer in Europe. Suggestions that Scottish football made Larsson look a better player than he really was were dispelled by two superb goals in the 2003 UEFA Cup final, a starring role for Sweden at Euro 2004, plus two La Liga titles and a Champions League win in two seasons at Barcelona.

Larsson's scoring record for Celtic is one of the finest in European football. He scored 242 goals in 315 games, including 53 in one season.

SEE ALSO '… BUT BARCA COME BACK TO WIN' (page 599).

DI CANIO SHOWS HIS SOFTER SIDE

Known for his spectacular goals and hot-headedness, Paolo Di Canio was also responsible for one of the most extraordinary acts of sportsmanship. With the scores level in the last minute of a heated Premiership game, Everton keeper Paul Gerrard injured himself making a clearance and the ball skewed straight to the Italian striker. However, instead of rolling the ball into the open Everton net, Di Canio caught the ball so that the stricken Gerrard could receive treatment.

West Ham United's fans, players and manager were horrified, but Di Canio was defiant. "There was evidently a problem and I couldn't go on," he insisted later. "It's not that he dropped the ball and faked an injury. In that case, I wouldn't have stopped." West Ham eventually finished seventh in the Premiership table, four points off a UEFA Cup place.

SEE ALSO 'DI CANIO GIVES FASCIST SALUTE TO SUPPORTERS' (page 586).

Often regarded as a controversial figure, Paolo Di Canio displays his Fair Play Award alongside FIFA president Sepp Blatter.

CLUBS TAKE CONTROL OF BUNDESLIGA

Since its launch in August 1963, the Bundesliga had been under the direct contol of German football's governing body, the German Football Association (DFB). This changed with the formation of the German Football League (DFL) in 2001, which brought all the Bundesligen under the immediate control of this new body. While remaining subordinate to the DFB, in the way the English Premiership is to the FA, the DFL manages Germany's professional leagues and is responsible for the issuing of licences to clubs, general fiscal oversight of the Bundesligen, and marketing rights for the top two leagues.

SEE ALSO **'FANS DESPAIR AT LACK OF FLAIR'** (page 407).

A huge inflatable, which formed part of the celebrations of the new German Football League is rolled off the pitch prior to a game.

ENGLAND GO FOR ERIKSSON

After Kevin Keegan's sensational resignation and with the English national team in disarray, the English Football Association looked to an overseas England manager for the first time in their history. Sven-Goran Eriksson was due to take over in summer 2001, but the Swede was released early from his contract with Lazio, where he'd previously won the Serie A title, and began his tenure with a 3-0 friendly win over Spain but with England faltering in their attempts to qualify for the 2002 World Cup campaign and an unconvinced national press he faced a battle to justify his appointment.

SEE ALSO **'GOTHENBURG WIN UEFA CUP'** (page 381).

Sven-Goran Eriksson had an impeccable pedigree as a club manager and became the highest paid England manager in history.

VALENCIA FANS TURN ON COACH

Despite leading Valencia to consecutive Champions League finals in 2000 and 2001, coach Hector Cuper was never popular with the club's fans. Cries of 'Cuper out!' in February 2000 were followed by the burning of Cuper effigies in March 2000, because of what the Mestalla crowd perceived as defensive tactics. "I like my teams to play attacking football, but I'm not going to commit suicide or give the opposition presents," responded the Argentinian. After rumours linking him with the Barcelona job, Cuper eventually joined Inter Milan after the 2001 Champions League final – and few were sorry to see him go.

SEE ALSO **'KHAN THE HERO AS BAYERN WIN CHAMPIONS LEAGUE'** (page 548).

Hector Cuper, the Valencia coach, stands on the touchline during his side's agonizing Champions League defeat at the hands of Bayern Munich.

SAMOA OUT FOR THE COUNT

Australia's triumph over American Samoa was, and still is, the biggest victory in international football history. So big, in fact, that the referee and match commissioner lost count of the number of goals scored and initially declared a 32-0 scoreline, before it was later changed to 31-0 by FIFA. The Oceania World Cup qualifier also saw the individual goal-scoring record broken by Archie Thompson, who scored 13 in only his third game for Australia. David Zdrilic also broke the previous record, netting eight times, with Con Boutsianis grabbing a hat-trick.

SEE ALSO **'IRAN QUALIFY AT AUSTRALIA'S EXPENSE'** (page 508); **'AUSTRALIA JOINS ASIA CONFERENCE'** (page 594).

Not only was Australia's 31-0 victory the biggest in international football but two players scored eight goals or more, including David Zdrilic.

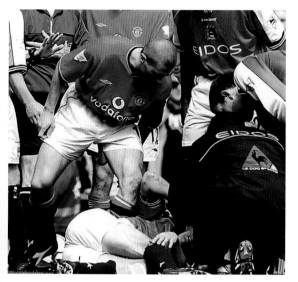

Having admitted that it was an act of revenge, Keane stands menacingly over the stricken Haaland shortly before receiving his red card.

ROY KEANE DELIBERATELY INJURES AN OPPONENT

Having suffered a serious knee injury taking a swipe at Leeds United midfielder Alf-Inge Haaland in 1997, Roy Keane "had waited long enough" to exact revenge on the Norwegian, now with Manchester City, who initially accused Keane of faking the injury. The Manchester United captain's knee-high tackle earned him a red card and a three-match ban, but Keane was suspended for a further five games and fined £150,000 when he later revealed in his autobiography that he had injured Haaland deliberately. Haaland retired from football shortly afterwards with an unrelated recurring leg problem, despite having initially threatened to sue Keane.

SEE ALSO **'MARADONA IS 'BUTCHERED"** (page 396); **'CHEEKBONE SMASHED BY CYNICAL CHALLENGE'** (page 587).

Boston Breakers' Maren Meinhart in action in the WUSA. The league attracted the best female players but unfortunately not the TV audiences.

WOMEN'S FIRST PROFESSIONAL LEAGUE

Founded in February 2000 on the back of the USA's victory in the 1999 FIFA Women's World Cup, the Women's United Soccer Association (WUSA) was the first ever full-time professional football league, succeeding the semi-professional W-League. Founded by 20 top US players in partnership with the Discovery Channel's John Hendricks, the WUSA also attracted the best female players from all over the world. The first game was played in April 2001, but after just three seasons, the eight-team league was suspended, with neither attendances nor television ratings as high as had been projected, and the five-year budget of $40 million having been spent in the first year.

SEE ALSO **'FIRST WOMEN'S EUROPEAN CLUB COMPETITION'** (page 532).

2001

STAMPEDE CAUSES AFRICA'S WORST FOOTBALL DISASTER

The Sports Stadium in Ghana's capital Accra,was packed with 40,000 fans when, with just five minutes remaining, Asante Kotoko from Ghana's second city fell 2-1 behind to fiercest rivals Hearts of Oak. Incensed by a perceived injustice, Kotoko fans began ripping up their plastic yellow seats and throwing them onto the running track surrounding the pitch. The police responded by firing 20 canisters of tear gas into the away end. Fans of both teams rushed to escape the fumes, some jumping over 20 feet from the stands to the terracing below. But the exits were locked and 126 people were killed in the crush.

SEE ALSO **'THE HEYSEL STADIUM DISASTER'** (pages 404).

Debris lies at the entrance of the stadium in Accra. The Ghanaian government announced a three-day mourning period after the disaster.

2001

The collapse of ISL sports agency threatened the FIFA presidency of Sepp Blatter but he overcame the scandal to win a second term.

ISL COLLAPSE IMPACTS ON FIFA

In December 1997 the sports marketing agency ISL was awarded the rights to market the 2002 and 2006 World Cup finals by FIFA, but less than four years later they were declared bankrupt in May 2001. The collapse of ISL left FIFA with debts of £21.4 million and also scuppered the 2001 World Club Championship. It also threatened to unseat FIFA president Sepp Blatter, but he survived with his job after he convinced members at an 'extraordinary congress' in Buenos Aires that FIFA was not damaged by the loss of its marketing partner. Blatter was re-elected for a second term as president in 2002

SEE ALSO **'BLATTER ELECTED TO FIFA TOP JOB'** (page 510); **'TELEVISION COMPANY COLLAPSE SPELLS TROUBLE FOR ENGLISH LEAGUE CLUBS'** (page 554).

Leeds United players applaud their travelling fans. The team's meteoric rise culminated in reaching a Champions League semi-final.

LEEDS UNITED – THE RISE BEFORE THE GREAT FALL

Having qualified for the 2000-01 Champions League with a third-place finish in the Premiership, David O'Leary's 'young' Leeds United team, littered with expensive signings, played some dazzling attacking football on their way to the semi-finals. However, their league form suffered and, having spent beyond their means 'chasing the dream', failure to qualify for the 2001-02 Champions League left the club with huge debts. With chairman Peter Ridsdale taking the brunt of the blame, Leeds were forced to sell their best players, including Rio Ferdinand to bitter rivals Manchester United for £28 million. They were later put into administration and were eventually relegated from the Premiership in 2004.

SEE ALSO **'LEEDS WIN LAST FIRST DIVISION TITLE'** (page 457).

BAYERN WIN GERMAN TITLE – WITH LAST KICK OF THE SEASON

Having trailed the leaders Schalke 04 – and early season pace-setters Werder Bremen – by as much as 12 points, in mid-February Bayern Munich coach Ottmar Hitzfeld declared, "We are now playing for third place." But with Schalke and Bremen faltering during the run-in, Bayern needed a draw away to Hamburg in the last game of the season to win the Bundesliga title. With 90 minutes up and Bayern trailing, Schalke were already celebrating when, four minutes into injury time, Patrik Andersson blasted in an equaliser and 'FC Hollywood' retained their Bundesliga title.

SEE ALSO **'RANGERS PIP CELTIC IN LAST DAY TITLE SHOWDOWN'** (page 570).

Steffan Effenberg holds up the Bundesliga trophy. Their title hopes written-off, Bayern Munich recovered to win the league on the last day.

KAHN THE HERO AS BAYERN WIN CHAMPIONS LEAGUE

Bayern Munich claimed their fourth European Cup – and their first for 25 years – in a game dominated by penalty kicks at the San Siro in Milan. Their Spanish opponents Valencia opened the scoring inside two minutes, Gaizka Mendieta converting from the spot after Patrik Andersson's questionable handball. Just five minutes later Bayern's Mehmet Scholl had a penalty brilliantly saved by Santiago Canizares, before Stefan Effenberg made amends five minutes into the second half following another dubious handball decision by Dutch referee Dick Jol.

With the scores at 1-1 after extra-time, both teams missed two of their first five penalties to take the shoot-out into sudden death. Thomas Linke then made it 5-4 to Bayern leaving Oliver Kahn, diving at full stretch, to save the decisive penalty from Mauricio Pellegrino and leave Valencia with a second consecutive Champions League final defeat. The following year Kahn would be named the world's best keeper at the World Cup, but even he couldn't prevent Germany from losing to Brazil in the final.

SEE ALSO 'MANCHESTER UNITED FIGHT BACK TO WIN TREBLE' (pages 526-7).

Bayern Munich goalkeeper Oliver Kahn saves the crucial penalty from Valencia's Mauricio Pellegrino to win the Champions League final.

The acquisition of Zidane heralded the start of Real Madrid president Florentino Perez's 'Galactico' buying policy. Other stars were to follow.

ZIZOU BECOMES A GALACTICO

In July 2001, at the Champions League gala at the Monte Carlo Sporting Club, Real club president Florentino Perez apparently took a napkin and wrote on it: "Do you want to play for Real Madrid?" The napkin was passed through several pairs of hands until it reached Zinedine Zidane. It was then passed back again with a one-word answer written on it in English: "Yes." The world's greatest player joined Real Madrid from Juventus for a world record £50 million a month later. Perez then continued his real-life game of Championship Manager by signing Brazilian striker Ronaldo from Inter Milan.

SEE ALSO **'ZIDANE'S WORLD PLAYER AWARD HAT-TRICK'** (page 573).

Despite the threat of the Copa America being abandoned, the tournament went ahead with hosts Colombia triumphing in the final.

KIDNAPPING THREATENS COPA

On 28 June Hernan Mejia Campuzano, vice-president of the Colombian Football Federation, was kidnapped, causing the South American Football Federation to withdraw Colombia's right to host the Copa America on security grounds. Brazil was put on stand-by as hosts, but when the authorities threatened to abandon the tournament altogether Campuzano was released – a day after being kidnapped. Argentina and Canada still withdrew because of concerns over their players' safety. They were replaced by Costa Rica and Honduras, who produced the shock of the tournament, beating favourites Brazil 2-0 in the quarter-finals and giving the disgruntled Argentinian public something to cheer about after all.

SEE ALSO **'FOOTBALLER'S MOTHER KIDNAPPED'** (page 585).

Rivaldo's last minute acrobatic bicycle kick ensured Champions League football and the revenue that entailed the following season.

RIVALDO'S LAST-GASP ACROBATICS WORTH MILLIONS

With the prize of Champions League football next season fast-disappearing and receiving possession 20 yards out with his back to goal, Rivaldo chested the ball and dispatched a perfectly-executed overhead kick into the top corner. This completed an astonishing hat-trick by the Brazilian number 10 and also came in the last minute of the final game of the 2000-01 Spanish league season, giving Barcelona a 3-2 win and a place in the following season's Champions League at the expense of Valencia, their opponents on the day, who only needed a draw to qualify themselves. Cue the first – and only to date – pitch invasion at the Nou Camp.

SEE ALSO **'BIRTH OF THE NEWLY BRANDED CHAMPIONS LEAGUE'** (page 545).

LIVERPOOL WIN 'OTHER TREBLE'

Two years after Manchester United won the treble of League, FA Cup and Champions League, Liverpool claimed their own trio of trophies – and in equally dramatic circumstances. First they won the League (Worthington) Cup on penalties, after Division One side Birmingham City had equalized Robbie Fowler's stunning opener with an injury-time penalty. Michael Owen then scored twice in the last ten minutes to give the Reds a 2-1 victory over Arsenal in the FA Cup final. And the UEFA Cup followed four days later as Spanish side Alaves were defeated 5-4 in extra-time, courtesy of an own goal Golden Goal.

SEE ALSO **'LIVERPOOL FIGHT BACK TO LEVEL EUROPEAN CUP FINAL'** (page 590).

Liverpool striker Michael Owen proudly showing off the FA Cup, one of the Reds' three trophies of the 2000-01 season.

The Munich scoreboard shows the result that few could have predicted, in what is regarded as England's finest performance on foreign soil.

GERMANY 1 ENGLAND 5

England's finest ever performance away from home came against perhaps their greatest enemy in a crucial World Cup qualifier in Munich on 1 September. The omens were not good for Sven-Goran Eriksson's team when Carsten Jancker stabbed the home side ahead after just six minutes. But Michael Owen soon volleyed England level from Nick Barmby's knock-down and Steven Gerrard fired them in front on the stroke of half-time. Michael Owen made it 3-1 just after the break, drilling home at the near post, and he completed his hat-trick on 66 minutes with a fine finish from Gerrard's through-ball. Emile Heskey finished the rout minutes later.

SEE ALSO **'AND THEN IT WAS ALL OVER'** (page 278).

BECKHAM SAVES ENGLAND

Having turned around their 2002 World Cup qualifying campaign after a stuttering start, England needed just a draw at home against Greece, who had already been eliminated, to reach the finals. But in a lacklustre display at Old Trafford, England fell behind in the first half and again in the second half after substitute Teddy Sheringham had equalized with his first touch. The play-offs beckoned for England, but deep into injury time captain David Beckham, in inspired form throughout the game, saved the day with a trademark free-kick from 25 yards, which flew into the top left-hand corner of the Greece goal.

SEE ALSO **'REVENGE FOR BECKHAM'** (page 560).

With one of his trademark free-kicks David Beckham almost single-handedly ensured England scraped through to 2006 World Cup.

In their first game since Algerian independence, the complexities of the fixture were increased with France's star player being of Algerian descent.

HISTORIC GAME ABANDONED DUE TO CROWD TROUBLE

The friendly international at the Stade de France in Paris in October was the first game between France and Algeria since Algeria had gained independence from French rule in 1962 and was made even more politically sensitive by the fact that France's star player Zinedine Zidane was of Algerian descent. With 15 minutes remaining in the game thousands of youths invaded the pitch after throwing bottles and pieces of wood at riot police. The players were led from the pitch and within minutes the match was abandoned. Seventeen people were arrested, three were later charged and the French Football Federation were fined US $77,000 by FIFA.

SEE ALSO **'ALGERIA BEAT WEST GERMANY'** (page 383).

The Scudetto badge as awarded to the winners of Serie A. Spezia had to wait 68 years to receive theirs.

SPEZIA ARE FINALLY AWARDED THE 1944 SCUDETTO

World War II meant that Italy's top division was split into regional rounds for the 1943-44 season, with a reduced number of matches for each team. After progressing to a three-way finals competition, Vigili del Fuoco della Spezia (Firefighters of La Spezia) beat a great Torino side in an epic encounter, as well as Venezia, to claim the title. However, because of the war Spezia were forced to play their home games in nearby Carpi, due to heavy bombing in Italy's north-west coast, the only Scudetto in Spezia's history was not declared official by the Italian Federation until 2002.

SEE ALSO **'WAR SUSPENDS COMPETITIONS'** (page 144).

Samuel Eto'o, Cameroon's most famous player, models the 'Indomitable Lions' sleeveless, FIFA regulation breaching strip.

CAMEROON'S SHIRTS CUT TO SIZE

Cameroon stunned the football world by unveiling a new sleeveless shirt for the 2002 African Cup of Nations and intended to wear it in the World Cup finals later that year. However, FIFA declared the shirt 'in breach of regulations' and the 'Indomitable Lions' were forced to wear black T-shirts under their 'vests' for the rest of the tournament. By the World Cup, the sleeves had returned. Undeterred, manufacturers Puma went one better at the Cup of Nations two years later with an all-in-one shorts and shirt design. Again FIFA intervened, threatening to dock six points from Cameroon's 2006 World Cup qualifying campaign until a more conventional design returned.

SEE ALSO 'MANCHESTER UNITED BLAME GREY KIT' (page 493).

Enrique may have played at the Bernabeu but he made it clear his heart lay at the Nou Camp, where he retired in 2004 having played 207 games.

ENRIQUE DECLINES INVITATION AND CEMENTS ALLEGIANCE

In 1997, three years before Luis Figo's move in the opposite direction sparked outrage in Catalunya, Luis Enrique left Real Madrid for bitter rivals Barcelona. The Spain midfielder was greeted with chants of 'hijo de puta' (son of a bitch) whenever he returned to the Bernabeu and the hatred increased over time as Enrique became Barca's captain and talisman, leading the club to league titles in 1998 and 1999. The final straw for Madrid supporters came in 2002, though, when Enrique cemented his allegiance to the Catalan club by refusing the invitation offered to former players to attend Real Madrid's centenary celebrations.

SEE ALSO 'REAL MADRID FORM – AND MAKE AN ENEMY' (page 49).

FIERCE RIVALS PLAY-OFF TO REACH CHAMPIONS LEAGUE FINAL

One of football's fiercest domestic rivalries took to the European stage for the first time in the Champions League semi-final. Barcelona dominated the first leg, but spurned several chances and were punished on 55 minutes when Zinedine Zidane put Madrid into the lead. As Barca continued to press, Steve McManaman doubled the lead to give Madrid their first win at the Nou Camp for 18 years. A car explosion before kick-off threatened to postpone the second leg, but it went ahead and Raul's stunning strike put the tie beyond Barcelona, who only had an own goal from Ivan Helguera to show for their efforts.

SEE ALSO 'AC MILAN WIN ALL-ITALIAN FINAL ON PENALTIES' (page 570).

Raul opens the scoring at the Bernabeu and puts the tie beyond doubt, with Real Madrid eventually winning 3-1 on aggregate.

TELEVISION COMPANY COLLAPSE SPELLS TROUBLE FOR ENGLISH LEAGUE CLUBS

With ITV Digital already struggling for viewers, the cost of a £315 million deal with the Football League proved too much for the ailing broadcaster and it was placed into administration in March 2002 after the League refused to accept a revised £185 million offer. Having budgeted with the TV deal in mind, many clubs were left facing financial difficulties, with several forced into administration. The Football League failed in an attempt to sue ITV Digital's parent companies, Carlton and Granada, to the tune of £150 million for breach of contract and leaving many clubs facing financial crisis.

SEE ALSO 'ISL COLLAPSE IMPACTS UPON FIFA' (page 546).

Lincoln City fans make their feelings clear as the impact of ITV Digital's collapse is felt throughout the lower leagues.

ZIDANE'S STUNNER SEALS CHAMPIONS LEAGUE TRIUMPH

Having won every domestic, international and individual honour the game had to offer, the finest footballer of his generation finally won European club football's biggest prize. And in the Champions League final at Hampden Park in Glasgow, the scene of Real Madrid's most famous European Cup triumph 42 years earlier, Zinedine Zidane scored a goal good enough to win any game.

Madrid took the lead in the ninth minute through Raul after Roberto Carlos' long throw-in, but another Brazilian defender, Lucio, equalized for Bayer Leverkusen with a header just five minutes later. Then just a minute before half-time the previously innocuous Zinedine Zidane confirmed his greatness with perhaps his greatest ever goal. From a cushioned Roberto Carlos cross the French midfielder met the ball first time and his left-footed, hip-high volley flew into the top corner from 25 yards, past helpless German keeper Hans Jorg-Butt. Zidane was named man of the match, yet his wonder goal might have come in a losing cause had Madrid's 66th-minute substitute goalkeeper Iker Casillas, who wouldn't turn 21 until five days after the final, not made three superb injury-time saves to deny the Germans.

However, the game's most memorable moment definitely belonged to Zidane. "We can spend all the time on the training ground planning for Real's tactics, but then something special happens that you cannot plan for and in this case it was Zidane's goal," said Leverkusen coach Klaus Toppmoller philosophically. Zidane himself was far more modest. "I had a pass from Roberto Carlos and slammed it in. It was a very nice volley."

SEE ALSO **'ZIDANE'S WORLD PLAYER AWARD HAT-TRICK'** (page 573).

Michael Ballack can only look on as Zidane's spectacular strike heads towards the top corner of the Bayer Leverkusen goal.

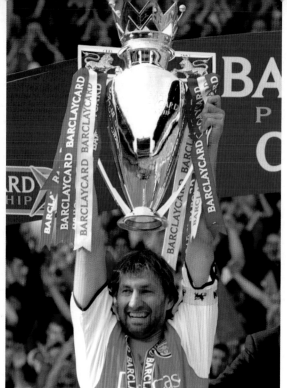

ADAMS' FAIRYTALE FAREWELL

Having made his Arsenal debut as a 17-year-old in 1983, Tony Adams became the most successful captain in the club's history, forming part of the most famous back four in English football. In total Adams won four League titles, three FA Cups, two League Cups and a European Cup Winners' Cup in a Highbury career spanning 19 years and 668 appearances. Only David O'Leary has played more game for the Gunners. In his last professional game 'Mr Arsenal' led his team to victory over Chelsea in the FA Cup final, clinching his second League and Cup double in four years.

SEE ALSO **'VIEIRA WINS FA CUP WITH HIS LAST KICK FOR ARSENAL'** (page 589).

In a perfect ending to his career Arsenal's Tony Adams lifts the Premiership Trophy. The FA Cup was to follow soon after.

Roy Keane's decision to quit robbed Ireland of their most influential player and there was little doubt where the Irish fans' sympathy lay.

IRELAND KICK OFF MINUS KEANE

"It's not been the best week for me and I dare say it's not been the best week for Roy Keane either," said Republic of Ireland manager Mick McCarthy after his team's 1-1 draw with Cameroon in their opening game of the 2002 World Cup finals. The team's captain and best player had walked out on the squad on the eve of the match after a furious bust-up with McCarthy. A last-minute equaliser from Keane's namesake Robbie gave the Irish a draw in their second game, against Germany, and they eventually reached the second round, where they went out to Spain on penalties.

SEE ALSO **'KEANE TAKES A BITE AT 'PRAWN SANDWICH BRIGADE"** (page 541).

BECKHAM MANIA HITS JAPAN

The 2002 World Cup finals were the first to be held in Asia, the first to be co-hosted and the first to witness David Beckham's extraordinary popularity in Japan. The England captain was greeted with autograph hunters and screaming girls everywhere he went, while his Mohican hairstyle was copied by thousands of football fans up and down the country. In Japan alone 150,000 copies of his autobiography were sold in June 2002, while one story claimed that the happiness Beckham created improved relations between Japan and their co-hosts South Korea. After the tournament one confectionary manufacturer even erected a three metre-high chocolate statue of Beckham.

SEE ALSO **'DAVID BECKHAM SIGNS FOR REAL MADRID'** (page 572).

2002

The spectacular opening ceremony for the 2002 World Cup took place in Seoul's newly constructed 64,000 capacity World Cup Stadium.

SENEGAL STUN FRANCE

The opening game of the 2002 World Cup finals produced the competition's biggest shock since Cameroon beat Argentina in the opening game of Italia 90. It couldn't have been scripted any better, as tournament debutants Senegal took on their former colonial masters and reigning World and European champions France, who had Senegal-born midfielder Patrick Vieira in their side. But inspired by flamboyant striker El Hadji Diouf the underdogs ran out deserved 1-0 winners.

The decisive moment came in the 30th minute, when Diouf beat Frank Leboeuf down the Senegal left and a mix-up between France goalkeeper Fabien Barthez and midfielder Emmanuel Petit allowed Papa Bouba Diop to scramble the ball across the line from close range, sparking a dance of celebration round the corner flag. Despite hitting the post twice France were poor without injured star Zinedine Zidane.

After a 0-0 draw with Uruguay in their next game, Zidane returned for the final group game against Denmark, but after a 2-0 defeat the holders were eliminated without scoring a goal, while Senegal reached the quarter-finals.

France's Emmanuel Petit and Bixente Lizarazu are beaten as Senegal's Papa Bouba Diop pounces to score.

SEE ALSO 'LOWLY CAMEROON BEAT MIGHTY ARGENTINA' (page 439); 'SOUTH KOREA SURPRISE ITALY' (page 561).

RIVALDO'S THEATRICS MAR BRAZILIAN WIN

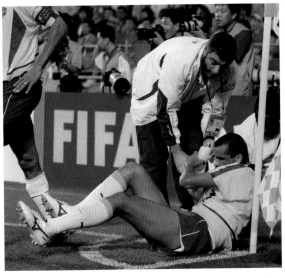

Rivaldo receives treatment at the corner flag after the ball was kicked in his 'face'. The incident led to Turkey having a second player sent off.

An excellent game between two excellent teams was memorable for one less than excellent incident. World Cup debutants and tournament dark horses Turkey took the lead against group C favourites Brazil through Hasan Sas's volley just before half-time, only to be pegged back by Ronaldo's volley five minutes after the break. With just four minutes left Alpay was then sent off for a professional foul and Rivaldo gave Brazil the lead from the resulting penalty. But when Hakan Unsal kicked the ball against Rivaldo's leg a minute later, the Brazilian fell to the ground clutching his face and Unsal was also given a red card.

SEE ALSO **'CHILE'S WORLD CUP 'PLOT FAILS'** (page 432); **'RIVALDO'S LAST-GASP ACROBATICS WORTH MILLIONS'** (page 550).

HEADS SAUDI ARABIA LOSE

Bernd Schneider celebrates Germany's eighth goal against Saudi Arabia. Making their height advantage count, six of their goals were headers.

Germany dispelled the myth that there are no easy games at the World Cup by putting eight goals past Saudi Arabia in their opening game without reply. Written off before the tournament began, the Germans took full advantage of a lack of height in the Saudi defence, with most of their play going through six foot seven striker Carsten Jancker and six of their goals coming from headers. Miroslav Klose benefited most from Saudi Arabia's defensive generosity, scoring a hat-trick – all from headers. Germany went on to reach the final while Saudi Arabia lost both their remaining games without scoring a goal, but conceding four.

SEE ALSO **'MIROSLAV KLOSE WINS GOLDEN BOOT'** (page 605); **'RECORD-BREAKING SAUDI KEEPER RETIRES'** (page 606).

David Beckham scores his redeeming winning goal from the penalty spot during England's group match against Argentina.

REVENGE FOR BECKHAM

Four years after getting sent off against Argentina at the World Cup, David Beckham scored the winning goal against the same opposition in the same tournament to put England in pole position in Group F and their opponents on the brink of elimination. On the stroke of half-time Michael Owen was tripped by Mauricio Pochettino and Beckham blasted the resulting penalty straight down the middle of the Argentina goal. England should have extended their lead at the beginning of the second half, but were hanging on in the end. "It feels better than it did four years ago," said Beckham.

SEE ALSO 'BECKHAM SEES RED' (page 515).

Nigeria's Julius Aghahowa performs his trademark acrobatic celebration. On this occasion it was in vain, thanks to Henrik Larsson's double.

AGHAHOWA CELEBRATES IN STYLE

"I thought his feet could have been closer together on landing," quipped ITV pundit Andy Townsend after Julius Aghahowa celebrated heading Nigeria into a 27th-minute lead against Sweden by performing seven back-flips. Having lost to Argentina in their opening game in Group F 1-0, Nigeria needed at least a draw against Sweden to stay in the 2002 World Cup. But their joy was shortlived as Henrik Larsson equalized for the Swedes seven minutes later and then scored the winner from the penalty spot midway through the second half to send the 'Super Eagles' heading for an early exit.

SEE ALSO 'ROGER MILLA DANCES INTO THE CORNER' (page 441).

SORRY ARGENTINA CRASH OUT IN FIRST ROUND

Well-fancied before the tournament, Argentina went into their final World Cup group game needing to win to qualify for the second round at the expense of their opponents Sweden, who only needed a draw to progress. Despite dominating possession Argentina created few clear-cut chances and were hit with the sucker punch in the 58th minute when Anders Svensson's superb long-range free-kick put Sweden into the lead. Argentina equalized through Hernan Crespo with two minutes remaining, but they couldn't find a winner. Sweden topped the group, England finished second and the tearful Argentina players headed home to an angry public.

SEE ALSO **'CAMBIASSO FINISHES OFF GOAL OF THE TOURNAMENT'** (page 600).

Argentina's Claudio Lopez sits on the floor in disbelief after Argentina go out in the first round. Sweden celebrate in the background.

SOUTH KOREA SURPRISE ITALY

After qualifying with two wins and a draw, South Korea were expected to go out in round two – even with a fanatical home crowd behind them. Christian Vieri's 18th minute header looked to be enough to send Italy through to the quarter-finals, but the Italians sat back and finally conceded an equalizer two minutes from time, when Seol Ki-Hyeon capitalised on a defensive error. In extra-time the Italians had Francesco Totti sent off and a goal wrongly disallowed for offside. Then, with penalties looming, Ahn Jung-Hwan caught Italy captain Paolo Maldini flat-footed to head home the winning golden goal.

SEE ALSO **'4 MILLION CELEBRATE SOUTH KOREA'S SUCCESS'** (page 562).

Korea's Ahn Jung-Hwan leaps higher than the Italian defence to score the goal that put the co-hosts through to the World Cup quarter final.

4 MILLION CELEBRATE SOUTH KOREA'S SUCCESS

Following their extra-time win over Italy in the second round of the World Cup, over four million South Koreans, including 1.76 million in Seoul alone, took to the streets in celebration. Even London's Trafalgar Square was invaded by 200 delighted ex-patriots and during the aftermath of victory in Daejeon fireworks illuminated the sky all over South Korea. On a more sombre note, two 20-year-old fans died of heart attacks caused by the excitement, while back in Italy Perugia president Luciano Gaucci said striker Ahn Jung-Hwan, the scorer of South Korea's winning goal, would no longer be welcome at the club.

SEE ALSO **'BECKHAM MANIA HITS JAPAN'** (page 557).

South Korean fans cheer on their team, who under Gus Hiddink, have been wildly outperforming expectations.

RONALDINHO BAMBOOZLES ENGLAND

Despite conceding the majority of possession to their opponents in the opening stages of the World Cup quarter-final with Brazil, England took the lead midway through the first half when Michael Owen capitalized on Lucio's piece of miss-control to chip the ball coolly over the advancing Marcos. England were looking increasingly comfortable, but in the final minute of the half Ronaldinho picked the ball up on the halfway line and went straight at the England defence. He wrong-footed Ashley Cole with a step-over and played the ball into the space vacated by the England left-back for Rivaldo to finish first time.

SEE ALSO **'RONALDINHO WOWS THE NOU CAMP'** (page 572).

Ronaldinho brought all his tricks when England faced Brazil in the World Cup quarter-final, creating one and scoring a spectacular second.

ONE FLEW OVER
THE SEAMAN'S HEAD

England said it was a fluke. Ronaldinho insisted it was deliberate. Either way, Brazil's winning goal in the World Cup quarter-final was a freak goal and England's goalkeeper was almost certainly to blame. Five minutes into the second half Ronaldinho's right-wing cross curled and dipped over and beyond the flailing David Seaman and into the top corner of the net. The Brazilian playmaker was then sent-off for a dangerous tackle on Danny Mills 12 minutes later, but in intense heat and humidity England rarely threatened thereafter, even with the extra man.

"It was a freak goal – a cross that ended up in the net," said captain David Beckham. "Seaman was f**king five yards off his line!" said BBC pundit Ian Wright afterwards, thinking the studio microphone was switched off. Meanwhile, down on the pitch the man in question was in tears. "It shows how much I care. I'm not ashamed of showing my feelings," said Seaman later. "Sometimes you look up to the sky and think: why me?"

SEE ALSO **'RONALDO REIGNS AS BRAZIL RULE'** (page 565).

England's David Seaman can only watch as he is beaten by Brazil's Ronaldinho for their winning goal from a free-kick.

Spain's Ivan Helguera is restrained by team-mate Xavi after a confrontation with the linesman following the penalty shoot out.

SOUTH KOREA MARCH ON AMID CONTROVERSY

The most controversial game of the 2002 World Cup finals was a quarter-final between Spain and co-hosts South Korea in Gwangju. The victims of several incorrect offside decisions, Spain were also denied two legitimate goals by mistakes from officials. First Kim Tae-Young's own goal was ruled out for a supposed push by Ivan Helguera. Then Joaquin was wrongly adjudged to have run the ball out of play before he crossed for Fernando Morientes to head home. South Korea created few chances, but were perfect from the penalty spot, winning the shoot-out 5-3. Several angry Spanish players confronted the officials after the match.

SEE ALSO **'SOUTH KOREA SURPRISE ITALY'** (page 561).

Hakan Sukur celebrates scoring Turkey's first goal in the first minute against South Korea. The goal set the tone for an attacking game.

TURKEY SCORE FASTEST GOAL IN WORLD CUP HISTORY

In the third/fourth place play-off game, Turkey scored the fastest goal in World Cup finals history on their way to a 3-2 victory over South Korea. After just 11 seconds, Hong Myung-Bo's error allowed Hakan Sukur to race clean through and open his account in the tournament with a smart finish. South Korea were level within eight minutes through Lee Eul-Yong's stunning free-kick, but two goals from Ilhan Mansiz put Turkey into a 3-1 half-time lead. Both teams continued to attack in the second half and Song's consolation goal meant South Korea's fairytale campaign had a happy ending.

SEE ALSO **'BRYAN ROBSON SCORES AFTER 27 SECONDS'** (page 382).

RONALDO REIGNS AS BRAZIL RULE

Shrouded in controversy after the 1998 World Cup, Ronaldo found redemption four years later as Brazil lifted the trophy for a record fifth time. Written off before the tournament, Ronaldo overcame a serious knee injury to finish top scorer with eight goals, including both in the final at Yokohama against Germany, to become Brazil's joint highest goalscorer at World Cup finals, joining Pele on 12. 'Ronie' first pounced on 67 minutes after Oliver Kahn spilled Rivaldo's 20-yard shot and the number 9 grabbed his second two minutes from time with a low drive from the edge of the box.

"I don't think sex could ever be as rewarding as winning the World Cup," he said afterwards. "It's not that sex is not great, but the World Cup is only every four years." The three-time World Player of the Year later described the victory as "the pinnacle of the mountain, because it came at the right moment – when 90% of people did not trust me; did not believe in me."

SEE ALSO **'WAS RONALDO FIT?'** (page 517).

Ronaldo hits the perfect shot – right into the far corner beyond Kahn's despairing dive.

CHARITY BEGINS AT HOME

Ecuadorian international Ulises de la Cruz grew up in the impoverished Valle de Chota and upon achieving football success he set up a charity in his own name to fund social improvements. The financial rewards that came with Ecuador's qualification for the 2002 World Cup paid for a vital clean water supply to stop the spread of disease, whilst his own performances earned him a move to Aston Villa. Since then de la Cruz has carved out a solid Premiership career and continues to send a proportion of his weekly wage home to Ecuador.

SEE ALSO **'TOTTI HELPS PAY WAGES OF ROMA'S YOUTH TEAM'** (page 574).

De La Cruz's childhood friend and fellow professional Augustin Delgado has also helped the local area by setting up a soccer school.

Northern Ireland's combative midfielder Neil Lennon is challenged by Bulgaria's Radostin Kichichev during a World Cup qualifier.

DEATH THREATS FORCE INTERNATIONAL RETIREMENT

On the eve of Northern Ireland's game against Cyprus, midfielder and former captain Neil Lennon announced his retirement from international football after receiving deaths threats. A Catholic who played for Celtic, Lennon had been booed by sections of the crowd during his last home international at Windsor Park after it was claimed he'd said that he wanted to play for a United Ireland team. The death threats were allegedly made by the Loyalist Volunteer Force – although they denied this – and were met with disgust from both sections of the Northern Ireland community. However, after 40 caps, Lennon never played international football again.

SEE ALSO **'WHEN FOOTBALL BECAME PURE MURDER'** (page 433).

Arriving in spectacular fashion. Everton's Wayne Rooney celebrates after scoring his stunning winning goal against Arsenal in 2002.

WAYNE ROONEY MAKES HIS MARK

In October, five days shy of his 17th birthday, Wayne Rooney became the youngest goalscorer in the history of the Premiership. Not only that, he did it against Arsenal's so-called 'Invincibles', his 30-yard shot flying past David Seaman and crashing in off the underside of the crossbar to give Everton a 2-1 victory. "Remember the name!" screamed ITV's Clive Tyldesley and soon nobody would be able to forget it. The player Arsene Wenger called a "special talent" has since lived up to his promise, becoming a vital player for England and Manchester United, who he joined from Everton in 2004 for £25 million.

SEE ALSO **'ROONEY STRUCK BY CURSE OF THE METATARSAL'** (page 581).

WIEGHORST PLAYS IT FAIR TO IRAN

Sometimes winning isn't everything. In February 2003, as Iran faced a Danish league representative team in Hong Kong, Jalal Kameli Morfradi mistook a whistle from the crowd as the signal for half-time and picked the ball up to give to the referee. However, after a quick word with coach Morten Olsen, Danish captain Morten Wieghorst deliberately put the penalty wide. "It was unfair to try and capitalise on it," said Wieghorst. "The Iranian player had no idea what had happened." Moralists look away now: two minutes into the second half Iran's Javad Nekounam scored the game's only goal... a penalty.

SEE ALSO **'HONESTY IS THE BEST POLICY FOR FOWLER'** (page 504); **'IRAN QUALIFY AT AUSTRALIA'S EXPENSE'** (page 508).

In an act of great sportsmanship Danish international Morten Wieghorst deliberately missed a penalty in a game the Danes would eventually lose.

FERGUSON BOOT HITS BECKHAM IN THE FACE

Minutes after Manchester United had been knocked out of the FA Cup by Arsenal at Old Trafford, Sir Alex Ferguson and David Beckham were involved in a furious stand-up row in the home dressing room. Ferguson blamed Beckham for Arsenal's second goal, but the England captain refused to back down and the United manager kicked out in frustration, sending a stray football boot rebounding off the wall and into Beckham's forehead. Ferguson apologised, but in the days that followed Beckham made no attempt to cover up the resulting cut above his left eye and it was the beginning of the end for his United career.

SEE ALSO **'DAVID BECKHAM SIGNS FOR REAL MADRID'** (page 572).

A plaster is visible over the left eyebrow of United midfielder David Beckham and reveals where he was struck by Ferguson's flying boot.

Mali President Alpha Oumar Konaré was quick to act when Cameroon's goalkeeping coach was suspected of voodoo activities before a games.

CAMEROON COACH ARRESTED FOR 'VOODOO CURSE'

Vodou (commonly Anglicised as voodoo) is an ancient West African faith system unconnected to zombies and dolls; a prayer or rite before a game is akin to a Catholic player crossing himself. However, before an African Cup of Nations semi-final with hosts Mali, Cameroon's goalkeeping coach Thomas Nkono was beaten, handcuffed and dragged away by local police who suspected him of leaving a charm on the pitch. With manager Winfried Schafer threatening to withdraw the team from the tournament, Mali president Alpha Oumar Konaré visited Nkono to apologise. Cameroon went on to retain the trophy, but CAF banned Nkono for a year for 'not displaying his accreditation properly'.

SEE ALSO **'IVORY COAST LEADER THREATENS NATIONAL TEAM WITH MILITARY SERVICE'** (page 532).

OLD TRAFFORD RISE TO ACKNOWLEDGE A MASTER

They've seen some fine football at Old Trafford, but in April 2003 Manchester United fans were quick to acknowledge a visiting master. Real Madrid were protecting a 3-1 first leg lead, but not by defending – not with Ronaldo up front. The Brazilian scored within 11 minutes and tormented £30m defender Rio Ferdinand all night en route to a stunning hat-trick, sealed by a 25-yard shot as the visitors lost 4-3, but went through on aggregate. Upon his substitution late on, he was given a moving ovation by all those at Old Trafford, from the cheap seats up to Alfredo di Stefano and Bobby Charlton in the directors' box.

SEE ALSO **'RONALDO BECOMES A HERO'** (page 610).

Ronaldo accepts the applause ringing out from all four corners of Old Trafford after his magnificent performance against Manchester United.

PETER THE GREAT HANGS UP HIS GLOVES

One of the greatest, if not the greatest, goalkeeper of all time, Peter Schmeichel had imposing presence, amazing reflexes and the ability to start attacks with his long throw-outs. He first shot to fame when his inspirational performances helped rank outsiders Denmark win the 1992 European Championships, going on to win 129 caps. At club level he made his name with Manchester United, winning the treble of League, FA Cup and Champions League in 1999, before joining Sporting Lisbon where he won the Portuguese title. Schmeichel returned to England for spells with Aston Villa and Manchester City, before retiring in May 2003, six months short of his 40th birthday.

SEE ALSO **'SUBSTITUTES DENMARK WIN EUROPEAN CHAMPIONSHIP'** (pages 460-61).

Peter Schmeichel leaves the field after his final match before retirement to a standing ovation from the blue half of Manchester.

RANGERS PIP CELTIC IN LAST-DAY TITLE SHOWDOWN

On the last day of the 2002-03 season, Rangers, who hosted Dunfermline, had the same points and goal difference as Celtic, who visited Kilmarnock. The biggest winner would take all. Michael Mols put Rangers ahead after three minutes and although the Pars levelled, Claudio Cannigia restored the lead, while Chris Sutton put Celtic in front. Sutton's second was matched by Shota Arveladze to put both challengers two clear at the break. Alan Thompson's penalty put Celtic temporarily top before two quick Rangers goals saw them resume command. Thompson's missed second penalty rendered Stilian Petrov's fourth goal academic, especially when Mikel Arteta's late penalty made it 6-1. Rangers had the title.

SEE ALSO **'REAL SOCIEDAD PIP MADRID TO THE TITLE'** (page 375).

Barry Ferguson leads the celebrations following Rangers 6-1 victory over Dunfermline, which was enough to win the title on goal difference.

Following an extremely tight game, Juventus' players stand dejected as AC Milan prevail in the penalty shoot-out.

AC MILAN WIN ALL-ITALIAN FINAL ON PENALTIES

The first all-Italian Champions League final was a typically Italian affair, a tactical battle between the country's biggest and best two clubs. Milan had the better of the first half, wasting three good chances, while Juventus went closest to scoring in the second period, Antonio Conte's header rebounding off the crossbar. After an uneventful extra-time period, the game was decided on penalties. Five spot-kicks were saved in the shoot-out, leaving Andriy Shevchenko to score the winning goal for Milan in sudden death. It was a sixth European Cup victory for the Rossoneri and a fourth for their captain Paolo Maldini.

SEE ALSO **'... AND BEAT MILAN ON PENALTIES'** (page 591).

ROMAN ABRAMOVICH
BUYS CHELSEA – AND SUCCESS

Roman Arkadievich Abramovich had been sniffing around Premiership outfits for a while before he bought Chelsea for £140m – a fine profit for previous owner Ken Bates, given that the club he had bought for £1 in 1982 was saddled with potentially lethal debts. These were effortlessly wiped out by the mysterious Russian who had lost both his parents by the age of four, but determinedly made money as his country converted to capitalism, eventually making billions by buying into oil firm Sibneft before selling his shares for 13 billion dollars – cash. Abramovich probably didn't have to dig too deep into his pockets for the money to write off the Blues' debts and buy a squad of multi-millionaire internationals, and those pockets were soon stuffed with a clutch of medals, the denim-wearing owner signalling his delight by clapping along to the Stamford Bridge Shed End's version of Kalinka. It's fair to say that his purchase of Chelsea wasn't universally popular, but the Abramovich era has indisputably brought – or as some would say 'bought' – success.

SEE ALSO **'CHELSEA END 50-YEAR TITLE DROUGHT'** (page 588).

Chelsea's new billionaire owner Roman Abramovich meets with fans before a game.

With the number 7 shirt taken by local hero Raul, Beckham opted for 23, the same number as basketballing legend Michael Jordan.

DAVID BECKHAM JOINS REAL MADRID

In July, after months of speculation linking him with a move away from Old Trafford, David Beckham finally left Manchester United, joining Real Madrid rather than fierce rivals Barcelona for a fee believed to be in the region of £24.5 million and a four-year contract worth a reported £5 million a year. "While we are sad to see David go after so many great years at Old Trafford, we believe this is a good deal for the club," said Manchester United.

Inevitably, there were also whisperings that Madrid's desire to sign him was as much a commercial decision as a football one. Indeed, Real Madrid shirts bearing Beckham's name and number sold out on the day his transfer was completed.

SEE ALSO 'GALACTICOS LEAVE ON A HIGH' (page 617).

RONALDINHO WOWS THE NOU CAMP

Two years after losing Luis Figo to arch-rivals Real Madrid, the Nou Camp crowd finally had a new hero and after an injury-hit first season the buck-toothed Brazilian playmaker inspired Barcelona to their first league title in six years. In his second, he was crowned FIFA World Player of the Year. He repeated the feat the following year when Barcelona retained their title and added the Champions League trophy with victory over Arsenal in Paris. So awesome was Ronaldinho's play that season that he was even giving a standing ovation by Real Madrid fans after scoring in a 3-0 win at the Bernabeu.

SEE ALSO 'RONALDINHO BAMBOOZLES ENGLAND' (page 562).

Having seen off Manchester United, who were also chasing the Brazilian, Barcelona unveil their new signing in a friendly with Juventus.

GERMANY'S WOMEN WIN THEIR FIRST WORLD CUP

Hurriedly switched to the USA from SARS-afflicted China, the fourth Women's World Cup was dominated by Germany's stately progress to the final: Tina Thune-Meuyer's squad scored 23 with only three conceded. Sweden had hammered them 4-0 in the 1993 third-place play-off and this time Hanna Ljungberg put the Scandinavians in front late in the first half, but the Germans' superiority was reflected in the corner-count of 24 to two. The excellent Maren Meinert equalised after 46 minutes and although Sweden doggedly held out until extra-time, Renate Lingor's 98th-minute free-kick was powered home by substitute defender Nia Kuenzer, who had barely played an hour in total during Germany's six finals games.

SEE ALSO **'FIRST WOMEN'S WORLD CUP'** (page 455).

Germany's Bettina Wiegmann holds aloft the trophy as her team-mates celebrate around her in Carson, California.

ZIDANE'S WORLD PLAYER AWARD HAT-TRICK

It's a mark of incredible consistency to be thrice named Player of the Year in any given sphere. When the bauble under discussion is the world governing body's global award, which had only been in existence for just over a decade, it's quite some achievement. Zinedine Zidane's effortlessly silky skills earned him a hat-trick of FIFA World Player of the Year titles in six years. The Frenchman's last award meant he equalled Brazilian striker Ronaldo's record of three victories and he was to grace the podium again in 2006 after finishing runner-up to Italy's World Cup-winning captain Fabio Cannavaro.

SEE ALSO **'ZIDANE'S HEAD-BUTT'** (page 603).

Three-times World Player of the Year, Zidane's exquisite skills and dramatic career have been the subject for a feature length film.

TOTTI HELPS PAY WAGES OF ROMA YOUTH PLAYERS

These days fans may call into question players' loyalty to their clubs more frequently, but when Francesco Totti shows his love for Roma, he means it. Despite constant speculation, one of his generation's greatest 'trequartistas' – a Unicef ambassador who has released a self-mocking joke book in aid of Roman charities – has stayed loyal to the Giallorossi, for whom nobody has played or scored more times. So it was no surprise that, when Roma went through financial strife in 2003, Totti reached into his back pocket to fund Roma's youth teams.

SEE ALSO **'CHARITY BEGINS AT HOME'** (page 566).

Born and raised in the Eternal City, Totti has only ever played for his boyhood team A.S. Roma making his debut when he was just 16.

Controversial Ecuadorian referee Moreno would be wise to stay away from Sicily after he disallowed Italy's match-winning golden goal.

REFEREE GETS IT IN THE NECK FROM ITALIANS

It's not just England fans who need a scapegoat in defeat. All of Italy was convinced that their 2002 World Cup exit was down to one man: Ecuadorian referee Byron Moreno, who disallowed a potential Italian golden goal and gave Francesco Totti a second yellow card for diving before South Korea scored the winner. A Sicilian town named some public toilets after him and Christmas saw a 'Hunt the Referee' board game, but by then Moreno had been suspended back home – after signalling six minutes of stoppage time, he played 13, awarded two penalties and sent off two players...

SEE ALSO **'WHEN FOOTBALL BECAME PURE MURDER'** (page 433); **'SOUTH KOREA SURPRISE ITALY'** (page 561).

An unfamiliar sight as Italian football's golden boy and Juventus' star striker Alessandro Del Piero gives evidence in court.

DEL PIERO QUIZZED IN JUVENTUS DOPING SCANDAL

In November 2004 Juventus team doctor Riccardo Agricola was charged with – and later acquitted of – sporting fraud after a three-year trial. He was given a 22-month suspended prison sentence. The case was sparked after former Roma coached Zdenek Zeman claimed in an interview in 1998 that Italian football was controlled, in part, by "pharmaceutical products". He went on to express his surprise at the "muscular explosion of certain Juventus players", between 1994 and 1998, including Gianluca Vialli and Alessandro Del Piero. Both players, along with Zinedine Zidane, were forced to take the stand, but after admitting to taking vitamins intravenously, were cleared of any wrongdoing.

SEE ALSO **'ITALIAN MATCH-FIXING SCANDAL'** (page 598).

ARSENAL'S UNBEATEN LEAGUE SEASON

They all laughed when Arsene Wenger said his team could complete the season unbeaten, as no top-flight team had achieved that since Preston in 1888-89 – but he was right. As his side powered to their third title in seven years, whispers grew that unlike the great sides of Revie, Busby, Shankly, Paisley, Ferguson et al, Arsenal hadn't lost a league game, painful defeats in the FA Cup semi-final and Champions League quarters serving to focus them. With the title long wrapped up, only already relegated Leicester stood in their way. Paul Dickov's goal shook Highbury, but Thierry Henry's penalty soothed the nerves before captain Patrick Vieira struck to make history.

SEE ALSO **'PRESTON PROVE INVINCIBLE'** (page 33); **'ARSENE WENGER ARRIVES AT HIGHBURY'** (page 503).

Thierry Henry celebrates with Edu during their unbeaten season. This win was particularly sweet as it came against local rivals Tottenham.

REAL SOCIEDAD FAIL IN TITLE FIGHT

Real Sociedad's brave bid for the La Liga title was eventually foiled by Real Madrid in the penultimate game of the season. Real Madrid thrashed local rivals Atletico Madrid 4-0, with Raul and Brazilian Ronaldo grabbing two goals apiece. In stark contrast, Real Sociedad fell to a 3-2 defeat against Celta Vigo, suddenly giving Real Madrid a two-point advantage. Both teams managed to win their final game, ensuring that Real Madrid ultimately claimed the title by just two points. Sociedad had been much inspired by 21-year-old Xabi Alonso, but conceding two injury-time goals to Villarreal and drawing 2-2 in late March was probably the turning point.

SEE ALSO **'REAL SOCIEDAD PIP MADRID TO THE TITLE'** (page 375).

Real Sociedad fell at the final hurdle in the race for La Liga. Star man Xabi Alonso stands on the far right of the back row.

FIFA CELEBRATES CENTENARY

2004 saw one of the most important anniversaries in football history as FIFA celebrated the centenary of its formation. The commemorations marked in particular England, as the origin of the laws of football; France, where FIFA was born; Uruguay as the first hosts of the World Cup in 1930; and Switzerland as the home of FIFA for more than 70 years. Frenchman Robert Guérin was the brain behind the formation of the world governing body for football and it was in Paris in July 1904 that seven founding members signed up to the foundation agreement and the initial committee was formed.

SEE ALSO **'FORMATION OF FIFA'** (page 55).

Legends from the past (Gordon Banks and Pele) and the present (Thierry Henry) gather at FIFA's lavish centennial celebrations.

'MINNOWS' MONACO REACH CHAMPIONS LEAGUE FINAL

It's normally a fairy tale for a team with an average gate of 10,394 to reach the Champions League final, but Monaco are hardly normal. That gate represents a third of the population of the principality, which has the world's highest percentage of millionaires. Still, kudos to Didier Deschamps in guiding Les Rouge Et Blancs to the world's biggest club game. Europe took notice when Deportivo la Coruna were crushed 8-3 in a group game, sat bolt upright when Real Madrid were defeated in the quarter-finals and applauded when Chelsea were well beaten in the semi-final. Porto took the final, but Deschamps had made his name as a coach.

SEE ALSO **'MOURINHO HELPS PORTO BECOME CHAMPIONS OF EUROPE'** (page 578).

Monaco's financial muscle means they are able to mount serious challenges for Europe's top prizes from the South of France.

FERGUSON'S LONG SILENCE

Manchester United manager Alex Ferguson is a man of passion – a characteristic that has served him well in his long and successful career. Yet this trait is responsible for keeping Man Utd's football knight off British TV screens, at least as far as the national broadcasters, the BBC is concerned. Enraged by a 2004 BBC3 documentary which probed the professional relationship between Ferguson and his son Jason, a football agent, Fergie refused to have anything further to do with the corporation. Instead, Saturday night viewers of the Match of the Day soccer round-up programme routinely gets United's Portuguese assistant coach Carlos Queiroz for post-match interviews.

SEE ALSO **'FERGIE DOESN'T FALTER'** (page 434).

Sir Alex Ferguson's self-imposed vow of silence following a BBC documentary about his agent son hasn't done his team any harm.

MOURINHO HELPS PORTO BECOME CHAMPIONS OF EUROPE

As coronations go it was subdued. After receiving his Champions League winner's medal, with Porto's players holding the famous trophy aloft, Jose Mourinho slipped from the field and confirmed his imminent move to Chelsea. Bobby Robson's former translator at Barcelona, who had led Porto to UEFA Cup glory the previous year, was never photographed with his jubilant team – but they had a lot to thank him for.

Although Brazil-born schemer Deco would soon move to Barcelona, while defenders Ricardo Carvalho and Paulo Ferreira accompanied Mourinho to Stamford Bridge, the charismatic Portuguese had cannily conquered Europe with a squad bereft of stars, but packed with players willing to follow their taskmaster tactician's orders to the letter. As so often in a run to glory which included a sharp win over Manchester United, Mourinho's men won the final despite having much less possession; with Porto 1-0 up, the coach spent a good five minutes telling 60th-minute substitute Dmitri Alenichev to play at the point of a diamond. Fifteen minutes later Alenichev had made it three without reply and a star was born.

SEE ALSO **'CHELSEA END 50-YEAR TITLE DROUGHT'** (page 588).

Jose Mourinho acknowledges the applause in what would prove to be his last game in charge of Porto before heading to the Premiership with Chelsea.

ZOLA GUIDES CAGLIARI TO PROMOTION

After seven hugely successful years at Chelsea, where he was idolised by the Stamford Bridge faithful, Gianfranca Zola opted to leave the club in 2003 in order to return to his native Sardinia and join Serie B side Cagliari. The move was to prove as spectacular as one of his trademark free-kicks when the diminutive Italian playmaker captained Cagliari to promotion. They ended the 2003-04 season as runners-up and sealed a return to the top division after an absence of four years. After one season in Serie A with Cagliari, Zola retired in 2005, but not before finishing his glorious career in typical style with a brace against Juventus.

SEE ALSO **'CHELSEA WIN EUROPEAN CUP WINNERS' CUP'** (page 509).

Evergreen Zola's return to the club where he started his career proved magical as he guided them back into Italy's top-division.

CALIFORNIA RESIDENT APPOINTED GERMAN COACH

Jürgen Klinsmann, taking his first managerial role, succeeded Rudi Voller as German national coach in July 2004. Germany had had a disappointing Euro 2004 and were desperate to perform well as hosts of the forthcoming World Cup, but Klinsmann's insistence on living in California, plus some poor results in the World Cup build-up, tested the faith of the German public. However, despite this and the bitter rivalry between Oliver Khan and Jens Lehman over the goalkeeping shirt, Klinsmann emerged a hero after leading an attack-minded German team to third place, only losing out to eventual winners Italy in the semi-finals. Shortly after the tournament, he chose not to renew his contract.

SEE ALSO **'FEUD BETWEEN KLINSMANN AND MATTHAUS'** (page 492); **'DAUM AND OUT IN GERMANY'** (page 540).

Klinsmann's appointment raised eyebrows but his tenure is generally considered to have revitalized the German national team.

FRANCE FIGHT BACK WITH TWO INJURY-TIME GOALS

As the clock ticked past 90 minutes, Zinedine Zidane broke English hearts in dramatic style. The French maestro firstly conjured up a curling free-kick from the edge of the penalty area after a foul by substitute Emile Heskey and then, even deeper into injury time, added a penalty as a back pass from Steven Gerrard let in an alert Thierry Henry who was brought down by England goalkeeper David James. As Zidane stepped up he vomited seconds before coolly slotting in the winner, to the simultaneous delight of the French and utter despair of the English team. It was 2-1 to the French in this Euro 2004 Group B match.

SEE ALSO 'ZIDANE WINS WORLD PLAYER AWARD HAT-TRICK' (page 573).

Zidane finds a gap in the wall to fire in France's equalizer in the dying minutes. Worse was to follow for England when he scored again.

"LET LJUNGBERG PLAY FORWARD BEHIND HENRIK AND ZLATAN"

It is probably unlikely that Swedish Prime Minister Goeran Persson's words had any bearing on the matter, but whatever the impact of his complaint something clicked as Sweden routed Bulgaria 5-0 in their opening Euro 2004 match. Persson had felt Sweden were too defensive, but such accusations appeared somewhat off the mark as the attacking talents of Henrik Larsson, Freddie Ljungberg and Zlatan Ibrahimovic inspired the Scandinavians to emphatic victory. The Swedish premier is evidently a football fan after previously adding his weighty signature to a petition aimed at coaxing Larsson out of international retirement in time for Euro 2004.

SEE ALSO 'KUWAITI PRINCE GETS INVOLVED' (page 384).

The trio of Ibrahimovic, Larsson and Ljungberg combine to fire Sweden to victory – just what their Prime Minister ordered.

Baros went on to score two more goals in the quarter-final against Denmark and ended Euro 2004 as top scorer with five goals.

CZECH REPUBLIC BEAT GERMANY

In this crucial final Group D match, Milan Baros came off the bench to grab the winner for the Czech Republic and sensationally knock Germany out of the competition. The Czechs had already qualified for the last eight and could afford to rest nine regulars. In contrast the Germans needed a victory and looked on course as the inspirational midfielder Michael Ballack put them ahead with a superb shot into the top corner. However, just eight minutes later Marek Heinz curled in a free-kick to bring the Czechs level and, with Germany desperately searching for an equaliser, Milan Baros entered the fray to devasting effect, stabbing in the winner.

SEE ALSO **'PANENKA THE SHOOT-OUT HERO'** (page 348); **'OLIVER BIERHOFF'S WINNING GOAL WINS FINAL'** (page 498).

Rooney is forced to withdraw and with him goes England's sole attacking threat. Toothless, they go out once again on penalties.

ROONEY STRUCK BY CURSE OF THE METATARSAL

After defeat by France in their opening game, England had moved through to the quarter-finals with successive victories over Switzerland and Croatia, thanks in no small part to the precocious talents of Wayne Rooney, scorer of four of England's eight goals. However, the curse of the metatarsal struck as England's great young hope was hit on the foot and suffered the now ubiquitous injury midway though the first half. Rooney's cracked fifth metatarsal perhaps cost England their best chance of victory and a place in the semi-finals as they became less adventurous and allowed Portugal to gain the initiative, although the match was ultimately decided by a penalty shoot-out.

SEE ALSO **'WAYNE ROONEY MAKES HIS MARK'** (page 567).

PIERLUIGI COLLINA RETIRES FROM INTERNATIONAL FOOTBALL

Pierluigi Collina's highly successful international referring career culminated in the Euro 2004 semi-final between the Czech Republic and Greece, after he had reached the mandatory retirement age of 45. It wasn't only the combination of baldness and those glaring eyes that made Collina stand out, for the Italian became renowned as one of the best and most respected referees in world football. He took charge of some of the biggest club and international matches in the calendar and, having been placed on FIFA's refereeing list in 1995, his career highlights included the 1996 Olympic final, 1999 Champions League final, 2002 World Cup final and 2004 UEFA Cup final.

SEE ALSO **'THREE YELLOWS FOR POLL'** (page 601).

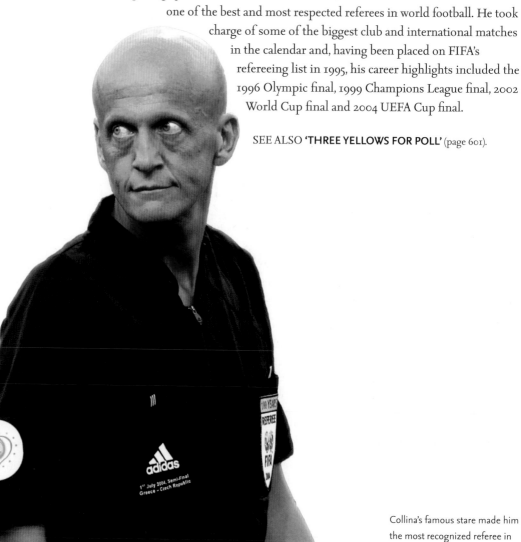

1st July 2004, Semi-Final
Greece – Czech Republic

Collina's famous stare made him the most recognized referee in world football.

OUTSIDERS GREECE WIN EUROPEAN CHAMPIONSHIP

After squeezing past the initial group stage by virtue of having scored more goals than Spain, Greece went on to shock the footballing world and seize the ultimate prize of the European Championship 2004. Utilizing their strengths of organisation, team-spirit and discipline under the expert guidance of German coach Otto Rehhagel, Greece knocked out the defending champions France in the last eight, disposed of the highly fancied Czech Republic team in extra-time in the semi-finals and finally defeated their Portuguese hosts for a second time in the tournament – each of the knockout matches incredibly won by the identical score of 1-0.

SEE ALSO **'SUBSTITUTES' DENMARK WIN EUROPEAN CHAMPIONSHIPS'** (pages 460-61).

Unfancied Greece utilized an old Italian tactic by grinding out 1-0 victories on their way to a shock victory. They were 150-1 rank outsiders at the outset.

IRAQ WIN FOURTH OLYMPIC PLACE

Against the back drop of the invasion of their country in 2003, Iraq not only managed to qualify for the 2004 Athens Olympic Games for the first time since 1988 – by winning their qualifying group, but also went on to beat Portugal, Costa Rica and Australia before succumbing to Paraguay 3-1 in the semi-finals. Iraq still had the bronze medal to play for, but eventually lost out by the slender margin of 1-0 to the Italians. It was still Iraq's most successful ever Olympic football tournament and the achievement was undoubtedly a remarkable one in the light of on-going hostilities in war-torn Baghdad.

SEE ALSO **'NIGERIA TAKE OLYMPIC GOLD'** (page 500).

Iraq's presence at the Olympics, let alone their performances, was an achievement in itself and a great demonstration of the Olympic spirit.

REFEREE FELLED

On 15 September Roma's Champions League group tie with Dynamo Kiev was sensationally abandoned after referee Anders Frisk was struck by an object thrown from the Roma crowd, just after he had signalled for half-time and with Dynamo Kiev leading 1-0. The Swede was in a clear state of shock as he was helped to the changing rooms with blood pouring from his head. The Italians within the Olympic Stadium had seemingly become incensed with Frisk after he had red-carded Roma defender Philippe Mexes, despite there being little doubt that the decision was correct. The game was left unfinished and Dynamo Kiev were awarded a 3-0 victory.

SEE ALSO **'ITALIAN FOOTBALL SUSPENDED'** (page 609).

Anders Frisk stares at the blood on his hand after being struck by an object thrown from the crowd whilst his shocked assistant looks on.

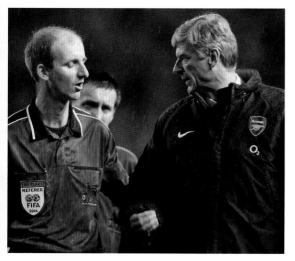

Mike Riley had the unenviable task of maintaining order at Old Trafford after a series of bad-tempered matches between Arsenal and United.

PIZZA FLIES IN OLD TRAFFORD TUNNEL

Matches involving Manchester United and Arsenal have often been fiery affairs, but there was a new twist to the tale in October 2004, when Arsenal arrived at Old Trafford protecting an astonishing 49 league matches unbeaten run. Manchester United went on to win the match 2-0, aided by a controversial penalty, and by the time the players disappeared down the tunnel at the final whistle tempers were frayed. It was then that pizza was allegedly thrown by an aggrieved Arsenal player supposedly landed on Sir Alex Ferguson. Perhaps revealingly, when the Old Trafford manager appeared for the post-match interview he was no longer attired in his match suit.

SEE ALSO **'ARSENAL'S UNBEATEN LEAGUE SEASON'** (page 575).

This was the most high-profile example of a worrying trend in Brazil. Players on the verge of lucrative moves to Europe are common targets.

FOOTBALLER'S MOTHER KIDNAPPED

On 6 November 2004, highly promising teenage Brazilian footballer Robinho was forced to stop playing for his club Santos after his mother, Marina da Silva Souza, was kidnapped. Shortly afterwards Robinho asked the police not to carry out an investigation so that he could negotiate with his mother's captors and, after paying a ransom of US $75,000 (£43,000), his mother was finally released 41 days later. Unsurprisingly, Robinho fled his native country at the end of the season and joined Spanish giants Real Madrid. Robinho's mother was the first of five footballers' mothers to kidnapped over the next few months.

SEE ALSO **'DI STEFANO IS 'KIDNAPPED"** (page 250); **'KIDNAPPING THREATENS COPA'** (page 549).

Di Canio's inflammatory gesture was clearly captured on camera – not the first time he has been in trouble with the football authorities.

DI CANIO GIVES FASCIST SALUTE TO SUPPORTERS

The Rome derby between Lazio and Roma is a fiery contest on most occasions, but the encounter between the two early in 2005 stays in the memory as a result of Paolo Di Canio's rather unusual choice of victory celebration. Having opened the scoring with an exquisite right-footed volley in a fully deserved 3-1 win for Lazio, the controversial Italian went on to perform a straight-arm Fascist salute during the immediate post-match celebrations which, he said, gave him, "a sense of belonging to my people". In his youth, Di Canio was also known to have been part of the notorious Lazio fan group known as the Ultras.

SEE ALSO **'ENGLAND TEAM GIVE NAZI SALUTE'** (page 137); **'DI CANIO BANNED FOR PUSH'** (page 520).

Disgraced former referee Robert Hoyzer arrives at court in Berlin to hear the corruption charges made against him.

GERMAN CORRUPTION SCANDAL

In German football's biggest ever match-fixing scandal, referee Robert Hoyzer was imprisoned for two years and five months in November 2005 after admitting attempts to fix nine matches. Hoyzer, who refereed in the German second division, was suspended in January 2005 following suspicions over his handling of a 2004 domestic cup tie between regional league team Paderborn and Bundesliga giants SV Hamburg. Paderborn won the match 4-2, helped by two penalties and a first half sending off for Hamburg striker Emile Mpenza. During the ensuing investigation it was discovered that Hoyzer had links with a Croatian betting syndicate who had bet large amounts of money on matches in which he had officiated.

SEE ALSO **'THE GREAT BUNDESLIGA SCANDAL'** (page 322).

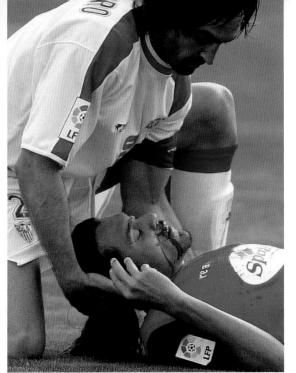

CHEEKBONE SMASHED BY CYNICAL CHALLENGE

In March 2005 fans at the La Liga clash between Real Mallorca and Sevilla witnessed one of the most brutal acts seen in recent times on a football pitch, when Sevilla hard man Javi Navarro's elbow thudded into the cheekbone of Real Mallorca's attacking midfielder Juan Arango. The 24-year-old Arango, who was immediately knocked unconscious and required assistance to breathe, subsequently spent three days under observation in hospital while recuperating from the effects, including a fractured cheekbone. Navarro, who only received a booking from referee Alfonso Pino Zamarano, was later given a five-match ban for his indiscretion; an act which Arango's father claimed was tantamount to "attempted homicide".

Navarro's woeful disciplinary record is often cited as the primary reason for his limited international career. He has only 2 Spanish caps.

SEE ALSO **'MARADONA IS 'BUTCHERED"** (page 396).

Remarkably this was the first time the two great European teams had met in the twenty years since the Heysel tragedy.

LIVERPOOL AND JUVE LINE UP FOR MINUTE'S SILENCE

For the first time since the European Cup final in 1985 where 39 Italians lost their lives, Liverpool and Juventus met in the first leg of a Champions League quarter-final tie on 5 April 2005. An emotional Anfield was determined to pay its respects to the visiting Juventus fans, after rioting by Liverpool supporters had led to the collapse of a wall and the tragic deaths in that Heysel Stadium final. Before kick-off, Liverpool fans presented a banner of friendship and this was followed by a minute's silence. However, both commemorations received a mixed reception from the visiting fans, with some turning their backs, leading to criticism in the Italian press.

SEE ALSO **'THE HEYSEL STADIUM DISASTER'** (page 404).

Inter's Materazzi and AC Milan's Rui Costa look on as a firefighter holds flares thrown by fans during their Champions League match.

FIREWORKS AS AC MEET INTER

In April the Champions League quarter-final second-leg tie between Italian giants AC Milan and Inter Milan had to be abandoned after fireworks were thrown onto the pitch by sections of the San Siro crowd. The match was initially suspended by referee Markus Merk after 73 minutes when a lit flare struck the AC Milan goalkeeper Dida on his right shoulder, with his team leading Inter 1-0. After a ten-minute stoppage Merk's attempts to re-start the game proved futile, with more missiles landing on the pitch. UEFA subsequently awarded AC Milan a 1-0 victory, as they progressed to the last four at their neighbours' expense.

SEE ALSO **'ITALIAN FOOTBALL SUSPENDED'** (page 609).

John Terry who came up through the Chelsea ranks, celebrates being the first Blues skipper to lift the League trophy since Roy Bentley in 1955.

CHELSEA END
50-YEAR TITLE DROUGHT

Chelsea romped to the 2004-05 FA Premiership crown, their first top-flight title win for exactly 50 years. In his maiden season in charge, Portuguese coach Jose Mourinho guided the Blues to a record 95 points, winning 29 games with just a single defeat. The club's Russian billionaire owner Roman Abramovich had bankrolled Mourinho to the tune of £200m on new player signings, such as the £24m spent on Ivory Coast forward Didier Drogba. However, Chelsea's triumph was largely inspired by their captain and Professional Footballers' Association Player of the Season John Terry, alongside 16-goal top scorer Frank Lampard, who scooped the Football Writers Association award.

SEE ALSO **'ABRAMOVICH BUYS CHELSEA – AND SUCCESS'** (page 571).

LYON SECURE FOURTH CONSECUTIVE LEAGUE TITLE

Having finished the 2000-01 season as runners-up, Manager Jacques Santini guided the previously unheralded Olympique Lyonnais team to their first-ever French League Championship crown in 2002. Just two weeks after the title triumph, Santini left the club, taking over as the France national coach. The resignation however had little effect on Lyon's new-found domestic supremacy, as new Manager Paul Le Guen arrived to deliver a hat-trick of Ligue 1 titles, helped by French internationals such as Sidney Govou, Florent Malouda and Sylvain Wiltord, as well as the brilliant Brazilian Juninho.

SEE ALSO 'FRENCH YOUTH SYSTEM ESTABLISHED' (page 472).

Lyon's Antonio Ribeiro Reis and Michael Essien celebrate their achievement which equalled the records of Saint-Etienne and Marseille.

VIEIRA WINS FA CUP WITH HIS LAST KICK FOR ARSENAL

In a final largely dominated by Manchester United, the 2005 FA Cup was ultimately decided on penalties for the very first time. With Jens Lehman and the woodwork coming to Arsenal's rescue on several occasions, the North Londoners somehow managed to force a penalty shoot-out. Lehman crucially saved the second United penalty, before the remaining spot kicks were scored to leave Arsenal captain Patrick Vieira with the opportunity to win the FA Cup. He found the corner of the United net with what was to prove his very last kick for Arsenal. Two months later, after nine successful years at the club, Vieira was sold to Juventus for £13.75m.

SEE ALSO 'TONY ADAMS' FAIRYTALE FAREWELL' (page 556).

Vieira had long been linked to Old Trafford. Sealing the FA Cup against Manchester United was a fitting end to his Gunner's career.

LIVERPOOL FIGHT BACK TO LEVEL EUROPEAN CUP FINAL ...

Three goals ahead at half-time and the 2005 European Cup final seemed to be over, with the trophy all but adorned in the traditional black and red ribbons of AC Milan. However, an incredible second-half Liverpool performance in Istanbul prompted an extraordinary turnaround, which Milan appeared powerless to prevent.

On 25 May 2005 the Italian giants were ahead within a minute, after Milan captain Paolo Maldini had slotted home following an Andrea Pirlo free-kick. Worse was to follow for Liverpool. First winger Harry Kewell limped off injured and then, with half-time approaching, Hernan Crespo grabbed two clinically taken strikes. Crespo's first was a tap-in following a cross from strike partner Andrei Shevchenko. His second was a sublime chip over the on-rushing Liverpool goalkeeper Jerzy Dudek, after a defence splitting pass from the influential Brazilian Kaka.

It looked as if Liverpool would have to settle for the UEFA Cup the following season, as the four-time European Cup winners had finished fifth in the Premier League, beaten to the fourth Champions League qualifying position by Merseyside rivals Everton and a vast 37 points behind champions Chelsea.

However, in an astonishing comeback, Liverpool levelled before the hour mark after scoring three times within five minutes. Firstly, a John Arne Riise cross found Liverpool talisman Steven Gerrard, who directed a fine header into the top corner beyond Milan's Dida. A second followed within two minutes as substitute Vladimer Smicer hit a low drive from the edge of the area and then a buccaneering run from Gerrard saw him hauled down in the area. Xabi Alonso saw his penalty attempt saved, but reacted smartly to convert the rebound, leaving the Milan players stunned.

At half-time in Istanbul Rafa Benitez famously told his shell-shocked team –'Give yourself the chance to be heroes'.

SEE ALSO **'TEN MAN ARSENAL TAKE CHAMPIONS LEAGUE FINAL LEAD...'** (page 598).

... AND BEAT MILAN ON PENALTIES

Liverpool sensationally beat AC Milan to win the Champions League after a penalty shoot-out – with goalkeeper Jerzy Dudek emerging the hero for Liverpool, saving two penalties to cap a breathtaking comeback. After somehow forcing their way back into the match with three second-half goals, Liverpool had taken AC Milan to extra-time. It turned out to be a long half an hour for the English side as Milan launched several attacks in a desperate effort to regain the lead. Dudek, particularly, distinguished himself with an incredible double save to somehow repel Andrei Shevchenko. Liverpool held on to force penalties and were soon 2-0 ahead as Dudek made his first crucial save from Andrea Pirlo. However, Milan came back into it as Tomasson and Kaka scored. Although Riise missed his spot kick, Smicer made it 3-2 to Liverpool, meaning that Shevchenko had to score. Dudek almost dived beyond the ball, but stuck out a hand above his body to thwart arguably the world's best striker and complete an unbelievable victory for Liverpool, securing their fifth triumph in Europe's premier club competition.

Jamie Carragher wins the race to be the first outfield player to congratulate the man-of-the-moment Jerzy Dudek.

SEE ALSO '... BUT BARCA COME BACK TO WIN' (page 599).

Fans converge on Old Trafford to protest against the rumoured takeover of the club by American billionaire Malcolm Glazer.

GLAZER TAKES OVER MANCHESTER UNITED

On 12 May 2005 Malcolm Glazer launched a formal takeover of Manchester United, worth £790m. The US tycoon secured the crucial 28.7% stake owned by Irish racing duo JP McManus and John Magnier and took total control on 28 June 2005. In 2004 some United supporters had formed a shareholders' association to buy club shares, fearing that the huge debt created by a takeover would mean increased ticket prices and a lack of player investment. Glazer's arrival was the catalyst for disenchanted fans to form FC United. The team kicked kicked off in August 2005 with a 5-2 victory in Division Two of the North West Counties League.

SEE ALSO 'UNITED ON CLOUD NINE' (page 613).

The blue glow tells you that it's 1860 Munich who are in action at the modern Allianz Arena on this occasion.

BAYERN'S DISTINCTIVE MODERN STADIUM OPENS

The completion of Bayern Munich's stunning new three-tiered stadium the Allianz Arena was marked by a full house of 66,000 to watch Bayern defeat a German national team 4-2. The futuristic arena, which cost £200m and was built in just two years, is shared by Bayern and their city rivals TSV 1860 Munich. When darkness descends on the stadium, the outside glows red if Bayern are playing or blue if TSV 1860 are at home. England international Owen Hargreaves scored the first competitive goal in the new stadium, as Bayern began the new era in style with a 3-0 victory over Borussia Moenchengladbach.

SEE ALSO 'BAYERN MOVE TO NEW STADIUM' (page 323); 'WEMBLEY RE-OPENS – AT LAST!' (page 616).

AUSTRALIA LAUNCHES NEW LEAGUE TO ATTRACT STAR PLAYERS

Sydney FC player David Zdrilic, right, contests Queensland Roar player Chad Gibson during their A-League game which Sydney won 1-0.

In a move designed to increase popularity and modernise the game, Australia unveiled its new A-League competition and Sydney FC signed former Manchester United striker Dwight Yorke on a two-year deal. The first season proved a success, with average attendances up to over 11,000; more than double that of the final National Soccer League season. Sydney FC went on to win the inaugural title and with Australia qualifying for their first World Cup since 1974 interest in the game reached new levels.

SEE ALSO **'FOOTBALL ARRIVES IN AUSTRALIA'** (page 27); **'AUSTRALIA JOINS ASIA CONFERENCE'** (page 594).

GEORGE BEST LOSES THE BATTLE

A sea of tributes were left outside Old Trafford and Windsor Park many bearing the number 7 shirt Best had worn for club and country.

In November 2005 George Best lost his long fight with alcoholism and died of multiple organ failure and a lung infection in a west London hospital. There were emotional scenes outside the hospital when his family announced to crowds that Best had passed away aged just 59 years old. At his funeral in Belfast a week later there was a huge outpouring of grief, but also a celebration for his career, as tens of thousands of mourners lined the streets in the rain for a memorial service at Stormont, which was televised live. He was buried in a private ceremony beside his mother at Roselawn Cemetery in the east of the city.

SEE ALSO **'EL BEATLE IS BORN'** (page 265); **'GEORGE BEST QUITS AT 26'** (page 319).

Lampard's career at West Ham was undermined by continued accusations of nepotism. At Chelsea he has proved his class.

LAMPARD PLAYS
164 CONSECUTIVE MATCHES

Beginning on 13 October 2001 and lasting for over four years until 26 November 2005, Frank Lampard set a Premiership record by playing in 164 consecutive league matches. The run, which broke goalkeeper David James' record of 159 consecutive appearances, ended when the England midfielder was taken ill before Chelsea's game at Manchester City. Lampard, an £11 million buy from West Ham United by previous manager Claudio Ranieri, proved to be great value as he went on to score 16 league goals in the 2005-06 season, breaking the record for most Premier League goals scored by a midfielder in one season.

SEE ALSO **'CHELSEA END A 50-YEAR DROUGHT'** (page 588).

Australia's Sasho Petrovski and Kuwait's Fahad Shaheen clash during their Asia Cup qualifying match in Sydney. Australia won 2-0.

AUSTRALIA JOINS
ASIA CONFERENCE

Australia left the Oceanic Football Confederation (OFC) on 1 January 2006 to become the 46th member of the Asian Football Confederation (AFC). One of the founder members of the OFC, Australia had qualified for the 2006 World Cup finals as an Oceanic team, but played in the finals as an Asian representative. Seeking a higher calibre of competitive football and favouring the Asian qualifying path for the World Cup, Australia had been campaigning to join the AFC for over 30 years. Along with increased revenue from sponsorship and television rights, the AFC hopes Australia will add weight to their campaign for an extra place in the 2010 World Cup.

SEE ALSO **'IRAN QUALIFY AT AUSTRALIA'S EXPENSE'** (page 508); **'AUSTRALIA'S FIRST WORLD CUP GOAL'** (page 599).

LUTON TOWN AND LIVERPOOL'S REMARKABLE CUP ENCOUNTER

In a remarkable third round FA Cup tie in April, captain Steven Gerrard fired Liverpool ahead before Luton stormed back to lead 2-1 at half-time. Luton goalkeeper Marlon Beresford then saved a penalty early in the second-half, before Kevin Nicholl scored another spot-kick to give Luton a two-goal advantage. A major shock looked probable, but Liverpool turned it round by scoring four goals in the final 30 minutes, with Xabi Alonso grabbing two stunning long-range strikes. The Spaniard's first effort from 40 yards was exceptional, but his second, a low drive from inside the Liverpool half into an open goal, was a special way in which to seal a memorable meeting.

SEE ALSO 'BECKHAM SCORES FROM THE HALF-WAY LINE' (page 501).

Shown live on BBC television, the incident-packed encounter was typical of the drama of the third round of the FA Cup.

Thierry Henry outwits Guti on his way to scoring a memorable goal against the favourites which proved enough to knock them out.

THIERRY HENRY'S SOLO GOAL AGAINST REAL MADRID

Thierry Henry showed Arsenal fans there was life after Patrick Vieira by scoring the only goal in a tense two-legged encounter with Real Madrid en route to the Champions League final. With the second-half barely underway, Cesc Fabregas picked up a loose ball and played in Henry who was standing just inside the Madrid half. The Frenchman set off towards the Madrid goal, shrugging off Ronaldo's challenge. After skipping past a lunge from Alvaro Mejia and then a sliding challenge from Madrid captain Guti, Henry rode a last-ditch tackle from Sergio Ramos before unleashing a precision left-footed shot into the bottom right corner past the diving Iker Casillas.

SEE ALSO '... BUT BARCA COME BACK TO WIN' (page 599).

2006

2006

LAST MATCH AT HIGHBURY

Arsenal's last match at their famous Highbury ground was certainly an emotional occasion, but it was also a crucial match as they needed to better the result of rivals Tottenham Hotspur in order to clinch the fourth Champions League position. It turned out to be a thrilling and ultimately glorious afternoon for the Gunners as a Thierry Henry hat-trick inspired Arsenal to a 4-2 win over Wigan, while across London, Spurs lost 2-1 at West Ham, ensuring Arsenal won the fourth-spot battle. As the clocked ticked down on Arsenal's 93-year association with Highbury, a parade of former legends helped to celebrate the end of an era in style.

SEE ALSO **'WOOLWICH ARSENAL MOVE TO HIGHBURY'** (page 73); **'HIGHBURY – THE FILM STAR'** (page 377).

Arsenal's Robert Pires loved Highbury so much he bought a flat in the new housing development built around the famous old stadium.

Bearing in mind the occasion and the match situation, Gerrard surely scored one of the all-time great FA Cup final goals.

GERRARD SAVES LIVERPOOL WITH LAST-MINUTE CUP FINAL GOAL

Liverpool and West Ham served up a thrilling contest in the last FA Cup final to be held at Cardiff's Millennium Stadium. After being pegged back to 2-2, underdogs West Ham had regained the lead and were moments from victory when Liverpool's inspirational captain Steven Gerrard let fly from 35 yards, striking the ball with such ferocity that Shaka Hislop in the West Ham goal had little chance of saving it. The game was ultimately decided by a penalty shoot-out in Liverpool's favour, with Jose Reina making three stops at West Ham's expense, but Gerrard's incredible strike was the turning point of the match.

SEE ALSO **'LIVERPOOL FIGHT BACK TO LEVEL EUROPEAN CUP FINAL'** (page 590).

TEN-MAN ARSENAL TAKE CHAMPIONS LEAGUE FINAL LEAD ...

Having seen off Real Madrid and Juventus, Arsenal faced much-fancied Barcelona in the UEFA Champions League final. After an eventful opening, Barca's Ronaldinho played a defence-splitting pass through to Samuel Eto'o, who was brought down by Jens Lehmann as he raced towards the edge of the 18-yard box. Ludovic Giuly tapped in the loose ball, but Norwegian referee Terje Hauge disallowed the goal and brandished the red card at Lehmann. However, the English team refused to buckle and the match took an unexpected twist as centre-back Sol Campbell rose above the Barcelona defence to head Thierry Henry's free-kick powerfully past Victor Valdes and put Arsenal 1-0 up at half-time.

SEE ALSO **'THIERRY HENRY'S SOLO GOAL AGAINST REAL MADRID'** (page 595).

Speaking to the press Hauge admitted, "In other circumstances I would perhaps have done something different with Lehmann."

Carlos Puyol leads the Barcelona team's celebrations as red and blue ticker tape pours down at the Stade de France, Paris.

... BUT BARCELONA COME BACK TO WIN

Expectations were high for Barcelona as they stepped out for the second half against a ten-man Arsenal side. Heavy rain couldn't dampen a thrilling 45 minutes as both sides had chances to score.

It was the introduction of Swedish veteran Henrik Larsson in the 61st minute that proved to be the catalyst for the Spaniards, as his deft touch played in Samuel Eto'o, who slotted the ball home.

The winner came from an unlikely source, as substitute Juliano Belletti exchanged a one-two with Larsson before firing a low drive between the legs of Almunia, leading the Catalans to their ninth European trophy.

SEE ALSO **'BARCELONA LOSE EUROPEAN CUP ON PENALTIES'** (page 409).

2006

OTILINO TENORIO, AKA SPIDERMAN

Ecuador international striker Otilino Tenorio was killed in May 2005, aged just 25, after a car crash in his native country. The tragic accident occurred only three days after he had represented his country in a 1-0 friendly victory against Paraguay in New York. Tenorio was nicknamed 'Spiderman' for the extrovert manner in which he celebrated his goals – he would put on a mask of the fictional super hero pulled from his shorts. As a tribute, Ivan Kaviedes replicated his former team-mate's trademark ritual by donning a Spiderman mask after scoring Ecuador's third goal in a 3-0 win against Costa Rica at the 2006 World Cup.

SEE ALSO **'CHARITY BEGINS AT HOME'** (page 566).

Ivan Kaviedes unveils his unique tribute to his former colleague, replicating his 'Spiderman' celebration in Hamburg.

2006

CAMBIASSO FINISHES OFF GOAL OF THE TOURNAMENT

Argentina recorded the most emphatic victory of the 2006 World Cup, thrashing Serbia-Montenegro 6-0. It was a scintillating show, with some truly memorable finishes, but one goal was breathtaking – when Esteban Cambiasso expertly fired in Argentina's second after a flowing 24-pass move. The Argentinians were passing the ball around patiently, probing for a weakness in their opponents. Eventually Javier Saviola passed to Juan Roman Riquelme, who moved the ball into Esteban Cambiasso's path. The midfielder then laid the ball into Hernan Crespo, who back-heeled a sublime return pass, before Cambiasso smashed home from 12 yards. It was a stunning goal, of which the watching Diego Maradona certainly approved.

SEE ALSO **'MARADONA SCORES AN INCREDIBLE SECOND'** (page 416).

Cambiasso finishes a perfect move but it was his penalty miss in the quarter-final shoot-out against Germany that sent Argentina home.

RONALDO RECORDS HIS 15TH WORLD CUP GOAL

Germany 2006 marked a real return to form for Ronaldo. After an injury-plagued spell with AC Milan, he has returned to South America.

Ronaldo, in his third World Cup competition, notched his 15th goal in a 3-0 win over Ghana to break the all-time World Cup finals goal-scoring record. The strike, after just five minutes, saw Ronaldo overtake Gerd Muller's 1974 record. Ronaldo had been criticised for appearing overweight and unfit during Brazil's first two games, but after two goals against Japan to equal Muller's record, the striker went one better. It was a typically stylish finish, involving a delightful step-over and feint to bamboozle the Ghana goalkeeper Richard Kingston with his right leg. He then eased the ball past the keeper with his left before stroking the ball home with nonchalant ease.

SEE ALSO 'LUCKY NUMBER 13 FOR JUST FONTAINE' (page 222); 'WAS RONALDO FIT?' (page 517).

REFEREE SHOWS THREE YELLOW CARDS TO ONE PLAYER

Unsurprisingly, among the 14 referees sent home by FIFA after the group games, Poll announced his immediate international retirement.

English referee Graham Poll sensationally entered the World Cup record books during the crucial Australia versus Croatia group match, when he issued three yellow cards to the same player. With Australia requiring a draw and the Croats a win in order to progress, the stakes were high, particularly as the climax approached. During the final 10 minutes Poll sent off one player from each side, both for two bookable offences. However, he also issued Croatia's Josip Simunic with two yellow cards, but neglected to produce the mandatory red. It wasn't until the final whistle that the official waved a third yellow card to Simunic and finally the overdue red.

SEE ALSO 'REFEREE GETS IT IN THE NECK FROM ITALIANS' (page 574).

Rooney was the third English player to be sent off in a World Cup, joining Ray Wilkins (1986) and David Beckham (1998).

ROONEY SENT OFF IN QUARTER-FINAL

It had been a belated start to the 2006 World Cup for England's Wayne Rooney after a battle to overcome a metatarsal injury. Regrettably for the striker and England, it was also an early end to the tournament during the quarter-final against Portugal. A scrappy but tense game was still goalless when, just after the hour mark, Rooney became embroiled with three Portuguese markers on the half-way line. Rooney then inexplicably appeared to stamp on defender Ricardo Carvalho, who was already on the ground. The Argentine referee Horacio Elizondo inevitably produced a red card, urged on in particular by Rooney's Manchester United team-mate Cristiano Ronaldo.

SEE ALSO 'BECKHAM SEES RED' (page 515).

Henry steals in unmarked at the far post to get on the end of Zidane's cross and fire past Dida from close range to give France the lead.

HENRY KNOCKS OUT BRAZIL

In a repeat of the 1998 World Cup final won 3-0 by France, Brazil were knocked out of the 2006 tournament in the quarter-finals by Thierry Henry's sixth World Cup goal. Although both teams had failed to set the competition alight, it was the French side that was beginning to play some attractive football, inspired by man-of-the-match Zinedine Zidane. After a goalless first period, a deep Zidane free-kick picked out an unmarked Henry and the Arsenal striker didn't disappoint, volleying past goalkeeper Dida from five yards after 57 minutes. The favourites were out. France had ended Brazil's record 11 consecutive World Cup victories, dating back to that 1998 final.

SEE ALSO 'FRANCE WIN WORLD CUP' (pages 518-9).

ZIDANE'S HEAD BUTT

It looked as if the World Cup final was destined to be Zinedine Zidane's glorious swansong, but it all turned sour for the temperamental French genius. With the final poised at 1-1 and with just 10 minutes of extra-time remaining, a quite extraordinary scene unfolded. The Italian centre-back Marco Materazzi, who had already headed the Italians level following an early Zidane penalty, and the Frenchman began to argue with each other near the half-way line, apparently trading insults. Zidane then suddenly turned and walked towards Materazzi, forcing his head into the Italian's chest with considerable strength. Materazzi was sent sprawling to the ground clutching his chest.

It appeared that the Argentinian referee Horacio Elizondo had little alternative but to dismiss Zidane in his final competitive match. However, Elizondo had not seen the off-the-ball incident and the fourth official appeared to relay the event to him before the red card was produced. This was an abrupt and controversial incident, which many saw as a shameful end to Zidane's glorious career.

SEE ALSO **'MARADONA SENT OFF AGAINST BRAZIL'** (page 385).

The aftermath of Zinedine Zidane's head butt on Marco Materazzi. An abrupt ending to an otherwise glorious career.

ITALY WIN WORLD CUP

Italy held their nerve to overcome 1998 champions France on penalties and win the World Cup for a fourth time. Having defeated the hosts Germany in the semi-finals, Italy were rocked after just six minutes of the final when Marco Materazzi was adjudged to have fouled Florent Malouda. Zinedine Zidane stepped forward and scored with a deft chip. However, just 12 minutes later Materazzi made amends, rising to connect with Andrea Pirlo's corner and heading convincingly past Fabien Barthez.

As the match ebbed and flowed, chances were spurned at both ends, before Zidane was sensationally sent-off for an astonishing head-butt at Materazzi's chest, but the shell-shocked French held on for a penalty shoot-out. Italy, though, emerged victorious, winning 5-3 on penalties.

SEE ALSO **'POZZOS' MOMENT OF TRUTH'** (page 141); **'FIRST EVER WORLD CUP PENALTY SHOOT-OUT'** (page 388).

As Cannavarro raised the Jules Rimet trophy, Italy became the most successful European side in World Cup history.

MIROSLAV KLOSE WINS GOLDEN BOOT

German striker Miroslav Klose clinched the 2006 World Cup Golden Boot award by scoring five goals during the competition. This made him the third German to win the award, after Edmund Conen (1934) and Gerd Muller (1970). Klose hit two in both group matches against Costa Rica and Ecuador, plus Germany's quarter-final leveller against Argentina, a match they went on to win on penalties. The Werder Bremen striker's total of five goals was the lowest total to win the Golden Boot since the Chile World Cup of 1962, but he now has 10 goals in World Cups after finishing equal second highest scorer during the 2002 tournament, again with five.

SEE ALSO **'HEADS SAUDI ARABIA LOSE'** (page 559).

Klose was linked to Europe's top teams but he opted to stay with Werder Bremen. In summer 2007 he signed for Bayern Munich.

RECORD-BREAKING SAUDI KEEPER RETIRES

Saudi Arabia goalkeeper Mohammed Al-Deayea announced his retirement following his country's exit from the 2006 World Cup, after making a world record 181 international appearances. Al-Deayea, who was close to being signed by Sir Alex Ferguson for Manchester United in 2001 before work permit issues prevented the transfer, played in the 1994, 1998 and 2002 tournaments and was an unused squad member during the 2006 tournament in Germany. Al-Deayea also retired as the holder of a somewhat less welcome record, having conceded 25 goals in World Cup finals, a total shared with Antonio Carbajal of Mexico.

SEE ALSO **'BILLY WRIGHT WINS 100TH CAP'** (page 227); **'HEADS SAUDI ARABIA LOSE'** (page 559).

Saudi Arabian Mohammed Al-Deayea came close to playing at Old Trafford when manager Sir Alex Ferguson attempted to sign him.

BARCELONA ANNOUNCE UNICEF SHIRT SPONSORSHIP

In July 2006, Barcelona announced a unique sponsorship deal with the United Nations Children's Fund (Unicef). The Catalan giants, famous for never having had a shirt sponsorship deal in their 107-year history, broke with tradition to help Unicef by donating a reported US $1.9 million a year to the children's charity for the duration of the five-year contract. After re-iterating Barcelona's mantra of being more than just a football club, their president Joan Laporta said, "It's an initiative with soul. Barca can help the children of the world." It remains to be seen whether Europe's other major clubs will follow suit.

SEE ALSO **'WANTED – A FOOTBALL CLUB!'** (page 44); **'LIVERPOOL GET A SHIRT SPONSOR'** (page 367).

As shirt sponsorship deals become more and more financially motivated, Barcelona's gesture seems all the more impressive.

HEALY'S HAT-TRICK HEROICS

In September 2006 during a famous 3-2 win over
Spain, David Healy became the first player since
George Best to score a hat trick for Northern Ireland
in Belfast. It was the latest spectacular performance
from the striker whose goal stunned England
at Windsor Park. It was Healy, too, who headed
in during a 1-4 defeat to Norway in 2004. Much
more than a consolation, it ended the longest goal
drought in international football – two years and
1,298 minutes long. Since then Northern Ireland has
enjoyed a resurgence and Healy, with 29 goals in his
56 appearances, is their all-time top scorer.

SEE ALSO **'ARMSTRONG PUTS NORTHERN IRELAND
INTO SECOND ROUND'** (page 384).

David Healy's goals helped Northern Ireland to their strongest
chance of qualifying for a major tournament since 1986.

SUPERSTAR BECKS JOINS GALAXY

On 12 January 2007 David Beckham revealed that he
would be swapping the Bernabeu for the Home Depot
Centre, as he announced that he would be leaving Real
Madrid in the summer to join the Major League Soccer
(MLS) team Los Angeles Galaxy. The move was reported
to make him the world's highest paid sports star, with a
salary of US $10 million a year and the potential to top
it up to US $50 million a year with endorsements and
profit-sharing. To make the transfer possible the MSL
introduced the Designated Player Rule, also known as the
Beckham Rule, for the 2007 season, which allowed each
team to sign one player who would ordinarily be outside
the team's salary cap.

SEE ALSO **'FOOTBALL'S GREATEST STAR LANDS
STATESIDE'** (pages 344–45).

Beckham was told by the Madrid coach that he would not play for them
again, but he won back his place by producing the form of his life.

PLATINI – FROM SOCCER PLAYER TO FOOTBALL POLITICO

Michel Platini

Michel Platini, France's greatest player of a golden generation, now holds the top position in European football as UEFA president.

French football's player of the 1980s, Michel Platini, completed the journey from grass roots player to the top of European soccer administration when he was elected UEFA president. After winning numerous accolades as goal-scorer and goal-maker in a brilliant career, as a UEFA board member Platini has dedicated himself to soccer administration. The 2007 presidential election result was close and after his victory Platini revealed he would push on with his controversial plans to reshape the Champions League with a new format from 2009.

SEE ALSO **'HAVELANGE ELECTED FIFA PRESIDENT'** (page 334); **'BLATTER ELECTED TO FIFA TOP JOB'** (page 510).

EURO 2012 GOES EAST

Four Polish cities and four Ukrainian cities will host the Euro group games. The final will be held in Kiev's 84,000 capacity Olympic Stadium.

When UEFA convened in Cardiff, few expected a joint Polish/Ukrainian triumph. Even in the shortlist of three it was considered the outsider, behind overwhelming favourites Italy and another dual effort, that of Croatia/Hungary. Italian football's recent corruption scandals and the upsurge in hooliganism may have cost them the tournament though Poland too has witnessed recent match-fixing investigations. Despite this and the daunting logistics of holding the tournament over an area so wide it incorporates two different time zones, Euro 2012 will be the first to be held in the old Eastern Bloc since the former Yugoslavia hosted in 1976.

SEE ALSO **'FIRST WORLD CUP ON AFRICAN SOIL'** (page 617).

The Inter team which includes Esteban Cambiasso, Marco Materazzi and Luis Figo, pose prior to their league match against AS Roma.

INTER CANTER TO CHAMPIONSHIP

As the other big European leagues headed towards nail-biting conclusions, Internazionale cantered to their fifteenth Scudetto with five matches remaining. A 2-1 away victory against lowly Siena coupled with defeat for nearest challengers Roma secured the third back-to-back title triumph in the club's history. Under Roberto Mancini, the Nerazzuri, including Hernan Crespo, Luis Figo and Zlatan Ibrahomivic, suffered only one defeat all season. Remarkably, it was World Cup hero Marco Materazzi who capped an incredible year by scoring both goals at the Artemio Franchi Stadium. The victory was dedicated to Inter legend and former club president Giacinto Facchetti, who died in September 2006.

SEE ALSO **'MILAN SPLIT CREATES INTER'** (page 61).

Getafe's Daniel Gonzalez Guiza celebrates after scoring the winning goal during the Copa del Rey semi-final second leg against Barcelona.

GETAFE DO THE UNTHINKABLE

Getafe staged one of the most startling comebacks in recent times, overturning a 5-2 first leg semi-final deficit to triumph against the mighty Barcelona 4-0 on the night and 6-5 on aggregate to land a place in the Copa del Rey final against Seville. Although 24-time champions Barcelona understandably felt confident prior to the incredible second leg, Argentine wonder-kid Lionel Messi was the only noticeable absentee. However, two goals in either half proved too much for Barcelona as Bernd Schuster led his side to a sensational comeback victory and a first-ever appearance in the Spanish Cup final.

SEE ALSO **'LIVERPOOL FIGHT BACK TO LEVEL EUROPEAN CUP FINAL'** (page 590).

UNITED ON CLOUD NINE

Manchester United deservedly won their ninth Premiership title in 2007. Cristiano Ronaldo was outstanding from August to May, and Wayne Rooney provided some memorable moments, but the title was won by the defence.

Everyone selected by Sir Alex Ferguson to play in front of goalkeeper Edwin van der Sar did their jobs solidly and effectively. Midfielder Paul Scholes had another great season and Ryan Giggs became the most decorated player in English club football. United proved, especially to strife-torn Chelsea, that football really is a team game.

SEE ALSO **'MANCHESTER UNITED FIGHT BACK TO WIN TREBLE'** (pages 526-27).

Paul Scholes, one of Manchester United's player of the season, sprays champagne at team-mates during the end of season celebrations.

MILAN'S SWEET REVENGE

AC Milan gained sweet revenge for their 2005 penalty shoot-out final heartbreak defeat to Liverpool as two goals from predatory striker Filippo Inzaghi sealed a 2-1 victory and a seventh magnificent triumph in Europe's premier club competition. Inzaghi scored his first when an Andrea Pirlo free kick took a crucial deflection off his shoulder and his tally was doubled with 10 minutes left when Kaka intervened to devastating effect, dissecting the Liverpool rearguard with a through ball for Inzaghi, who rounded Reina and finished coolly into an empty net: 2-0 to AC Milan. A late Dirk Kuyt header proved only a consolation and Milan sealed a 2-1 win.

SEE ALSO **'LIVERPOOL FIGHT BACK TO LEVEL EUROPEAN CUP FINAL...** (page 590).

Veteran AC Milan captain Paolo Maldini collects his fifth European Cup of a long and distinguished career, thanks to Inzaghi's two goals.

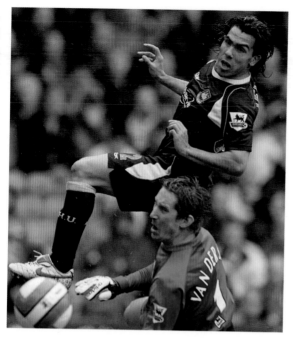

Carlos Tevez guides the ball past Manchester United goalkeeper Edwin van der Sar to secure three points and Premiership survival.

TEVEZ LANDS HAMMER BLOW

On the final day of the season, West Ham travelled to already-crowned Champions Manchester United knowing victory would secure one of the Premiership's greatest escapes and they got their win courtesy of a Carlos Tevez strike. Tevez spearheaded the Hammers revival, but his arrival at Upton Park in a joint deal with Javier Mascherano had been under investigation. A Premier League panel found the club guilty of transfer irregularities and fined them a record £5.5million, but did not impose a points deduction, despite the demands of other teams in the relegation dogfight for a harsher sentence. It had looked as though West Ham were doomed regardless until Tevez found his form and ensured the team's Premiership survival – much to the dismay of the relegated teams.

SEE ALSO **'VILLA AND ARDILES SPEARHEAD BRITAIN'S FOREIGN LEGION'** (page 364).

The new Wembley opened four years late and as a result England games continued to be played at major club grounds across the country.

WEMBLEY REOPENS – AT LAST!

Over four years late and costing a budget-busting £798 million, the new Wembley Stadium in London staged its first senior international match. The honour of putting the new stadium and turf through its paces went to Brazil who were entertained by England in a game that ended 1-1. The showpiece stadium had been a long time coming – it had been due to open in 2003 – and in the meantime major soccer events moved to Wales, with England internationals shared among major club grounds. The £798 million bought England a 90,000-capacity stadium, uninterrupted views for fans, a roof that closes over seats and a 315m steel 'tiara' spanning the whole structure.

SEE ALSO **'WEMBLEY CLOSES... AND COACH RESIGNS ON TELEVISION'** (page 539).

Coach Fabio Capello celebrates with Roberto Carlos and David Beckham, after Real Madrid's title-clinching 3-1 victory over Mallorca.

GALACTICOS LEAVE ON A HIGH

Real Madrid said farewell to the last of the Galacticos, Beckham left for LA Galaxy and Roberto Carlos went to Fenerbahce after 11 seasons at the Bernabeu, with their 30th Spanish championship. Beckham had been told he had no future at Real by coach Fabio Capello, but earned a recall. And his form – combined with Ruud van Nistelrooy's goals – was such that Real were unbeaten in 20 games. Needing a final-game victory Real were losing 1–0 at home to Mallorca at half-time. Van Nistelrooy limped off, but Madrid equalised before Beckham, too, went off. His replacement was Juan Antonio Reyes and he promptly scored the two goals that gave Real the title.

SEE ALSO **'SUPERSTAR BECKS JOINS GALAXY'** (page 604).

Jose Mourinho contemplates his future with the spectre of his successor Avram Grant behind him.

THE "SPECIAL ONE" BIDS FAREWELL

A row too far ended Jose Mourinho's controversial reign as manager of British Premiership club Chelsea. Fiery Portuguese Mourinho, the self-styled "Special One", who won the Premiership title two years running for the London club after a 50-year gap, quit after a reportedly heated row with owner Roman Abramovich. The clash came after a disappointing 1-1 Champions League home draw with Rosenborg from Norway when Mourinho threw his normal cautious team selection to the wind and played a three-man strike force. Chelsea had also made their worst start to a season since 2001. Mourinho emerged nine months later as manager of Italian Serie A club Inter Milan.

SEE ALSO **'CHELSEA END 50-YEAR TITLE DROUGHT'** (page 588).

Derision from England fans rained down on Steve McLaren after he failed to qualify for the Euro 2008 finals.

ENGLAND EURO FAILURE COSTS McLAREN HIS JOB

Thirteen agonising minutes stood between England's qualification for Euro 2008. England, roared on by home fans, needed only a home draw with Croatia to go through to the following summer's finals but in the 77th minute they found themselves 2-3 down from which they failed to recover. England's earlier comeback from 0-2 down to 2-2 had been in vain and its manager, Steve McLaren, was sacked within 24 hours. Three weeks later Italian Fabio Capello signed a four-and-a-half year contract to become the new England manager with the immediate target of securing a place in the 2010 World Cup finals.

SEE ALSO **'ENGLAND GO FOR ERIKSSON'** (page 543).

POMPEY'S 69-YEAR WAIT FOR MAJOR HONOUR

Provincial side Portsmouth ended one of the longest gaps between major honours when they won the English FA Cup at Wembley. It had taken Portsmouth, nicknamed Pompey, 69 years to repeat their FA Cup triumph of 1939. Ironically it was a player who has not been able to command a regular spot in the starting line-up who sealed the 1-0 victory over Welsh club Cardiff City. Nigerian international Nwankwo Kanu will never have an easier chance to be a hero. After John Utaka's near-post cross was fumbled by Cardiff goalkeeper Peter Enckelman it gave the predatory Kanu a two-yard tap-in.

SEE ALSO **'PORTSMOUTH WIN LEAGUE WITH EX-SERVICEMEN'** (page 169).

A tap-in goal from Kanu just two yards out was enough to end Portsmouth's long wait for the FA Cup.

VETERAN HERO GIGGS MAKES UNITED CHAMPS AGAIN

Manchester United's 17th league title was wreathed in poetic justice as their current longest serving player clinched the match at Wigan. The Reds 10th Premier League championship, while a team effort, was about Welsh international Ryan Giggs. His cool 80th-minute finish came on the day he equalled Sir Bobby Charlton's appearance record of 758 games for the club. Giggs' team-mates stood aside as he was given the honour of lifting the Premiership trophy. For Manchester United manager Sir Alex Ferguson and his all-conquering team it was the first leg of a unique treble as they were to go on to become European and World club champions.

SEE ALSO **'GIGGS' RUN TAKES UNITED TO THE FINAL'** (page 523); **'MANCHESTER UNITED FIGHT BACK TO WIN TREBLE'** (page 526).

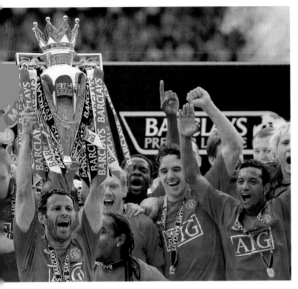

Ryan Giggs lifts the Premiership trophy on the same day the midfielder equalled Bobby Charlton's appearance record of 758 games for United.

TERRY SLIP ENDS CHELSEA'S CHAMPIONS' LEAGUE DREAM

In a cruel twist of fate, Chelsea's "Mr Reliable" failed his team on one of the biggest football stages. When Manchester United and Chelsea faced each other in Moscow's Luzhniki Stadium it was the first European Champions' League final between two English teams. With the score deadlocked at 1-1 after 120 minutes of play the match went to a tense penalty shoot-out. Chelsea captain and inspiration Terry stepped up for a shot that would take the trophy to London but he slipped in his run-up and hit the post. It was a let-off that Manchester United would capitalize upon and they went on to win the final 6-5 on penalties.

SEE ALSO **'MARTIN PALERMO MISSES THREE PENALTIES'** (page 528); **'CHELSEA END 50-YEAR TITLE DROUGHT'** (page 588).

Usually ever-dependable, John Terry's penalty shoot-out slip destroyed Chelsea's Champions League-winning dream.

EARLY DUTCH EURO 2008 HOPES FADE

Legendary former captain Johann Cruyff looked on from the stands as the Netherlands rekindled the days of Dutch "Total Football" in Euro 2008's so-called "Group of Death." Arguably the toughest group in the draw, Group C pitched the Netherlands against 2006 World Cup finalists Italy and France. Playing with style and panache, the Dutch beat Italy 3-0, then with goals from Kuyt, Van Persie, Sneijder and Robben, blitzed France 4-1. Unrated Romania were dispatched 2-0 as the Dutch topped the group while conceding only one goal but scoring nine. Hopes of taking the European Championship ended at the quarter final stage when the Netherlands were beaten 3-1 by Russia.

SEE ALSO 'TOTAL FOOTBALL ARRIVES' (page 296); 'HOLLAND SHOW THEIR PEDIGREE' (page 425).

The Dutch celebrate the return of their famous free-flowing style, however, it was short-lived as they were beaten 3-1 in the quarter-finals by Russia.

Despair for Croatia's players after Turkey's late comeback. Croatia looked to have won a place in the quarter-finals until Semih Senturk's equaliser.

TURKEY'S LAST-GASP SURPRISE FOR CROATIA

Turkey were literally seconds from elimination from Euro 2008 when a desperate punt sparked a sensational turnaround of fortunes. Opponents Croatia looked to have won the quarter-final in Vienna with a goal by Ivan Klasnic a minute from the end of extra time. The Croatians celebrated wildly but were stunned only seconds later – in the 30th minute of extra time – when Turkish substitute Semih Senturk latched on to a long clearance by his goalkeeper Rustu and volleyed into the net. The equaliser forced a penalty shoot-out which Turkey won 3-1 to secure a semi-final clash against Germany.

SEE ALSO 'TURKEY SCORE FASTEST GOAL IN WORLD CUP HISTORY ' (page 564).

TORRES HELPS END SPAIN'S 44-YEAR WAIT FOR SUCCESS

Fernando Torres chips the ball past German goalkeeper Jens Lehmann to open the scoring in the Euro 2008 final.

A single chipped goal by star striker Fernando Torres saw Spain land its first major title in 44 years. The Liverpool player struck after 33 minutes to defeat Germany in the final of the Euro 2008 championship at a packed Ernst Happel Stadium in Vienna, Austria. Other goal-scoring chances had fallen to Torres, Silva, Iniesta, Ramos and Senna but it was significant that Torres should be Spain's hero following a spectacular English Premier League season as Liverpool's top scorer. Midfielder Xavi was the architect of Spain's winner with a pass that wrong-footed the German defence. Torres met it, shrugged off a defender's challenge and lifted the ball past goalkeeper Jens Lehmann. The Spanish national side had flattered to deceive in decades of major tournaments, only winning the equivalent of Euro 2008, the European Championship, once before in 1964. At Euro 2008, Spain's youthful side had a testing route to the final but were regarded as worthy winners. They beat Italy and the holders Greece as well as putting seven goals past Russia in a group match and the semi-final.

Spain's 1-0 victory over Germany ended a wait of nearly half a century for a major honour.

SEE ALSO **'SPAIN PROVE THEIR METTLE IN EUROPE'** (page 253); **SPAIN TRIUMPH IN EURO THRILLER'** (page 534).

WORLD-RECORD BID FOR KAKA COLLAPSES

A record-busting transfer bid for Brazilian striker Kaka, whose ramifications threatened to change the financial complexion of football, failed. English Premier League club Manchester City, backed by the huge wealth of its new Abu Dhabi-based owners, made a £100m bid for AC Milan's Kaka. Even more astounding was the value of the total package which, including the player's salary, was a reported £243m. It sparked weeks of world press speculation and pleas from Milan fans for Kaka – real name Ricardo Izecson dos Santos Leite – to stay. Finally the bid was rejected with deeply-religious Kaka, saying he was unmoved even by the reported £500,000-a-week salary on offer.

SEE ALSO 'MARADONA SIGNS FOR BARCELONA IN RECORD DEAL' (page 378); 'ZIZOU BECOMES A GALACTICO' (page 549).

At the end of 2008/09 season Kaka opted to transfer to Real Madrid for less money, but still a world record transfer of £56 million.

HOFFENHEIM'S METEORIC RISE TO THE TOP

In January 2009 an unknown name arrived at the top of Germany's Bundesliga, eclipsing such illustrious names such as Bayern Munich. Eighteen years ago Hoffenheim's team was way down at the eighth level of German football, but after seven promotions and £163m of investment by a villager-made-good they burst to the pinnacle of the Bundesliga. The side from rural south-west Germany was confidently looking forward to facing Barcelona, Real Madrid, Manchester United or AC Milan in the 2009-10 European Champions League. Hoffenheim, a quiet farming community of 3,286 people, has been consumed by football fever since software billionaire Dietmar Hopp returned to his rural roots to pump millions into Hoffenheim. He has even bankrolled a new 30,000-capacity all-seater stadium in nearby Sinsheim.

SEE ALSO 'CALAIS REACH FRENCH CUP FINAL' (page 533).

Seven promotions and £163m of investment have taken Hoffenheim to the top of the Bundesliga and made them strong contenders for the title.

Such was David Beckham's impact at AC Milan, the Italian club soon became keen to make his loan move permanent.

BECKHAM LANDS ITALIAN JOB

England's David Beckham continued to amaze and confound his critics with his world travels. The former Manchester United and Real Madrid midfielder is unique in splitting his talents between two clubs more than 6,000 miles apart. Having used LA Galaxy's close season break to sign on a loan period for Italy's AC Milan, Beckham wowed the Milan faithful with goal-scoring performances and wanted to stay. After much haggling over his talents – and a reported cash input from Beckham himself – the two clubs agreed Beckham could split his time between them. While the American league had not been a happy hunting ground for Beckham, his Italian form revived his international chances and he became England most-capped outfield player.

SEE ALSO **'BECKHAM MANIA HITS JAPAN'** (page 557); **'SUPERSTAR BECKS JOINS GALAXY'** (page 608).

THREE-IN-A- ROW TITLES FOR THE RED DEVILS

Even for supporters bred on success, the cheers were deafening as Manchester United celebrated one of the greatest feats in English soccer. They sealed a hat-trick of Premier League titles with a goalless draw with Arsenal and finally saw off the title pretensions of Liverpool, who had been United's closest rivals for much of the season. To further rub salt into Liverpool's wounds the latest Red Devils' triumph equalled the Scousers' record of 18 English top-flight league wins. Eleven of United's league titles – including a previous three-in-a-row – have come in the Premier League era under manager Sir Alex Ferguson.

SEE ALSO **'MANCHESTER UNITED FIGHT BACK TO WIN TREBLE'** (page 526); **'VETERAN HERO GIGGS MAKES UNITED CHAMPS AGAIN'** (page 611).

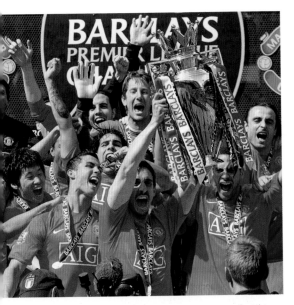

United's Gary Neville holds aloft the Premier League trophy. This was the club's 18th and record-equalling English league title.

NEWCASTLE TAKE A TUMBLE

An own goal cost an estimated £50m as Newcastle United, one of the most fanatically-supported teams in English football, were relegated from the Premier League. On the last day of the season Newcastle, temporarily managed by former England striker Alan Shearer, needed a point against Aston Villa to survive their season of unprecedented turmoil but were beaten 0-1 by a deflection off midfielder Damien Duff into his own net. Dropping to the Coca-Cola Championship was estimated to slash annual revenue by around £50m. Newcastle, put up for sale by its owner Mike Ashley, had been riven by strife throughout the 2008-09 season with fan discontent over four managerial changes, underachievement on the field and lack of investment in new players.

SEE ALSO **'PROMOTION AND RELEGATION ADD TO THE COMPETITION'** (page 43); **'DENIS LAW SENDS UNITED DOWN'** (page 331).

Even the intervention of Newcastle United legend Alan Shearer failed to save the Magpies from relegation in what was a season of turmoil.

BARCELONA – EUROPE'S BEST

Midfielder Lionel Messi inspired Barcelona to their third European Champions' League crown with a 2-0 win over England's Manchester United in Rome. The Catalan team put in by far the better performance as it thwarted United's bid for successive European titles. Messi, arguably the best player in the world at the time, headed home a 70th minute Xavi cross to put the match beyond doubt. Barcelona weathered a confident United start before taking the lead in the 10th minute through striker Samuel Eto'o. Barca then proceeded to hand United a silky-smooth demonstration of how the "Beautiful Game" should be played before Messi put the trophy in Catalan hands for the third time since 1992.

SEE ALSO **'KOEMAN FREE-KICK WINS EUROPEAN CUP'** (page 458); **'... BUT BARCELONA COME BACK TO WIN'** (page 597).

Lionel Messi leaps to head home Barcelona's second against Manchester United in a Champions League Final they dominated.

25-SECOND GOAL MAKES FA CUP HISTORY

The fastest goal in the long history of the FA Cup was not enough to take the trophy for Everton. Frenchman Louis Saha shot Everton into the lead just 25 seconds after the kick-off at Wembley Stadium against Chelsea. Although the Chelsea defence was rattled at so early a lapse, the London side worked their way back into the game and secured a first-half equaliser through Didier Drogba. With 18 minutes of the game left, midfielder Frank Lampard hit the winner but Chelsea were denied a win by a bigger margin when the referee disallowed a spectacular strike from Florent Malouda which crossed the Everton goal line after hitting the underside of the crossbar. Interim manager Guus Hiddink left Chelsea with at least one piece of silverware before AC Milan boss Carlo Ancelotti took over the permanent role.

SEE ALSO **'FA CUP INAUGURATED'** (page 19); **'POMPEY'S 69-YEAR WAIT FOR A MAJOR HONOUR'** (page 610).

Guus Hiddink celebrates with the Chelsea team following their FA Cup triumph. The Dutch coach was credited with revitalising the Blues.

FIRST WORLD CUP ON AFRICAN SOIL

With African football an increasing force in the global game, FIFA decided to debut the World Cup on the African continent with the 2010 event. South Africa beat off competition from Egypt, Morocco, Tunisia and Libya for the honour. African players now make an impact in the top leagues of Europe and their birthplace was the last major continent not to have hosted a World Cup. The choice of South Africa as a World Cup venue is the culmination of a vigorous campaign to have this fact recognised.

SEE ALSO **'URUGUAY APPOINTED FIRST HOSTS'** (page 111); **EURO 2012 GOES EAST'** (page 605).

South Africa 2010 games will be played in Cape Town, Durban, Pretoria, Port Elizabeth, Bloemfontein, Nelspruit, Polokwane and Rustenburg.

INDEX

PICTURE CREDITS

The publishers would like to thank the following sources for
their kind permission to reproduce the pictures in this book.

PHOTOGRAPHY SUPPLIED BY **PA Photos**

Except for the following:
Getty Images: 252; /AFP: 77, 125, 138, 141, 192, 331; /Gunnar Berning/Bongarts: 532; /David Cannon: 432; /Central Press: 312; /Tim
Clary/AFP: 477; /Stu Forster; 562; /HO/AFP: 69; /Hulton Archive: 32, 152, 301; /Keystone: 165; /Keystone/Hulton Archive: 288; /Hoang
Dinh Nam/AFP: 520. **Action Images**: /Ivan Alvarado/Reuters: 453; /Albert Gea/Reuters: 550. **Offside**: /L'Equipe: 302, 305, 338; /Witters:
262. **Private Collection**: 14, 40, 44, 45, 65, 70, 96, 99, 102, 104. **AKG London**: 450. **Topfoto.co.uk**: 251

Every effort has been made to acknowledge correctly and contact the source and/or copyright holder of each picture and
Carlton Books Limited apologises for any unintentional omissions which will be corrected in future editions of this book.

Special thanks go to Liz Parsons and Geoff Kirby at PA Photos for all their hard work on this project.